The *Leaders Praise*
Successful E-Mail Marketing Strategies:
From Hunting to Farming

"From Hunting to Farming" is a Master Class for e-mail marketing in the 21st Century. The book is destined to become the new must-read strategy playbook for e-mail marketers today and required reading for CMOs and CFOs looking to grow their businesses through this effective and efficient channel. Arthur Hughes, the premier author on database marketing strategy, makes a compelling business case for the "Farming" approach to e-mail marketing with a wealth of charts and examples for effective measurement. Each chapter addresses the key tactics and best practices for a "How-To" guide for delivering a state-of-the art e-mail communication strategy. It's an enjoyable read offering a thought-provoking look at the promise of how the medium can benefit your company.

Rob Befumo
Director of E-mail Marketing
Publisher's Clearing House

Successful E-Mail Marketing Strategies delivers a dynamic new framework for thinking about your subscribers. The real-world examples included throughout the book will get you buzzing with new ideas for jumpstarting or revitalizing your e-mail marketing efforts."

Heather Johnson
Manager of Online Strategy
AirTran Airways

What's missing for many e-mail marketers is plain old attitude. The two Arthurs make it easy to see the difference between primitive "hunting" and customer-centric "farming." The data, technology, expertise and opportunity abound to make all e-mail marketing wildly successful, getting to the heart of what makes it work: creating great subscriber experiences. This is a game-changing attitudinal shift. If you want your e-mail marketing to succeed, learn how to farm.

Stephanie Miller
Vice President
Return Path

This book is a must-read for new and seasoned e-mail marketers alike. Hughes and Sweetser have written a powerful manual filled with innovative strategies and eye-opening statistics to help you bring your e-mail marketing program to the next level.

Megan O'Donnell
Manager, Email Marketing
OfficeMax

When they write, ". . . e-mail permits an entirely new and better way of building relationships with our customers . . ." the authors of *Successful E-mail Marketing Strategies*, Arthur Middleton Hughes and Arthur Sweetser have hit the *enter* key right on the head. Their useful exploration of the fast-expanding world of e-mail marketing provides numerous actionable strategies that cannot help but make e-mail marketing more profitable and effective. Best of all, their exposition of the medium makes clear what Obama's campaign has proven so stunningly: *involvement* of the audience through the new language of marketing success and using this powerful electronic medium has come of age.

Peter J Rosenwald
Partner: International Associates—
Strategic Marketing Consultants
Author, *Accountable Marketing*

Combine all of your webinars, training events and reading materials. Now throw them all away. This is the single most important marketing book you need for today and beyond. Live, breathe and learn the techniques to take your campaigns from flat to fat based on methods from people who have truly lived through the ups and downs of the changing face of marketing.

Melanie Singleton
senior marketing manager
Norvax, Inc., a Fortune 500 Company

E-mail marketing is unique because it can be a truly personalized communication between a company and a single recipient. That's immensely powerful, but only if a marketer understands the science of learning from the customer. At the same time, they must be able to accurately measure the lifetime value of a subscriber in order to properly allocate resources. Hughes and Sweetser explain how to measure that value in elegant and accurate language. They build upon that to help the marketer determine the ROI of their e-mail communications with easy- to- understand calculations that can be used by all e-mail marketers to measure their own success and continually improve upon it.

Stefan Tornquist
Research Director
Marketing Sherpa

Successful
E-mail Marketing
Strategies:

from HUNTING to FARMING

By
Arthur Middleton Hughes
&
Arthur Sweetser

2009

© 2009 Arthur Middleton Hughes and Arthur Sweetser

Editor: Richard Hagle
Interior design: Sans Serif Inc., Saline, Michigan 48176

Published by: .

Racom Communications, Inc.
150 N. Michigan Ave.
Suite 2800
Chicago, IL 60601
312-494-0100
www.racombooks.com

ISBN 13   978-1-933199-16-0

PREFACE

E-mail marketing began in the early 1990s. In 1995 the number of advertisements sent by e-mail was greater than the number sent by regular mail. It became a serious marketing discipline in 1998 with the founding of several e-mail service providers (ESPs), such as e-Dialog and Responsys, who assisted major companies with their e-mail marketing. Since then, more than a dozen books have been written on e-mail marketing, including those by Chris Baggott, Bill Nussey, Jim Sterne, Kim Macpherson, Shannon Kinnard, Herschell Gordon Lewis, and John Arnold. So why do we need another?

The reason is there has been a seismic shift in the e-mail marketing industry. Stephanie Miller of Return Path summarized this shift by saying, "E-mail 'batch and blast' marketing is in distress. It simply no longer performs. Subscriber inboxes are overflowing with permission-based e-mail that is irrelevant. Our research shows that 60 percent of subscribers just ignore the e-mails, deflating marketer hopes for relationship building and sales."

We think Stephanie is right. Like Stephanie, we are e-mail marketing practitioners. Our company provides e-mail services for more than 140 major e-mail marketers. As we see it, there are two basic ways to approach e-mail marketing today. The first is the traditional way involving massive identical e-mail campaigns sent to relatively unknown subscribers. The campaigns are analyzed by opens, clicks, conversions, and unsubscribes. We call this approach hunting for sales. The second way involves personalized, relevant e-mail communications to individual subscribers based on a database of demographic and behavioral information. We call this approach farming.

Most e-mail marketers today are engaged in hunting. They know little about their subscribers except their e-mail addresses. They are unaware of their subscriber's ages, incomes, lifestyles, offline purchases, children in the home, or any of about a hundred relevant facts that are usually known to database marketing professionals. Like hunters, they set out their traps (e-mails) in a vast wilderness of relatively unknown subscribers, hoping that some of them will be caught. It is getting harder to succeed because there are more traps set by a growing number of hunters.

Farming, on the other hand, is quite different. Each permission-based e-mail subscriber is listed in a marketing database with a wealth of demographic, behavioral, and preference data. It is possible today to send a different promotional e-mail to every single customer—an e-mail tailored to what we can learn of the customer's preferences, behavior, and lifestyle. Furthermore, marketing e-mails can be interactive. They can permit customers not just to read them but to explore them in depth—to ask questions and get answers within the e-mail, to express opinions and preferences, and to make purchases right in the e-mail.

These personalized, triggered, interactive marketing e-mails can produce amazing results in increased retention and sales that beat anything that could come from any other form of marketing, including e-mail batch-and-blast hunting campaigns.

Most e-mail marketing books have been written with hunting in mind: how to create better traps (e-mails) to catch more game (customers). This book is written to help marketers understand the motivation and preferences of their farm livestock (their subscribers) so they can build loyalty and repeat sales.

This book dives deeply into the entire business of e-mail marketing based on farming subscribers. We cover triggered messages, interactivity, retention and loyalty building, relevance, lifetime value, segmentation, viral marketing, and testing. We show how offline and online purchasing history can be combined into a single database to create a 360-degree picture of each subscriber so we can speak to her as if we knew her, because, in reality, we do. We show how to use subscriber databases and e-mails to talk to subscribers with the intimacy of the corner grocer who knew each customer by name, knew their families, knew their preferences, and built customer loyalty by daily conversations.

The methods we present here are new for e-mail marketers, but they are based on time-tested principles. E-mail marketing based on farming brings to the electronic age marketing methods that worked when the world was much smaller and personal loyalty was important in marketing. This type of e-mail marketing is a highly profitable new system that allows marketers to build and maintain one-on-one relationships with thousands of customers and create bonds of loyalty that keep customers buying for a lifetime.

This book is filled with tables and charts that supplement the text. All these materials can be downloaded by our readers for free at www.dbmarketing.com.

We welcome you, our readers, to the world of e-mail marketing by farming.

Arthur Middleton Hughes and Arthur Sweetser

ALSO BY
ARTHUR MIDDLETON HUGHES

Customer Churn Reduction and Retention for Telecoms: Models for all Marketers (Racom Communications, 2008)

Strategic Database Marketing, 3rd ed. (McGraw-Hill Publishing Company, 2006)

The Customer Loyalty Solution (McGraw-Hill Publishing Company, 2003)

Strategic Database Marketing, 2nd ed. (McGraw-Hill Publishing Company, 2000)

The Complete Database Marketer, 2nd ed. (McGraw-Hill Publishing Company, 1996)

Strategic Database Marketing, 1st ed. (McGraw-Hill Publishing Company, 1994)

The Complete Database Marketer, 1st ed. (McGraw-Hill Publishing Company, 1991)

Don't Blame Little Arthur; Blame the Damn Fool Who Entrusted Him with the Eggs (Database Marketing Institute, 1998)

The American Economy (Norvec Publishing Company, 1968)

CONTENTS

1

E-mail Marketing:
Something New and Wonderful

E-mail marketing is everything that a marketer dreams about: it's cost-effective, personal, individualized, popular, interactive, measurable, and convenient. Due to e-mail's omnipresence across business and personal demographics, it offers an incredible reach. Due to technology's innovative abilities to use databases to customize each outgoing message to each recipient, e-mail is customizable on a massive scale. Finally, with tracking ability enabled by codes embedded into e-mail messages, or with unique URLs or other tracking mechanisms, marketers can measure the response (on an individual and aggregate levels) to outgoing campaigns.

Shannon Kinnard, *Marketing with E-mail*

Something new, sophisticated, and wonderful has happened to the marketing industry: e-mail marketing. New because it's only about 10 years old, having started in a big way only in 1998. Sophisticated because it permits marketers to do very targeted and interactive marketing. And wonderful because, when used correctly, it produces more bottom-line results per dollar than any other marketing method ever developed.

Today more than 93 percent of major US corporations use e-mail marketing, according to JupiterResearch.[1] The rest of them, plus smaller companies, are definitely looking at it, thinking about it, and planning to introduce it. Unfortunately, only about 31 percent of e-mail marketers reported in a JupiterResearch survey that they use click-through data to follow up with more targeted messages.[2] The rest of the marketers aren't varying their marketing message based on e-mail recipients' behavior. They blast identical e-mails to millions of unknown subscribers. They don't use the segmentation and interactivity that would permit them to get the real benefits e-mail marketing can provide.

Television ads blast exactly the same offer and copy to everyone. Individually targeted TV ads for digital subscribers are theoretically possible, but their implementation is somewhere off in the future. Individually targeted e-mail marketing is here now, even though most companies don't take advantage of it.

It's possible today to send a different promotional e-mail to every single customer, an e-mail tailored to what we can learn of the customer's preferences, behavior, and lifestyle. Marketing e-mails can also be interactive. They permit customers not just to read them but also to explore them in depth, to ask questions and get answers within the e-mail, to express opinions and preferences, and to make purchases right in the e-mail.

These personalized, triggered, interactive marketing e-mails can produce amazing results, in terms of increased retention and sales, that beat anything that could possibly come from any other form of marketing.

E-mail marketing produces three types of sales. The most obvious are online sales. In many e-mails, you can buy the product by clicking on links within the e-mail itself. In this way, suppliers know not only who is buying what but also the actual message that caused a customer to buy the product. But e-mails produce two other important conversions: retail and catalog purchases. As a result of e-mails, consumers drive to shopping malls and buy products. This can be measured by providing e-mail recipients with coupons they can take to the store. But a vast quantity of retail and wholesale sales resulting from e-mails come about without a coupon. An e-mail is really like a TV or a radio advertisement. It produces action, but it's often hard to pin down the exact sequence of steps.

In the same way, e-mails can produce catalog and telephone order sales. According to Miles Kimball, many catalogers send an e-mail when they send out a catalog, saying, "Look in your mailbox for our spring catalog." Miles Kimball found that an e-mail plus a catalog produced about 18% more dollars per book than the catalog alone.[3]

Online shopping is becoming a mainstream activity. Forty-nine percent of US adults had shopped online as of September 2007, according to a survey by the Pew Internet & American Life Project[4], up from 22 percent in 2000. E-mail promotions increase the number of online sales. Among more affluent Americans, online shopping is even more common. Sixty-six percent of adults with household incomes between $60,000 and $100,000 and 79 percent with incomes above $100,000 have purchased on the Web, according to the survey.

Most people have become used to e-mails. According to a study by

Merkle[5], consumers check e-mail more frequently. Forty-four percent of consumers check their primary e-mail account more than three times a day, a 38 percent increase from just three years ago. Half of the respondents (52%) "couldn't live without it," up from 45 percent three years ago. And over half of the respondents (58%) believe e-mail is a great way for companies to stay in touch, up from 45 percent three years ago.

Finally, e-mails permit companies to build customer retention and loyalty. They permit real conversations rather than simple promotions. They are as close to a face-to-face meeting as you can get, short of the real thing.

This is the message of this book: e-mail permits an entirely new and better way of building relationships with our customers. We used to talk about building close, long-lasting relationships, but very few companies were able to achieve them. Now we have the tools we need to reach every customer individually and engage her in a dialogue, a conversation with benefits for both parties. We can learn each customer's personal preferences, then deliver to her exactly what she wants instantly. It's what the old corner grocers used to do.

Before there were supermarkets, all the groceries in America were sold in small grocery stores. In many cases, the proprietor could be seen at the entrance to his store, greeting the customers by name. "Hello, Mrs. Hughes. Are your son and his family coming for Thanksgiving again this year?"

These guys built customer loyalty by recognizing them by name, greeting them, knowing them, doing favors for them. "I just got a shipment of California grapes. I put some aside for you." They knew what their customers were interested in, and they discussed that with them. But most of these veterans no longer exist. Supermarkets came in; prices went down, and quality went up. The corner grocer had 800 SKUs in his store. Today's supermarkets have more than 30,000 SKUs.[6] He had a few hundred customers. Companies today have hundreds of thousands or millions of customers.

As a result of losing these guys, their loyalty-producing familiarity and friendship had become much more difficult to create and sustain— until e-mail marketing came along. Using the techniques in this book, a large corporation can now build relationships with its customers that re-create the recognition and loyalty that corner grocer built. We do this through creative use of our Web sites and e-mails. Using e-mail marketing, we return to methods that worked wonderfully in the old days. They build loyalty, repeat sales, cross sales, and profits.

Most marketers have not realized this yet. They use promotional e-

mails as if they were TV or print ads: blasting the same thing at everyone and not providing a way for the consumer to respond or engage in
a dialogue. They don't realize that promotional e-mails can be funda-
mentally different from blasted ads, they can be interactive dialogues
that give consumers a chance to express their opinions and do some research on their own. Using a promotional e-mail like a TV ad is a terrible waste of an opportunity to engage in a dialogue with your
customers. In addition, it fails to deliver on the relationship expectation
that customers have when they give you their personal e-mail address.

A TV, newspaper, or direct mail advertisement is only one way:
from you to consumers. They may be paying attention to it or they may
be ignoring it. The only way you can find out what they think about
what you're saying to them is if they react to your ad: getting on the
phone, going online, or walking into your store. Promotional e-mails
can also be only one way if you use them to simply blast ads at consumers. But e-mails have the power to be much more than blasted ads.
They can and should be individually targeted and interactive. Customers like to be engaged with rather than lectured to. Most of them
prefer a dialogue to a one-way blast.

It sounds so simple. Why don't marketers do this? Because it's not
as simple as it sounds. The dialogue has to be about something the customer is interested in. If the customer's interest is major league baseball,
to start a conversation about knitting or global warming might not be a
useful beginning. Our corner grocer would sense that right off the bat.
He would know what to talk about.

How can you get inside a successful corner grocer's brain and make
your e-mails as productive as his daily conversations? That's really
what this book is about. By the time you have finished reading this, you
will understand and be able to apply the ideas and methods of modern
e-mail marketing. You will be successful in winning the friendship, loyalty, and patronage of your customers for a long time to come. To get
from here to there, you will need to do a number of things.

Build a database to hold all the information you'll need to create effective e-mails

We haven't yet built a computer as complex and wonderful as the
human brain, but that's no reason not to try. The corner grocer kept
thousands of pieces of information in his head, information about
every customer and what each one was interested in, what her children
were doing, what not to talk to her about (the other party's candidate!).
To support your e-mails, you need to build a database that stores every-

thing you've learned and that serves up information to draft the outgoing e-mails so they seem like the continuation of a conversation to subscribers.

Get your customers' e-mail addresses and names, and use them to personalize your conversation

Good Web sites and good e-mails say, "Hello, Arthur." Poor Web sites and e-mails don't have any personalization. Why is personalization important? The corner grocer learned and used his customers' names. Personalized e-mails and Web sites have been tested hundreds of times. Communications that use the recipient's name are opened more, clicked more, and sell more.[7] Of course, you must get the name correct. Everyone has horror stories about e-mails with junk in the name field. So should you be a shrinking violet and not use personalization, foregoing the profits from it, because your database has a few bad entries in the name field? No way. Get busy. Clean up your database and get on with it.

Create segments

What do you discuss in your e-mails? You can never know exactly what is in all of your customer's minds, but you can make a stab at it. Depending on your business, and the questions you ask when you acquire the customer's e-mail address in the first place, you can create marketing segments: college students, families with young children, affluent seniors, or small businesses. To do this, of course, you have to learn your subscriber's home address so that you can append the data needed to create the segments. Alternatively, your segments might be based on the products your customers expressed an interest in. Chapter 7 is devoted to how to create segments and how to design e-mails that appeal to each segment.

Keep track of your customer's lifecycle

There is a big difference between buyers and people who have never bought anything from you. When they buy something, welcome them and thank them. From then on, use their name. If they buy a lot, tell them how much you appreciate their business. Remind them of what they bought in the past. They have probably forgotten about it. It can be a great conversation starter.

Make every e-mail interactive

With the software available today, there is no excuse for a promotional e-mail to just lay there. It should be filled with interactive links: preference centers, polls, surveys, drill-downs, and paths to more information. A good e-mail should be like a Nintendo game, with scores of pathways the user can explore. Every marketing e-mail should be an adventure.

Three marketing movements

There have been three great marketing movements in the past sixty years: mass marketing, database marketing, and e-mail marketing.

Mass marketing began in 1950 with the advent of television. Within five years, most consumers in most households watched TV every night. The result was an explosion of mass purchasing of consumer products and services. In the US, more than $80 billion was projected to be spent on TV and radio advertising in 2008[8]. Mass marketing is alive and well today.

Database marketing began around 1985. The idea was to create prospect and customer databases and use them to send personalized direct mail and phone calls to individuals and households, keeping track of what they bought and how successful each campaign was. Unlike TV or radio, direct marketing made it possible to measure the success of each offer, list, and campaign. Control groups that didn't get the messages were set aside, so it became possible to know with some precision which messages were working and which weren't. Coupons were used to bring consumers into stores. Database marketing worked so well that by 2008, marketers in the US spent more than $64 billion on direct mail, 20% more than on TV.[9]

E-mail marketing took off in 1998 with the creation of such companies as e-Dialog and Responsys. Marketers started sending promotional and transactional e-mails to consumers, getting them to buy products online or in their stores. Today, about 80 percent of all US and UK consumers have e-mail addresses that they use from time to time. On the other hand, 18 percent of US households have no access to the Internet and don't plan to go online.[10] Millions provide their e-mail addresses to their suppliers, giving them permission to send them transactional and promotional e-mails. JupiterResearch reported that about one-half of online consumers who had signed up to receive promotional messages made either online purchases (48 percent) or offline purchases (50 percent) because of these messages. Companies are projected to spend about $1.5 billion on e-mail marketing in 2009[11].

By 2008, online retail sales had reached $129 billion[12]. These sales, however, were only about 3 percent of total retail sales.

EXHIBIT 01-01 Annual e-commerce

	Annual e-Commerce Billions	% Total Retail Sales
2000	$22.28	0.80%
2001	$31.60	1.10%
2002	$38.72	1.30%
2003	$49.24	1.70%
2004	$63.64	2.00%
2005	$77.64	2.30%
2006	$96.52	2.70%
2007	$114.36	3.10%
2008	$129.64	3.40%

What makes these numbers more significant are studies concerning the behavior of retail shoppers. Ninety percent of those who use the Web, who are themselves three quarters of all US households today, say they consult the Internet regularly or occasionally before making offline purchases.

EXHIBIT 01-02 Internet Research before buying offline

How often do US Online Shoppers Research Products Online Before Buying in a Store

	Men	Women	Total
Regularly	50.50%	30.60%	43.30%
Occasionally	41.50%	52.50%	47.30%
Never	8.10%	10.70%	9.40%

Stores Magazine Survey of 7,675 Consumers in 2007
BIGResearch sponsored by Microsoft

This shows the actual impact of e-mail promotions on retail purchasing decisions is about four times the total value of online sales. E-mails may be responsible for influencing more than 12% of total retail sales, about one half of a trillion dollars annually.

E-mail marketing is possible because the Internet exists and because millions of consumers have PCs and cell phones equipped to receive e-mail. A major driver of e-commerce growth is the extension of broadband connections to more US homes. With broadband, Web pages load five to ten times faster than with dial-up connections, making online shopping much easier. Fifty-eight percent of all US homes, nearly 68 million households, had broadband connections by 2008, up from 48 percent in 2006, according to Forrester Research.

Pew reports that broadband users are more likely than dial-up users to shop online—74 percent to 59 percent. The US, Canada, Australia, the UK, and many other countries have become "wired nations" in which virtually all consumers can be reached by e-mail as well as by phone or direct mail.

A 2007 JupiterResearch survey of 630 large US corporations showed that each one was sending an average of 5.2 million marketing e-mails to their customers each month. The effect of this marketing on consumers is reflected in a 2006 JupiterResearch survey that showed 27 percent of the e-mails received by consumers were opt-in marketing e-mails from commercial sources.

EXHIBIT 01-03 Source of e-mails to consumers

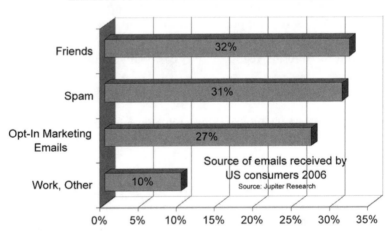

What are these marketing e-mails used for?

A 2007 JupiterResearch report of 200 major corporation executives showed how e-mail marketing messages are used by their corporations in customer communications.

The eight different commercial e-mail categories shown in Exhibit 01-04 can be divided into two broad categories: promotional e-mails and transactional e-mails. Promotional e-mails say, "Here is what we have. Review it, and click on anything that interests you. You can buy it online by clicking here right now, or go to one of our stores to get it." The transactional e-mails occur after a purchase is made. "Thank you

EXHIBIT 01-04 Purpose of corporate customer e-mails

Question: For which of the following applications does your company use email as
a tool to interact with your clients, prospects and partners? Select all that apply.
Asked of 200 executives in 2007 by Jupiter Research

for your order of Grand Prix Supremes Shoes, Mr. Hughes." "Your
Grand Prix Supremes Shoes were shipped today, Mr. Hughes. The
tracking number is . . ."

Some interesting statistics

E-mails deliver sales at an average cost per order of less than $7.00,
compared to $71.89 for banner ads, $26.75 for paid search ads, and
$17.47 for affiliate programs, according to Shop.org's State of Retailing
Online 2007.

Forrester reported that 95 percent of companies used or were planning to use e-mail as a marketing tool in 2008. The average company
that used e-mail marketing sent 23 million e-mail messages per year.

The average company loses about 30 percent of its e-mail subscriber list per year, according to EmailStatCenter.com.

Quris.com reported that 40 percent of e-mail subscribers will go
"out of their way" to patronize a company whose e-mail programs they
like.

Over 147 million people in the US use e-mail almost every day, according to eMarketer.

Why are most marketing e-mails like blasted TV ads?

The exciting information presented thus far about marketing e-mails is
really only a peep at the future. It's not an accurate view of the present.
Almost all US corporations send marketing e-mails today but only a
small number of those use their full capabilities. Why?

Many companies today are driven by the need for this quarter's sales to be higher than last quarter's. If the sales don't go up, the company's stock price will go down. The pressure is on to increase sales. To achieve e-mail marketing's full results, companies must capture customer names, addresses, demographics, and preferences; put them into newly constructed marketing databases; and contract with an e-mail marketing firm to use the information to create and send individually targeted interactive e-mails to each subscriber. "Great idea," these companies say. "We will look at that after we get next quarter's sales up where they should be." So marketers continue to blast identical TV-type ads in their e-mails on a daily basis to every consumer who foolishly provides her e-mail address to them.

It's not that complicated. It doesn't cost that much more to send individually targeted interactive e-mails so customer retention and sales can be doubled or tripled over their present levels. In this book we'll explain in detail how to do this.

How valuable is e-mail marketing?

The Direct Marketing Association reported that for every dollar spent on e-mail marketing in 2008, marketers returned an estimated $57.25 on the investment.[13]

In the twenty-two chapters that follow, we'll provide you with detailed information about how to arrange and send highly profitable personalized, targeted marketing e-mails to all your customers. We'll explain the difference between hunting for sales, using e-mails as hunters use guns, and farming your subscriber base, using database marketing and e-mails to communicate with your customers, studying and reaching out to each subscriber as a farmer studies and cares for his livestock. Underlying the chapters in this book is the notion that using e-mails for farming is more profitable than using them for hunting.

In the following chapters, we will explain how to:

- Acquire customers' e-mail addresses with proper permission, gaining in the process information about their preferences and lifestyle and putting them into a marketing database used to support future communications.
- Measure the relevance of your e-mails and resulting lifetime value derived from them.
- Test and measure the effectiveness of your marketing e-mails, including sophisticated analytics.

- Create interactive promotional and transactional e-mails using segments and preference information derived from your database.

- Use viral marketing and loyalty programs, and determine the appropriate frequency of customer contacts.

- Understand how business-to-business e-mail marketing differs from consumer marketing.

E-mail marketing isn't just a way to increase profits by reducing costs and selling more products and services, although those things are, and must be, the primary results. Marketing e-mails are tools that provide management with customer information and provide customers with company, brand, or product/service information. Customer information is used in various ways to increase customer retention and acquisition rates, the essence of business strategy. The information derived from e-mail customer interactions that you can store in the customer database provides a measurement device essential for the evaluation of strategy.

Looked at from the customer's point of view, e-mail marketing is a way of making customers happy; of providing them recognition, service, friendship, and information for which they will reward you with loyalty, retention, and increased sales. Genuine customer satisfaction is the goal and hallmark of satisfactory e-mail marketing. If you are doing things right, your customers will be glad that you are sending them promotional and transactional e-mails. They will want to log on to your Web site. They will appreciate the things you do for them. If you can develop and carry out strategies that bring this situation about, you are a master marketer. You will keep your customers for life and be happy in your work. You will have made the world a better place to live in.

Notes

1. David Daniels, *Maturation of Email: Controlling Messaging Chaos Through Centralization* (New York: JupiterResearch, 2007), 5.
2. David Daniels, *The ROI of Email Relevance: Improving Campaign Results Through Targeting* (New York: JupiterResearch, 2007), 7.
3. Arthur Middleton Hughes, *Strategic Database Marketing,* 3rd ed. (New York: McGraw-Hill, 2006), 243.
4. John Horrigan, *Online Shopping: Internet Users Like the Convenience* (Pew Internet & American Life Project, 2008), http://www.pewinternet.org/ppf/r/237/report_display.asp.
5. *A View from the Inbox 2008* (Merkle 2008), http://www.merkleinc.

com/userassets/Documents/WhitePapers/ViewFromTheInbox2008.pdf, 5.

6. *The Future of Food Retailing in the U.S.* (Package Foods, March 2008), http://www.mindbranch.com/Future-Food-Retailing-R567-681/.

7. Jeanne Jeannings, "Dear John: Tips for Testing Personalized E-Mail Salutations," The ClickZ Network (February 13, 2006), http://www.clickz.com/showPage.html?page=3584001: "A personalized salutation provided a 13.0 percent lift to the [click-to-open rate]. This was over three times what we'd seen when we tested a generic salutation against the control in [a previous test.]"

8. Bert Coen, *Insider's Report* (New York: Universal McCann, December 2007), 5.

9. Ibid.

10. "One in Five U.S. Households Has Never Used E-mail" (Parks Associates, May 13, 2008), http://newsroom.parksassociates.com/article_display.cfm?article_id=5067.

11. David Daniels, *US Email Marketing Forecast, 2007–2012* (New York: JupiterResearch, 2007), 11.

12. Stephanie Miller, "Email ROI, or Kicking Our Baby Out of the Nest" (MarketingProfs, August 19, 2008), http://www.marketingprofs.com/8/email-roi-kicking-baby-out-of-nest-miller.asp.

13. Ibid.

2

E-mail Marketing: Hunting or Farming

E-mail "batch and blast" marketing is in distress. It simply no longer performs. Subscriber inboxes are overflowing with permission-based e-mail that is irrelevant. Our research shows that 60% of subscribers just ignore the e-mails, deflating marketer hopes for relationship-building and sales. Worse, half of subscribers unsubscribe or complain to their ISPs, completely severing the relationship and hurting deliverability across the board. Using our old direct marketing friend, data, marketers can finally respond to the fact that response rates have steadily declined year over year and start to provide custom, relevant e-mail experiences for their important subscriber segments. With CRM systems finally providing intelligent and actionable methods for determining a subscriber's place in your sales and product lifecycle, marketers can more easily create relevant subscriber experiences, which is the key to driving response.

Stephanie Miller, VP of Strategic Services Return Path Inc.

Despite the agreement in the industry about the importance of relevance, the vast majority of permission-based commercial e-mails sent today are blasted content for subscribers about whom nothing is known other than their e-mail address. E-mail is so inexpensive compared to any other channel of advertising—TV, radio, print, or direct mail—that marketers' main problem has been how to get it out the door quickly, not whom to send it to or what to say to them.

If you look at the typical e-mail marketing shop today, it's creating content that's sent out as fast as it's written. In many e-mail marketing situations, less than 10% of opt-in e-mail subscribers buy anything at all from the company sending the missives. The companies send the same e-mails to buyers that they send to non-buyers. People who have made a dozen purchases get the same e-mails as people who have never bought anything.

E-mail marketing is just one frantic campaign after another, and sales are down. Solution? Send more e-mails. People are unsubscribing. Solution? Frenetically try to get more subscribers and send more e-mails to those who are still here. How can we measure the success of e-mail programs conducted at this breakneck pace?

There are two basic ways to look at e-mail marketing: as hunters and as farmers. All e-mail marketers measure e-mail campaign performance. Only advanced e-mail marketers also measure subscriber performance. Subscriber performance measurement is more expensive. However, it yields the most opportunities for increasing retention and profits. Most e-mail marketers aren't there yet.

North America: hunting and farming

The two approaches to e-mail marketing are analogous to the difference between buffalo hunting and cattle farming. For centuries, North American natives obtained their protein by hunting for game, such as buffalo, deer, rabbits, and wild turkeys. Some hunters came back empty-handed. Some were successful. When the Europeans began to arrive, hunting wild game could no longer sustain the growing population's need for protein.

The newcomers introduced a different method of obtaining a balanced diet: raising cows, pigs, chickens, and other livestock. Starting with rudimentary farming methods, farmers gradually became more successful at producing milk, eggs, and meat. They studied their herds, learning to care for them and meet their needs. Farming in the US today is generally highly scientific and profitable. In most large commercial dairy farms, for example, the farmer keeps track of every cow: her health, feed, days in milk, pounds of milk, percentage of butterfat, percentage of protein, and pedigree going back for a few generations.

The direct mail industry has become more like farming than hunting. High postal rates have made it uneconomical to send direct mail to just anyone. Instead, efficient direct mailers build customer and prospect databases. They use database marketing to send their mail to consumers and businesses they know a lot about: age, income, presence of children, type of housing, mail responsiveness, and (for business) Standard Industrial Classification (SIC) code and annual revenue. They select from the right lists, augment their databases with appended data. They use predictive analytics. It's very scientific and profitable.

Most of the e-mail marketing industry, however, is more like hunting than farming. E-mails are so inexpensive that sending e-mails to millions of nonrespondents is a trifling matter. You set out your e-mail traps, and enough people respond to make you a nice profit. But this situation is beginning to change.

Subscribers are sick of receiving so many e-mails, even those they originally subscribed to. Even worse, almost three quarters of the e-mails received by the average consumer consists of unwanted spam. These unwanted e-mails are routed by the consumer's ISP (AOL, MSN, Yahoo, etc.) to a spam folder, where they are quickly deleted. But even the volume of legitimate (non-spam) promotional e-mails has become a growing annoyance for many consumers. Many e-mail marketers are blasting millions of daily e-mails to everyone on their opt-in list. Some consumers ignore these messages. Others delete or unsubscribe from them, and others classify them as spam.

Most e-mail marketers measure their success by measuring their campaigns. They send out 1 million e-mails, and within 24 hours they know how many opens, clicks, and conversions they've achieved. The national average open rate for opt-in permission-based promotional e-mails is below 23% and falling.[1] Some e-mail marketers have seen the handwriting on the wall and are turning to database marketing.

Database marketing is analogous to farming because when doing it, you study the customers and prospects (your domestic livestock) instead of the campaigns (the traps for wild animals). You create a database of business or consumer prospects and customers. You append demographics to their records from compiled sources like AmeriLINK. The appended records now have more than 100 fields of relevant demographic and behavioral data, including gender, age, income, children, wealth, length of residence, own or rent, type of dwelling, occupation, education, and ethnicity. In these databases you also record your prospects' on- and offline behavior: Did they open, click, download, complete a profile or preference form? Did they buy something online, from a catalog, or from a retail store? What was it, when was it, how much did they pay? What promotions have they received? Where do they live?

Armed with this data, you can create subscriber segments, such as affluent retired, college students, families with young children, condo dwellers, home office owners, major league sports attendees, frequent travelers, and golfers. You can create marketing messages specifically for each profitable segment. E-mailers who have done this find that a personalized customized message to a profitable segment has much higher open, click, and conversion rates than a one-size-fits-all blasted e-mail promotion.

Why, then, are only a small portion of e-mail marketers using database marketing? The principal reason is that e-mail is so inexpensive ($6 per thousand compared to $600 per thousand for direct mail) that it seems to be more profitable to blast than to customize. Most e-mail marketers don't even know the street address or Zip Code of their registered e-mail recipients. Some ask simply for the e-mail alone in their registration form. Others get the name and e-mail. They have discovered that the more data they ask for, the fewer registrations they get. If your prospect list contains only a name and an e-mail address, however, it's impossible to get appended demographics. You have no idea who these people are, making it very difficult to send relevant e-mails.

Database marketing to the rescue

Some advanced e-mail marketers are turning to database marketing because blasted e-mails have begun to lose their effectiveness now that everyone is doing it. Open, click, and conversion rates are falling. Unsubscribes, undeliverables, and spam designation rates are going up. The return from the hunt is falling because too many hunters are chasing the same subscribers.

E-mail marketing based on database marketing (farming), on the other hand, is becoming more productive. E-mail recipients open e-mails from trusted sources that consistently send them personalized, customized content of interest to them. Marketing Sherpa reported in 2008 that e-mails directed at specific segments early in the year had open rates as much as 20% higher than nonsegmented blasts.[2] The same report showed that click rates for segmented e-mail campaigns during the last quarter of each year were five times higher than nonsegmented blasts.

But if e-mail is so cheap to send, why concern yourself with open and click rates? Why not blast everybody? The reason is that consumers are increasingly opening e-mails based on their prior experience with the sender and the sender's previous e-mails. If they trust you and have gained value from opening and reading your previous e-mails, they will open your new ones. If they have had bad experience with your e-mails in the past, they are unlikely to give you another chance.

The best way to build trust and good experiences is to segment your subscribers and send customized content to the members of each segment. The e-mails contain content that you've learned is of particular interest to these segment members. You can only do this through database marketing. This is the future of e-mail marketing: putting your prospects and customers into marketing databases, using the databases to create marketing segments, and designing custom marketing strategies for each segment. We are learning to study our subscribers one by one, analyzing them as a farmer analyzes his livestock, rather than setting out traps (e-mail blasts) as a hunter does in the wild.

In the meantime, however, even if we want to use database marketing so we can send relevant e-mails, we still have to continue with our existing e-mail campaigns. We still have to measure the performance of each campaign. The next two chapters cover these aspects of e-mail performance measuring.

What do subscribers want from e-mail marketing?

The basic goal of all e-mail marketing is to create profits from selling products to consumers and businesses. A successful long-term way of doing this is to build a relationship with every person (consumer or business person) who is interested in your products, services, and company. The purpose of this relationship is to sell products and services, building a long-term relationship that is fruitful and rewarding to both the customers and your company. If you want readers to continue to open and read your e-mails, they should contain content readers consider interesting and valuable. What can you put in these e-mails to make them valuable?

Recognition

People like to be recognized as individuals, with individual desires and preferences. They like being called by name. They want the e-mails they read to demonstrate that you have paid attention to what they have told you in their preference profiles and what they have purchased. They don't want to have to repeatedly enter their name and address when the company sending the e-mail already knows what it is.

Service

Subscribers want thoughtful services provided in e-mails that are helpful to them. Once a customer has made a purchase, subsequent e-mails to the customer should reflect that action. She can look up the delivery status of her purchases, for example, by clicking a button on any e-mail she receives.

Convenience

People today are very busy. They don't have time to drive a couple miles to buy something. They want to do business from where they are by reading and clicking on e-mails from companies that remember their names, addresses, credit card numbers, and purchase history.

Helpfulness

Anything you can do to make customers' lives simpler is appreciated. You have to think, every day, "How can I be more helpful to my customers?" Only those who come up with good answers will survive. E-mails should be filled with personalized, helpful services.

Information

Customers are more literate today than ever before. They use the Internet. Technical information is as important to many of them as the product itself. Our e-mails should be loaded with links that permit subscribers to find out anything they want to know about anything. Your e-mails should be gateways to the world.

Identification

People like to identify themselves with their products (like their cars) and their suppliers (like their sports teams). Companies can build on that need for identification by providing customers with e-mails that reflect a warm, friendly, helpful institution and staff they can identify with.

E-mail marketing involves listening to the customer

Unlike direct mail, e-mail is two-way. Each outgoing e-mail to subscribers should be loaded with relevant links that permit recipients to respond, express opinions and preferences, order products, or change their address or order. The e-mails make these things easy to do by having the results of customer input entered automatically into database records. Business rules built into the database permit companies to take action based on customer input, which helps customers and is less costly than having customer service reps doing things that computers can do more efficiently. At the same time, live help is always available when customers want it. The result is that with a first-class e-mail communications system, customers are more loyal. They stay with you for a lifetime. Profits are up while costs are kept lower because of the e-mail service's efficiency.

Information available to hunters and farmers

One big difference between hunting and farming is the amount of data collected about each subscriber. With hunters, the data is minimal—

often limited to the e-mail address and Web activity. With farmers, there is a wealth of information. Getting the data costs money, as does maintaining the database. Here is a shorthand way of comparing the two techniques:

EXHIBIT 02-01 Hunter data vs. farmer data

Information	Hunters	Farmers
Basic Information	E-mail address	E-mail, home address
Name	Sometimes	Always
Promotion History	Sometimes	Usually
Web Activity	Opens, clicks, conversions, RFM	Opens, clicks, conversions, RFM
Offline Activity	Rarely	Often
Profile	Yes, if they provide it	Appended data plus provided data
Preferences	Yes, if they provide it	Yes, if they provide it
Lifecycle Information	Limited	Complete data
Physical Location	Rarely	Street address, city, state, Zip Code, phone
Personal Information	Rarely	Age, children
Marital Information	None	Marital status, name of spouse
Residence Information	None	Housing type, own vs. rent, length of residence, home value
Financial Information	None	Income, wealth, credit
Ethnic Information	None	Ethnicity, language
Educational Information	None	High school, college, grad school
Occupation	None	Yes in most cases
Lifestyle Information	None	Extensive, Prizm clusters
Segment Information	Not much	Complete data
Lifetime Value	Only on buyers	Always
Predictive Modeling	Not possible	Often
Descriptive Modeling	Not possible	Often
Conversions per E-mail	Less than 1%	More than 1%
Database Cost	As low as possible	About $0.50 per name per year
Success Measure	Campaigns	Campaigns and subscriber performance

We know that most of the readers of this book are still at the hunter stage: just getting started and very excited about the possibilities but not wanting to spend too much money. By the time you have finished reading this book, however, you will be wild to become farmers so you can realize the profits that come from successful subscriber management.

Acquiring subscribers

The race is continually on to acquire registered subscribers, both to add to our marketing programs and to replace those who are lost due to un-subscribing and undeliverability. We first try to get people to visit our Web sites using every trick we can think of: banner ads, direct mail, TV, radio, print, search engines, store visits, catalog orders, sweepstakes, co-registration, rented lists, and so on.

For every 200 people who visit our Web site or are registered by other means, a few will give us their e-mail address. Most marketers today stop there. The best marketers take the next step and ask for a double opt-in (described in chapter 18): they send an e-mail to the registrant asking her to click on the e-mail to affirm that she really agrees to accept our e-mails.

At that point, most hunter e-mail marketers stop. They have met all the CAN-SPAM requirements. They can send subscribers as many e-mails as they have promised, or as many as they can get away with. They don't ask for more, because they know the more they ask, the more subscribers will drop out. The goal is a very large marketing audience. It is hard to build that audience if you push your luck by asking for too much information.

Farmers take the process one step further. At confirmation, serious farmers ask for the subscriber's street address. With the street address, the farmer can have more than 100 pieces of relevant data appended to more than 90% of all consumers and businesses. With consumers, we can learn their exact age, their estimated income, wealth, housing type, whether they rent or own, length of residence, marital status, children, ethnicity, direct mail responsiveness, credit worthiness, and dozens of other facts. For business customers, we can learn annual revenue and number of employees. These data cost just $0.04 to $0.05 per subscriber.

With this appended data we know much more about each subscriber than we did before. Today, about 30% percent of all marketers use the detailed information collected from subscribers to put them into marketing segments and develop custom marketing strategies for each segment.[3]

Both hunters and farmers can, of course, ask people to complete a profile and a preference form. Their responses permit marketers to create segments and really targeted personalized e-mails. The problem is that only a small percentage, perhaps less than 10%, of all subscribers will fill out either of these forms. If they do, we can use that information. But for the bulk of all subscribers, we have to make do with appended data based on postal address, which, on the whole, is quite valuable.

Subscriber lifetime value: hunting

To illustrate why farming subscribers is so much more profitable than hunting for customers, let's compare lifetime value tables for hunting and farming (for more on lifetime value, see chapter 6). The first table is for a retailer's hunting database of 2 million subscribers who are sent a weekly e-mail blast. Each month about 1.10% of the recipients unsubscribe and about 1.75% bounce, becoming undeliverable. These numbers are typical numbers derived from actual case studies. The retailer knows only his subscribers' e-mail addresses. He doesn't know their names, addresses (unless they bought something), not even their Zip Codes. The retailer does very well despite knowing so little:

EXHIBIT 02-02 Lifetime value of subscribers using hunting

Hunting LTV Total Subscriber List		Acquisitiion Year	Year 2	Year 3
Subscribers start of year		2,000,000	1,316,000	873,824
Unsubscribe Rate		1.10%	1.10%	1.10%
Bounce Rate		1.75%	1.70%	1.65%
Subscribers end of year		1,316,000	873,824	585,462
E-mails Delivered	52	86,216,000	56,935,424	37,941,438
Open Rate		20%	22%	24%
Opens		17,243,200	12,525,793	9,105,945
Open conversion rate		1.5%	2.0%	2.5%
Online Orders		258,648	250,516	227,649
Total Revenue	$138	$35,693,424	$34,571,189	$31,415,511
Cost of Operations	55%	$19,631,383	$19,014,154	$17,278,531
Acquisition Cost	$14	$28,000,000	$0	$0
Transaction E-mails	2	517,296	501,032	455,297
Cost of e-mails	$6.00	$520,400	$344,619	$230,380
Total Costs		$48,151,783	$19,358,773	$17,508,911
Profits		-$12,458,359	$15,212,417	$13,906,599
Discount Rate		1.00	1.15	1.36
NPV Profits		-$12,458,359	$17,494,279	$18,912,975
Cumulative NPV Profit		-$12,458,359	$5,035,920	$23,948,895
Lifetime Value		-$6.23	$2.52	$11.97
E-mails producing sales		0.30%	0.44%	0.60%
Unique Buyers		111,219	107,722	97,889
Percent Buyers		5.6%	8.2%	11.2%

In the first year (the acquisition year), subscribers received 86.2 million e-mails, of which 17.2 million were opened. Of the e-mails that were opened, 1.5% resulted in a purchase whose average order size was $138. In this simplified chart, we don't calculate the offline sales made to retail stores or catalog call centers as a result of the e-mails. In all, the e-mails were responsible for $35.6 million in revenue in the first year.

Looking at the costs, you can see that 55% of the revenue went to operating costs. It cost $28 million to acquire these 2 million subscribers through a variety of means: banner ads, search engines, direct mail, TV, radio, and print. The e-mails were very inexpensive—only $520,400. By the third year, the lifetime value of each subscriber was $11.97. Less than half of the original 2 million subscribers were still on the list, and the conversion rate of a delivered e-mail was only 0.6% in the third year.

Remember, our retailer had no information about these 2 million subscribers, except their e-mail address, how they were acquired, when they signed up, what they purchased (if they did), and which of them opened their e-mails. In the first year the 258,658 orders were placed by 111,219 subscribers, who represented just 5.6% of all subscribers. Almost 95% of the subscribers who received these weekly e-mails never bought anything at all during the first year. Some buyers bought several times, but most bought only once.

The illustration shown here isn't unusual. It is typical of a modern e-mail marketing hunting operation. After the first year, the list is profitable, with a total net present value profit of $23.9 million in the third year. To keep it going, of course, the retailer has to constantly add new subscribers. It has to blast out an e-mail every week.

Here is how the subscriber acquisition cost could be determined:

EXHIBIT 02-03 Cost to acquire subscribers by hunting

Acquisition spending for Hunting

	Visitors	Cost
Come to website	8,000,000	$28,000,000
Provide e-mail	2,400,000	
Valid on first try	2,000,000	
Total Cost		$28,000,000
Total Cost Each	2,000,000	$14.00

Using various means, the retailer attracted 8 million visitors to his Web site at a cost of $28 million. Of these visitors, 2.4 million provided their e-mail addresses. On the first try (a welcome e-mail) to these sub-scribers, 2 million resulted in an acceptance by the subscriber. Net cost of a valid e-mail address? $14.

Subscriber lifetime value: farming

Let's contrast this situation with that of a similar retailer who sends e-mails to 2 million subscribers based on farming. In this case, the retailer knows a lot more about his subscribers. He obtains the subscribers' name and street address, he uses a double-opt-in acquisition process, and he appends demographic and behavioral data to the subscribers who survive the acquisition process. To get these subscribers, he had to spend a lot more money:

EXHIBIT 02-04 Cost to acquire subscribers by farming

Acquisition spending for Farming

	Visitors	Cost
Come to website	9,000,000	$31,500,000
Provide e-mail	2,400,000	
Double Opt In	2,000,000	
Append Data	2,000,000	$80,000
Total Cost		$31,580,000
Total Cost Each	2,000,000	$15.79

To end up with 2 million valid double-opt-in subscribers, the re-tailer had to attract 9 million visitors to his Web site. Of these visitors, 2.4 million were willing to provide their name, street address, and e-mail address. The double-opt-in process involved sending an e-mail to the 2.4 million subscribers to get their confirmation that they want to receive his e-mails and to provide him with their street address. Two million confirmed.

When the retailer got those names, he appended demographic data to their records at $0.04 each. He created a relational database with all that information. When the database was set up, he used analytics to create five segments of approximately 400,000 subscribers each, devel-oping marketing strategies and content for each segment. The database and analytics cost about $6 million. In addition, it was necessary to de-velop different creative for each segment—offering different products to each segment. He personalized his e-mails and sent more transac-tional messages and a large number of triggered messages, such as birthdays, Next best product (NBP) suggestions (covered in chapter 4), and so forth.

These additional steps added to the cost of sending e-mails. As with the previous table, the numbers in this table are illustrative of the methods that e-mail marketers use to measure their success with subscribers:

EXHIBIT 02-05 Lifetime value of subscribers using farming

Farming LTV Divided in Segments		Acquisition Year	Year 2	Year 3
Subscribers		2,000,000	1,424,000	1,048,064
Unsubscribe Rate		0.80%	0.70%	0.65%
Bounce Rate		1.60%	1.50%	1.40%
Net Subscribers		1,424,000	1,048,064	790,240
E-mails Delivered	52	89,024,000	64,273,664	47,795,911
Open Rate		24%	26%	28%
Opens		21,365,760	16,711,153	13,382,855
Open Conversion Rate		2.5%	3.0%	3.5%
Online Orders		534,144	501,335	468,400
Total Revenue	$145	$77,450,880	$72,693,514	$67,917,989
Cost of Operations	55%	$42,597,984	$39,981,433	$37,354,894
Acquisition Cost	$15.79	$31,580,000	$0	$0
Transaction E-mails	3	1,602,432	1,504,004	1,405,200
Triggered E-mails	12	24,000,000	17,088,000	12,576,768
Cost of e-mails	$8.00	$917,011	$662,925	$494,223
Database & Modeling	$3.00	$6,000,000	$6,000,000	$6,000,000
Total Costs		$81,094,995	$46,644,358	$43,849,117
Profits		−$3,644,115	$26,049,156	$24,068,872
Discount Rate		1.00	1.15	1.36
NPV Profits		−$3,644,115	$29,956,529	$32,733,666
Cumulative NPV Profit		−$3,644,115	$26,312,414	$59,046,080
Lifetime Value		-$1.82	$13.16	$29.52
E-mails Producing Sales		0.6%	0.8%	1.0%
Unique Buyers		201,372	189,003	176,587
Percent Buyers		10.1%	13.3%	16.8%

The table shows the lifetime value of subscribers acquired for farming. As you can see, this subscribers performed much better than the subscribers marketed to by hunting techniques. The e-mails were personalized and customized to offer each subscriber her NPB. As a result, the number of people unsubscribing and the bounce rates were much lower.

More of these people opened their e-mails, because they proved to be more relevant to their lives and interests. More people placed online orders. The open conversion rate was more than 3% by the third year. Approximately 16.8% of subscribers bought something by the third year. Average order size was higher, too: $145 instead of $138.

The overall effect of shifting from hunting to farming, using the numbers from our examples, can be seen in this table:

EXHIBIT 02-06 Gain from shifting from hunting to farming

Gain from Shifting from Hunting to Farming		Acquisition Year	Year 2	Year 3
Hunting LTV		−$6.23	$2.52	$11.97
Farming LTV		−$1.82	$13.16	$29.52
Gain		$4.41	$10.64	$17.55
With 2,000,000 Subscr.	2,000,000	$8,814,244	$21,276,494	$35,097,185

This table illustrates how to measure e-mail success. Marketers similar to those in our examples could increase their net profits by $35 million by the third year. These are net profits after all costs have been subtracted. The gains come about by:

- Reducing the unsubscribe and bounce rates
- Segmenting the audience and developing a marketing strategy for each segment
- Determining a NPB for each customer, and using that in the e-mails
- Improving the open rates through delivering relevant, personalized e-mail content

This chart, in a nutshell, is what this whole book is about: boosting profits by moving from a primitive method of e-mail marketing (hunting) to an advanced one (farming).

Takeaway thoughts

- E-mail marketing today is one frantic campaign after another. Getting out the door fast is the goal.
- There are two ways of looking at e-mail marketing: as a hunter setting out traps (e-mails) in the wild, or as a farmer taking care of his flock (double-opt-in subscribers) and maintaining them with tender loving care.

- Most e-mail marketing today is done by setting out traps and hoping for a catch.
- Subscribers today are getting sick of the volume of e-mail they receive, even of mail they have subscribed to.
- Subscribers are looking for recognition, service, convenience, helpfulness, information, and identification. Relevant e-mails can provide these things.
- E-mail involves listening to subscribers and acting on what they say.
- Most readers of this book are at the hunter stage. By the end of the book, they will want to become farmers.

Notes

1. Tad Clarke, *Email Marketing Benchmark Guide 2008* (Warren, RI: Marketing Sherpa, December 2007), 178, http://www.marketingsherpa. com/#, 178.
2. *Dirty Dozen* (Warren, RI: Marketing Sherpa), http://www.marketing sherpa.com/MSEmailEmailMistakes08.pdf.
3. Tad Clarke, *Email Marketing Benchmark Guide 2008* (Warren, RI: Marketing Sherpa, December 2007), 178, http://www.marketingsherpa. com/#, 73.

3

E-Mail Campaign Performance Measurement

Business-to-consumer (B-to-C) and business-to-business (B-to-B) marketers alike are failing to use metrics at even a high level to gauge the effectiveness of their mailings. Although B-to-C marketers are slightly more engaged with using the barometer-oriented metrics . . . than are their B-to-B counterparts, many fail to use these metrics at least once a month. Barometer-oriented metrics are useful, particularly for trending mailing performance over time. Marketers should seek to use aggregate click-through, click-to-conversion, profit-per-mailing, and revenue-per-subscriber information as KPIs [key performance indicators] for each mailing. Additional measures, such as average order value (AOV), will vary based upon the offer, merchandise selection, and even time of year. While valuable, AOV is a variable that should be used via merchandising and creative tactics to affect the primary barometer-oriented KPIs.

JupiterResearch

We describe many types of e-mail campaigns in this book, including newsletters, sales promotions, surveys, viral promotions, triggered mail, and transactional mail. We can sum these up by listing several types of marketing e-mails

- Promotional e-mails
- Newsletters
- Transaction e-mails
- Triggered e-mails
- Welcome e-mails
- Reactivation e-mails
- Thank-you e-mails
- Surveys

You can probably come up with additional types of e-mails that are useful in your business. You should have segmented your customer database so that you don't send the same promotions to seniors that you send to college students. Businesses get different promotions from those sent to consumers, and so on.

In chapter 13, you will learn that every time there is a purchase, you have a sequence of messages, including a thank-you message and a order shipped message.

Finally, you will have triggered, or event-driven, e-mails that you send, such as birthday greetings, suggestions for a product that complements one the customer just purchased, a thank-you for a completed survey, a white paper requested by the subscriber, and a confirmation of a registration.

You may also have an active reactivation program going on at all times. Most of this must be conducted by direct mail, rather than by e-mail, to avoid being considered as spam. As a matter of course, you should send a postcard or other direct mail piece to those undeliverable registrants whose names and addresses you have in your database. After a suitable interval, you may find that a direct mail piece to someone who has unsubscribed is productive. Philosophy.com sent a "we've missed you" reactivation trigger e-mail to those who hadn't purchased in the last 90 days. Results: 67% opened the e-mail, 55% clicked through, and 11.5% converted. The reactivation e-mails generated $3.34 for each delivered e-mail.

What can you measure?

E-mail marketing's measurement potential is almost limitless. There has never been anything like it in the marketing field. Comparing e-mail's measurement possibilities with those of previous marketing forms is like comparing business in 1870 with business today. In 1870, there was no electricity, telephone, radio, television, automobiles, aviation, or fast mail service which would have permitted mass marketing. By 1970, we could measure a direct mail list's pulling power, offer, and copy. By 1990, we could measure the response by various demographics or Zip Code. Today with e-mail, we can measure all of the above and just about anything else that you can imagine. What can we measure in an HTML (Hypertext Markup Language) e-mail campaign?

- Effectiveness of the sender and subject lines
- Offer, copy, text placement, images, and video

- Opens, clicks, downloads, conversions, deliveries, and unsubscribes
- Demographics and geographics of recipients by all of the above
- Success of campaigns by all of the above
- Success of our entire e-mail marketing program by all of the above
- Value of an opt-in e-mail address
- Cost of a delivered e-mail
- Number of sales produced
- Volume of sales produced
- Profits from conversions due to e-mails
- Effect of e-mails on offline sales
- Conversions per campaign
- Effectiveness of reactivation campaigns
- Revenue per delivered e-mail
- E-mails produced by store visits, catalog purchases, and Web site registrations
- Return on investment

How e-mail works

E-mails were the first use of the Internet back in 1971, long before Web sites existed. The Internet was created by connecting many computers to wired networks so that each computer could receive information from other computers digitally. The networks rely on switches (routers) that help the little boats (digital packets) that hold the information contained in e-mails, Web sites, video, or telephone conversations. A packet can leave one computer and travel halfway around the world through many different networks and arrive at another computer in a second or two.

To create a packet, the e-mail software (or client) breaks up the e-mail into packets of about 200 bytes. A byte consists of eight bits (a bit is a zero or a one). Each packet is put into a frame that contains extra bits with the information necessary for routing the packet from one computer to another. The main advantage of packet-switching is that it allows millions of computers to use the same worldwide network of communication lines. Sharing allows for very efficient use of the worldwide network.

With the Internet, computers aren't connected directly to other computers. Instead, each packet is independently routed over common lines to its destination. When a packet is ready, the host computer sends it over a telephone line or cable to a router. The router examines the destination address in the frame and passes the packet along to another router, chosen by a route-finding system. A packet may go through a few or thousands of routers in its travels from one computer to another. When the packets reach their final destination, they are reassembled in the correct numerical order at the destination computer.

Exhibit 03-01 illustrates one of the billions of electronic packets that travel every minute of the day all over the world on the Internet. The packet begins and ends with an electronic flag so that the routers can know where each packet begins and ends. It has an electronic address of the destination computer and a packet number with control bits to ensure that the data in the packet is not corrupted. The payload is a group of bits that contain the information that the packet is transporting from the source to the destination computer. This information may be a little section of a Web page, of a TV picture and sound, of a VoIP voice conversation, or of an e-mail.

EXHIBIT 03-01 A packet in its frame with its address and control bits

Flag: Packet Ends Here	Packet # & Controls	Payload: Webpage, TV, VoIP or Email	Address: To where?	Flag: Packet Starts Here

All packets travel at close to the speed of light: 186,000 miles per second. Because of the various lines and routers involved, a packet may take a few seconds to get where it is going.

How HTML works

HTML is used to create the colorful e-mails and Web sites we are all familiar with. The images shown in a typical HTML e-mail may not actually be in the e-mail itself. They may be located on the server of the company sending the e-mail. Each image has its own particular URL, which is called up by HTML code when you view the e-mail. The HTML code uses your PC to send a packet back to the server saying in effect, "Send us this URL." The server creates a group of packets containing the image and sends them to your PC so that the image is shown as a picture on your screen.

Something else happens, as well. When the server receives the request for the URL, it learns you have opened the e-mail, since both packets contain your address. Every time a user opens an HTML e-mail, the sender knows the e-mail has been opened, who opened it, and when. When you click on a link in an HTML or text e-mail (e.g., to see a different page or section of the e-mail), you see new information because a packet has been sent to the server asking for the new page. The server sends it and records the fact you clicked on a link. Packets sent back may also include your input (such as your name, a product order, or your response to a survey question).

Many times the recipient's messaging client is set up to protect the recipient's privacy. If this is the case, the user may see a yellow line at the top of the e-mail that lets the user know the images have been blocked (as in Outlook). When you click on that notice to unblock the images, you also send a message to the sender that you have done something with the e-mail (opened, clicked, downloaded, etc.).

The messaging client shows you an inbox: a list of all messages that have arrived for you. The inbox displays the message headers: who sent the mail, the subject of the mail, and the message's time, date, and size. You can use the header to select a message to read, skip it, delete it, or mark it as "junk," or spam.

Outlook also shows you a preview pane. The preview pane shows the first few lines of the message text, either to the right of or below the message header. Many e-mail receivers go through a series of steps before they actually read or delete an e-mail. They look at the sender and the subject lines. If they are interested in knowing more, they look at the preview pane to get an idea of what is inside. Only if that view peaks their interest will they actually open the e-mail.

EXHIBIT 03-02 A client with a preview pane

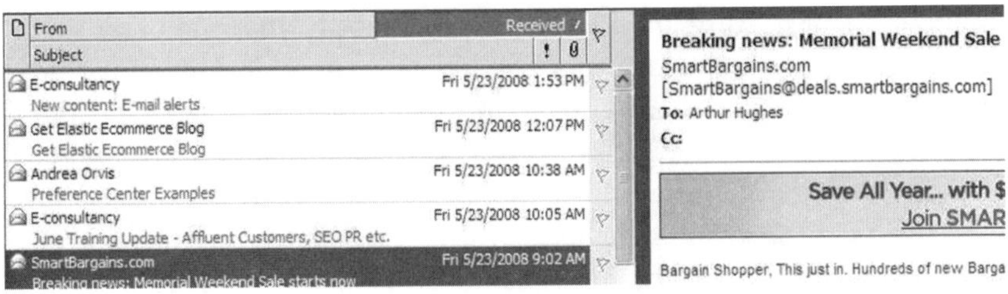

Many e-mails are sent and received as just text, with no HTML. In the case of text e-mails, the sender doesn't know whether you have opened the e-mail, since text e-mails don't send packets back to the sender. There is no way to track text e-mail opens. You can, however, check the clicks or conversions in a text e-mail. This can be done if the user clicks on a hyperlink to a URL in the text. But in this case, the

Web site owner can't know it was the text e-mail that led the viewer to his site. All he knows is that some unknown person has visited his site for some unknown reason.

Text e-mails are fine for spreading the word about something but aren't much use in tracking the effectiveness of the word-spreading process. However, it is possible to encode the links in a text message with codes that identify the subscriber. So while you can't track text opens, you can tell who clicks on the links in a text message.

Measuring deliverables

In a campaign, we send out a million e-mails to a list of people who have provided us with their e-mail addresses, with permission to use the addresses for commercial promotions to them. We have previously verified this permission by sending each person an e-mail to his address, asking him to click on a link that sends a packet back to us, indicating he has received the e-mail (verifying the address's correctness) and wants to hear more from us, thus verifying that this is truly an opt-in situation. This is called the double opt-in system, which we highly recommend. Only about 20% of all e-mail marketers today use the double opt-in method. The others send promotional e-mails to people who have provided them without the verification step.

Despite this authentication, a percentage (from 2% to 10%) of every batch of promotional e-mails you send out, which may even have just been confirmed recently, still bounce. Why?

Most e-mails bounce because the addresses are no longer valid. About 30% of all e-mail addresses change every year. This happens because consumers switch to new e-mail providers, create new accounts, or move to new companies. Users seldom notify their commercial e-mail marketers when their e-mail addresses change. In fact, some people actually change their e-mail addresses just to get rid of these marketing messages. Even if an address is valid, a mailbox may be temporarily unavailable because the owner has exceeded the allotted disk space or a mail server may be temporarily unavailable because it is processing a large volume of mail. If the address doesn't exist anymore, of course, the failure will be permanent.

When you send an outgoing e-mail, it goes to a message transfer agent (MTA) at the company that sends your e-mails for you, which transfers messages from one computer to another. Each MTA has a mail queue with a certain number of slots available to process outgoing messages. Each slot holds an outgoing e-mail until that e-mail has been delivered successfully or until the MTA determines that it can't be delivered. If your outgoing list has lots of bad addresses, the rate that your mail can be delivered will drop, since many slots will be filled with e-mails with bad addresses that the MTA repeatedly tries to deliver.

When an e-mail bounces, it comes back to your MTA's automated bounce handler. The bounce handler sends a series of bounce messages to the addressed domain to test whether the bounce was temporary or permanent. The bounce handler tracks what happens to the messages it sends and responds accordingly. e-Dialog uses a three-strike rule. If there are three or more consecutive soft (temporary) bounces over more than 14 days, they are automatically converted into a hard (permanent) bounce.

Since messages can bounce for many different reasons, the bounce handler doesn't take the subscriber off the list right away. Instead, it waits for about 10 days after the first bounce, then sends a warning message to the subscriber. At the end of every marketing promotion, your e-mail service bureau will give you a report on which e-mails were delivered and which had permanent bounces. You will then get a deliverability rate, such as 95.30%.

This is much better than what the US Postal Service (USPS) can do for third-class (bulk-rate) mail. If a bulk-rate letter can't be delivered, the local post office just chucks it out without telling you. You can't find out how many letters were delivered or which customers didn't get their mail. Of course, if you want to pay the price, you can send your letters by first-class mail which is always forwarded or returned to you if it can't be delivered. Most marketers can't afford to use first-class mail; it is too expensive for promotional mail. Even USPS bulk-rate mail with all of its deliverability problems costs about 100 times more per message than e-mail.

Why do large e-mailers outsource their e-mails?

Most marketers outsource the entire e-mail creation and sending process to an ESP, giving the provider instructions (usually digitally) as to who is the audience for the e-mails, what the content of each e-mail should be, what triggers will be used, and so on. Other firms develop the content but outsource e-mail sending, using an ESP's software.

Why would you outsource these functions? First, e-mail delivery is a highly specialized function, which requires special software and staff training. Even after 10 years, the ESP function is still new and changes every year in new directions that are hard to predict. Today, more than 50 US ESPs specialize in e-mail delivery for clients, and at least eight of them are large companies that have attracted corporations with more than $1 billion in annual sales as clients. Experienced ESPs, with 100 or more clients, have developed considerable experience they use to advise and support each client. This experience isn't available to a company that does its e-mail delivery internally.

E-Mailing a new client

Sending e-mails is a very complex business that can easily go wrong unless done by professionals with experience. For one thing, ISPs could mistake mass e-mails from legitimate mailers for spam. The mistake could cost the mailer thousands of dollars until the situation is corrected.

For example, e-Dialog handled the first mailing for a new client with 16 million opt-in e-mail addresses. It wanted to warm up the ISPs so they wouldn't be concerned about getting so many e-mails from one source all at once. First, it created a cell for each major ISP. Within each cell it segmented the audience by length of time on the list (6 months, 7-12 months, etc.). It sent e-mails gently to each ISP, keeping the number sent at or below 480,000 per day for the 10 largest ISPs and 240,000 per day for the remaining ISPs. The first e-mails were to those subscribers added to the file most recently. It took approximately 11 days to mail the whole 16 million for the first time.

What services do ESPs provide to their clients?

- Strategic guidance on strategies and tactics that have been proved to work elsewhere and could be adapted for use with a client's e-mail marketing program
- IP warming
- Deliverability monitoring, showing daily real-time results
- The ability to provide information on industry trends and best practices, stemming from the ESP's experience with many other clients
- The ability to deliver triggered e-mails, which have much higher ROI than regular e-mails but often require complex software
- Sophisticated analytics support
- The ability to integrate data from multiple channels
- Specialized software, typically some sort of campaign builder or campaign insight software

What an ESP usually includes

A typical major ESP sends e-mails for 100 or more different clients, so an experienced staff is important. They have made mistakes in the past (everyone does) and have learned from them. They know what they are doing. That may not be true of an individual company's e-mail marketing staff. In-house staff has to learn to use highly specialized e-mail marketing software. The training takes time and resources.

Any company doing its own e-mail delivery will also have only a small trained group that knows how to send mass e-mails. If someone is out sick, on vacation, at a conference, or gets a promotion, the company may not have enough staff to get out today's promotion. An experienced ESP, on the other hand, servicing 100 or more clients, has a sufficiently large staff that it can always move people around to get out today's jobs.

The ESP should be able to keep up with constant innovation, as well. In the e-mail world, scores of new ideas are being tried all the time. Some work well, some don't. But overall, e-mail marketers are learning more about viral marketing, links, interactivity, subject lines, deliverability, microsites, JavaScript, HTML techniques, and so on. The e-mail marketing industry just doesn't stand still. A typical ESP manages e-mails for 100 or more clients. Some of these clients have e-mails on the cutting edge of technology. In the course of creating these e-mails, the ESP staffers learn how they work and will be able to suggest some of these advanced ideas to other clients. Since they built these new techniques, they will know how to apply them. A small in-house staff, unfortunately, will not be exposed to these new ideas. Result: their e-mail techniques may fall behind the industry.

Measuring opens

When an e-mail arrives in your subscribers' inboxes, your subscribers have several choices: they can open it and look at it, they can open it and unsubscribe, they can delete it, or they can send it to a spam folder, where it will eventually be deleted. If it's an HTML e-mail and subscribers open it, a Web beacon[1] sends a packet to your Web service, either your ESP or your internal e-mail-sending software, saying the e-mail was opened. (If it was a text e-mail, of course, no message is sent.) Your Web service tracks the packet announcing the e-mail opening. It will update that subscriber's database record. That is more than you can expect with direct mail. Most consumers today toss out direct mail promotions without even opening them. There is no way you can tell what they did with your letter, postcard, or catalog, unless they contact you by mail, phone, or e-mail.

A few hours after each e-mail campaign is sent out, your Web service will begin producing reports on open rates and bounces. These are crucial measures of the success of any e-mail marketing campaign.

Some open rates are as low as 5% or 10%. Few are as high as 50%.[2] Each company's situation is different, so there is really no such thing as an average open rate. One thing is certain: the overall average open rate for promotional e-mails is falling. Every year it is lower than the year before.

How is an open calculated? Some common ways are:

- Unique opens divided by e-mails delivered (about half of e-mail marketers use this method)
- Total opens divided by e-mails delivered (about 8% use this method)
- Unique opens divided by e-mails sent (about 15% use this method)
- Total opens divided by e-mails sent (about 5% use this method)

The rest have another method altogether. These differences, combined with differences in what is considered "delivered," mean the open rate for the same mailing can range from 12% to 35%! In this book, we calculate the open rate as unique opens divided by e-mails delivered. This is the method most major ESPs use.

Exhibit 03-03 should be taken with a grain of salt. There are no absolutes in the e-mail industry. Irrelevant e-mails don't get opened in any industry. Relevant, important e-mails can get open rates of 40% or more, no matter what the industry. It is useful, however, to see others'

EXHIBIT 03-03 Open rates by industry

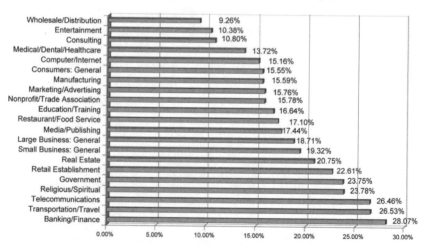

Wholesale/Distribution	9.26%
Entertainment	10.38%
Consulting	10.80%
Medical/Dental/Healthcare	13.72%
Computer/Internet	15.16%
Consumers: General	15.55%
Manufacturing	15.59%
Marketing/Advertising	15.76%
Nonprofit/Trade Association	15.78%
Education/Training	16.64%
Restaurant/Food Service	17.10%
Media/Publishing	17.44%
Large Business: General	18.71%
Small Business: General	19.32%
Real Estate	20.75%
Retail Establishment	22.61%
Government	23.75%
Religious/Spiritual	23.78%
Telecommunications	26.46%
Transportation/Travel	26.53%
Banking/Finance	28.07%

Source: MailerMailer 2007

open rates to know if you are missing something. In general, open rates are coming down, year after year.

There are two reasons an open rate may be misleading. First, many

EXHIBIT 03-04 Average open rates by year

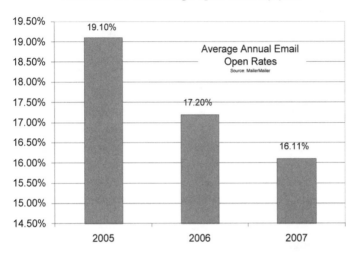

e-mail clients block images. Until the user unblocks them, no packet is sent to the sending computer saying that the e-mail has been opened.

Second, about 40 percent of all clients have a preview pane, which allows users to see a small portion of an e-mail before they open it. When the preview pane opens, however, a packet is sent back and the e-mail is registered as an open, whether the user reads it or not.

According to Loren McDonald of EmailLabs:

> Various companies report "industry average" e-mail metrics such as open, click-through, and bounce rates. We all love these statistics, but let's be clear—they are not industry averages. What the statistics usu-ally are is a snapshot [of] the average results from one company's client base. Unless your profile is similar, then the "average statistics" are probably not a good benchmark for your company's program. Factors that influence these "average" statistics include: types of e-mails sent (newsletter, notification, e-commerce, etc.), industries, sophistication of senders, size of lists, source of addresses, amount of personalization, nature of relationship with recipients, and how they define their metrics.
>
> So how do you use these reported industry stats? I suggest using them as goals rather than clear benchmarks. For example, if your first newsletter generates a 25% open rate but you read of a 40% industry

average, establish internal targets and steps to achieve open rates of 30% and 35%.

Measuring click-throughs

If your HTML e-mail is good, it has lots of interesting things for recipients. Each interesting thing is accompanied by a link. There are descriptions of products subscribers can read. There are surveys they can take. There are videos they can watch. There are forms they can fill out and shopping carts they can fill with products.

Each of these things is a link, which is usually blue underlined text or an image they can click on. Hidden behind the link is the URL of the image, form, file, or video. Clicking on the link sends a packet to your site saying, "Send us this item." The site will send the image. Your MTA keeps track of it all: "Arthur Sweetser just clicked to see the video of the Super Bowl ad." Your database will be updated with all that information.

Click-throughs are a vital measurement of e-mail marketing success. They are way stations on the road to a purchase or a visit to one of your retail stores. The more click-throughs, usually the more interesting your e-mail is to your subscribers and the more likely you are to sell something. The click-through rate (CTR) can be measured as a percentage of opens or a percentage of delivered e-mails. In most cases it is measured based on opens.

What do they measure?

In 2007, Marketing Sherpa surveyed 1,210 e-mail marketers, asking them what metrics they tracked in their e-mails. (See Exhibit 03-05.)

Monthly new-subscriber sources

People are constantly moving and changing their e-mail addresses. About 30% of any e-mail file becomes obsolete every year. In addition, of course, many customers who sign up for e-mail newsletters and promotions get tired of them and unsubscribe. As an e-mail marketer, you will find your subscriber list is constantly melting away. To keep it up, you have to continually add permission-based e-mail addresses. There are many sources of new e-mail names, which can be summed up into six categories:

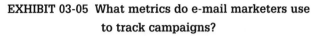

EXHIBIT 03-05 What metrics do e-mail marketers use to track campaigns?

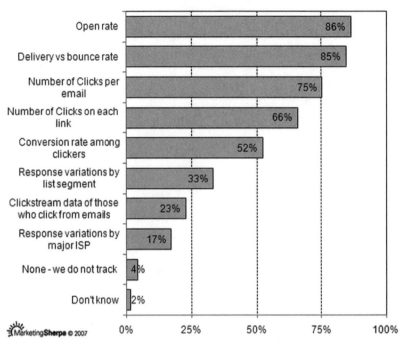

- Web site visitors who register their e-mail addresses on the site
- Viral marketing subscribers who are recommended by friends
- Online sales customers (an e-mail is usually a requirement for an online purchase)
- Store visitors who register their e-mail addresses while in the store
- Catalog purchasers who give their e-mail addresses when buying
- Reactivated customers who are enticed to come back after having disappeared or unsubscribed (note: these folks are usually reached by a direct mail to avoid consumers considering the e-mail to be spam)

Each of these acquisition sources has a different rate of registration. Most people come to your Web site but fail to register their address. Most online purchasers, however, give their e-mail address as part of the purchase process. Online catalog purchasers give you an address. Those who use mail or phone often don't. And store visitors seldom give you an e-mail address, unless you offer some sort of discount to the visitor or an incentive to your sales clerk to get the addresses. The monthly source of your new e-mails can be entered as shown in exhibit 03-06.

EXHIBIT 03-06 New-subscriber sources

Catalog Registrations	244.336
Retail Store Registrations	123,556
Website Registrations	99,766
Reactivated Subscribers	1,266
Total New Subscribers Added	468,924
Amount spent to acquire new subscribers	$156,244
Cost of acquiring one opt in subscriber	$0.33

Web sites have counters that measure visitors. When a visitor registers her e-mail address, that fact is stored in her database record, and your software adds one to a counter showing the number of Web site registrations this month. Viral marketing is so important that we have devoted an entire chapter to it (chapter 18). Not everyone is doing viral marketing today, but it's a great way to add to your database.

When people come to your stores to shop, they should be offered an opportunity (with some reward) for registering their e-mail address with you. To be successful, provide a reward for your store clerks when they sign customers up. The same principle applies to catalog sales. All catalogs today provide at least two ways to buy: online or over the phone. Online, your buyers will give you their e-mail address. On the phone you can reward your customer reps for capturing the e-mail addresses. This process is explained in detail in chapter 8.

Finally, send direct mail to those who have purchased in the past but whose e-mail address has ceased to work for you. If you reward them, some of them will come back, register, and buy. The amount spent in Exhibit 03-06 is an estimate of what you pay to acquire a typical name, whether to the subscriber or to an employee for getting the name.

Measuring list growth

If you can add a lot of permission-based e-mail addresses in a month, you can't assume your registration database will increase at that rate. While you are adding people, many people on your existing database will be unsubscribing or changing their e-mail addresses without letting you know.

Suppose you begin with a database of 1 million. If you are like most e-mail marketers, you will find that only about half of these are actually active e-mail addresses you can market to. Why? When customers unsubscribe, you have to stop sending them e-mails. But instead of wiping them off your list, you mark them as unsubscribers and keep them on the list. You want to use their records as a suppression file for the next few weeks to be sure you honor their request. When e-mails become undeliverable, you don't just wipe them off the database, either. In some cases, you may have their name and address; you may want to send them a direct mail letter, postcard, or catalog to try to get them back at some point. Possibly, they've changed their e-mail address but still want to get your newsletter. In life's fast pace, they didn't notice that your newsletter wasn't getting through to their new e-mail address. They may even have been an active buyer. So you keep them in your database. You may pay an outside service to append their new e-mail address so that you can reconnect with them.

In this way, over time, your database fills up with inactive e-mail addresses.

EXHIBIT 03-07 Growth of inactive e-mail addresses

Address List including Inactives	1,879,880
Mailable e-mail addresses start of month	619,878
Percent Mailable	33%
Dropped because undeliverable	5,882
Unsubscribed in Month	10,234
Lost in the month	16,116
New Subscribers Added	44,337
Mailable e-mail addresses end of month	648,099

During a month, you lose some subscribers through unsubscribes and many from changes of address. If you can accumulate enough new names to compensate for the losses, you are doing well. The actives are the only ones that you can send newsletters and promotions to.

The Television-E-mail Paradox

E-mail marketing has one thing in common with TV advertising: it builds the brand. E-mail produces millions of orders for products and services, some of which can be tracked directly to the particular message that produced the sale. With television, ads can't be tracked as easily. This situation leads to a paradox:

We can't be sure of any specific result for TV ads, so we spend a lot of money on them. We can be absolutely sure of some of the results of e-mail promotions, so we spend much less on them.

Television advertising can be very powerful, but it can't be measured with e-mail advertising's exactitude. TV advertising is typically brand building. Because of TV ads, millions of people recognize Geico's gecko and its cavemen. They also remember the banker who said, "I lost another loan to Ditech!" We know that ads like these drive millions of people to call or go to a Web site or drive to a mall and buy. What we almost never find out is that Sarah Williams bought a specific product through a TV ad on a specific program as a result of a specific ad on a specific day,. We marketers accept the idea that blasted TV ads work, but we also accept the idea that how they work in any particular case can never be proved. As a result, billions of dollars are spent on preparing and broadcasting TV ads and programs with no proof of exactly what happens when they are viewed.

When e-mail marketing and search engine marketing came along, something quite different happened. For the first time, we could prove that as a result of a particular e-mail or search engine placement, Sarah Williams bought a particular book from Amazon.com on a certain day. Because we can know these things, many companies have based their e-mail marketing budgets only on the resulting online sales. What a mistake!

The fact is that e-mail promotions are in many ways like TV ads. They build the brand. They lead recipients to visit a Web site, make a phone call, purchase from a catalog, or purchase at a mall—just like a TV advertisement. Seventy percent of online users today research products using, e-mails, Web sites, and Google, before they buy offline. But normally that offline sale can't be tracked to the e-mail that produced it. Furthermore, a significant number of e-mail promotions never sell anything online. Are these marketers crazy?

Major companies don't take an e-mail promotion's ability to generate offline sales into account when they determine their e-mail promotion budget. They know that e-mail promotions build the brand. They just don't use that knowledge in budgeting. As a result, e-mail budgets in most corporations are far lower than they would be if the true effect of e-mail promotions were taken into account.

Measuring on- and offline sales from e-mail promotions

In this analysis, we can begin with a verifiable fact: a particular group of e-mail campaigns resulted in a certain number of online sales. We then make an estimate of the offline sales through catalogs, retail store visits, phone calls, and indirect sales. An indirect sale occurs when a

customer buys a pair of Nike sneakers from, say, Macy's Web site or retail store rather than from a Nike-owned store or Web site. These retailers rarely, if ever, report to product manufacturers which products
they sell, how much they've sold, to whom, when, and through what
channel. Yet for many products, indirect sales are far greater than direct sales.

To know e-mail promotions' true effect, we have to estimate all
sales that result from those promotions. This isn't as difficult as it might
seem at first—and is much easier than learning a TV ad's effect.

If the e-mail marketer has a catalog sales department, he can learn
which catalog sales were assisted by e-mail promotions with a simple
coding system. The numbers can be backed up by verifiable statistics.

Many e-mail marketers with retail stores already include promotion codes in their e-mails. These codes can be entered into the POS system at the stores so the retailer will learn which e-mail produced which
retail sale. Other retailers use the 10-day rule: If Arthur Sweetser received an e-mail about a specific product and that same Arthur
Sweetser bought that product at a company-owned retail store within
10 days, then that e-mail gets credit for the sale.

Indirect sales can also be estimated with some precision, much
more precision than sales resulting from TV ads. For example, many retailers include electronic coupons in their e-mails. Such coupons may be
effective in selling products in their stores, and retailers can learn a lot
from e-mails with such coupons. The product manufacturers, however,
will probably learn nothing. By doing a bit of research, any company
sending promotional e-mails can make an informed guess about the offline sales that result from their e-mail promotions. For example, let's
say an athletic shoe manufacturer knows its overall annual shipments
of these shoes:

EXHIBIT 03-08 Method for computing indirect product sales

Where Shipped	Pairs	Percent
Shipments to Company Owned Stores	8,557,300	25.84%
Shipments to Company Website Warehouse	7,668,200	23.16%
Shipments to US Retailers (Indirect)	12,556,900	37.92%
Shipments Overseas	4,334,006	13.09%
Annual Shipments	33,116,406	100.00%
Indirect Sales as % of Online		163.75%

Exhibit 03-08 shows that each online order for the product is
matched by 1.64 indirect sales of the same product. This ratio, once determined, can be used in estimating indirect sales. The online sales are

known, the indirect sales must be determined. You can further refine this number by comparing indirect sales with online sales attributable to e-mail promotions.

It's also useful to know how many people have been influenced by an e-mail promotion. When customers come into a department store as a result of an e-mail promotion, for instance, they may buy the promoted product. But some of them will buy other products as well. This almost always happens, and you can count on it if you drive traffic to your stores. With a little research, you can estimate the total orders per e-mail-driven customer. This number can be used to estimate indirect orders or unique customers resulting from an e-mail.

Once armed with the estimated number of buyers resulting from an e-mail promotion, you can estimate the percentage of those subscribers in your database who become buyers as a result of your e-mail promotions.

These numbers can, and should, be used to estimate e-mail promotions' true effect. They should be used to determine the e-mail promotion budget. Far too few companies do this kind of analysis. With this book, you will realize the power of e-mail marketing and adjust your budget accordingly.

Measuring order value and margins

If we are going to determine our success in e-mail marketing, we have to know how much gross and net revenue is generated. We have to know things like this:

EXHIBIT 03-09 AOVs and margins

Average Order Value (Page Two)	$117.92
Net margin on an online order	65.00%
Net margin on a catalog order	60.00%
Net margin on a retail order	50.00%
Net margin on an indirect order	30.00%

The AOV may be difficult to establish in many instances, but it is vital to measuring e-mail marketing's effectiveness. One customer may buy a $4,000 HDTV set, while another buys a $2.00 pair of socks. Adding these together doesn't seem to make sense, but try it: Add up all the online sales in a month or a year; say it's $118.3 million. Then add up the online transactions; we'll say 1,003,368. Divide the sales total by the transactions, and you get $117.92. You may have no product whose sale price is $117.92, but that average number is a really good way to measure your e-mail marketing effectiveness. Use it.

The net margin on a sale is also a difficult number for many marketers. In a retail store, there is often a 100% markup. That means you buy a case of canned string beans for $10.68 and mark it up 100%. You sell the case for $21.36, or $0.89 per can. A 100% markup means your net margin is 50%. But you have other costs to consider: salaries, rent, utilities, advertising, and so on. Your cost to sell that case of string beans may be quite high. A typical supermarket today earns a profit of only about 1% of the sale price of any item. In Exhibit 03-09, the net margin on a retail order (60%) represents the cost of goods sold plus all other variable costs for a retailer. The margin leaves out only the e-mail marketing costs. Determining the average cost per sale in insurance, automobile rental, or airline travel may be complex. Don't make it a massive research project. Look at your annual report. Take the total profit before taxes made by your firm as a percentage of total sales, subtract from 100% and you get the average cost per sale: $100 million in sales minus $8 million profits is $92 million. Your average cost per sale (rate) is 92%. That's good enough for a chart like this.

Measuring e-mail delivery costs

What you pay for e-mail marketing is really based on two numbers: internal and outsourced e-mail service:

EXHIBIT 03-10 E-mail Mailing Expenses

Outsourced e-mail expenses	$22,090
Internal e-mail Expenses	$20,000
Total e-mail Expenses in Month	$42,909
New Subscriber Acquisition Spending	$104,556

In most cases you pay a specific dollar amount for the development of the month's e-mail campaign creative. If the creative is done in house, the marketer can enter the total cost of salaries and overhead as part of internal e-mail expenses. Most ESPs encourage their clients to manage their own programs, using advanced self-service software that's used to select the names for each campaign, the content, the personalization, the links, and so forth. In other cases, the ESP does everything, based on general instructions from the client's e-mail marketing staff.

E-mail delivery is usually paid on a per-thousand basis, anywhere from $2 to $6, depending on how many e-mails are sent. Some ESPs charge based on e-mails sent, others based on e-mails delivered. These numbers are multiplied by the delivery rate to come up with the cost.

Underlying any e-mail marketing program is the e-mail customer marketing database, such as in our earlier example the 1 million names, including actives and inactives. This database permits segmentation, personalization, and tracking of visits to your Web site, purchases, and preferences. This database is so important we have devoted a significant part of the next chapter to discussing how it is set up and maintained.

Measuring this month's results

After we have entered all the data listed so far in this chapter, we can now see some monthly results that jump out at us. Take a look at these numbers:

EXHIBIT 03-11 Monthly e-mail results

E-mails Delivered	10,115,783
E-mails delivered per campaign	595,046
HTML e-mails Opened	1,358,446
Online Orders	143,995
Revenue from Online Orders	$16,941,012
Cost of online goods sold & Overhead	$10,164,607
Net profit from online orders	$6,776,405
Offline Orders from e-mails	60,565
% Offline Orders per delivered	0.60%
Offline revenue from e-mails	$7,125,490
Cost of goods sold plus overhead	$3,919,020
Net revenue from Off Line orders	$3,206,471
e-mail spending this month	$147,465
Net Profit from E-mail Operations	$9,835,410

We delivered 10.1 million e-mails during the month—newsletters, promotions, transactions, triggered, and so forth. We made 143,995 online sales at an average price of $117.92 each, giving us a total online revenue of $16.9 million. We learned something else: 0.60% of the e-mails delivered resulted in an offline purchase. That's a reasonably good outcome. Some marketers can get that number considerably higher. But 0.60% is a profitable number, as we will see.

With these numbers, we are at last able to measure our e-mail promotions' effectiveness in a way the CFO can understand.

EXHIBIT 03-12 Annual status levels of buyers

Group	Buyers	Dollars	Per Buyer	Orders	AOV
One Time Buyers	45,236	$4,563,323	$100.88	45,236	$100.88
2 Time	12,470	$2,657,539	$213.11	24,940	$106.56
3 Time	4,979	$1,582,429	$317.82	14,937	$105.94
4 Time	2,348	$980,293	$417.50	9,392	$104.38
5 Time	1,225	$653,713	$533.64	6,125	$106.73
6 Time	697	$451,484	$647.75	4,182	$107.96
7 Time	506	$370,171	$731.56	3,542	$104.51
8 Time	347	$284,338	$819.42	2,776	$102.43
9 Time	246	$224,195	$911.36	2,214	$101.26
10+ Time	689	$1,038,207	$1,506.83	8,957	$115.91
Total	68,743	$12,805,692	$186.28	122,301	$104.71

Annual buyer status levels

Before we finish with the monthly statistics, let's compare this month with the previous 12 months so we can get some averages. Here is a typical chart that shows these relationships:

Exhibit 03-13 includes numbers from the earlier charts in this chapter. The AOV is $117.92, and the average orders per buyer during the year is 1.8. It also provides the basis for segmenting customers by purchasing status (see chapter 4).

ROI calculation

We now can put all of the data in Exhibit 03-13 into a table that gives important information about our e-mail programs' success. Only e-mails can produce numbers like these.

These are wonderful numbers. Unfortunately, most e-mail marketers don't have numbers like these for their campaigns. They are a picture of what the most successful e-mail hunters have available from an advanced ESP. Yet the statistics e-mail farmers get from their campaigns are much more useful. We'll cover them in the next chapter.

Where do the data come from?

All the data described in this chapter are known to someone in any e-mail marketing operation. The problem is the data aren't all normally known to any one individual. They are spread between the e-mail

EXHIBIT 03-13 E-mail marketing ROI

E-mail Spending This Month	$147,465
ROI per $1 spent on e-mails	$66.70
Cost per Delivered e-mail	$0.015
Cost per Opened e-mail	$2.435
Cost per Unique Click	$0.221
Cost per Off Line Order	$0.021
Cost to acquire one opt in subscriber	$2.36
Orders per campaign	3,563
Average revenue per campaign	$419,146
Cost per Campaign	$8,674
Average Profit per campaign	$578,554
Offline Revenue per delivered	$0.704
Monthly Revenue per Active Sub.	$6.32
Annual Revenue per Active Sub.	$75.87
% Buyers of 12 Month Subscribers	1.55%
Monthly Profit per Active Sub	$15.87
Value of an Opt-in e-mail Address	$190.40

marketers, the ESPs, the Web site managers, the retail store VP, the CFO, IT professionals, and others. How can the information be assembled so we can produce the kind of effectiveness measures shown here?

E-mail marketing managers should make the first move. They should fill in all the information they have at their command right away. That will show what they don't know. At that point, they should form a committee of all involved in e-mail marketing to discuss how the missing data can be made available on a regular, automatic basis so the reports shown above can be produced each month.

An alternate solution is to have your ESP collect the data and send it to everyone involved on a monthly basis. Most of the data can be collected from existing sources. Some of the numbers have to be estimates based on research. Data that have to be estimated at first include:

- Web site and viral subscription rate
- Store visitors and their subscription rate
- Catalog purchaser subscription rate
- Direct mail sent to lost subscribers and the reactivation rate
- Average cost per sale
- Percentage of offline sales from online

For the first round of reports, make reasonable estimates of each number so the reports can be prepared. It will soon become clear whether these initial estimates are realistic—and what can be done to get the data to make them representative of the actual situation.

Putting all the data on one chart

All the campaign data discussed in this chapter can be put together to get a monthly view of e-mail marketing's ROI. It could look something like this:

EXHIBIT 03-14 Monthly e-mail marketing report

A. Costs of Service			E. Opens, clicks & on and off line sales		
Outsourced Email Expenses	$22,909	A1	HTML e-mails Opened	1,358,446	E1
Internal e-mail Expenses	$20,000	A2	Percent Opens of Delivered	13%	E2
Total e-mail Expenses in Month	$42,909	A3	Clicks	445,332	E3
New Subscriber Acquisition Spending	$104,556	A4	Percent Clicks of Opens	32.78%	E4
B. e-mails Sent			Unique Clicks	667,889	E5
Campaigns in Month	17	B1	Unique Clicks as % of Avg Subs.Mailed	108%	E6
Total e-mails Sent	10,213,031	B2	Percent offline orders per click	13.6%	E7
Total e-mails Delivered	10,115,783	B3	Estimated Offline Orders from e-mails	60,565	E8
Deliverability Rate	99.05%	B4	Estimated off line orders per buyer	1.2	E9
C. Monthly List Growth Measures			Est Off Line Buyers from e-mails	50,471	E10
Total Addresses in T-Master	1,879,880	C1	Percent offline buyers of mailable e-mails	8.14%	E11
Mailable e-mails (T-M less suppressions)	619,878	C2	Online Orders	143,995	E12
Percent Mailable	33%	C3	This month unique online buyers	121,445	E13
Undeliverable Dropped in Month	5,882	C4	Orders per online buyer	1.19	E14
Percent Undeliverable of Mailable	0.95%	C5	**F. Value Costs and Margins**		
Unsubscribed in Month	10,234	C6	Average Order Value	$117.65	F1
Percent Unsubscribed of Mailable	1.65%	C7	Cost of Offline Goods plus Overhead	55.00%	F2
Lost in the month	16,116	C8	Cost of Online Goods plus Overhead	60.00%	F3
New Registrations in Month	44,334	C9	**G. Return on Investment and Costs**		
Mailable e-mail addresses end of month.	648,096	C10	e-mail Spending This Month	$147,465	G1
Percent change in mailable addresses	4.55%	C11	ROI per $1 spent on e-mails	$66.70	G2
D. This Month's Results			Cost per Delivered e-mail	$0.015	G3
e-mails Delivered	10,115,783	D1	Cost per Opened e-mail	$2.435	G4
e-mails delivered per campaign	595,046	D2	Cost per Unique Click	$0.221	G5
HTML e-mails Opened	1,358,446	D3	Cost per Off Line Order	$0.021	G6
Online Orders	143,995	D4	Cost to acquire one opt-in subscriber	$2.36	G7
Revenue from Online Orders	$16,941,012	D5	Orders per campaign	3,563	G8
Cost of online goods sold & Overhead	$10,164,607	D6	Average revenue per campaign	$419,146	G9
Net profit from online orders	$6,776,405	D7	Cost Per Campaign	$8,674	G10
Offline Orders from e-mails	60,565	D8	Average Profit per campaign	$578,554	G11
% Offline Orders Per Delivered	0.60%	D9	Offline Revenue per Delivered	$0.704	G12
Offline revenue from e-mails	$7,125,490	D10	Monthly Revenue Per Active Sub.	$6.32	G13
Cost of goods sold plus overhead	$3,919,020	D11	Annual Revenue per Active Sub.	$75.87	G14
Net Revenue from Off Line Orders	$3,206,471	D12	% Buyers of 12 Month Subscribers	1.55%	G15
e-mail spending this month	$147,465	D13	Monthly Profit per Active Sub	$15.87	G16
Net Profit from e-mail Operations	$9,835,410	D14	Value of an Opt-In e-mail Address	$190.40	G17

This is as complete a picture of e-mail marketing campaign performance as you are likely to get. Every e-mail marketer should have a chart like this produced automatically every month. It should go to the CFO, the CEO, and the CMO. Arising from this form should be graphs that compare the performance of each value month by month. Graphs can be prepared that show progress—or lack of it. (See Exhibit 03-15.)

This chapter has covered the information you can derive from hunting for sales using e-mails. The next chapter covers farming: the measurement of customer performance.

EXHIBIT 03-15 Monthly revenue and active subscribers

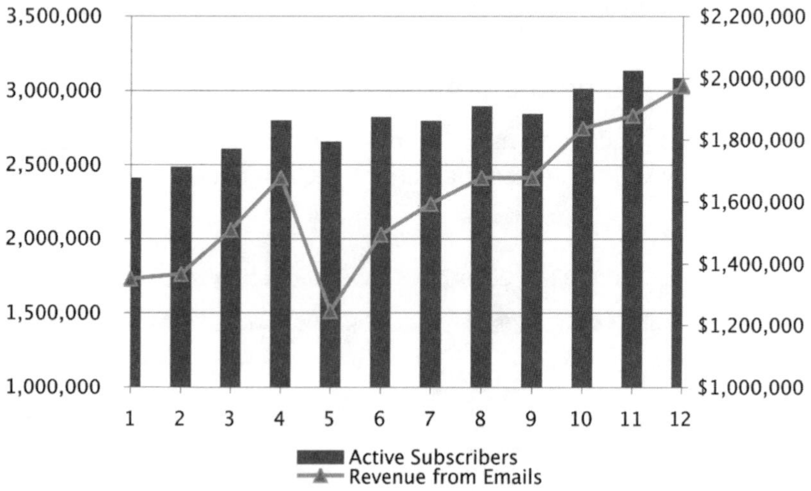

Active Subscribers
Revenue from Emails

Takeaway thoughts

- The measurement potential for marketing e-mails is almost limitless.
- You can measure the performance of only HTML e-mails; you can't measure text e-mail performance.
- E-mails are sent and received by means of digital packets, which travel on the Internet.
- HTML e-mails have interesting fonts, color, and images. Text e-mails don't.
- HTML images are usually stored on the e-mail sender's server. Each image has its own URL.
- When a subscriber opens an HTML e-mail, a packet is sent back to the sender.
- The packet tells the sender that the e-mail has been opened, by whom, and when.
- Thirty percent of e-mail addresses become undeliverable every year.
- The overall industry open rate for e-mails is about 16% and falling.
- CTR is measured when subscribers click on links in their e-mails.

- To maintain a valid marketing list for e-mails, new subscribers have to be constantly added, since so many disappear each month.
- E-mails produce both on- and offline sales.
- It is possible to determine e-mail marketing's ROI and an opt-in e-mail address's value.

Notes

1. A Web beacon is an object embedded in a Web page or e-mail. It is usually invisible to the user. It allows the site owner or sender to see if a user has viewed the page or e-mail. One common use is in e-mail tracking.
2. The exceptions to the 50% maximum for opens are transaction and triggered e-mails. Transaction e-mails (e.g., "Your order has just shipped" or "Print out your boarding pass") have open rates of over 90% in many cases.

4

Farming Subscribers

> To engage customers, you need to understand who your likely customer is and to market to that customer based on what you know about him. The more you can build your marketing around what you know about the customer, including when and where he communicates and does business with you, the greater your chances of marketing success. Moreover, customers who engage with your brand through multiple channels are known to be of even higher value and to stick around longer than single-channel customers. Stores, contact centers, e-mail, Web sites, direct mail, all are proven channels, and more channels, such as RSS and mobile, are cropping up all the time.
>
> John Rizzi, CEO, e-Dialog

For the first decade of e-mail marketing, hunting was almost the only method used to attract customers. Traps were put out into wild to catch subscribers. Some subscribers were caught in the traps and became customers. Marketers became experts at designing the traps and adding lures, such as catchy subject lines, to bring in more business. The system still works. Billions of dollars are still being made in this way.

In the past few years, however, some e-mail marketers have been experimenting with farming; they study the farmyard animals (the subscribers) as individuals and design e-mails for each subscriber. This process is more complicated than hunting. It requires learning a lot about each subscriber and putting that knowledge into a marketing database. The database is used to create subscriber segments that, in turn, are used to craft personalized messages designed to appeal to each subscriber. If done correctly, the farming process can be more profitable than hunting. A key reason is that too many hunters and too much hunting are reducing the success rate (the e-mail open rate, for example) for everyone.

You can use the data from the subscriber database to measure the lifetime value of each subscriber and put each one into a particular segment. The e-mail messages you send to each subscriber can be personalized because you have collected relevant information about each subscriber and stored the information in the marketing database in such a way that you can easily use it to create communications to each subscriber. The marketing database enables you to have meaningful, individual dialogues with hundreds of thousands or millions of customers, just as the old corner grocer had with his individual customers.

As you know by now, there are two ways of measuring an e-mail marketing program's effectiveness: campaign performance measurement and subscriber performance measurement. Campaigns are easier to measure. Tracking systems have been set up so that e-mail marketers can count opens, clicks, conversions, and unsubscribes.

Subscriber performance measurement is more difficult, more expensive, but much more profitable in the long run. You learn each subscriber's physical mailing address. You track everything a subscriber does on your Web site, while reading your e-mails, while shopping at your retail stores, and when calling your catalog desk. You add all this to your subscriber database. You then use the database to manage these customers. The goal is to understand these subscribers, maintain contact with them, build their loyalty to your company, and boost sales through personalized communications.

The farming process centers around the customer marketing database because it contains all your subscribers, customers, and former customers. It may contain not just the subscriber's e-mail address also many other fields as well, including:

- Name and street address
- Date of birth, income, wealth, education, marital status, children
- Type of housing, house value, own vs. rent
- Purchases made online, from catalogs, and in retail stores
- Promotions and transactional e-mails sent
- Record of clicks, downloads and Web visits
- Lifetime value, recency, frequency, monetary (RFM) cell code, Next best product
- Loyalty program points, subscriber preferences, and special interests
- Segment and status level into which the subscriber has been put
- Source of the subscriber and the source date
- Whether the subscriber is an advocate or a hand-raiser

Depending on the products you sell, you may not want or need all these data fields. There is no need to collect and keep data you don't use.

The basic idea is to put all you know about the various individuals who have registered their e-mail address with you or bought something from you into a relational database[1]. When you send promotional e-mails, you select names from this database. Relevant e-mails are constructed using several different factors, including:

- The segment you have placed the subscriber in (described in chapter 7)
- The lifecycle of the subscriber—is she a new customer, a multi-channel customer, a lapsed customer, and so on
- The available triggers, that is events in the subscriber's life that can be used as a reason for messages, such as a birthday
- The subscriber's name, which can be used in the body of the e-mail
- The subscriber's preferences and profile, which can be used to create relevant content in each e-mail
- Interactivity, such as lots of links in the e-mail that make the e-mail an adventure for the reader
- Testing and measurement, which are built into each e-mail campaign, comparing the success of new marketing ideas in e-mails against the performance of control group e-mails

Each of these factors requires data be stored, usually in the customer marketing database. In many companies, constructing such databases is very difficult. This is mainly for historical reasons: the data stemming from promotions and purchases in different channels are collected by different business units and stored separately. Many modern companies have already created a data warehouse that has all the information on a particular customer. Other companies have not reached that stage yet. In these companies, data storage looks something like Exhibit 04-01.

Companies often have multiple channels for customers to buy products and services through, and orders from different channels are fulfilled by different business units. One group manages the Web site. Another handles the catalog call center. A third runs the retail stores. Each has its own database out of necessity, which are often incompatible with one another. There may also be still another group that sends promotional and transactional e-mails to subscribers. This group may

EXHIBIT 04-01 Multiple customer-data storage locations

The customer buys through several different channels

Web and Email	Retail & Wholesale	Phone, Fax & Mail

outsource its e-mail delivery function to an ESP, which is simply given a list of e-mail addresses and told, "Send today's special to this list."

The result of these separate groups each using their own database is that no one has a comprehensive picture of the customer. In 2007, 24% of large corporations had six or more independent business units sending e-mails to their subscribers, according to JupiterResearch.[2] Many of these units don't check with the others when designing or dispatching the e-mails to the same group of subscribers. The customer soon realizes that she is dealing with several different groups within the company that don't know about or appreciate her purchases from other channels. She is apparently the only one who knows what she buys from this company. When one of your best online customers visits one of your retail stores or calls the catalog desk to ask a favor, she may be considered a nuisance by the sales rep who knows nothing of this customer's history with your firm.

Why do customers leave? Most people (68%) leave a supplier because of how they are treated rather than because of price or quality issues.[3] You may be treating your best buyers like strangers when they shop in another channel. Channels affect customer behavior. Those customers who use multiple channels typically spend more than those who use fewer channels. J.C. Penney Corp., for example, found that 80 percent of people who visited its JCP.com Web site also made purchases at its brick-and-mortar stores, and 30 percent of online visitors shopped the chain's catalog.[4] The effect of multichannel purchasing is illustrated by numbers compiled by a major US retailer (Exhibit 04-02).

EXHIBIT 04-02 Spending by multichannel customers

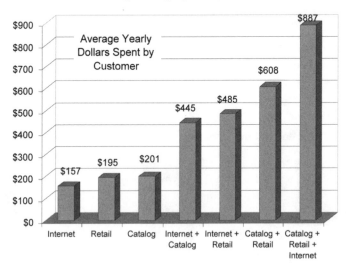

Knowing how much each customer spends with you and how much she is worth to you can help you develop programs to assure that you retain your very best customers. You can't really afford to risk their leaving just because some other channel didn't recognize their importance to your company.

A solution to the multichannel database situation is to create a single customer marketing database that receives input from all parts of your organization, updated frequently.

The process looks something like Exhibit 04-03.

EXHIBIT 04-03 A consolidated customer database

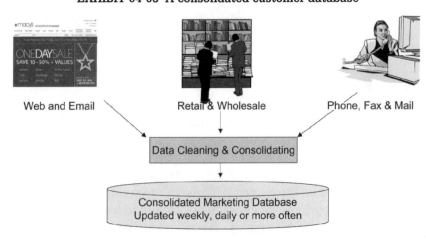

This database is then used by all channels in their interactions with customers and prospects. The Web site, the call center, the retail POS system, and customer service person will all be able to identify the gold customers, for example, when they show up—even if the customer earned that status from another channel or from a combination of channel purchases. A customer may come to the Web site for the first time, but when she registers and logs in to the Web site, what she sees will reflect what she has bought from a retail store or the catalog. She is treated like an old friend. Now that builds customer loyalty.

How to collect subscriber data

To farm your subscribers, you must know a lot of information about them. How can you get it? There are at least four methods that work. First, capture events. Keep track of everything they do: open, click, and buy in any channel. This data comes from the operational databases.

You can also gather preferences. Ask customers what they prefer. The advantages and methods of getting subscriber preferences and profiles are spelled out in chapter 11.

Third, you can infer their preferences. By studying what your customer does on your Web site, in your e-mails, with your catalog, or in your retail stores, you can infer what she is interested in. Clicks and conversions can be made to tell a powerful story.

Finally, you can append data, which you can get from one of the four major consumer data compilers in the US.[5] For about $0.04 for each subscriber, you can get demographic data appended to a consumer's entry that contains an accurate street address. This data is never 100% accurate, but it is much better than nothing.

Using data to create segments

Demographic and behavioral data can be used to create meaningful segments, in both e-mail and non-e-mail activities (Exhibit 04-04).

The care and feeding of subscribers

Now that you have the data on your subscribers stored in a well-built database, your job is to make the subscribers happy with your company and its services. You want them to read your communications, be loyal, and purchase lots of products. You divide them into useful segments, such as college students, seniors, married with children, and home-office workers. Then you develop a marketing strategy for each segment. Their database records will be the focal point for all future contacts and communications.

EXHIBIT 04-04 Consolidated database uses

Email Campaigns

Phone Campaigns

Direct Mail Campaigns

Customer Segmentation

Consolidated Customer
Marketing Database

Status Level Rewards

Models and Analytics

Website Recognition

Defection Prediction

When subscribers come into a retail location, the POS system should make personnel aware of their status. Circuit City, for example, asks customers for their home phone number. Entering that on a POS system brings up the essential facts from its database record. At a bank, the teller might find the customer is category five in the bank's profitability index and her NPB is a certificate of deposit. That information is used in conversations by in-person staff, call center personnel, the e-mail marketers, and the Web site, which would feature items of presumed interest to the customer when she logs in.

Every subscriber should feel as if she has been noticed and is appreciated by your company. You call her by name in your e-mails. You remember her past purchases in a way she can see in her online account. New purchase suggestions designed just for her appear in every promotional and transactional e-mail she receives from you. If you are clever, you can do what Netflix does for its subscribers (Exhibit 04-05).

Your subscriber will soon realize she isn't seeing the same e-mails everyone else is. She is corresponding with a company that knows her preferences, appreciates her as a customer, and helps her make purchasing decisions.

Once you have relevant information in your subscriber file, you will be amazed at what you have learned. Instead of just e-mail addresses and names, you now have real people with ages, incomes, children, occupations, and homes. You may want to make use of all the data in every e-mail. Don't. Subscribers don't want you to seem as if you know

EXHIBIT 04-05 Netflix.com suggestions

too much about them, particularly if you have obtained the data from somewhere else. Figure out ways to use the data that will increase your conversion rate but not make you seem like Big Brother.

To begin with, you can stop sending e-mails about lawn mowers to people who live in high-rise apartments or condos. Stop sending e-mails about baby food to houses whose occupants are all over 60. Start sending e-mails about life insurance that are relevant to subscribers' incomes. For example, a bank sends messages offering $2,000 worth of life insurance to all of its depositors. Some of these depositors have incomes of less than $20,000. Others have incomes of more than $150,000. The $2,000 offer makes sense for the low-income depositors, but it makes no sense for the high-income depositors, most of whom already had policies of $300,000 or more.

What's wrong with sending an e-mail offering a $2,000 life insurance policy to a consumer whose income is $150,000? It's not relevant. The consumer opens the e-mail and sees that his bank does not understand him at all. He may not open another e-mail from that bank in the future as a result. It has lost the chance to sell him a $100,000 home equity loan with a silly life insurance e-mail.

Before you had a customer database, you had no way of knowing your offer wasn't relevant to some of your depositors. You sent e-mails to everyone on your list and hoped for the best.

Hand-raisers and other subscribers

Chapter 8 describes the subscriber acquisition process. In that chapter you will find dozens of ways to get consumers and businesspeople to give you their e-mail addresses so you can communicate with them. But not all subscribers are alike. Some you acquire because they gave their e-mail address to a partner who gave it to you. Some subscribers may not even remember when or how they gave you their address. Others are hand-raisers—people who are really interested in your company or organization and what you have to offer. These folks are more likely (at first, at least) to open your e-mails and read them. They may be more likely to buy what you are selling. If you can distinguish them from the crowd, you should go out of your way to make them feel at home. You should treat them really well.

Throughout this book we stress that you should be sure your subscribers really want to get your e-mails. We recommend the double-opt-in process, which allows you to be fairly certain that you have a hand-raiser. If your subscriber database contains folks who haven't confirmed they really want your messages, you can't get the true benefits of subscriber farming from them as described in this book.

How can you identify hand-raisers from other customers? One of the best ways is to find people who will recommend your company to others. A satisfied, happy customer is most likely to recommend you to others. Not only is it cheaper to use referrals than other customer acquisition methods, but you will get similar profile prospects to your existing customers. Reader's Digest uses the referral route to garner millions of new customers. A person who will recommend others is a hand-raiser.

Hunting vs. farming

With your database, you can begin farming subscribers and give up hunting for them. Determine what type of person would buy each of your products or services. One way to do this is to consult your database of existing customers. Figure out the characteristics of those who bought the product compared to those who didn't buy it (see chapter 19 for details on analytics). Create a profile of the typical buyer, and use it to select subscribers from your database that fit the profile. Create e-mails just for them. To make sure you are doing this correctly, also create a control group: subscribers selected at random from your database without regard to demographics or behavior.

Exhibt 04-06 illustrates how you can use the data.

From a database of 2 million subscribers, 273,334 people were selected who matched the buyer profile of a particular product and sent a promotional e-mail. Of these people, 842 people purchased the product. At the same time, 20,000 randomly selected subscribers were sent

EXHIBIT 04-06 E-mails based on profiles vs. random selection

E-mail Based on Profile Vs. Random Select	Number	Opens	Open Rate	Clicks	Click Rate	Sales	Conv. Rate	Unsub. Rate	Unsubs
Match the Buyer Profile	273,334	48,653	17.8%	3,990	8.20%	842	21.10%	0.10%	273
Selected at Random	20,000	840	4.2%	27	3.20%	3	11.20%	1.30%	260
Effect of Random Select	273,334	11,480	4.2%	367	3.20%	41	11.20%	1.30%	3,553

the same e-mail. Three of them bought the product. What would have happened if we had randomly selected the original 273,334? The bottom line of Exhibit 04-06 tells us: 41 people would have bought the product and 3,553 people would have unsubscribed because of this irrelevant (to them) e-mail.

What is wrong with a random select?

You have a limited number of chances to be relevant to your subscriber base. Every time you send them something they aren't interested in, you turn some of them off, and your unsubscribe rate goes up. By targeting the right consumers, you not only sold about 800 more units but also saved more than 3,000 subscribers from unsubscribing due to an irrelevant e-mail.

Conclusion: send relevant e-mails. Don't send irrelevant ones.

What do you do with the non-selected subscribers?

In our example, you have 2 million registered subscribers and have sent e-mails to only 273,334 of them. Every one of those 2 million subscribers has some interest in your company and products. If they had no interest, they wouldn't have subscribed. What products or services can you offer them?

You can ask them, of course. In your preference forms (see Chapter 11), you can ask specific questions that will point you in the right direction. This might be the best solution, except that in most cases only a small group of subscribers will take the time to fill out a preference form. And many customers aren't really aware of all the products you have to sell. One purpose of promotional e-mails is to educate your customers about products they might not have seen before and therefore didn't list in their preference questionnaires.

So what will you offer to the remaining 1,726,666 subscribers? This is where farming your subscribers becomes very useful. In the following sections, we will discuss several techniques: link categorization, collaborative filtering, and the NPB (next best product).

Link categorization can be very powerful

In chapter 15 you will learn how important it is to include lots of links in your e-mails. Every time a link is clicked, the subscriber's e-mail client sends a packet back to your server that in effect says, "Show this subscriber the link's landing page." Your e-mail tracking software will keep track of who clicked the link and what the link was. It will store this information in the subscriber's database record. Your job is to categorize the links so you can use the information later.

From the links, you can learn (or infer) what each subscriber is interested in. In designing the next e-mail to this subscriber, you should first research all the links she clicked. If you have a good categorization system, you will know that she is interested in books on, say, interior design, European furniture, and the September Conference. In addition to anything else you plan to communicate with her about, these three subjects should be included in some way.

This is powerful information. Such an advanced farming technique makes the subscriber feel that you are really paying attention to her and her interests, just as our corner grocer would.

Collaborative filtering is another answer

With collaborative filtering, the idea is to make automatic predictions (filtering) about a user's interests by collecting taste information from many similar users (collaborating). Both Amazon.com and Netflix use this technique. The underlying assumption of collaborative filtering is that those who agreed in the past tend to agree again in the future. For example, a collaborative filtering for music tastes could predict which music a user will like, given a partial list of that user's tastes (likes or dislikes). These predictions are specific to the particular person but uses information gleaned from many subscribers.

Netflix asks each member to report on movies they liked and those they didn't like. From the reports of millions of people, it is able to create "soul mates"—people who have likes and dislikes in common. For example, if Netflix knows Arthur Sweetser likes Jane Austen, Alfred Hitchcock, and "Curb Your Enthusiasm" and dislikes "Lost" and "Desperate Housewives," it can pair Arthur with others, soul mates, who also have these likes and dislikes. Knowing that, it can predict that

Arthur is likely to want to see a new movie based on what his soul mates thought of that particular movie.

Collaborative filtering is very powerful. It can produce outstandingly successful results. GUS, the largest cataloger in the UK, used this software to increase its cross-sale rate from 20% to 40% by correctly identifying the next product customers would like to hear about, based on their soul mates' preferences. (The cross-sale rate is a measurement of the sales of a second product after the customer has bought the first product she called up to buy.) Before using collaborative filtering, GUS call center agents had been using intuition and rules of thumb to suggest a second product to callers. The collaborative filtering software calculated the appropriate cross-sell product for each particular caller, and put it on the agent's screen while she was processing the first order. Many of the suggestions seemed counterintuitive, such as suggesting bath towels to a woman ordering a dress. But these suggestions worked. They doubled the cross-sale rate.

Collaborative filtering software is expensive. It requires large files with millions of members who expressed opinions on or made purchases. Most marketers aren't in a position to use collaborative filtering. But collaborative filtering is a goal that all marketers at large companies should keep in mind for the future. We are just getting started in sophisticated e-mail marketing. Always keep your eyes and ears open for new profitable ideas. If you are not ready for collaborative filtering, however, you can use NBP analysis right now.

NPB product determination

Suppose you have a dozen products you want to promote to your subscribers. In the past, you might have had a "product of the month" with a special sale for your subscribers each month. With your subscriber database, however, you can do some analytics instead. Suppose you have promoted a particular product to a group of subscribers at some time in the past. Of subscribers getting the promotion, only 3% buy it. To do this type of analysis, your database has to have demographic and behavioral data in most of the records. You select 6,000 buyers of the product who bought it as a result of an e-mail and 30,000 of those who got the same e-mail but did not buy.

Using segmentation and analytics, you can calculate the likelihood of a particular customer being interested in buying each of your products, based on the segment she is in and the percentage interest in each product demonstrated by members of that particular segment. You can

EXHIBIT 04-07 NBP for Janet Westman

Janet Westman	Purchase Likelihood	Profit Potential	Promotion Percent	Promotion Index
Product A	4.5%	9	40.5%	147
Product B	3.7%	8	29.6%	107
Product C	9.0%	2	18.0%	65
Product D	0.6%	6	3.6%	13
Product E	10.3%	5	51.5%	187
Product F	8.8%	1	8.8%	32
Product G	2.7%	11	29.7%	108
Product H	8.0%	3	24.0%	87
Product I	4.5%	12	54.0%	196
Product J	2.3%	4	9.2%	33
Product K	6.0%	10	60.0%	217
Product L	0.4%	7	2.8%	10
Total	60.8%	78	331.7%	1,202
Average	5.1%	6.50	27.6%	100

The promotion percent is the profit potential times the purchase likelihood. The promotion index is calculated as the promotion percent divided by the average promotion percent times 100.

put together a NBP calculation for each subscriber that looks something like Exhibit 04-07.

Analytics shows us the likelihood that Janet Westman will buy each of the 12 products. We have determined how profitable each product is to our company and assigned an order to the products from most profitable (Product I) to least profitable (Product F). Multiplying profitability by purchase likelihood, we have determined the index of Janet's NBP: Product K and Product I are the most likely. We can show this as a graph, as in Exhibit 04-08.

This graph can be done in a number ways, depending on the products and the industry. In banking, we might compute Janet's NBP based on her income, age, wealth, and housing type. For example, a home equity loan might be ideal for Janet based on her age and income, but she rents an apartment and doesn't own a home.

The graph illustrates that it is possible to use demographics and behavior to create a NBP for every subscriber on your database. As a result of promoting customers by their individual NBPs instead of blasting everyone with your product of the month, you can greatly increase the open, click, and conversion rates and reduce the unsubscribe rate. Why does this work? Because the subject line suggests to a subscriber a product that you are quite sure she is likely to buy. This tech-

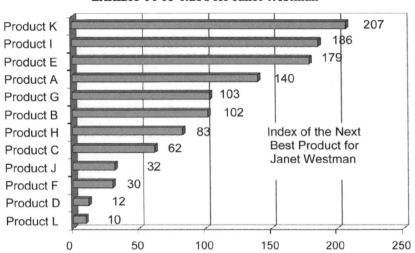

EXHIBIT 04-08 NBPs for Janet Westman

nique teaches your subscriber that your e-mails are relevant to her needs, and she will be disposed to see what you have to say each time.

Let's compare the two methods of treating customers. Exhibit 04-09 is a lifetime value table (details of how lifetime value is calculated are explained in full in chapter 6) of customers sent promotional e-mails 52 times per year, based on the "Special of the Week."

This table details a weekly campaign sent to 2 million subscribers over three years. Assume we have done the analysis necessary to determine for each customer her NBP. To get from here to there, we have appended data to each customer record at a cost of $60 per thousand records and have done the analytical analysis to put all customers into segments and determine their NBPs. This work is not without cost. Exhibit 04-10 is an estimate.

The additional cost per subscriber is $0.79 per year. The results of NBP e-mail campaigns might look like Exhibit 04-11.

By sending each subscriber e-mails based on her calculated NBP, we have reduced the unsubscribe rate and increased the open rate, the conversion rate, and the average order size. The additional cost of calculating the NPB and the database are included. The result is an increase in the subscriber lifetime value from $6.56 to $37.01. The bottom-line meaning of this shift in the e-mail program looks like Exhibit 04-12.

From this we can see that the increased profits by the third year would be more than $60 million. This is pure profit. All the costs have been subtracted.

EXHIBIT 04-09 Subscriber lifetime value for the "Special of the Week"

E-mail Blast of Special of the Week		Acquisition Year	Year 2	Year 3
Subscribers	52	2,000,000	1,620,000	1,328,400
Annual Unsub & Undeliver		19%	18%	17%
E-mails Sent		94,120,000	76,658,400	63,205,272
Open Rate		14%	14%	14%
Opens		13,176,800	10,732,176	8,848,738
Conversion rate		2%	3%	4%
Sales		263,536	321,965	353,950
Revenue	$119.38	$31,460,928	$38,436,215	$42,254,494
Costs	60%	$18,876,557	$23,061,729	$25,352,696
Acquisition Cost	$12	$24,000,000	$0	$0
Transaction E-mails	3	790,608	965,896	1,061,848.57
Total E-mails		94,910,608	77,624,296	64,267,121
E-mail Cost /M	$6.00	$569,464	$465,746	$385,603
Total Costs		$43,446,020	$23,527,475	$25,738,299
Profit		-$11,985,093	$14,908,740	$16,516,195
Discount Rate		1	1.15	1.36
NPV Profits		-$11,985,092.58	$12,964,122	$12,144,261
Cumulative NPV Profit		-$11,985,093	$979,029	$13,123,290
Lifetime Value		-$5.99	$0.49	$6.56
E-mails Producing Sales		0.28%	0.42%	0.56%

EXHIBIT 04-10 Extra cost of NBP

Extra cost of Next Best Product	
Customers	2,000,000
Append data	$120,000
Analytics	$150,000
Creative	$300,000
Database Cost	$1,000,000
Total Extra Cost	$1,570,000
Per Subscriber	$0.79

EXHIBIT 04-11 Subscriber lifetime value based on NBP e-mails

E-mails sent by Next Best Product		Acquisition Year	Year 2	Year 3
Subscribers	52	2,000,000	1,680,000	1,428,000
Annual Unsub & Undeliver		16%	15%	14%
Remaining Subs		1,680,000	1,428,000	1,228,080
E-mails Sent		95,680,000	80,808,000	69,058,080
Open Rate		19%	20%	21%
Opens		18,179,200	16,161,600	14,502,197
Conversion Rate		4%	5%	6%
Sales		727,168	808,080	870,132
Revenue	$124.32	$90,401,526	$100,460,506	$108,174,786
Costs	60%	$54,240,915	$60,276,303	$64,904,872
Acquisition Cost	$12	$24,000,000	$0	$0
Transaction E-mails	3	2,181,504	2,424,240	2,610,395.42
Total E-mails		97,861,504	83,232,240	71,668,475
E-mail Cost /M	$6.00	$587,169	$499,393	$430,011
NBP Additional Costs	$0.79	$1,580,000	$1,327,200	$1,128,120
Total Costs		$80,408,084	$62,102,897	$66,463,003
Profit		$9,993,441	$38,357,609	$41,711,784
Discount Rate		1	1.15	1.36
NPV Profits		$9,993,441.28	$33,354,442	$30,670,429
Cumulative NPV Profit		$9,993,441	$43,347,884	$74,018,313
Lifetime Value		$5.00	$21.67	$37.01
E-mails Producing Sales		0.76%	1.00%	1.26%

EXHIBIT 04-12 Profit from e-mails based on NBP

Lifetime Value Comparison Of two e-mail programs	Acquisition Year	Year 2	Year 3
Special of the week	-$5.99	$0.49	$6.56
Next Best Product	$5.00	$21.67	$37.01
Difference	$10.99	$21.18	$30.45
Times 2 MM Subscribers	$21,978,534	$42,368,854	$60,895,023

Making different offers to different segments

NBP analysis isn't all we can do in the farming of customers. We can make different offers for the same product, based on the loyalty segment of each customer. We can test and measure targeted offers to each segment. We can experiment with different rewards. For example, what works best for a segment: offering 15% off on the next purchase or $15 off (with minimum purchase of $50)? How do such offers affect purchase behavior over the next six months?

Marks and Spencer, one of the world's great retailers, gets a strong response from its better customers who are invited to a special evening of shopping in their stores prior to Christmas. No special prices are offered. On the contrary, the sense of exclusiveness and privilege brings these special customers out in large numbers.

Using the database, you can see customers who were visiting retail stores regularly but who have stopped coming. An e-mail saying, "We've missed you" can add a personal touch and make a significant difference.

> Customers like to be treated like the individuals that they are. We were pleasantly surprised that our customers did not mind receiving different offers than those of their neighbors. This had been a major concern in our organization. Customers accepted the fact that the offers were based on their purchases.
>
> Scott Ukrop, Ukrop's Markets

Retaining subscribers

So far we have talked about sending e-mails to promote online product sales. E-mails have other, equally important roles in farming subscribers: providing them information, reactivating them, and building their loyalty. When you blast identical e-mails to all subscribers, it is difficult to build loyalty. Loyalty can be built in transaction e-mails, of course. When a customer has bought a product, you thank her for her order. You let her know when it is shipped, and you ask her to rate the success of her purchase. These benefits are listed in chapter 13.

You build loyalty in promotional e-mails and newsletters—filled with interesting information—rather than in sales pitches. The development of subscriber loyalty is described in chapter 17.

Conclusion: Farming beats hunting every time

No matter how clever your one-size-fits-all e-mails are, personalized, segmented, targeted e-mails based on farming a subscriber database will be more relevant and profitable. You can prove that by testing on a small scale. Once you know that farming works better, get busy and do it.

Takeaway thoughts

- Customer performance measurement requires a marketing database that includes data from all channels: online, catalog, and retail.
- Most customers leave because of the way they are treated, rather because of price or products.
- Multichannel customers spend much more than single channel customers.
- Demographic data can be appended to any consumer file for which you have the street address.
- E-mails based on profiles or individual customer behavior produce many more conversions than e-mails based on a random select.
- Link categorization can help you determine what customers are interested in.
- Collaborative filtering is used by Amazon.com and Netflix to select customers for targeted e-mails.
- Next best product (NBP) determination can be used by any company.
- E-mails sent based on NBP can produce millions more in sales and profits than blasted e-mails.
- Farming customers beats hunting for them, every time.

Notes

1. A relational database is a collection of data items organized in tables from which data can be accessed or reassembled in many different ways without having to reorganize them. It is accessed by structured query language (SQL). Relational databases are easy to extend. New categories can be added without requiring that existing applications be modified. The database consists of tables containing data in columns and rows.

2. David Daniels, Maturation of Email: Controlling Messaging Chaos Through Centralization (New York: JupiterResearch, 2007)
3. Bryan Ong, "Why Customers Leave (Part 2),"*A Marketing Blog by Marketing Journal* (December 9, 2005), http://marketingjournal. blogspot.com/2005/12/why-customers-leave-part-1.html.
4. Elaine Misonzhnik, "On and Off the Web," *Retail Traffic* (January 1, 2008), http://retailtrafficmag.com/management/technology/sephora_catalog/index.html.
5. While there are only four major compilers of US consumer data, their data is resold by service bureaus all over the country. If your subscribers are businesses, there are also major business data compilers, including Dun & Bradstreet and InfoUSA.

5

The Importance of
Relevant E-mails

The tone of a good direct mail letter is as direct and personal as the
writer's skill can make it. Even though it may go to millions of people,
it never orates to a crowd but rather murmurs into a single ear. It's a
message from one letter writer to one letter reader.

Harry B. Walsh

Forrester Research reports[1] that about 72% of North American online
consumers "delete most e-mail advertising without reading it." Why?
E-mails are deleted because the consumer is either (a) overloaded today
with other matters or (b) uninterested because she believes the e-mail
doesn't contain content that is relevant to her current interests. She
bases her deletion decision on what she can see (where the e-mail is
from, the subject line, and the preview pane) and her prior experience
with marketing e-mails from this particular company. Nearly three-
quarters of respondents to a Merkle study[2] ranked irrelevancy as their
top reason for unsubscribing from a company's e-mail program.

Relevance makes all the difference. Even if your recipient were really busy, if the e-mail subject jumped out at her as being particularly
relevant, she would open it. Most mailers today understand the importance of relevance. They just don't know how to create it or to define it.
They feel like Justice Potter Stewart, who said, "I shall not today at-
tempt further to define . . . pornography . . . But I know it when I see
it"[3]

Actually, relevance *can* be defined. Relevant e-mail has content
that relates to the recipient's location, interests, attributes, behavior,
and other factors that grab her attention. Relevance increases e-mail
productivity by improving opens, clicks, conversions, revenue, and
profit. Relevant e-mails help get the subscriber involved. Relevant e-
mails are:

- Customized to the preference and situation of the addressee by including content appropriate to that particular person
- Timed using triggered messaging to coincide with the subscriber's behaviors or milestones
- Able to stimulate the subscriber by interactivity
- Flexible enough to recognize and adjust to the subscriber's interests and responses expressed within the e-mail itself

The Six Factors of Relevance

The relevance of an e-mail can be measured by six factors, each of which contributes to making a particular e-mail message relevant to the reader.

Segmentation

Subscribers are divided into segments based on their particular demographics, lifestyle, preferences, locations, or behavior. Different marketing strategies are constructed for each segment.

Lifecycle management

Customer lifecycles could be defined as prospects, first-time buyers, multibuyers, advocates, or lapsed customers. E-mails to each group might be different. Lifecycle management can also entail the lifecycle of a product or a service. How long have they had the car? When does the lease run out? When does this product need an upgrade?

Triggers

Trigger e-mails are based on a subscriber's life events, such as making a first purchase, having a birthday, achieving gold status, or becoming an advocate by using viral marketing. For example, the customer buys something, and we thank her and suggest she also buy a complementary product. The customer bought something at this time last year, and we send her an e-mail reminding her of last year's purchase. Triggers are successful if they are timed right. Automation can be used to send an e-mail at just the right time for this particular subscriber. Triggers activated by business rules are converted into software.

Personalization

We use the subscriber's name in the e-mail salutation. Then we vary the e-mail's content based on what we have learned about her preferences, previous purchases, clicks, downloads, and so on.

Interactivity

Every e-mail should be an adventure: full of links to products, polls, surveys, drill-downs, and downloads. What do we want the customer to do when she gets this e-mail? How can links in the e-mail help her achieve her and our objectives?

Testing and measurement

Every single e-mail campaign should contain at least one test. Test the audience, subject line, offer, content, and frequency. Study the tests, draw conclusions, and make changes to make the e-mails better and better. Use control groups to measure the success of any initiative compared to the performance of those who didn't get the e-mails. Testing should tell you: did it work? And did it work better than your usual message?

Are these factors valid?

Relevance sounds like a nice idea, but how do we know that relevant e-mail marketing programs, as defined by these six factors, are more successful than other e-mail marketing programs?

JupiterResearch has answered this question. It used actual e-mail performance data to establish that relevant e-mails produced more conversions, revenue, and profit than one-size-fits-all broadcast e-mails did. Its results are shown in the following graph. In its research, Jupiter established that targeting tactics (Exhibit 05-01) such as segmentation

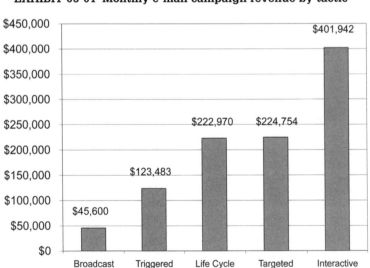

EXHIBIT 05-01 Monthly e-mail campaign revenue by tactic

with dynamic content produced 5 times more revenue and 16 times more profit than did broadcast campaigns.

JupiterResearch also found that specific applications of relevance increased e-mail conversion rates. For example:

- Marketers testing on a regular basis were more likely to have conversion rates exceeding 3% than were those who did not.[4]

- Use of personalization increased by eight percentage points; the probability of conversion rates exceeded 3%.

- Half of marketers who used messages triggered by subscriber activity produced conversion rates exceeding 3%. This compares with only 38% and 32% of marketers who sent their e-mail messages on a standard weekly or monthly schedule who achieved 3% or better.

How to measure your e-mail marketing program's relevance

The relevance of e-mail marketing programs is measured on a scale of 0 to 3. The success of each of the six relevance factors is graded by the criteria in Exhibit 05-02:

EXHIBIT 05-02 Relevance grading factors

Score	Description
3	Uses this factor on more than half of e-mail programs in a sophisticated way
2	Uses the factor on between one quarter and one half of e-mails
1	Uses this factor in less than one quarter of e-mails in an unsophisicated way
0	Does not use this factor at all

Using this score card, more than 70 major e-mail marketers graded their own e-mail marketing programs in 2007. Their programs' average score was 1.4 out of a possible 3.0. These marketers recognized their programs' shortcomings, and as a result of the scoring, many of them took action to correct and improve their programs.

Relevance is so important that there are chapters in this book that

EXHIBIT 05-03 Relevance ranking of 72 companies

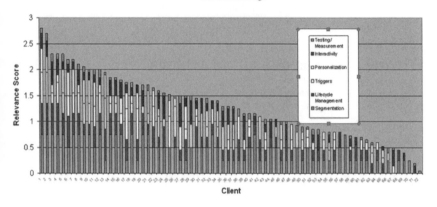

Client Rankings

explore the relevance factors in depth. There are chapters on segmenta-tion (chapter 7), triggering (chapter 14), interactivity (chapter 15), test-ing (chapter 16), and lifecycle management (chapter 17).

Why is e-mail relevance important to profits?

E-mail responders are better customers than other Internet shoppers. According to Forrester[5], those who buy from e-mails:

- **Spend more money online.** Consumers who buy products adver-tised in e-mails spend 138% more online than their peers who don't.

- **Buy impulsively.** Compared with 29% of all online consumers, more than half of consumers who buy products advertised through e-mail promotions prefer to buy immediately on credit rather than wait to complete a purchase.

- **Will pay for convenience.** Of consumers who think using e-mails is a great way to find out about new products or promotions, 47% are willing to pay a premium for products that save them time and hassles.

- **Embrace social computing.** Of consumers who buy products ad-vertised through e-mail, two thirds have submitted ratings and reviews of products; compared with just half of all online con-sumers. In addition, three quarters of these e-mail readers have forwarded an online ad to a friend.

- **Spend more money offline.** Consumers who read their e-mails use the information gained to shop offline in stores and catalogs. Overall, their spending exceeds that of consumers who don't receive and read e-mails.

Why relevance is difficult to achieve

Few e-mail marketers today deliver highly relevant e-mails to their subscribers. In fact, as we have already noted, almost all e-mail marketers are still hunting for customers instead of farming them. Most of them are sending batch-and-blast e-mails with the same content to every subscriber and every customer. Why?

When e-mail marketing was first invented in the early 1990s, no one knew exactly how to make it work. Marketers soon realized, however, that it was incredibly cheap to deliver e-mail compared to any other marketing method. In hundreds of companies, management set up small e-mail marketing operations to see what could be accomplished. In a few months these primitive shops produced online and offline sales with very little expense. Management saw success and built this early success into their quarterly marketing plans. Each plan projected the sales expected from e-mail marketing during the next quarter. Each quarter the goals were increased by a substantial percentage. The investors were informed. E-mail marketers were told, "Get busy and meet the next quarter's numbers."

To meet these goals, e-mail marketers found themselves on a never-ending treadmill. They had to acquire more and more subscribers and send them more and more e-mails, at first monthly, then weekly, and finally daily. Sales went up. But subscribers became unhappy. The novelty soon became a nuisance. Unsubscribe and bounce rates began to go up. Spam filters were created and soon caught many of these marketing e-mails in their nets. Subscribers deleted millions of marketing e-mails unread and marked others as spam.

Industry leaders recognized the problem: most e-mails were irrelevant to subscribers' interests or lives. The e-mails needed to be redesigned. To do that, e-mail marketers had to collect information on their subscribers, put it into databases, and use the databases to create more relevant content for their subscribers. Unfortunately, these recommendations came too late. The e-mail batch-and-blast methods had been built into the quarterly sales projections of thousands of companies. They couldn't afford to revise their methods. They didn't have the staff or the time to make the needed changes. Relevance seemed like an unattainable goal. There is a way out, however.

How to achieve relevance

To succeed, marketers must achieve relevance bit by bit. There are seven steps e-mail marketers can take that will gradually convert their e-mails into communications that their subscribers will be delighted to receive. The program described in the balance of this chapter is a universal one that all current e-mail marketing units can and should adopt if they are to retain their subscribers and save their programs.

Determine your e-mail program's relevance

Do what many e-mail marketers have already done: calculate your own e-mail program relevance. Take an honest look at the product you are delivering. Your efforts should produce a chart something like the chart in Exhibit 05-04.

EXHIBIT 05-04 E-mail program relevance scores

Factors of Relevance	Score	Weight	Weighted Score
Segmentation	1	25%	0.25
Lifecycle Management	1	20%	0.20
Triggers	1	20%	0.20
Personalization	1	15%	0.15
Interactivity	0	15%	0.00
Testing	1	5%	0.05
Total			0.85

The chart shows that you have no interactivity; your e-mails are strictly promotions with no significant links. However, you do segment some of your audience and manage the customer's lifecycle, Lifecycle is really a particular form of segmentation, whereby you treat subscribers who have never bought differently from one-time buyers, multibuyers, and lapsed buyers—all of which describe varying states of the customer lifecycle. You do some testing, personalize your e-mails, and send a few triggered e-mails. That's a start.

Some aspects of relevance are more important than others, hence the factors are weighted. Segmentation, for example, has the highest weight (25%). Experience shows that designing and directing e-mails to specific subscriber segments is a very important way of making an e-mail relevant to its audience. Knowing that your subscriber is 68 years old allows you to put her in a different segment than an 18 year old and design her e-mails with that in mind. Experience has also shown that segmentation is more important than personalization (15%), especially in creating a message that is really relevant to the recipient. Weights help you to focus on improving the most important factors.

In terms of triggers, you may send a thank-you message to buyers and use their name in e-mails sent to them. Finally, you have a subject-line testing program going on. These are all good first steps. Overall, however, your total relevance score of 0.85 out of a possible 3.0 is not a very high score. Changes should be made.

Design a program to increase your relevance score

What can you do to make your e-mail marketing messages relevant? You're already doing first step: reading this book. Each chapter contains specific suggestions that you can do to improve your relevance, together with case studies of what others have done. In later chapters, you will see how to do segmentation, triggering, interactivity, testing, lifecycle management, and personalization. To get from here to there, you will need to collect a lot of information from your subscribers (chapter 11). You will also have to build a marketing database.

All of these things will involve expending resources. It you don't already have an ESP, now is the time to get one. Experienced ESPs can help you with the tactics and strategies that lead to relevance. Consult Forrester Research and JupiterResearch, experts on e-mail marketing, about choosing an ESP. These research companies have dozens of white papers and reports that you can consult as guidelines on how to design a really good e-mail marketing program.

With the help of an ESP, you should determine the specific objectives and milestones you will need to establish to be able to send relevant e-mails to your subscribers. Create a chart that looks like the one in Exhibit 05-05.

Determine the cost of making improvements

Once this chart is completed, determine how much it will cost to reach your goals. There will be staff costs, external contractor costs, and premiums for subscribers, such as free shipping or bonus coupons, to get them to subscribe. You will want to reward your customer contact personnel (e.g., store clerks and telesales personnel) for capturing subscriber e-mail addresses and home postal addresses. You will want to calculate subscriber lifetime value and the next best product for each subscriber. You will also need analytics help in setting up the segments and in determining the actions you should take as a result of the many tests you will run. You will probably need more staff, including segment managers.

Develop a chart that looks like Exhibit 05-06.

EXHIBIT 05-05 E-mail marketing scores and goals

Factor	Current Score	Weight	Goal	Weighted Score	What must be done to reach the goal
Segmentation	1	25%	2	0.50	Build DB. Append Data. Collect Preferences Create Segments. Develop marketing strategy for each segment. Appoint segment managers.
Lifecycle Management	1	20%	2	0.40	Set up levels: subscriber, buyer, two time buyer, advocate, lapsed. Different e-mails for each lifecycle.
Triggers	1	20%	2	0.40	Create triggers: birthday, last year's buys, reminders, viral e-mails
Personalization	1	15%	1	0.15	Use name in copy, change website and e-mail based on preferences and previous purchases
Interactivity	0	15%	1	0.15	Make every e-mail an adventure, filled with links, contests, quizzes, puzzles, treasure hunts, downloads, white papers, shopping carts, excitement
Testing	1	5%	1	0.05	Build a test into every single e-mail campaign: have weekly reviews on the outcome of each test. Revise the e-mails due to these reviews
Total Weighted Score	0.85	100%		1.65	

Calculate the ROI for relevant e-mails

Start by calculating your existing subscriber lifetime value (explained in chapter 6). Then figure out what the lifetime will be when you deliver relevant e-mails to your subscribers. Into your calculations build the cost of acquiring more subscribers and collecting important profile and preference information from them and from your existing customers. You will end up with a chart that looks something like Exhibit 05-07.

EXHIBIT 05-06 Cost of reaching relevance goals

Costs of Gearing Up To Send Relevant E-mails	Size	Cost Per Unit	Annual Cost	3 Year Investment
Subscriber Database	2,000,000	$0.50	$1,000,000	$3,000,000
Subscriber Premiums*	1,000,000	$2.00	$2,000,000	$6,000,000
Staff Premiums**	200,000	$5.00	$1,000,000	$3,000,000
Additonal Staff	3	$65,000	$195,000	$585,000
Analytics Cost	1	$50,000	$50,000	$150,000
Software***	1	$25,000	$25,000	$75,000
Appended Data	1,000,000	$0.06	$60,000	$180,000
Total			$4,330,000	$12,990,000

* To get them to give you their e-mails and home addresses
** To reward them for getting subscriber e-mails and addresses
*** For Next Best Product, LTV, Triggers, etc.

EXHIBIT 05-07 ROI from improved relevance

Difference between now and When Relevance is achieved	Number of Subscribers	Average Lifetime Value	Annual Profit or Investment
Current Situation	1,000,000	$26.44	$26,440,000
LTV & Profit when goals reached	2,000,000	$136.35	$272,700,000
Annual Investment required			$4,330,000
Return per $1 Invested			$62.98

Gain management approval

Armed with these calculations, your next goal is to get management approval for the steps needed to reach relevance and the profits that come from relevance. Explain to management that you are shifting from hunting to farming and that the shift will take some time. Let them know how e-mail relevance is defined and how improved relevance will lead to increased ROI from your e-mail programs. Make sure they understand that, as a result of the measurement process, you will probably have to make some modifications to the existing e-mail programs. These modifications may include capturing new subscriber information, building a comprehensive database, storing subscriber data in the database, and using it to segment the subscribers, personalization, and so on. You will design new content and triggers for each segment. You will create personalized e-mails for each segment. You will need additional resources to do these things.

Identify the data you need

You will undoubtedly have to store more data than you do now, including:

- Subscriber demographics
- Subscriber behaviors
- The subscriber's physical address and phone number
- The segments you have put each subscriber in
- Subscriber lifetime value
- Customer RFM cell code (see chapter 7)
- Subscriber's profile, preference, and survey results
- Subscriber's trigger events
- Total number of e-mails sent to subscriber by periods
- Subscriber's Web site activity, such as departments she has visited and what she clicks on or downloads
- Subscriber's gift registry status (did she record birthdays or other occasions for which she wants notification?)
- Subscriber lifecycle, including if she is an advocate and the person she has identified in a viral marketing program
- Exact source of each e-mail address

Develop and activate your plan

With management approval, you are now ready to develop and write programs for the business rules that will implement your plan. These include triggers, such as welcome, congratulations, thanks, and happy birthday messages; viral marketing; and reactivations. You will need help from your ESP to do this. Most large companies outsource their e-mail marketing programs to experienced ESPs rather than try to do all the actions listed in-house. Constructing a database, creating segments, implementing business rules, and sending millions of e-mails are complex and specialized operations that are best carried out by professionals who have done it many times. ESPs have experience doing these things for many different companies. There is a lot to learn, and e-mail marketing is too important for on-the-job training.

Once the database is created and populated and the business rules are written, the operation should be thoroughly tested before you go live with millions of e-mails to thousands of subscribers.

The marketing department should have sole responsibility for e-mail content. You have to move very fast with daily tests and daily modifications based on what the tests are telling you. Get someone who is experienced and competent and put her in charge. Depend on her to do a good job. Give her the flexibility to try new things.

If your corporate Web site is run by IT or an advertising agency rather than by the marketing department, it may be very stiff and formal. It may lack cookies and personalization. Links from your e-mails to the corporate Web site may destroy the relevance you are trying to create in your e-mails. Rather than linking to this type of Web site, set up microsites that you can link to in your e-mails. Let a microsite house your registration page, preference and profiles, shopping carts, product search, and so on. Links to these pages are essential to making your e-mails interactive.

In the Internet world, nothing stands still for long. A killer e-mail that astounded everyone becomes old hat very quickly. Subscribers will think, "I've seen all that. It was great. But I want something new, and this company is not going to give it to me. I'll just unsubscribe while I'm thinking about it." You will need to analyze your results against your goals and expectations for the program, then share your analysis with your ESP and with others in your company—and possibly with your subscribers. For programs that didn't work well, you should either restructure the programs or get rid of them and use the budget elsewhere.

Improve each relevance factor

Create a plan to improve each relevance factor. Let's take personalization as an example. The scoring rules are in Exhibit 05-08.

EXHIBIT 05-08 Personalization score criteria

	Personalization Description - Weight 15%
3	Dynamic content: highly personalized program
2	Personalization using more than one component
1	Uses customer name only
0	No personalization

Steps toward personalization

Make a list of the things that should be done. For example:

- Welcome visitors to your Web site by name: "Welcome Back, Susan." You do the Web site personalization with cookies.
- Provide a similar salutation, using the subscriber's name, in each e-mail.

- Organize e-mail content around what you know about the customer: her previous purchases, what she clicked on in previous visits to your Web site or in your e-mails, and her expressed preferences.

- Provide plenty of opportunities for her to share her opinion and preferences.

- Thank her with an e-mail whenever she completes a form.

Personalization results

What kind of results can you expect from personalization? Williams-Sonoma tested personalized images and saw conversions increase 50%. Golfsmith saw revenue jump 167% when it used personalization. Network Solutions applied personalization to the its individual account renewal program. Result? Open rates increased by 50%. In addition, the personalized renewal program achieved 60% better conversion rates than the previous broadcast e-mail programs sponsored by the company.

Harvard Business School Publishing used behavior-generated data to create a reply-to-buy program. The e-mail content was personalized with links to landing pages prepopulated with products geared to the subscriber's interests. When subscribers clicked on links in the e-mail, the data was captured for further personalization in subsequent e-mails. As a result, Harvard Business School Publishing achieved much higher conversion rates and ROIs over its previous standard campaigns.

How relevance affects open rates

In 2006, JupiterResearch reported the average untargeted e-mail campaign had an open rate of about 20%, a CTR of about 9.5%, and a conversion rate of only about 1%. On the other hand, targeted (relevant) e-mail campaigns had a 33% open rate on average, a 14% CTR, and a 3.9%conversion rate.[6] Your rates will be different, of course, but the principle is the same: relevant e-mails do much better. Let's look at these numbers in an actual e-mail promotion setting, applied to a typical mailing to 2 million subscribers (Exhibit 05-09).

Note that to get the targeted results shown here, the 2 million subscribers would have had to be broken down into several segments based on their previous behavior and demographics. As a result, subscribers would not have been sent 2 million identical messages, as untargeted subscribers did. They would have had to be sent individually

EXHIBIT 05-09 Extrapolation of JupiterResearch conversion rates

	Delivered	Open Rate	E-mails Opened	CTR Rate	Clicked	Conversion Rate	Conversions	Net Rate	Net AOV	Net Revenue
Untargeted	2,000,000	20%	400,000	9.50%	38,000	1.00%	380	0.02%	$ 42.10	$15,998
Targeted	2,000,000	33%	660,000	14.0%	92,400	3.90%	3,604	0.18%	$ 42.10	$151,712

Source: JupiterResearch
Kristina Knight: October 30, 2006 Jupiter: Make Emails Relevant. Bizreport.com
Actual Jupiter rates — delivered and resulting numbers are illustrative.

targeted marketing messages featuring products that were of particular interest to each subscriber or subscriber segment.

That 3.9% conversion rate is a *wonderful* number. Compare it to direct mail, where a 2% conversion rate is usually considered a success. When you realize you can send about 350 e-mails for the cost of one direct mail postcard, you see the significance of a conversion rate like 3.9%.

JupiterResearch reported the average consumer received about 304 opt-in promotional e-mails per week in 2007.[7] These represented 26% of the total inbox mail of the average consumer. The fact that 20% of those permission-based e-mails were opened and read doesn't mean 20% of your e-mails will be opened and read. You may get a fraction of 1%, while other marketers get 30% or more. What makes some marketers successful while others fail? Relevance. Following are several case studies in relevance.

But I'm already a customer!

I got this e-mail this week from a company encouraging me to buy the '08 edition of its coupon book. You may be saying, "What's the big deal? You got an e-mail." The funny thing is that I already responded last month to one of its other renewal e-mails and purchased the'08 book.

As a recipient of this e-mail, it made me wonder why the company couldn't take the time to exclude individuals who have already renewed their memberships from their future prospecting e-mails. I could understand being included again if the copy said something like, "Hey, we know that you have already bought your new '08 book, but they also make great gifts. Here is an offer for $5 off each additional copy you buy." That would be relevant to me because it would be targeting individuals who have already purchased at least one '08 edition. Nothing turns a customer off more than when a company acts like it doesn't realize you are already a customer.

Delta pays me for my time

A consumer reports: "Delta is reaching out to all of its SkyMiles members, asking them to update their profiles and read and react to future e-mail correspondence from Delta. In exchange for my time, it will give me SkyMiles toward my mileage plan. Here is the initial e-mail I received asking me to enroll so that I can start receiving messages that are relevant to me:

> As a Delta Air Lines SkyMiles member, you are invited to earn thousands of miles in just minutes a day. It's free. It's easy. All you have to do is to read and react to messages that are relevant to you. Plus, earn over 250 miles today just for enrolling and completing your profile, FREE.

The preference form included this interesting section:

> Because we respect and value your time, you may limit the number of minutes you make available for e-Miles earning opportunities each day. Please choose the number of minutes you would like to make available each day."

Don't they know where I live?

Another consumer reported: "I received an e-mail from bebe telling me to 'change to a bikini for the beach look.' I was shocked when I opened this e-mail, because Seattle just had one of the coldest days in this winter season. Some of us had to work from home due to the snowy and icy roads. After I shoveled some inches of snow from my driveway, shopping for new bikini was the last thing on my mind! Maybe bebe was trying to be optimistic, but it looked as if it knew nothing about where I lived. This mailing almost made me want to hit the unsubscribe button due to the lack of relevancy. There was no mention of my name in the e-mail. The whole message didn't make me feel like a valued customer."

In the next chapter you will learn how to determine the lifetime value of subscribers who receive your e-mails.

Takeaway thoughts

- Relevant e-mails get opened. Irrelevant e-mails don't.
- Relevance can be defined and quantified.
- The six factors of relevance are: segmentation, lifecycle management, triggers, personalization, interactivity, and testing.

- JupiterResearch has proved that relevant e-mails produce 10 times as much revenue as broadcast e-mails.

- Marketers who test e-mail regularly are more likely to have conversion rates reaching 3%.

- Marketers grading their own e-mails gave them a score of 1.4 out of 3.0.

- To improve e-mail relevance, score your current programs, identify shortfalls, identify the data you need, get approval of management, and measure your results.

Notes

1. Shar VanBoskirk and Julie M. Katz, *Email Marketing Comes of Age* (Cambridge, MA: Forrester Research Inc., March 2, 2007).
2. *A View from the Inbox 2008* (Merkle 2008), http://www.merkleinc. com/user-assets/Documents/WhitePapers/ViewFromTheInbox2008. pdf.
3. *Jacobellis v. Ohio*, 378 US 184 (1964).
4. *Conversion* is defined here as the number of unique sales as a percentage of e-mails delivered.
5. Shar VanBoskirk and Julie M. Katz, *Email Marketing Comes of Age* (Cambridge, MA: Forrester Research Inc., March 2, 2007).
6. Kristina Knight, "Jupiter: Make Emails Relevant," *Bizreport.com* (October 30, 2006), http://www.bizreport.com/2006/10/jupiter_make_emails_relevant.html.
7. "Email Marketing Statistics and Metrics" (EmailLabs), http://www.emaillabs.com/tools/email-marketing-statistics.html.

6

E-mail Subscriber Lifetime Value

In our experience, once companies understand the potential value of customer retention, they tend to fall into a trap. Eager to produce rapid improvement, they short cut their analysis of customer cash flow. Understandably but foolishly, they conclude that getting bogged down in the details of a proposition they already accept as fact—that improving customer retention will improve profits—is a waste of time and money. The omission usually comes back to haunt them. The only way to put loyalty at the heart of daily decision making is to take the economic effects of loyalty seriously, measure them rigorously, and link them firmly to reported earnings. The best way to reduce misunderstandings between different parts of the organization, and to surface and resolve them when they do occur, is to make loyalty numbers so trustworthy that everyone accepts them as a basis for investment and strategy decisions.

Frederick Reichheld, *The Loyalty Effect*

Customer lifetime value (LTV) has become the standard method for measuring the success of customer marketing programs. LTV predicts the future performance of a group of customers or subscribers based on their past and current spending behaviors. It also permits you to determine the value of an e-mail name. It is particularly useful for those who extensively e-mail their customers.

Customer LTV is the net profit you receive from a given subscriber over a period of years. How can you increase LTV? There are many ways, but an important one is by communicating intelligently with your customers. If you have something relevant and interesting to say and you don't waste their time with irrelevant messages, not only will they listen, they are also more likely to stay with you and buy more products and services rather than drift away.

This has always been true, even before e-mail. The problem was the traditional personal communication channels—direct mail, telephone calls, and personal contacts—were expensive. Once you had a million customers, using any of these contact methods runs into serious money. You couldn't afford to communicate more than a few times a year.

Not so with e-mail. E-mail allows you to converse personally with thousands or millions of customers on a regular basis at comparatively little expense.

To understand LTV, let's look at an LTV table for a typical retailer before and after the company sets up a relevant e-mail communication program using a professional ESP. The retailer sells via the Web and retail stores. We will trace the LTV of 1 million customers who were recruited about the same time and trace their purchasing experiences with the retail chain over three years.

To begin, the retailer sends an e-mail blast to these 1 million customers every week. At this time, the retailer has scored his own e-mail marketing program using the methods outlined in chapter 5, receiving a relevance score of 1.6 out of 3.0. This is typical of many e-mail marketers today. Exhibit 06-01 is the resulting LTV table.

This chart shows the three-year history of 1 million of the retailer's subscribers. We aren't looking at subscribers who join up before or after this period, just those who joined in year 1. The company may be growing or declining; this chart isn't concerned with that.

The e-mails sent to subscribers encourage them to shop both online and in the chain's retail stores. The retailer sent one e-mail communication to each subscriber each week, with the following results in the first year:

- A number of subscribers unsubscribed; others became undeliverable. This is normal in any e-mail promotion program. The numbers are typical of e-mail marketing situations.
- 42.6 million e-mails were delivered.
- The open rate was 16%, with 2% of those opened resulting in a purchase for a total conversion rate of 0.32%.
- There were 136,448 online orders.

In addition to these online sales, the e-mails prompted many subscribers to visit the retail stores. The retailer discovered that for every online sale, e-mail generates 1.20 times the number of in-store sales. As a result:

- 300,186 orders, online and off-, resulted from the e-mails in year 1.

EXHIBIT 06-01 LTV table

E-mail Subscriber Lifetime Value

E-mail Programs Relevance 1.6 Campaigns Per Year	Rates 52	Acquisition Year	Year 2	Year 3
Subscribers beginning of the year		1,000,000	640,000	409,600
Unsubscribes - Monthly Rate	0.90%	108,000	69,120	44,237
Undelivers - Monthly Rate	2.10%	252,000	161,280	103,219
Subscribers at the end of the year		640,000	409,600	262,144
Promotional E-mails Delivered		42,640,000	27,289,600	17,465,344
Percent e-mails opened		16%	17%	18%
Percent orders per open		2.0%	2.5%	3.0%
Online Orders:		136,448	115,981	94,313
Estimated Retail Orders:				
% of Online	120%	163,738	139,177	113,175
Total Orders		300,186	255,158	207,488
Revenue: Average Order:	$152.00	$45,628,211.20	$38,783,979.52	$31,538,219.58
Cost of Goods Sold	50%	$22,814,106	$19,391,990	$15,769,110
Selling Costs	$6.00	$1,801,114	$1,530,947	$1,244,930
Customer Acquisition Cost	$12.00	$12,000,000	$0	$0
Transaction e-mails Delivered				
(Per Order)	2.00	600,371	510,316	414,977
Cost of e-mails sent (per thousand)	$1.80	$77,833	$50,040	$32,185
DB, Segmenting & Marketing	$2.00	$2,000,000	$1,280,000	$819,200
Total Cost		$39,293,423	$22,763,292	$18,280,401
Gross Profit		$6,334,788	$16,020,688	$13,257,819
Discount Rate		1.00	1.16	1.35
Net Present Value Profit		$6,334,788	$13,810,938	$9,820,607
Cumulative NPV Profit		$6,334,788	$20,145,726	$29,966,333
Subscriber Lifetime Value		$6.33	$20.15	$29.97
Dollars Per Delivered		$1.07	$1.42	$1.81
% Online Conversion Per e-mail		0.32%	0.43%	0.54%

- The average order size was $152 for each of the three years.
- Total revenue was $45.6 million in year 1.
- Subscriber acquisition cost was $12 per subscriber, or $12 million total.
- Database, segmenting, and marketing costs were $2 per subscriber.
- Year 3 subscriber LTV was $29.97.
- At the beginning of the third year, only 409,600 of the original 1 million subscribers were still on the list, due to unsubscribes and delivery issues.

For explanation of the discount rate, see the appendix.

We get the acquisition cost by adding the money spent on a wide variety of methods used to acquire subscribers: radio, TV, print, banner ads, search engines, direct mail, staff resources, and so on, and dividing that total by the number of subscribers actually acquired in a given year. It is worth spending some time to get this number correct, as it will affect all subsequent calculations. (These calculations are found in chapter 8.)

The database cost includes updating and maintaining the database and performing the analytics: RFM, LTV, NBP and segmentation scoring. The database also has to keep a lot of unsubscribed and undeliverable subscribers for some time. Unsubscribers have to be kept in a suppression file to make sure the e-mails to these folks actually stop. Undeliverables should be kept because it is possible those subscribers have changed their e-mail addresses but are still interested in hearing from you. If you have retained postal addresses, you might reactivate them with a postcard. If they are worth $12.00 or more, certainly a postcard would be money well spent.

Becoming Relevant

How do you improve your e-mail communications? Communications work only if they are relevant to receivers' lives and interests. Every week the average consumer receives hundreds of irrelevant e-mails. They lead busy lives. If they were to read all the commercial e-mails sent to them, they would do little else all day. So they classify some of the e-mails as spam, they unsubscribe when it seems appropriate, and they delete almost all the rest. For the average person to open an e-mail, the subject line has to promise something interesting or important inside. The content has to live up to the subject line within about three seconds, or that e-mail is gone forever.

As explained in chapter 5, e-mail marketing programs' relevance can be quantified on a scale of 0 to 3, with 0 being totally irrelevant and 3 being extremely relevant to recipients. For this initial LTV example, let's assume our retailer was sending relatively untargeted e-mail blasts with a relevance score of 1.6.

Let's also assume that as a result of reading this book, our retailer has gotten religion. His marketing staff has adopted many of the strategies and tactics recommended, so he is able to increase his relevance score from 1.6 to 2.4.

EXHIBIT 06-02 LTV relevance

Factors of Relevance	Score	Weight	Weighted Score
Segmentation	3	25%	0.75
Lifecycle Management	2	20%	0.40
Triggers	2	20%	0.40
Personalization	3	15%	0.45
Interactivity	2	15%	0.30
Testing	2	5%	0.10
Total			2.40

The retailer develops a full-fledged segmentation and personalization program for his e-mail communications and brings the other four factors up. He makes progress. How would this increased relevance improve his customers' LTV? Exhibit 06-03 illustrates the new results.

EXHIBIT 06-03 LTV with a relevance of 2.4

e-mail Subscriber Lifetime Value e-mail Programs Relevance 2.4 Campaigns Per Year	Rates 52	Acquisition Year	Year 2	Year 3
Subscribers beginning of the year		1,000,000	712,000	506,944
Unsubscribes - Monthly Rate	0.60%	72,000	51,264	36,500
Undelivers - Monthly Rate	1.80%	216,000	153,792	109,500
Subscribers at the end of the year		712,000	506,944	360,944
Promotional e-mails Delivered		44,512,000	31,692,544	22,565,091
Percent e-mails opened		20%	22%	24%
Percent orders per open		3%	4%	5%
Online Orders:		267,072	278,894	270,781
Estimated Retail Orders: % of Online	120%	320,486	334,673	324,937
Total Orders		587,558	613,568	595,718
Revenue: Average Order:	$161.00	$94,596,902	$98,784,392	$95,910,664
Cost of Goods Sold	50%	$47,298,451	$49,392,196	$47,955,332
Selling Costs	$6.00	$3,525,350	$3,681,406	$3,574,310
Customer Acquisition Cost	$17.00	$17,000,000	$0	$0
Transaction e-mails Delivered (Per order)	4.00	2,350,234	2,454,271	2,382,874
Cost of e-mails sent	$1.80	$84,352	$61,464	$44,906
Segmenting and Modeling	$4.00	$4,000,000	$2,848,000	$2,027,776
Database Cost	$2.00	$2,000,000	$2,000,000	$2,000,000
Total Cost		$73,908,154	$57,983,066	$55,602,325
Gross Profit		$20,688,749	$40,801,326	$40,308,339
Discount Rate		1.00	1.16	1.35
Net Present Value Profit		$20,688,749	$35,173,557	$29,858,029
Cumulative NPV Profit		$20,688,749	$55,862,306	$85,720,335
Subscriber Lifetime Value		$20.69	$55.86	$85.72
Dollars Per Delivered		$2.13	$3.12	$4.25
Online Conversion per delivered e-mail		0.60%	0.88%	1.20%

A lot of things have changed as a result of sending more relevant e-mails. Going down the chart, we see that fewer customers have unsub-scribed and that the delivery rate has gone up. The open rate has gone up, as has the order rate—and the overall conversion rate is now 0.6% in year 1, rising to 1.2% in the third year. The average order size has in-creased from $152 to $161. These changes have boosted the retailer's sales and revenue considerably. They are typical of the improvements that come from increased relevance.

Of course, these improvements cost money. The retailer is sending twice the number of transactional messages. He is now spending $6 per customer per year on his database, segmentation, and creative triggered e-mail program instead of $2 per customer—an increase of $4 million overall. Without a LTV chart like this, it is doubtful the marketing manager would have been able to get a $4 million increase in his e-mail budget approved.

So what has relevance done for this retail chain (Exhibit 06-04)?

EXHIBIT 06-04 Result of boosting relevance

Difference Lifetime Value Campaigns Per Year	Rates 52	Acquisition Year	Year 2	Year 3
LTV with Relevance of 1.6		$6.33	$20.15	$29.97
LTV with Relevance of 2.4		$20.69	$55.86	$85.72
Increase		$14.35	$35.72	$55.75
With 1,000,000				
Customers	1,000,000	$14,353,961	$35,716,580	$55,754,002

Overall profits have gone up by $55 million by the third year. These are net profits, not revenue. All costs have been subtracted. This is the type of result that comes from a well-organized customer communica-tions program featuring relevant e-mails.

How to get the data

LTV tables assume you have a way of getting the necessary data. Many e-mail marketers currently can't do that. A typical Web site registration asks only for the e-mail address. Some ask for gender, others ask for the type of product the subscriber is interested in. Few ask for the impor-tant information: name, street address, and possibly phone number. Without the street address or phone number, you can't be sure the peo-ple who are buying are the same people you are sending e-mails to.

Without the name, you can't be sure those visiting your Web site are the ones who originally registered with you. Why is this important? Because without knowing who is visiting the Web site, you can't create relevant e-mail messages for them.

Many marketers send millions of e-mails to consumers who never have and never will buy anything from them. One company sent e-mails to opt-in registrants three times a week. During one calendar year, it sent 93,591,274 e-mails to 570,679 individual consumers. Only 153,602 of the recipients (27%) made any purchase at all. The remaining 73% didn't buy anything that the retailer had any record of. When the next year started, it continued to send e-mails to the non-buyers. Why?

There are several reasons. First, the bulk e-mails were very inexpensive, so the retailer could continue to send e-mails three times a week to the 417,077 non-buyers. At a cost of $7.80 per thousand ($1.80 plus $4.00 plus $2.00), the e-mails to these non-buyers cost the retailer $507,499 per year. The sales to the 153,602 buyers brought in more than $21 million, so $507,499 was probably money well spent. Some of the non-buyers would buy in the coming year, thus paying off part or all of the send cost.

Second, the retailer hadn't done the analysis we have done here, so he hadn't identified the non-buyers. This is a more common situation than you might think. Many mass e-mailers don't do much analytics. They don't know which e-mail subscribers are buying and which aren't.

Finally, the most powerful reason is this retailer sells online and offline. He has several hundred large retail stores. Since the e-mail file contained only the consumer's e-mail address and nothing else, he had no way of knowing whether recipients made retail purchases at his stores. The chances are that thousands of recipients were spurred by the e-mails to visit the stores to make purchases, but how could he prove that without data?

How you can get purchase data

In our LTV example, we have estimated that for every online purchase, customers make 1.20 purchases in the chain's retail stores. This number can be estimated by surveying buyers. It isn't a very accurate way of measuring the impact of e-mail marketing, because it is missing a very important part of the use of e-mail marketing data: testing to make campaigns better.

Successful e-mail marketers get their subscribers to register all the vital information: name, address, e-mail, and phone number. Ama-zon.com does that, even though Amazon has no retail stores.

Since you have the registrant's name, you can say, "Welcome back, Susan. If you're not Susan, click here" on the Web site when she ar-rives. You can send personalized e-mails. The e-mails and the Web site will have content designed just for Susan based on her preferences and previous purchases. You can also offer one-click purchasing, making it easy for Susan to buy anything she wants.

Does saying, "Welcome back, Susan" on the Web site and personal-izing the e-mails help sales? It is very easy to find that out. Do an A/B split test. Welcome half of your registrants back, recommending pur-chases to them. Don't welcome the other half. Treat them in the e-mails and on the Web site as perfect strangers. Measure the difference in sales between the two groups. You will soon find out the value of personal-ization.

For offline purchases, you can come close to getting a handle on the effect of e-mails on retail sales when armed with the appropriate data. There are several methods: routinely ask all retail customers to provide their home phone when making any purchases. Set up your retail POS system to include the phone number with every purchase. A really good POS system puts the customer's record on the screen at that cash regis-ter as soon as the phone number is entered. The clerk sees this and says, "Susan Collins, 431 Ocean Drive?" If she says, "No," the clerk can correct the record immediately to find out who she is, entering a correct phone number. If she is a new customer, the clerk can enter her data in the POS system.

Then comes the tricky part: the e-mail address. "Can you give me your e-mail address? We like to have it to advise you about specials and to let you know about product recalls. As a new customer, we can give you a $5.00 credit when your e-mail is entered and validated." Few customers will turn this offer down. If they do, just skip it and com-plete the purchase. Since you are using a double-opt-in e-mail registra-tion system (see chapter 8), you will send her an e-mail to verify her address before it goes into your database. You may also reward the store clerks for all the correct addresses they provide to the system.

The e-mail address is validated with a welcome e-mail. When the customer receives the e-mail and clicks on it, her address is validated. The welcome message invites her to print a coupon for $5 toward a fu-ture purchase at the store. The coupon has a barcode and a unique number. If she uses the coupon at a store, the clerk's scanner can read the bar code, giving her the $5 credit, and making sure the coupon isn't used a second time. If the customer wants to make her next purchase online, she can enter the coupon number, getting the $5 off her next purchase. The unique number also ensures the coupon is used only once.

Making e-mail campaigns better

Now that you have set up a system to ensure that all online and most offline purchases are registered in your marketing database, you are in a position to do what few marketers can today: measure both the effectiveness of each e-mail campaign and the contribution from each subscriber.

As we explain in chapter 7, your e-mails to each customer should be personalized. Content is determined by the customer's segment and by previous purchases. Your e-mail this week to Susan features a "Famous American Maker Lightweight Wool Blazer" for $179.99, plus other items. If Susan buys this blazer on- or offline, you know that your e-mail was successful. But what if Susan buys something else? Was it because of the e-mail or for some other reason?

Many marketers have a 10-day rule to cover this situation. If the consumer makes a purchase, online or offline, within 10 days of receiving a promotional e-mail, the e-mail gets the credit. This isn't completely accurate, but it's a lot better than nothing.

Armed with this data, you can measure each e-mail campaign's success. You will soon find out that some campaigns do much better than others. By asking why some campaigns succeed and others fail, you will become better at e-mail marketing. Some e-mail marketers have conversion rates (percentage of e-mails that result in a sale) of less than 1%. Others have rates of more than 5%. The difference may be attributed to the collection and analysis of campaign data and the corrective steps taken as a result of the analysis.

Why dogs bark

There is a flaw in the reasoning behind the discussion so far in this chapter. The discussion assumes that the purchases come about because of the e-mails. That may be true of some purchases, but certainly not all of them.

Anyone who has owned a dog knows that when a dog hears a strange noise in the middle of the night, it may start to bark, waking up everyone in the house. But dogs bark for dozens of other reasons: to be let out, to be let back in, because they are happy, because they are angry. Noises in the night are only one cause of barking.

In the same way, consumers buy from an online or a brick-and-mortar store for many reasons besides receiving a relevant e-mail. They buy because of online, television, or print advertising. They buy because they need the item or because they were in the mall or on the Internet anyway and decide to look in the store to see what is available. After all, consumers have been buying products from merchants for thousands of years before e-mails were invented.

A more accurate way of depicting customer LTV would be to measure the purchases based on all causes of customer behavior, rather than based solely on e-mail relevance. Let's do a new set of LTV tables, based on all factors that influence customer purchases. Exhibit 06-05 is a picture of the retailer before any e-mails are sent.

We are looking at 1 million customers who came to the Web site or the stores and made a purchase because of search engine marketing, banner ads, print, TV, direct mail advertising, or just because the stores were there, inviting customers to come in and buy. Bear in mind these people are *customers* not *subscribers*. The difference is that all 1 million customers actually bought something in the first year. This is generally not true of subscribers. Millions of consumers and businesses subscribe to e-mail lists but never buy anything.

EXHIBIT 06-05 Customer LTV with no e-mails sent

Customer Lifetime Value Offline and Online with No E-mails Sent		Acquisition Year	Year 2	Year 3
Customers		1,000,000	520,000	270,400
Customers lost in year (loss/mo.) 4%		480,000	249,600	129,792
Average Customers in Year		760,000	395,200	205,504
Online & Offline Visits / Yr.		1.2	1.3	1.4
Revenue per Visit		$100	$110	$120
Revenue		$91,200,000	$56,513,600	$34,524,672
Cost of Goods Sold	50%	$45,600,000	$28,256,800	$17,262,336
Customer Acquisition Cost	$15	$15,000,000		
Marketing Costs	$12	$12,000,000	$6,240,000	$3,244,800
Total Costs		$72,600,000	$34,496,800	$20,507,136
Gross Profit		$18,600,000	$22,016,800	$14,017,536
Discount Rate		1	1.16	1.35
Net Present Value Profit		$18,600,000	$18,980,000	$10,383,360
Cumulative NPV Profit		$18,600,000	$37,580,000	$47,963,360
Lifetime Value		$18.60	$37.58	$47.96

These customers saw TV and print ads. They received some direct mail. They used a search engine to find the Web site, but no promotional e-mails were sent to these customers.

Of the 1 million customers who made purchases during the year, 200,000 of them bought twice in the first year. The average purchase was $100, rising to $120 made by the 205,504 loyal customers who were still shopping in the third year.

Bear in mind that this table tracks only those 1 million who we put on our database so we could track them.

How do we know what they did? If we want to keep track of customers, we have to set up some sort of a system. If they are members of our loyalty program (see chapter 17), we can track them that way. If not, we might use their home telephone number. Many companies routinely ask for home phones as a means of identification for offline buyers. POS systems have to be set up to use that number to pull up a customer's record on the screen. Then the clerk can say, "Arthur Sweetser, right?" and check Arthur's street address. If Arthur isn't in there, the clerk can ask for the street address and the e-mail address, "so we can identify you in case of product returns or in case we find there is something wrong with the product we are selling to you." Few customers will balk at giving this information when making a purchase. For those who do, just skip it.

Armed with the phone number, you can track most of your offline sales. The sales clerk, if she captures the e-mail address, can be rewarded when that address is verified in the double-opt-in process. Even if you only get a phone number, there are plenty of service bureaus that will do a reverse append: getting you the names and addresses of the people who use that phone number (the hit rate is generally about 60%, which is much better than nothing).

Now let's see the effect of sending e-mails to those 1 million buyers. We assume that all of the 1 million buyers have given us their e-mail address with permission to use it. For that reason, the 1 million people in this chart *aren't exactly the same 1 million as those in Exhibit 06-05.* It isn't easy to get people to give you their e-mail address. These 1 million buyers are more profitable customers. They are probably more affluent, and they buy larger amounts. Many of them may be multichannel customers, as well.

As you can see, these customers, stimulated by e-mails, placed more orders than the previous group. Why? Because these are both customers and e-mail subscribers, and many of them are multichannel customers. Multichannel customers are more affluent and spend more money.

One effect of the e-mails has been to reduce the churn rate. Rele-

EXHIBIT 06-06 LTV with weekly e-mails

Customer Lifetime Value Offline and Online with Weekly E-mails Sent		Acquisition Year	Year 2	Year 3
Customers With Opt-In E-mails		1,000,000	760,000	577,600
Annual Loss of Customers				
(loss per month)	2%	240,000	182,400	138,624
Average Customers in Year		880,000	668,800	508,288
E-mails Sent	50	44,000,000	33,440,000	25,414,400
Offline & Online Visits per Year		1.5	1.6	1.7
Revenue per Visit		$120	$130	$140
Revenue		$158,400,000	$139,110,400	$120,972,544
Cost of Goods Sold	50%	$79,200,000	$69,555,200	$60,486,272
Marketing Costs	$12	$12,000,000	$9,120,000	$6,931,200
Customer Acquisition Cost	$15	$15,000,000		
E-mail Address Acquire	$10	$10,000,000		
E-mail costs plus database cost	$4	$4,000,000	$4,000,000	$4,000,000
Total Costs		$120,200,000	$82,675,200	$71,417,472
Gross Profit		$38,200,000	$56,435,200	$49,555,072
Discount Rate		1	1.16	1.35
Net Present Value Profit		$38,200,000	$48,651,034	$36,707,461
Cumulative NPV Profit		$38,200,000	$86,851,034	$123,558,495
Lifetime Value		$38.20	$86.85	$123.56

vant, personalized e-mails remind customers of where they have shopped before. They invite customers to come back. They show them new products that they didn't see on the first visit. E-mails in many ways are much better than print or TV ads. Why? Because print and TV ads are limited in what they can show. TV ads usually show only one or two products. Print ads are limited to what they can show on a page.

An e-mail, using links, can show hundreds or thousands of products—depending on what the viewer is interested in seeing and how much time the viewer wants to spend. The net effect of the e-mails, therefore, has been highly positive.

The year 3 LTV is up from $47.96 to $123.56. To get that increase, we have spent $10 per subscriber to get their e-mail address. We sent 25 million e-mails in the third year. The cost of the database, segmentation, analytics and e-mails was $4 million per year. Typically database costs continue even after subscribers have unsubscribed. The reason:

you keep them as a suppression file and later you may want to try to re-activate them.

How have profits increased from setting up the e-mail marketing program?

EXHIBIT 06-07 LTV before and after e-mails

Customer Lifetime Value Before and After Weekly E-mails Sent	Acquisition Year	Year 2	Year 3
Before	$18.60	$37.58	$47.96
After	$38.20	$86.85	$123.56
Change	$19.60	$49.27	$75.60
With 1,000,000 customers	$19,600,000	$49,271,034	$75,595,135

Net profit increased by $75 million in the third year. If we take the steps necessary to increase e-mail relevance to a higher level, we will increase our profits by a corresponding amount.

In the next chapter, we will explore LTV further by determining the LTV of customer segments and determine the individual LTV of each customer. This will permit us to create customer status levels—silver, gold, and platinum—which can help us further increase our profits.

The value of an e-mail name

Direct mail campaigns typically operate by renting response names from companies that have sold products to consumers (or businesses) or renting compiled names from one of the four companies that maintain lists of all consumers in the country. Such rented names have a market value. To rent compiled names, you may pay $50 to $80 per thousand names for one-time use. For response names, you may pay $80 to $200 per thousand names. A name and address have value.

This situation doesn't exist in e-mail. To avoid sending spam, you must have the consumers' permission to use their e-mail addresses (see chapter 8). There are, to be sure, e-mail addresses listed for sale on the Internet. Because of the danger of spam, except in special circumstances most reputable marketers don't rent e-mail names in the same way they do direct mail names. That doesn't mean, however, that e-mail addresses don't have a value to the company that has been granted permission to mail. They have a real value that can be measured using a LTV table.

The LTV for year-three customers who didn't get e-mails was

$47.96, while it was $123.56 for customers who did get e-mails, a $75.60 difference. Each e-mail address, therefore, was worth $71.20 over three years. Note that this LTV includes the cost of paying $10 to acquire the e-mail name in the first place. There are many ways of determining a subscriber name's the value, but this one is as good as any.

The importance of knowing the e-mail name value

Whatever method we use, having a handle on e-mail names' value can be very important. It gives impetus to efforts to acquire more e-mail addresses so we can send more e-mails. E-mails are so inexpensive to send that, once acquired, they can boost the revenue and profits of any company that acquires them and uses them properly.

We will continue to use LTV charts throughout this book to illustrate the significance of the actions we recommend.

Takeaway thoughts

- Customers' and e-mail subscribers' LTV can be calculated.
- You must build a subscriber database and be able to track specific subscribers' performance from year to year.
- The LTV depends on the relevance of the communications sent.
- More relevant e-mails result in lower unsubscribes and bounces.
- Increased relevance increases opens and average order size.
- E-mails produce online and offline sales.
- Consumers buy as a result of many stimuli in addition to e-mails.
- Compare the LTV of customers who don't received e-mail from that of customers who do receive e-mail.
- Once you know an e-mail name's value, you have a reason to acquire more.

7

E-mail Marketing to Subscriber Segments

Segmentation needs validation through testing, and e-mail allows for greater precision and flexibility in testing than other forms of marketing. E-mail testing is more cost-effective than its offline counterparts, and results are obtained much faster. Segmenting and testing cycles that can take weeks in direct mail campaigns can be done in a matter of hours online.

Segmenting is basic marketing. At the very heart of the process is the effort to improve your knowledge about customers and prospects. The act of segmentation requires you to understand what makes each customer unique from the universe of recipients and how subsets of customers vary from one another. You must understand such things as:

- What messages will be most likely to cause them to react favorably to your product or service?
- Are there groups within your database more receptive to a discount offer and others more likely to purchase when free shipping is offered?
- Is a portion of your target audience early adopters who need to be among the very first to hear about your new products?
- How often do they want to hear from you?
- How engaged are they with your products or services?

Bill Nussey, Silverpop.com

Successful e-mail marketing's goal is to become profitable through acquiring and retaining customers who, as a result of your efforts, are happy and loyal and buy a lot. As we know by now, for marketing e-mails to be effective, they must be relevant to each subscriber. Relevance is in the eye of the recipient, not the sender. So how do you find out what your subscribers consider to be relevant to them? One way is to put subscribers into segments based on their preferences, behavior, and demographics and develop e-mail messages relevant to each segment.

JupiterResearch reports that marketers who segment their lists (by things like what customers buy or where people click on their Web site) can improve conversion rates by up to 355% and increase revenues by as much as 781%.[1] Despite these wonderful numbers, only about 58% of retail e-mailers send e-mails to segmented groups of customers based on their preferences or purchase data. Does segmenting work for those companies who use it? The technique is considered to be very effective by 67% of those same merchants.

Primitive subscriber segmentation

Most of the advanced segmentation tactics at the end of this chapter are impossible for most e-mail marketers today, because they have been hunting for sales, not farming them. All they know about most of their subscribers is the subscriber's e-mail address. You can't do much segmentation with that. There are some things that you can and should do to send more relevant e-mails, however, even if you are in this primitive situation.

Primitive subscriber segmentation can be broken down into six methods:

- **Purchase behavior.** *Easy:* buyer vs. non-buyer; *medium:* one buyer vs. multiple buyers vs. non-buyers. This is really considered lifecycle management when we calculate relevance.
- **E-mail activity.** *Easy:* active clicker vs. non-clicker; *medium:* active clicker/opener vs. opener vs. inert.
- **Web activity.** *Easy:* added items to cart vs. never visited site; *medium:* no visits vs. added items to cart vs. browsed multiple categories.
- **Tenure on database.** *Easy:* new e-mail addresses (within 30 days) vs. older addresses; *medium:* new vs. 30-90 days' old vs. more than 90 days on the database.
- **Channel shopped.** *Easy:* on Web vs. at store; *medium:* on Web via e-mail vs. on Web not via e-mail vs. at store, thanks to e-mail vs. at store.
- **Click categorization.** *Easy:* number of clicks on opened e-mails; *medium:* number of repeated clicks on opened e-mails; *advanced:* audience segmentation based on categories of items clicked on.

First, separate subscribers into buyers and non-buyers. Many e-mail marketers have a million or more subscribers, but less than 10% of them have ever bought anything online. At a minimum, your segmentation scheme should be buyers and non-buyers. You have little excuse for treating them alike; buyers should be treated better.

You can easily prove this idea's validity by setting up a control group of buyers who get the same blasts non-buyers get. The remaining buyers get welcome, thank-you, and preferred buyer messages based on what they bought and on what you learned in the online fulfillment process. If you shipped a product, you probably have the buyer's complete name and street address. With this information, you can get appended data (described later in this chapter) and personalize their e-mails. Basic rule: treat buyers better and they will buy more.

Inactives as a segment

Every e-mail subscriber database has a huge segment: inactive subscribers. These people don't open or open but don't click. Set a time limit for inactivity, then separate these subscribers from the rest of your list. Send them something to wake them up. If you don't, they will be gone. Plus, continuing to send them e-mails they never open may brand you as a spammer. So get busy. Get them active or get rid of them.

Marketing Sherpa surveyed 1,210 e-mail marketers in 2007 to show their use of segmentation.

EXHIBIT 07-01 How e-mail marketers use segmentation

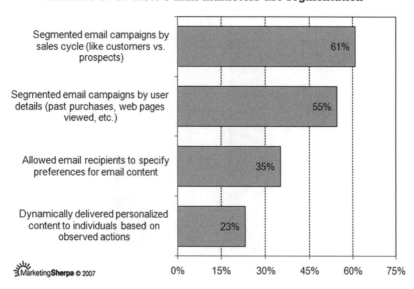

MarketingSherpa © 2007

As you can see, only 23% of responders segmented subscribers by their observed actions. This is usually a very effective type of segmentation but is harder to do.

Acquisition segments

Save the origin of every e-mail subscriber. Consider putting subscribers from a particular source: a sweepstakes, a partner program, or a direct mail promotion, into a segment of their own, particularly if the source might be meaningful to the subscriber. You can begin with these segments by saying, "You may be wondering where we got your e-mail address. Do you remember when you signed up for . . . " That is better than having recipients assume you are a spammer. This isn't a segmentation scheme that will yield great long-term results, but it can help you decide whether certain sources are good or bad for you.

Multibuyer segments

Try treating multibuyers better than single buyers. Exhibit 07-02 shows the results discovered by one major retail e-mailer over one year.

This retailer sent the same blasts to everyone: single, multi, and non-buyers. As you can see, 15,368 multibuyers spent 50% more than the 33,957 single buyers. The multibuyers are so important that they

EXHIBIT 07-02 Single buyers vs. multibuyers

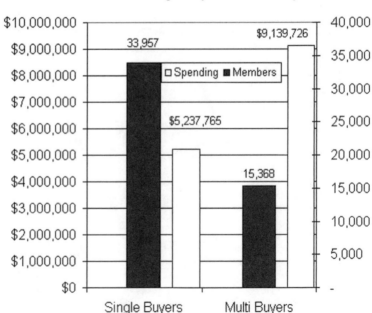

EXHIBIT 07-03 Multibuyers by status level

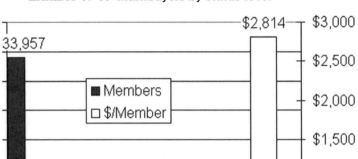

could be divided into different status levels based on the average annual purchase per household. Exhibit 07-03 shows the breakdown.

As you can see, the 510 "platinum" customers spent an average of $2,814 per year with the retailer, compared to $154 per year spent by the one-time–buyer households in the bronze group. Reaching out to platinum customers with a personalized thank-you or other messages would certainly help retain these customers. In this same year, 105,103 consumers unsubscribed from the retailer's list, many of whom had made one or more purchases before they disappeared. No effort was made to see why these buyers went away.

Another primitive segmentation scheme would be to treat openers, clickers, and cart-abandoners better than non-openers. Treating openers better than non-openers can pay off in terms of increased conversions.

Design a really good preference profile

Another thing a primitive segment marketer absolutely must do: have a preference profile button on every page of your e-mails. Your goal is to maximize the revenue from your existing subscriber base, and one route to increased opens, clicks, and conversions is to move as fast as you can to base your e-mails on *advanced segmentation*. The more information you have on each subscriber, the faster you can move this particular subscriber to advanced status. The preference center should ask for the information you need to make that leap, such as street address, the category of products the subscriber is most interested in, and demographics (income, presence of children, type of home, own vs. rent, length of residence). Have a brainstorming session and pick out the 5 or 10 most useful pieces of information you would like to have—and could use in e-mails.

Once you have designed this profile, how do you get subscribers to fill in the blanks? Remember, subscribers only do what is in their own best interest. As you design your preference profile, think like a subscriber and say, "What's in it for me to fill out this form?" If you have been doing your homework, you can prove that subscribers who fill out a preference profile—and get more relevant e-mails as a result—are more likely to open, click, and buy.

Subscribers who have provided this kind of information to you have a dollar value that exceeds that of subscribers about whom you know only the e-mail address. Determine what that dollar value is.

Suppose you figure out that the dollar value of e-mail-address-only subscribers is $4.91 each per year, but preference-profile completers are worth $18.22 each. You are on your way to creating an incentive. Offer your e-mail-only-subscribers $X or X% off their first order (try both to see which works best) if they complete the preference profile. Soon you will be moving hundreds, thousands, or millions of subscribers into a position where you can do some of the advanced segmentation tactics described in the remainder of this chapter.

Caution: set up business rules so you don't look ridiculous to your subscribers. For those who have given you their profiles, don't offer an incentive for providing them a second time. This seems obvious, but many e-mailers forget simple concepts like this. If you do, you make it clear to your subscribers that they are corresponding with a rather stupid machine instead of an intelligent human being.

If you determine you need a lot of data, you may want to break your preference survey into two parts, each with its own benefit, so you don't scare subscribers with a time-consuming preference form.

Intermediate subscriber segmentation: RFM and clusters

Before you get into advanced segmentation, there are a couple intermediate methods that work and will boost toward understanding your subscribers and creating relevant e-mails for them. They are recency, frequency, and monetary (RFM) analysis and cluster analysis.

Segmentation using RFM codes

Some e-mail marketers use RFM to classify their segments. This is particularly useful when they don't have the street addresses of a large number of their e-mail subscribers. RFM was developed more than 50 years ago by direct mail marketers and is alive and well today.

The basic concept is that customer react to your communications in a predictable pattern based on their previous behavior. Those who have joined more recently are more likely to respond (open, click, and buy) than those who joined a long time ago. The same idea applies, less powerfully, to how often they purchase and how much money they spend.

There are two systems of RFM coding: proportional and hard coded. With hard-coded RFM, you create arbitrary classifications, such as joined 0–6 months ago, 7–12 months ago, and more than 12 months ago, for example. Frequency is divided into one-time, two-time and three-time (or more) buyers. Monetary can be divided in a similar way: under $100, $101–$300, and more than $300.

The trouble with hard coding is that many times the classifications are arbitrary, with some groups having far too many subscribers and some far too few. It is necessary, then, to constantly redo the classifications.

Proportional RFM coding is easier. To do this for recency, for example, you code everyone in your subscriber database by date of most recent response. The response could be a registration, a purchase, or an open. Sort your entire database by that date each month. Divide it into five equal groups (each 20% of the file), and classify the most recent as 5, the next group as 4, and so on. Marketers who have done this get a graph after every e-mail promotion like Exhibit 07-04.

From this graph, you can see that those recent responders, classified as 5s, had almost three times the response rate of the 4s, the 4s had a higher response rate than the 3s, and so on. This a universal graph. You will find the same results with your e-mail marketing file.

Graphing frequency

For purchases, you can classify subscribers by the number of times they have made a purchase. Typically, most of your e-mail subscribers have never bought anything. Some have bought once, some many times. Put a number into everyone's database record representing the number of purchases. If you don't sell anything online, you can classify frequency by number of opens.

Sorting your file by frequency, you again divide the file into five

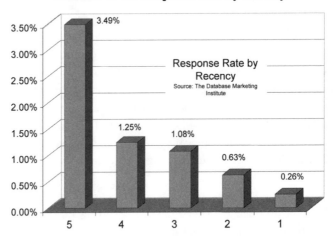

EXHIBIT 07-04 Response rate by recency

equal groups, coding those who have the highest number of purchases (or opens) as 5s. Lower 20% groups become 4s, then 3s, and so on. After any e-mail campaign, you can graph the response by frequency. It will look something like Exhibit 07-05.

Monetary segments

Finally, if you have data on actual purchases, you can put the total amount spent into each subscriber record (with most of the spending being, probably, zero), sort the file by the spending and classify every-

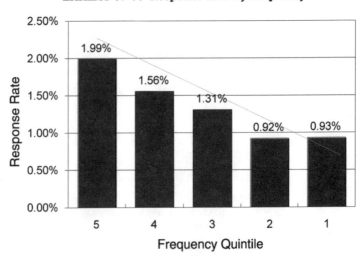

EXHIBIT 07-05 Response rate by frequency

EXHIBIT 07-06 Response rate by monetary amount

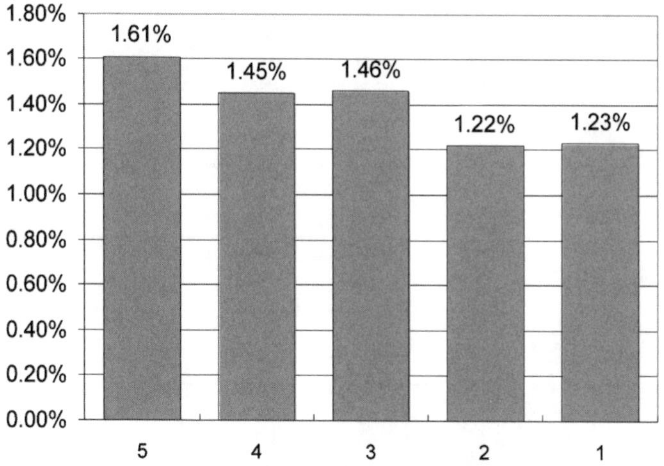

one as either 5, 4, 3, 2, or 1. After any e-mail promotion campaign, a graph of opens based on monetary will look something like Exhibit 07-06.

As you can see, monetary isn't as predictive (there is little difference between the quintiles) as recency or frequency. This holds true for low-ticket items, whereas a monetary graph for a high-ticket item, such as an automobile or a condo, would look quite different. It would show that previous monetary behavior was predictive of current monetary behavior.

Developing RFM cell codes

The next step is the most significant. You can develop RFM cell codes for your entire subscriber database, dividing them into 125 cells based on recency, frequency, and monetary.

In a promotion to 45,246 subscribers, 1,893 (4.18%) made a purchase, with the average order size being $25.96. Exhibit 07-07 shows the buyers broken down by three-digit RFM cell code. As you can see, RFM is quite predictive of response and conversions.

RFM was originally developed for nonprofit mailers. It is still widely used by direct mailers where the cost of a third-class letter is so high ($500 to $700 per thousand) that RFM helps you to decide who not to mail to—because the profit from the response won't be sufficient to pay for the letter.

This reasoning doesn't apply to e-mail, where the cost is $2 to $6

EXHIBIT 07-07 Response rate by RFM cell

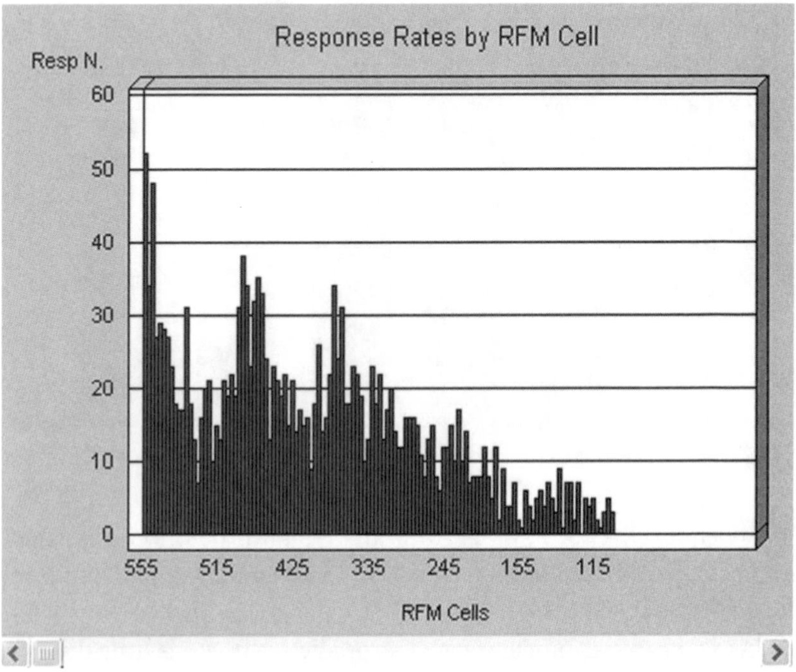

per thousand. You might as well mail them all. So why would e-mail marketers want to use RFM? There are a number of important reasons.

First, you don't want to mail to people who you know (from RFM analysis) are unlikely to respond. To these folks, your e-mail will seem like spam. It will be irrelevant to them. As a result, you may be branded as a spammer and have all of your e-mails blocked by an ISP.

Second, RFM can help you determine e-mail content. Let's say you have had several orders from a customer in the past two years, and the orders have been from different product categories. A month ago, this customer purchased $100 worth of men's clothing, and two months ago, she purchased $300 worth of women's clothing. In this e-mail, should you pitch men's or women's clothing to this customer? RFM can help you make this decision.

Third, some companies, such as FedEx, use RFM to determine which customers to offer discount coupons to. With RFM, they can see patterns in customers' shipping patterns. If, for example, the customer only ships products at Christmas time, there is no point in sending him offers to mail in April. Nor does it make sense to make him offers in the Christmas season because he is going to ship then anyway. RFM can help you to see shifts in customer behavior patterns so you can reach out to those who may be slipping away.

Finally, RFM helps you become more relevant to your subscribers. Clearly a message to those coded 555 (bought recently and very often and spent a lot of money) should be quite different from those coded 111 (opted in a long time ago, purchased only once, and spent very little).

Prizm cluster segmentation

Some marketers, like the women's dress chain described below, have had success in segmenting by appending Prizm segments, or clusters, to their customer file of names and addresses.

Claritas has been developing consumer segments since 1974, when the Prizm lifestyle segmentation system was first introduced. The segments have catchy names and are based on such factors as income, age, lifestyle, and purchasing habits. The current version, Prizm NE, contains 66 clusters organized into 14 groups.

Following are a few cluster descriptions:

- **15. Pools & Patios**—Formed during the postwar Baby Boom, Pools & Patios has evolved from a segment of young suburban families to one for mature, empty-nesting couples. In these stable neighborhoods graced with backyard pools and patios—the highest proportion of homes were built in the 1960s—residents work as white-collar managers and professionals, and are now at the top of their careers.

- **17. Beltway Boomers**—The members of the postwar Baby Boom are all grown up. Today, these Americans are in their forties and fifties, and one segment of this huge cohort—college-educated, upper-middle-class and home-owning—is found in Beltway Boomers. Like many of their peers who married late, these Boomers are still raising children in comfortable suburban subdivisions, and they're pursuing kid-centered lifestyles.

- **18. Kids & Cul-de-Sacs**—Upscale, suburban, married couples with children—that's the skinny on Kids & Cul-de-Sacs, an enviable lifestyle of large families in recently built subdivisions. With a high rate of Hispanic and Asian Americans, this segment is a refuge for college-educated, white-collar professionals with administrative jobs and upper-middle-class incomes. Their nexus of education, affluence and children translates into large outlays for child-centered products and services.[2]

EXHIBIT 07-08 Best-performing clusters

Cluster	Index
Rustic Elders	159.8
Blue Highways	148.5
New Eco-topia	146.0
Grain Belt	142.9
Back Country Folks	142.8
Hometown Retired	135.7
Shotguns and Pickups	134.1
Agri-Business	133.2
Gray Power	132.4
River City, USA	130.7

Service bureaus, such as KnowledgeBase Marketing and Acxiom, often have the Claritas Prizm NE database in-house. You can send them your customer file and have them append segmentation data to it. By doing this you can determine which segments have a propensity to buy your product and which don't. Have data appended to your test group of 100,000 to see if it helps in segmentation. If not, drop it.

As a test, a nonprofit mailer that appealed to a certain group of older donors used Claritas' previous segmentation system (Prizm 62) to generate market research information for a nationwide mail campaign. It applied Claritas cluster coding to a sample of its prospect file and donor base. The results were quite revealing. The mailer discovered its best donor segments were those in Exhibit 07-08.

The index was created by comparing the percentage of the population in the area being mailed with the percentage of the donors. An index of 100 means the percentage of donors was equal to the percentage of the population mailed. The bottom clusters were those in Exhibit 07-09.

EXHIBIT 07-09 Worst-performing clusters

Cluster	Index
Young Literati	61.1
Urban Gold Coast	61.1
Latino America	57.9
Hispanic Mix	57.5
Inner Cities	55.8
Norma Rae-Ville	54.5
Southside City	54.1
New Beginnings	47.8
Military Quarters	42.2
Towns and Gowns	32.6

Advanced subscriber segmentation

Once you have accumulated the necessary data on a portion of your subscribers, you can move on to advanced segmentation based on subscriber farming.

If you knew what each customer considered to be relevant to her, you would create that content in your e-mails. Say you have the opt-in e-mail addresses with profile and preference data on 1 million customers. How will you create e-mail content that each customer would consider relevant?

We recommend creating less than a dozen customer segments and designing particular e-mail content for each segment.

You can break segmentation marketing into four main tasks:

1. Getting data about and from your customers that can be used to put them into segments and to design content for the e-mails sent to them
2. Creating workable segments based on your customer base and the information you can collect
3. Designing marketing programs for each segment, managing the segments, and sending relevant e-mails to each segment
4. Creating reports on each segment, reviewing your success, then revising your marketing program based on the reports

Customer purchase activity: the when

Every time a customer opens an e-mail, clicks, or buys a product or service, the data should be stored in your customer marketing database. But how can you categorize purchase events so they are useful for creating segments? You will want to know when your customer bought: time of day, day of the week, or the season of the year. Some people buy all the time. Some buy certain products only at certain times, such as Christmas. People who buy during the day may not be employed or may be buying using computers at work. They may even be buying for their companies.

To decide on how to categorize the when part of purchases, you have to look ahead and think, "How will I use this information to create segments?" The answer to this question tells you what is important to study in when people purchase. As long as you keep the time, day, month, and year, you can run analytics later and decide how to use the data to create useful segments.

Segmentation by opt-in date and time

A major online retailer of bags and accessories, eBags, decided to identify the day and time it should send promotional e-mails to generate the highest response rates and online sales. Larry Martine, then eBag's director of retention marketing, decided the best time to reach each customer would be the same day and time the customer had originally opted in. Martine and his team reasoned that if the customer's schedule afforded her time to opt in, it might also be the best time for her to consider an offer and make an online purchase.

To test this segmentation strategy, eBags sent promotions to recipients on the same day of the week and time of day as they had originally opted in. The results were amazing. Compared with a control group's results, the test group's click-throughs were 20 percent higher and conversion rates increased by 65 percent. The average order size was 45 percent higher, while the average revenue per recipient was 187 percent more than the control group.

This is really a great segmentation idea. Most marketers keep track of the date and time that subscribers subscribed already! See if you can match these outstanding results.

Customer purchases: the what

Many operational systems record purchases by item number. For example, a customer bought item 241830, color blue, size 14, quantity 1, for $89.95. Actually, 241830 is a cocktail dress made in China. There is a lookup table that tells you that. It's a mid-price woman's garment that was on sale (the regular price is $109.85).

But how will you use this information to create a segment?

To make sense out of the data, get a spreadsheet file of a couple thousand transactions. As you look at the records, think about how to categorize them, then sort them in different ways until something clicks in your head. Aha! Some people buy only sale items. Some buy top-of-the-line merchandise. Some buy women's apparel. You are on your way to creating segments that you can use for e-mail marketing.

You may already have a classification scheme. For insurance, you have life, health, casualty, file, homeowners, and auto. The same is true for bank customers: savings, checking, money market, home equity loans, mortgages, and credit cards. But you have a problem using these categories alone: some people have one product; some have several. That could be the basis of segmentation.

You can create temporary segments to support particular campaigns. For example, if you are selling homeowner's policies, you may want to sell such policies to people who have your auto or health coverage. Ad hoc segments like this can work, particularly if you have a control group to prove that what you are doing is working. The main goal is not to have segments that last a long time but having segments that, at the time you develop a campaign, enable you to draft relevant e-mails.

Once you have spent a week or two doing this kind of analysis, you can come up with a method of categorizing purchases that enables you to put your customers into different segments for some campaigns based on purchase data. Armed with this method, you can develop some business rules that enable your database managers to categorize purchases by your scheme. We can't be any more specific than that. Classifying the what to create segments calls for imaginative marketers who put some time and thought into the process.

Segments and status levels

It may or may not work to segment customers by total sales. Silver, gold, and platinum may be great for customer status levels: it gives them something to work toward. It may not be as useful for you in planning your e-mail campaigns. What do you say to the silver people? "Buy more." What do you say to the gold people? "Buy more." How can your e-mail marketing programs be personalized when they all have the same message? If, however, gold members have certain privileges (such as free shipping) that silver members don't, you can sell silver members on the possibility of moving up to a higher status.

As a marketer, you will find marketing segments more useful. You can look at a segment to identify common interests so your e-mails are relevant. You can look at a status level as a customer trying to earn recognition, increased status, and perks.

For an airline customer, for example, status levels can have real value. You can earn preferential treatment in upgrades and seating choice. You get on the plane first. You get bonus miles when you fly. Your business may not be able easily to provide different levels of service based on status level the way airlines can. But that's no reason not to try. What about free shipping for gold members, letting the silver members know what is in store for them if they were to move up?

A retailer developed a highly successful segmentation scheme based on analysis of the when and the what of purchase behavior. It looked at not just how much customers spent but also when they bought and what they bought. Some customers bought only at Christmas. Others bought only necessities. Some bought only sale items. On the other hand, there were customers who were fiercely loyal to the chain. Others

EXHIBIT 07-10 Status levels and marketing segments

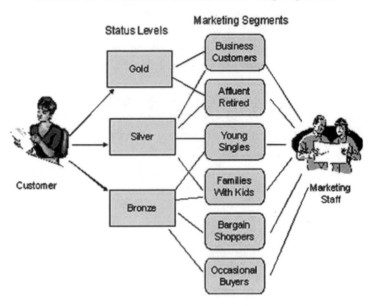

wanted to be the best dressed people on the planet. In total, the retailer broke its customers down into three large status levels: gold, silver, and bronze, each divided into three smaller marketing segments. Exhibit 01-11 illustrates the segmentation.

EXHIBIT 07-11 A retailer's segmentation scheme

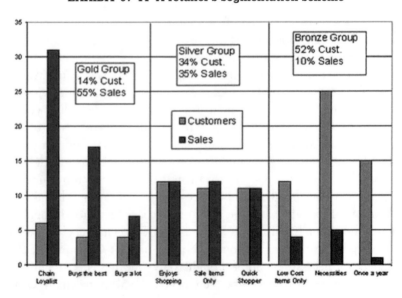

Study this chart carefully. It wasn't developed by some college pro-fessor to explain a theory but by a major national retail chain with 54 million customer records, of which 16 million purchased in the previ-ous 12 months. The chain has $9 billion in sales and 3,000 stores na-tionwide. The vast majority of the customers are women.

The data came from two sources: the chain's proprietary charge card customers and credit card customers. The transactions were run through the chain's POS system and nightly matched against a credit card database using reverse append. The system captured the transac-tions of 60% of customers, representing 70% of the sales.

All customer records were coded for RFM plus Claritas Prizm clus-ter codes, which yielded lifestyle and demographic data. The segments were developed based on a very sophisticated analysis of its customer's habits. The retailer answered the following questions:

- Who are our best customers?
- What percentage of sales do they generate?
- How big is their clothing budget and the chain's share of their wallet?
- What are their demographic characteristics?
- When and what do they buy in our category?
- Who buys full price, and who buys only sale items?
- When and what do they buy from the competition?

Armed with lots of statistics from its marketing database, the retailer went through five steps to create the segments:

- Determine the behavior that drives each segment
- Identify naturally occurring clusters of customers, each with a unique buying pattern based on 24-month purchasing history
- Enhance these clusters with lifestyle data and demographics
- Conduct an in-depth survey of each cluster for competitive infor-mation and fashion attitudes
- Emerge with a multidimensional picture of each customer seg-ment

Once the nine marketing segments were developed, the chain's ana-lysts created detailed picture of each. Here are five.

1. **The Chain Loyalist** (6% of customers and 31% of all sales) has a median age of 32 and an annual clothing budget of $2,700.

The chain gets 40% of these women's clothing wallets, with a visit to a chain store every six weeks.

2. **The Enjoys Shopping** (10% of customers and 11% of sales) with a median age of 30 has a $1,400 annual clothing budget of which the chain gets 20%. She shops the chain five times a year.

3. **The Buys a Lot** (4% of customers and 7% of sales) is 35 years old and has a $2,800 annual clothing budget, of which 21% is spent at the chain twice a year.

4. **The Low Cost Items Only** (12% of customers and 4% of sales) has a median age of 45 and an annual clothing budget of $800, of which the chain gets 12% in her twice a year.

5. **The Once a Year Shopper** (15% of customers and 1% of sales) have a median age of 38 and a clothing budget of $1,500, of which the chain gets only 3%.

Once the segments were identified and backed up with statistical analysis, they had to develop a marketing strategy for each segment. In essence, they decided to put their marketing money where it would do the most good. They allocated their marketing budget to each of the major groups.

For the gold group (14% of customers and 55% of sales), the goal was retention. These were the most valuable individuals to the chain. It allocated 60% of its marketing budget to programs designed to retain this loyal group. It let them know how valuable they were to the store and provided special services and status perquisites. These special services included:

- Status-based loyalty benefits
- Private sales with advanced notice
- Personalized gifts with purchases
- Seasonal merchandise previews
- Image-based mailings and catalogs
- In-store recognition and special services

Those who dropped out of the group received reactivation mailings. Those who spent less than they had been spending got telephone calls to find out why.

For the bronze group (52% of customers and 10% of sales), the retailer decided not to waste resources. These people didn't spend much money in the store; $1 spent here wouldn't do anywhere near as much good as $1 spent on the gold customers. So, it allocated only 5% of its entire marketing program to bronze customers. They got clearance announcements and gift certificate promotions.

The silver group (34% of customers and 35% of sales) was right in the middle. Here, the goal was to encourage them to move up to gold status. The retailer felt it could motivate those who enjoyed shopping to spend more time in the store and could encourage the sale shoppers with sale offers. The programs included performance-based frequency programs, notice of sale events, bring-a-friend events, and gift certificate promotions. Those who showed definite trends toward loyalty were rewarded with gold membership.

The chain experimented with special programs for the quick shoppers so they could find what they wanted quickly—more quickly than with its competitors. It allocated 35% of its marketing budget to silver customers.

So how did the retailer measure success? By measuring retention and migration against control groups and specifying goals for each group. It watched attrition and retention: were the retention programs working on the gold group? It measured migration upward and downward: how many silver people could it get to become gold? How many slipped down to bronze status? Incremental sales per program and per season were also important. The store had regular seasonal programs. It could measure the effect of these programs on each of the nine segments. It watched frequency of seasonal purchases. Christmas was always the big season, but what about spring and fall buying? How did each segment respond to those seasons? And what about dollars spent per trip and per season? The shopping basket was a key measurement of success.

The retailer measured the number of departments a person shopped per trip and per season. It was possible to make offers to people who had only visited one or two departments to get them to go to a new department. Did these shoppers keep buying in the new department after the promotion was over?

It also measured the number of items a person bought per trip and per season. Bundling is a technique that will never go out of style. If you buy a dress, you have to buy matching shoes and perhaps a belt. To make bundling work, you have to start with the buyers to make sure you have something to offer. Next, you develop POP displays and train the sales force to make the bundling work. The real test is noting segment responds to bundling and which doesn't. Maybe you are motivating the wrong segment.

Finally, the retailer measured its share of customers' wallet. It con-

EXHIBIT 07-12 Purchases traced to e-mails, before segmentation

E-Mails before segment marketing				Average		
				Store	Visit	Total
Segment	Customers	Mails	e-mails	Visits	Spend	Spend
Chain Loyalist	240,000	30	7,200,000	64,800	$510.00	$33,048,000
Buys the Best	150,000	30	4,500,000	31,500	$465.00	$14,647,500
Buys a Lot	170,000	30	5,100,000	53,295	$380.00	$20,252,100
Enjoys Shopping	450,000	30	13,500,000	160,380	$151.00	$24,217,380
Items on Sale	430,000	30	12,900,000	103,200	$98.00	$10,113,600
Quick Shopper	490,000	30	14,700,000	86,436	$95.00	$8,211,420
Low Cost Items	470,000	30	14,100,000	68,808	$93.00	$6,399,144
Necessities	1,004,000	30	30,120,000	47,891	$78.00	$3,735,482
Once a Year	596,000	30	17,880,000	32,899	$68.00	$2,237,146
Total	4,000,000	30	120,000,000	649,209	$189.25	$122,861,772

ducted a continual review of share of wallet to see how it varied with each segment.

Applying segments to your subscriber base

Let's see how using such a segmentation scheme would work for a retailer with a large number of retail stores. You, as the retailer, have an e-mail database of 4 million subscribers, and before segmentation you sent identical e-mails to all 4 million subscribers 30 times a year, as shown in Exhibit 07-12. You receive 649,209 store visits per year that you can trace to the e-mails, with an average purchase of $189.25.

Now you set up segments similar to those discussed earlier. How might your subscriber's behavior vary by segment? Once you create these segments, you will send different e-mails to each segment, in fact to each subscriber. You send personalized e-mails using different frequencies based on segment members' desires, and the products featured are based on subscriber preferences, previous purchases, and data on what others in the same segment have purchased. Your campaigns might look like Exhibit 07-13.

In this chart, the top three segments (Chain Loyalist, Buys the Best, and Buys a Lot) are the most valuable customers. Their loyalty must be preserved. Experience shows that sending them 30 e-mails per year may be excessive, leading to a loss of some of their business. To keep their loyalty, you mail to them only 18 times a year.

For the next four segments (Enjoys Shopping, Items on Sale, Quick Shopper, and Low Cost Items), you continue your current e-mail pro-

EXHIBIT 07-13 Purchases traced to e-mails, after segmentation

E-Mails after segment marketing

Segment	Customers	Mails	e-mails	Average Store Visits	Visit Spend	Total Spend
Chain Loyalist	240,000	18	4,320,000	71,539	$663.00	$47,430,490
Buys the Best	150,000	18	2,700,000	34,020	$604.50	$20,565,090
Buys a Lot	170,000	18	3,060,000	56,549	$494.00	$27,935,107
Enjoys Shopping	450,000	30	13,500,000	200,880	$181.20	$36,399,456
Items on Sale	430,000	30	12,900,000	131,580	$117.60	$15,473,808
Quick Shopper	490,000	30	14,700,000	124,468	$114.00	$14,189,334
Low Cost Items	470,000	30	14,100,000	99,574	$111.60	$11,112,481
Necessities	1,004,000	8	8,032,000	44,979	$78.00	$3,508,378
Once a Year	596,000	8	4,768,000	31,469	$68.00	$2,139,878
Total	4,000,000	19.5	78,080,000	795,058	$224.83	$178,754,021

gram. The bottom two segments (Necessities and Once a Year) don't buy very much or very often. Experience shows that throwing e-mail at these determined occasional shoppers may do more harm than good (through being classified as junk mail), so you reduce their mailings to eight times a year and only in those periods in which these two segments normally buy.

There is another benefit to segmentation. Since we are sending fewer e-mails and more relevant e-mails, customized for each segment and each person within the segment, our unsubscribe and undeliverable rates will go down.

You spend $2 million a year on segmenting and customizing e-mails for the nine segments. When we compare the two approaches, including costs, we find that fewer e-mails sent equals higher customer spending, as shown in Exhibit 07-14.

EXHIBIT 07-14 Segmentation ROI

	E-mails Sent	Number Visits	Average Spend	Resulting Sales
Before	120,000,000	649,209	$189.25	$122,861,772
Segmented	7,808,000	795,058	$224.83	$178,754,021
Increase	-112,192,000	145,849	$35.58	$55,892,249
Reduced loss of subscribers				$7,762,905
Total Gain				$63,655,154
Segmentation Cost				$2,000,000
Return per $1.00				$31.83

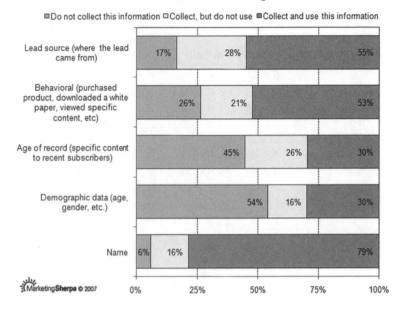

EXHIBIT 07-15 Uses of data in segmentation

⊞ Do not collect this information ▢ Collect, but do not use ■ Collect and use this information

Lead source (where the lead came from)	17%	28%	55%
Behavioral (purchased product, downloaded a white paper, viewed specific content, etc)	26%	21%	53%
Age of record (specific content to recent subscribers)	45%	26%	30%
Demographic data (age, gender, etc.)	54%	16%	30%
Name	6% 16%		79%

MarketingSherpa © 2007   0%   25%   50%   75%   100%

Appended demographic data

If you have a consumer's name and street address, you can go to any one of the four companies (KnowledgeBase Marketing, Equifax, Experian, and InfoUSA) that compile information on consumers and get demographic data appended to your customer file. The data include about a 100 fields of information, including date of birth, marital status, income, wealth, length of residence, type of housing, value of home, own vs. rent, presence of children, and occupation. This information can be really useful in creating segments. After all, you wouldn't send the same series of e-mails to a couple over 65 that you would to college students or to families with young children. For financial services, age and income are usually the most important segmenting factors. Only about 30% of e-mail marketers are collecting and using demographic information today as shown by a Marketing Sherpa survey (Exhibit 07-15).

We recommend you get the demographic data for a file of 100,000 customers. Categorize these customers' purchases by the when and the what, and see if by blending all three together you can create a meaningful segmentation scheme like the one shown earlier. While you do this, keep thinking, "How can I use this information to help create relevant e-mails for these folks?"

Creating supermarket customer segments

Almost all US supermarkets have loyalty programs, but few are success-ful with them. One successful program was from Kroger, which linked up with British firm dunnhumby a few years ago.

Dunnhumby helped UK grocer Tesco move from England's third-largest retailer to its biggest retailer, with a market share double that of its closest UK competitor. Tesco promoted its Clubcard, a shopper loy-alty program that provides discounts to specific customer segments, such as pet owners, and gives customers money-back vouchers they could use in the store. The analysis and segmentation was done by dunnhumby.

Kroger, with $66 billion in sales from over 3,600 stores, asked dunnhumby to analyze what it needed to provide shoppers with a more customized shopping experience. Kroger recognized when it began that the average American household belongs to 12 different customer loy-alty programs. Such programs usually do little to generate loyalty. They accumulate massive POS data, but most retailers lack the know-how to convert the data into actions that would delight shoppers, increase sales, and get a return on their investment.

The Kroger system was similar to collaborative filtering. Dunnhumby assigned a score to the products that Kroger sells based on attributes like price, quality, freshness, and package size. Its computers then found customers whose shopping carts had similar scores. It grouped those shoppers into segments. It then set up seven segments for Kroger, each of which received customized mailings. Three of the seg-ments were budget shoppers, watching the waistline, and family-fo-cused.

The program had a second benefit as well: consumer-product man-ufacturers paid fees to learn which segments were buying their brands. Clients included Unilever, Procter & Gamble, Kraft, General Mills, PepsiCo, Clorox, and Kellogg's. There were 60 clients in all. To protect privacy, the data provided to them didn't include personal information, like addresses.

Nationwide, US coupon redemption has dropped from 7 billion to 2.6 billion per year, according to the research firm CMS. But coupon redemption rates at Kroger are far higher than the normal 1% to 3% for untargeted offers. Using the new system, Kroger managed to per-suade its most loyal shoppers to shop a few more times a month and spend a little more on each trip.

Segmenting by subscriber ability to pay

In 2008, DirecTV CEO Chase Carey said the company had a new focus on "quality subscribers."[3] It found these subscribers by analyzing their income, age, home ownership, education, and other metrics. DirecTV segmented customers to figure out who was valuable and who wasn't and went after the valuable ones. "We developed in the last couple of years a much more sophisticated customer segmentation set of tools that are unique to us," he said.

By early 2008, DirecTV's monthly churn hit an eight-year low of 1.42%—well below other telecoms. To do this, DirecTV avoided taking on subscribers it deemed less than desirable. It mainly did this with two policies: requiring that customers have a credit card and that they commit to contracts for 18 months (up from 12 months).

Those policies caused gross subscriber additions to fall from 1.02 million in 2007 to 986,000 in 2008, while the net gain in subscribers stayed the same (275,000). In 2008, DirecTV had a total of 16.8 million US subscribers, a 6% increase from the previous year.

"We're going after the customers we want and in some ways creating higher hurdles for the customers we don't want," he said. "We think it's the right place to be and we feel good about it."

Segment management

Reviewing the information you have collected on your customers, you can begin to put them into segments. Customer segments should:

- Be easy to grasp so anyone can understand what you are talking about
- Be big enough in numbers and spending to make it worthwhile learning what motivates them
- Be sufficiently responsive so behaviors can be modified by opportunities and rewards
- Make efficient use of available data to support segment definition and marketing efforts
- Be measured in performance against control groups
- Be significant enough to justify an organization devoted to it, even if it's just part of a person's time

A well-defined segment is one that a segment manager can understand. He sees what these folks are doing and predicts what they will do. He dreams up strategies to get them to buy more services or to become more loyal. He can run promotional e-mail tests with controls to see what promotional e-mails are working with them and what strategies are not working. He can manage them.

Defining the segments requires insight, analytics and anecdotes. Insight requires experienced marketing strategists who develop hypotheses about each possible segment, including the rewards necessary to modify member behavior.

Analytics involves using statistical analysis, which supports or rejects each hypothesis: Does such a segment exist? How much are they spending now? What is their income? When do they purchase in our category? How much would it cost to change their behavior?

Anecdotes are success or failure stories that illustrate what your company or other companies have done to modify the behavior of segments like this one. They provide a clue as to what kind of actionable strategy is likely to work. Start with an anecdote, and develop a hypothesis that can be tested before any rollout.

Each segment must have its own marketing strategy with different messages and rewards. Segments differ in profitability as well as needs. Start developing your advanced segment strategy development by understanding each customer segment: its size, potential value, and the best way to reach them. Then map the content, offers, channel, and contact strategy with that segment. Build testing and learning steps into this process so that all decisions can be refined and optimized along the way. The strategy for each segment should involve several steps. First, targeted e-mails to members of the segment. Communications should support both your short-term sales and long-term marketing objectives. These may differ. For example, if you have a segment that normally pays full price, it may not be in your long-term best interest to send them bargain offers, even though your message may generate some immediate sales. You may be training them to wait for bargains, and you may lose their normal full-price business.

Next, use the channel that works best for each customer. E-mail messages, of course, are less expensive than direct mail. Some segment members may be stimulated to buy more if they get an e-mail saying, "Look in your mailbox this week for an invitation to have lunch with Walter Driscoe, manager of the Park Ridge store."

Third, assign segment managers, at least on a part-time basis, to see if your staff can come up with really creative ideas to change the behavior of each segment. Then set up a reporting system based on these segments so you can learn each month how the segment is doing. Give your segment managers budgets so they can experiment with promotions and rewards to their segment members.

Finally, define a reasonable goal for each segment. Set up a compensation scheme for success.

The impact of segmentation

Marketing Sherpa analyzed open rates, comparing financial services marketers who used segmentation to those who did not.[4] Results showed that average open rates for segmented e-mails with finance-oriented lists were 42.2% compared to nonsegmented blasts, which had a 10.5% open rate. The effect on click rates was even more dramatic. The segmented e-mails had a 15.6% CTR for those who had been subscribers for 30 days or less. Nonsegmented e-mails had only a 1.3% CTR.

Language segmentation

There are over 40 million Hispanics in the US, and nearly 8 million of them use the Internet. If you are a typical mass retailer, you can be sure that 4% to 8% of your subscribers would prefer to read their e-mails in Spanish. Of course, to produce copy in Spanish is usually not a cheap project. Review the economics. Adding a question about it to your customer preference questionnaire might help you decide whether this is something to look into.

Scoring segments for relevance

No matter how you set up your segments, if you use them to send differentiated e-mails, you will improve opens, clicks, and conversions because your e-mails will be more relevant to your subscribers. You can grade your relevance on a basic three-point scale. Segmentation represents 25% of the basic relevance scoring (see Exhibit 07-16).

EXHIBIT 07-16 Three-point relevance scale

Segmentation Description Weight 25%	
3	Uses model with behavior & demographics
2	Uses multiple elements: gender, age, income
1	Uses one element alone
0	No content based segmentation

Takeaway thoughts

- There are three types of subscriber segmentation: primitive, intermediate, and advanced.

- Most e-mail marketers today are at the primitive level.
- At a minimum, buyers should be treated better than non-buyers.
- Multibuyers are better than single buyers.
- Various segmentations include purchase behavior, e-mail activity, Web activity, tenure on the database, and channel shopped.
- All e-mails should have a preference profile button to move subscribers to the advanced level as soon as possible.
- Recency, frequency, and monetary and Prizm clusters are two powerful segmentation methods.
- When customers buy can be as important as what they buy.
- Segmentation by e-mail open date and time can be productive.
- Major retailers create sophisticated marketing segments based on how much people buy, how often, and whether the items are on sale.
- Segmentation success lies in more opens, less attrition, more retention, and migration to higher levels.
- If you have the street address, you can append valuable demographic data.
- Segments should be easy to understand, big enough to yield useful data, and responsive to your e-mails. Justify putting someone in charge of it.

Notes

1. Derek Gehl, "E-Business Trends: It's All About the Customer," *Entrepreneur.com* (November 16, 2006), http://www.entrepreneur.com/ebusiness/ebusinesscolumnist/article170460.html.
2. Claritas, http://www.claritas.com/claritas/Default.jsp?ci=3&si=4&pn=prizmne_segments#15, accessed October 22, 2008.
3. Linda Moss, "DirecTV Adds 129,000 Subs In Q2," *Multichannel News* (August 7, 2008), http://www.multichannel.com/article/CA6585353.html.
4. Tad Clarke, *Email Marketing Benchmark Guide 2008* (Warren, RI: Marketing Sherpa, December 2007), 178, http://www.marketing sherpa.com/#, 178.

8

Acquiring Permission-Based E-mail Addresses

It all begins with The List. The possession of a large database of loyal customers and qualified prospects is the foundation upon which successful e-mail programs are built. All elements of sophisticated e-mail marketing—segmentation, personalization, dynamic content, lifestyle marketing and more—depend upon the quantity and quality of the e-mail list. But adding addresses to the company's database continues to be difficult. More than half of all marketers rank the task of developing a qualified e-mail list as their top challenge. E-mail marketers are eager to learn how others are adding to their lists, which tactics work and which are more effort than they're worth.

Silverpop's "2006 List Growth Survey"

You can't do any of the wonderful marketing programs outlined in this book if you don't have an opt-in list of subscribers who want to be on your list, receive your e-mails, and open your messages. But how do you acquire such a list? This chapter explores a number of techniques that work well and a number that don't.

The right way to get an e-mail address

How do you acquire permission-based e-mail addresses legitimately? A few ways include:

- Offline transactions, including retail store and phone contacts
- Online transactional e-mails
- E-mail appends
- Web site visits
- Direct mail marketing
- TV and print ads
- Internet banner ads

- Co-registration
- Search engine marketing
- Viral marketing
- In-store promotion
- Special events and trade shows
- Social networking Web sites

First, we must recognize that acquiring e-mail marketing lists is not at all like acquiring direct mail lists. It is easy to acquire direct mail consumer addresses. There are 40,000 lists for rent in the US that contain the addresses of consumers who have bought something from someone. The price is reasonable—from $70 to $150 per thousand names and addresses for a one-time mailing. There are also several national consumer name and address compilers, such as KnowledgeBase Marketing, that will rent you the addresses (and demographics) of about 95% of all the consumers in the country. Renting consumer names and addresses has a 50-year history. The business is legal, ethical, and widely used.

When e-mail began, most marketers thought the same rules would apply. And by 1998, several companies began to acquire and sell consumer e-mail addresses to other businesses. The whole industry soon ran into a buzz saw of consumer anger and legislative restrictions, particularly the CAN-SPAM Act of 2003. Many leading e-mail service companies, such as e-Dialog, were active in helping draft and encourage the passage of this law. Today, e-mail subscriber names aren't rented in the same way as direct mail subscriber names.

Why the difference? Several reasons. First, home addresses are public knowledge (collected by governments for tax and property ownership purposes) and can be changed only by the relatively expensive cost of moving. E-mail addresses can be and are created or abandoned at any time with no cost to the user. Scores of Web sites offer free e-mail addresses to anyone who wants them.

Unsolicited direct mail maybe a nuisance to some people, but it is kept within manageable limits by costs ($0.60 or more per piece). Marketers are anxious to make every mailed piece profitable, so they constantly prune their lists to concentrate on the most likely responders. Unsolicited e-mail, however, is more of a nuisance to everyone. According to Marketing Sherpa's *Email Marketing Benchmark Guide 2008*, e-mail is so cheap to send that more than 91% of all e-mail delivered is still spam, and everyone who uses the Internet pays for it. Spam makes the Internet work harder and slower and uses up disk space in millions of PCs and servers throughout the world. It requires increased network bandwidth to handle the heavy load of unsolicited, unwanted e-mail. All Internet users are forced to spend a portion of every day looking at and deleting spam.

The spam industry has become a criminal enterprise, banned by law in most countries. Some spammers use massive networks of hijacked computers, called botnets, to initiate attacks. They run autonomously and automatically, infecting more than 1 million computers worldwide each day, with 50,000 or more active at any instant.[1] Botnets run on groups of hijacked (zombie) computers controlled remotely. Newer bots can automatically scan the Internet and propagate themselves using weak passwords. Botnets today are a significant part of the hidden Internet. At any given time, up to one quarter of all online personal computers are unwittingly part of one or more botnets.

The CAN-SPAM Act 2003

Because of widespread consumer reaction to spam, Congress passed the Controlling the Assault of Non-Solicited Pornography and Marketing (CAN-SPAM) Act of 2003, which was further spelled out by the Email Sender & Provider Coalition (ESPC) in 2005 and 2008. ESPC rules state that commercial e-mail must not be sent to an individual unless prior "affirmative consent" from the individual has been obtained. According to CAN-SPAM, affirmative consent is the recipient's express consent "to receive the message, either in response to a clear and conspicuous request for such consent or at the recipient's own initiative."

In short: you may not send commercial e-mail to an individual unless you have already received the individual's express permission to do so. This means all automated methods of e-mail address acquisition are illegal.

Few of us meet criminals in our daily offline lives. On the Web, however, we meet them every day. ISPs try to screen these spammers out. They are constantly looking for illegal and unethical e-mail communications on behalf of their customers. They design software to ensure these messages don't get through to their customers' inboxes. In general, they do a good job of it.

As a responsible e-mail marketer, you don't want your e-mails to be considered spam by any ISP. If they think your e-mails could be spam, you won't be able to contact thousands or millions of your subscribers. This is an additional reason why you have to be very certain you acquire subscriber e-mail addresses in a legal, ethical, and responsible way.

EXHIBIT 08-01 Cost of sending a message via various channels

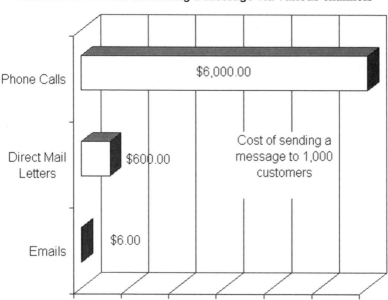

The cost of sending e-mails

Before you launch any e-mail acquisition programs, make sure you know what a permission-based e-mail is worth to your company. Having opt-in e-mail addresses gives you access to customers and other registered Internet users for almost nothing. Compare the cost of communicating via e-mail with the communication costs through other channels.

Exhibit 08-01 demonstrates that e-mail communications are tremendously inexpensive compared to any other method.

The value of an e-mail address

True, e-mails are much more inexpensive to send than other communications. But what are they worth? An e-mail address's value depends on your net profit from using it. If you use it to send uninteresting e-mails to someone who never opens the e-mails, the e-mail address is probably worthless. On the other hand, if you use it to send relevant e-mails that are opened and read and that lead to sales, that address can be very profitable indeed.

The best way to determine an e-mail address's value is to understand the average potential revenue and profit margin of an e-mail sub-scriber, then to adjust that for the average lifetime of an active e-mail address. Next, put the address into a segment, create an e-mail market-ing program for the segment, and see what happens. By a marketing program, we don't mean a one-shot e-mailing. We mean a complete re-lationship-building program, including a welcome e-mail, transaction e-mails after each purchase, surveys, profiles and preferences, perhaps a birthday greeting, and promotional e-mails at various points during a year or more. Upon this process you can build your segmentation strat-egy. Based on your experience, you can develop a lifetime value table. This table will establish the addresses' value.

Examining a relatively large segment or your whole program is vital to the process. You can't accurately know the value of just one ad-dress; there are too many reasons for a subscriber to stop opening your e-mail. Let's assume you have collected 600,000 addresses of con-sumers who have visited your site or one of your retail stores and bought one or more pairs of shoes that sell for an average of $106.56. You have 800 retail stores, and you have a store locator on your site and in all of your e-mails. Through research, you have determined that for every online sale you make, your e-mail subscribers make 1.45 of-fline purchases in your stores.

Your collected 600,000 permission-based e-mail subscribers have agreed to receive e-mails about special discounts, gifts with purchase, express checkout, order tracking, new product arrivals, and new brand arrivals. Exhibit 08-02 illustrates one method of computing each e-mail address's value.

This chart tells us that for this retailer, an opt-in e-mail address is worth $56.40 in the third year when sending 52 campaigns a year. Note that the overall conversion rate for e-mails delivered is 1.47% in the first year and grows with the length of time subscribers are in the database. The offline sales number can be derived from research. For example, comScore fielded a study in April 2007 that examined the im-pact of online search and display advertising on in-store sales for five major retailers. The study showed that consumers exposed to online advertising tend to research online prior to purchase and this behavior ultimately leads to increased in-store sales.

Note that although you started out with 600,000 e-mail addresses, you've lost half of them by the third year. Acquiring e-mail names is a never-ending process. It is like trying to fill a bucket that has a sizeable hole in the bottom. If we don't constantly add new names, in a few years the bucket will be empty again. (The acquisition methods are dis-cussed later in this chapter.)

EXHIBIT 08-02 An e-mail address's value

Value of an e-mail Name	Campaigns 52	Acquisition Year	Year 2	Year 3
Subscribers		600,000	427,200	299,040
Unsubscribe Rate		0.80%	0.70%	0.60%
Undeliver Rate		1.60%	1.80%	2.00%
Average Subs in Year		513,600	363,120	252,390
Promo E-mails Delivered		26,707,200	18,882,240	13,124,268
Open Rate		20%	22%	24%
Opens		5,341,440	4,154,093	3,149,824
Click Through Rate		15%	16%	17%
Click Throughs		801,216	664,655	535,470
Conversion Rate		20%	22%	24%
Online Orders		160,243	146,224	128,513
Off Line Orders	145%	232,353	212,025	186,344
Total Orders		392,596	358,249	314,856
Total Revenue	$106.56	$41,835,013	$38,175,010	$33,551,101
Goods and Order Costs	55%	$23,009,257	$20,996,255	$18,453,105.50
E-mail acquisition cost	$16	$9,600,000		
Marketing Cost	$2	$1,200,000		
Transaction Eamils	3	1,177,788	1,074,747	944,569
E-mail Cost Per 1000	$4.00	$111,540	$79,828	$56,275
Total Costs		$33,920,797	$21,076,083	$18,509,381
Profit		$7,914,216	$17,098,926	$15,041,720
Discount Rate		1	1.15	1.36
NPV Profie		$7,914,216	$14,868,632	$11,060,088
Cumulative NPV Profit		$7,914,216	$22,782,847	$33,842,936
Lifetime Value		$13.19	$37.97	$56.40
Net Revenue per E-mail		$0.30	$0.91	$1.15
Overall Conversion Rate		1.47%	1.90%	2.40%

Now that you know your opt-in e-mail address is worth $56 by the third year, you can determine how much to spend to acquire more addresses. You can afford to provide benefits, discounts, or cash rewards to your customers and to your employees. If you give away $5 to $10 to acquire an opt-in address, you are still $46 to $51 ahead.

Not all e-mail addresses have the same value. If you send a promotion to some customers, you may get a sale from 50 of 1,000. The same promotion sent to others on your list may net just 1 out of 1,000. Why this difference? Check the source of the e-mail address. E-mail addresses acquired through sweepstakes entries are often of very low quality: a promotion sent to them will seldom result in sales. The most valuable e-mail addresses usually come from customers who have actually bought from you, and bought quite recently. Unfortunately, most marketers have the e-mail address of only a percentage of their active offline customers.

Acquire e-mail addresses from regular commercial transactions

The best way to acquire the most valuable e-mail addresses is to acquire them as a part of the purchase process. If a customer buys from you over the Web, from a catalog, or at a retail store, you must find a way to get a valid e-mail from them *then and there*. You can tell the customers you want to send them:

- A confirmation of their purchase
- Access to your loyalty program
- Coupons or other savings
- Early notice of discounts, sales, and happenings
- A way of returning the product if it is unsatisfactory
- A means of buying more when they run out
- Customer service help if they have any problem with the product
- Detailed information about the product and its history
- Upgrades when they become available

Come up with a dozen reasons why consumers would want to be on your e-mail list, and put them in your product literature. Make sure all your sales personnel know these reasons by heart. Think like a customer, not like a seller. What's in it for them?

To make transaction e-mail name acquisition work, it may be a good idea to offer incentives to your staff and customers. After all, if customers are giving you something worth $56, what is wrong with paying something to get it? We'll break the idea down into two parts: staff incentives and customer incentives.

Staff incentives

Depending on your business, you may have a few or many ways your staff can get e-mail addresses from your customers. Anyone who calls customer service for any reason should be asked in the course of the phone call to provide their e-mail address so the customer service rep can send them the details on their conversation. The rep enters the customer's e-mail address, name, and other data into your system while talking on the phone. When the call is over, the system automatically sends an e-mail to the customer thanking her for the phone call and asking her to "click here" to verify that she wants to receive promotional literature (spell out what you'll send her). This is called the double-opt-in process and is the one we recommend in most cases (see below for more information). Sometimes a pre-checked negative opt-in may be sufficient.

When the customer does click on the link, her name is entered into your opt-in database and, if you do it right, the customer service rep gets a monetary reward added to her next paycheck. The payment is made only if this is a new and valid e-mail. The same process works for all sales personnel in your retail stores and can even apply to your product installation staff.

Since an e-mail address has a value, acquiring it is like selling a product. Use all your regular sales incentives. Why not a monthly contest for the employee who acquires the most opt-in e-mail addresses? E-mail marketing may be your company's best profit making channel, so take it seriously.

If you don't have retail locations or your POS system can't be easily modified to accept e-mail addresses, you have to seek other methods. You could promise customers rewards on receipts and other literature that would drive customers online to fill in the addresses themselves.

This is a great way to acquire customer e-mail addresses, but a two-week delay in sending e-mails is inexcusable. By the time your coupon arrives, the customer has forgotten all about the store visit and may consider the e-mail as spam. Companies are finding ways to get these confirming e-mails out the next day. How? You could have a PC at the store for employees to enter these e-mail addresses into the system in their spare time. (This method may only work for big-ticket items where staff would have the time to do data entry.) You could make it the manager's responsibility to go to a company Web site and enter these e-mails. Offer employees an incentive for speedy data entry. Of course, your best solution is to update your POS system to permit it to accept e-mail addresses along with other transaction details.

The reason for double opt-in

In the double-opt-in process, you will lose people who fail to click the second time. However, the people who do opt in are much more likely to want your e-mails and will read them and buy your products.

Double opt-in is a foolproof way to make sure new e-mail names are clean and that the risk of spam complaints from them is low. Double opt-in will protect you from having typos on your list. It also proves that your employees have entered valid e-mail addresses into the system. They don't get credit for mickeymouse@aol.com.

Let's face it. Double opt-in may not maximize short-term revenue. If that is your goal, you may not want to use it. But it does help maximize customer retention and loyalty, which may turn out to be more important in the long run than short run. You really have to think through your goals before you decide on your customer acquisition method.

Customer incentives

If you offer consumers an incentive for providing their e-mail address, be sure it is something related to your product. If you offer a premium, such as a T-shirt, consumers may sign up to get the premium, then unsubscribe. A better offer would be a download of information or a coupon that will bring consumers into your stores or back to your Web site. Entry into a sweepstakes can generate lots of e-mails, but you will find these e-mails tend to be from folks looking to get something for nothing. They are much less likely to buy than consumers whose addresses are obtained in a more direct way.

Downloads of interesting information and whitepapers can help particularly in acquiring business-to-business (B2B) subscribers. Many of these downloads are really valuable. Let your visitors know the value of what they're downloading, so when they provide their permission they feel they're making a good exchange, valuable information for valuable information. Try including thumbnails of the documents to let subscribers know what they'll learn from the download and what they can do with the information.

Be clear about what will happen with their information. Will you be calling them? Or just sending them e-mails? How often?

Subscriber benefits

One great way to get permission e-mail addresses is to offer subscribers a lower price than nonsubscribers. On its site and in its e-mails, electronic bookseller eReader.com offers two prices next to each title: a sale price and a discounted price for its newsletter subscribers.

You don't have to hurt your margins by discounting everything you sell, however. Instead, discount only certain products, and offer a valuable discount in the welcome e-mail. E-mail subscribers should get exclusive promotions, such as letting them take advantage of sale pricing one day before everybody else.

Every contact with customers or Web site visitors should include an opportunity and a reason to sign up for e-mails. It should be in every e-mail. It could include a mention of e-mail-only discounts and special offers. Certainly when you ship goods to a customer, the package should include some literature about the benefits of being on the e-mail list. But—and this is vital to good e-mail practice—don't tell folks who are already signed up to sign up. For those subscribers you might say, "We already have you enrolled as an e-mail subscriber. If you plan to change your e-mail address click here."

How to word the permission message

What do you say to customers to get them comfortable with providing you with their e-mail address? Your approach should be to let them know the benefits *to them* of the communications they will receive and let them know specifically what to expect.

In asking for the e-mail address, don't ask for too much information. Studies have shown that asking for more than just the e-mail address at first you may reduce your acquisition rate by 20% or 30%. Get the name and the e-mail address. Make sure subscribers enter the address twice. If they get it wrong, you may have lost them forever. To do segmentation, you will need more than just an e-mail address, but you don't need to get it all at once. The additional data can come later. If you ask for the e-mail address online, there is standard content you should always include, whether on the sign-up page or on another page you link to:

- A sample e-mail
- Bullet points that answer the question, "What's in it for me?"
- Your privacy policy
- The word "Subscribe" on the response button
- How often they will hear from you—and their frequency choices
- How the customers can control the content they receive

Proof of permission

Some people will always complain about the activities of large corporations (and some small ones), and they may label your e-mail spam. You may find yourself defending your e-mail address collection procedures to an ISP if there are spam complaints. For this reason, you must keep a record of when and how each customer's e-mail address got on your mailing list. These data should be stored in the database record of each customer. All good ESPs do this automatically, which is another reason you should outsource your e-mail delivery process.

For online acquisition methods you may want to keep this information to prove that you have received permission from your subscribers:

- E-mail address
- Date and time permission was obtained
- IP address used
- Level of permission obtained or method used

Transactional e-mails to acquire permission

Just because a customer bought something from you and you send her an e-mail to confirm the purchase doesn't mean she has given you permission to send promotional e-mails to her. However, those transactional e-mails are ideal opportunities to ask for that permission. Order confirmations, account statements, and product and service updates get opened *four times* more often than other types of e-mail.

There are rules governing the use of permission requests in transactional e-mails. Marketers who push too hard risk drawing the attention of the Federal Trade Commission. Return Path recommends no more than 50% of the space in a transactional e-mail be devoted to a permission request. This is certainly enough space to ask the recipient to subscribe to your e-mail communications.

For example, Avis Budget Group enrolled tens of thousands of customers into its e-mail newsletter by having its call-center reps ask if customers would like to receive an e-mail confirmation of their car rental reservation. The confirmation e-mail included a request for renters to receive promotional e-mail messages. The transactional messages yielded an 87.1% open rate, and CTRs for permission for further e-mails ran as high as 61.6%.

"The open rates were expected, since we're sending transactional messages," said Dawn Perry, director of CRM, Avis Budget Group, "but the click-through rates on promotional content have been surprisingly encouraging."

Feature e-mail permission on your Web site

One of the most overlooked spots to ask for an e-mail address is on the company Web site. It is amazing how many companies fail to take advantage of this. Yet this is where most of your registrations come from. There is usually a battle within any company on how to use the valuable space at the top of the page. As of this writing, only about 25% of major Web sites included a pitch for permission e-mails above the fold. Having a registration link is something, but it isn't really a pitch. Acquiring an e-mail is as important to your bottom line as selling a product. Devote as much effort and space to e-mail registration as you do to product sales. Take a look at how Pizzeria Uno uses the space on the top right of its home page.

EXHIBIT 08-03 Pizzeria Uno's home page

Even better is to create a box for the subscriber's e-mails in the top left corner, with a one-click subscription function. And it should be on the first line, not the second.

Besides having an e-mail registration request on your home page, you should ask for e-mail address on every page people can visit. When they register, give them a choice of subject matter and frequency.

People will come to your site from banners, search engines, and TV and print ads. When they get to your site, you must get them interested in signing up for e-mails.

Some companies put registration at the bottom of the page. But this doesn't get as good results as putting it at the top.

Make registration easy

No matter where subscribers enter their e-mails address on your site, make the process as painless as possible.

Place as few barriers to entry you can during registration. A few companies still require users to sign up for a full account before allowing them to opt in to e-mail lists. What a mistake. Smart companies require only an e-mail address, but they follow that up by gathering more information later in the opt-in and welcome e-mails.

Let's say you are a sports site and have several newsletters, covering baseball, football, soccer, and tennis. Encourage users to sign up for the baseball newsletter in the baseball section, the football newsletter in the football section, and so on. This seems obvious, yet many companies put the newsletter choices somewhere else—in a newsletter option page.

When subscribers click that registration button, make sure something positive and easy happens right away. Exhibit 08-04 shows how Uno does it.

EXHIBIT 08-04 Uno's Insider's Club application

EXHIBIT 08-05 Uno's "sign me up" button

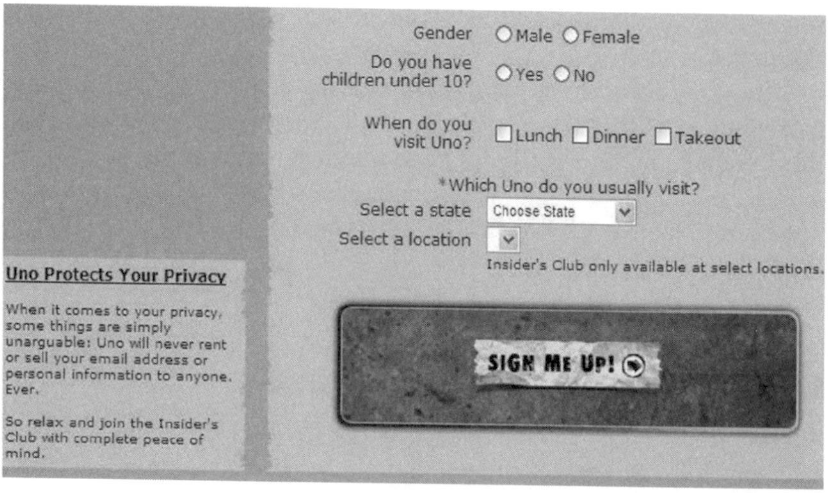

Looking at this form, you can see it is designed to encourage sign up. Is asking for all the information a good idea? Requiring a full address as well as a birthday may discourage to the subscriber. To find out, test your registration form both ways. The bottom of this form also includes a privacy link and a simple "sign me up" button, as seen in Exhibit 08-05.

Get your retail staff to acquire e-mail addresses

When I took my car to one of those quick-lube places, I watched the attendant as he clicked through the screens for my transaction and just skipped the one asking for my e-mail address. Why didn't he ask me? Probably because some people, when asked in the past, grumbled about spam and peppered him with questions he didn't know the answer to. Also, he must have had no incentive to capture my address. These issues are very easily overcome with little cost; it just takes commitment and a clear plan supported at all levels.

—John Rizzi, CEO, e-Dialog

You should insist that employees in all your channels collect e-mail addresses. Make sure you provide the staff with short, easy answers to overcome objections, such as "I'll just get spam." ("No, you will get discounts you can use the next time you come in.") A countertop sign that explains the benefits of providing an e-mail address and the promises of a subscription helps your clerks quickly handle objections. Even better, give your store or contact center managers measurable goals and incentives to collect e-mail addresses. If you do, you may see results skyrocket.

You may have to set up a short training course for customer-contact employees that teaches them how to get e-mail addresses. Help them understand the security of your systems; that customer e-mail addresses, credit card data, and personal information will be safe and that your company won't sell their address to anyone but will only use it to send them your own e-mail messages. Train your staff to remind customers that they can opt out from your e-mails at any time.

Case study: carwash customer e-mails

A Marketing Sherpa case study[2] looked at Bubbles Car Wash in Houston, which sends e-mails to stimulate customers to come in for more washes. Bubbles tried to capture e-mails while the customers were having their cars washed, but the data quality was so poor that it was almost unusable. To improve results, the company adjusted its POS system to recognize any customer whose e-mail wasn't on file. Those people's receipts included a coupon for a premium car wash—worth $28.95—if they went to the Web site and used the coupon code to enter their valid e-mail address. The result? The system increased its e-mail list by 71.4%. The e-mails sent monthly to subscribers produced $70,000 per weekend in increased revenue due to the e-mails.

Getting addresses from e-mail appends

Situation: You have customers who have bought from you in the past, but you don't have their current e-mail addresses. Either you never had them (they bought from a catalog or retail store) or you had them, but they are currently undeliverable. What should you do? One possibility is to pay an outside service to append the addresses for you.

Use these services with caution. In some cases, you don't have these customers' e-mail addresses because *they don't want you to have them.* When they bought from your catalog, the sales clerk said, "Can I have your e-mail address?" They answered, "I would rather not give that to you." If you suddenly begin to send them e-mails, how does that make you look?

In this book we are teaching you how to use the most cost-effective, profitable sales channel. Don't ruin it by doing anything that even appears to be shady.

However, several reputable services will append e-mail addresses to your customer database. One of the best is Fresh Address, the original developer and US patent holder of e-mail change of address (ECOA) technology. It can help with both business-to-consumer (B2C) and B2B e-mail appending. It also does reverse appending.

Using a service like Fresh Address, you can keep yourself out of trouble. Such services will send an opt-in message for you as a part of their basic service and will in most cases not give you the appended address without guarding themselves and their lists by first sending a negative opt-in. Before you send any customer an e-mail promotion using an appended address, be sure your customer has been given a chance to opt in and hasn't rejected the opportunity.

If you do append e-mails to your existing customer file, the next step is vital. Use that e-mail to send a request for permission (double opt-in). If the consumer says "yes," you are home free. If she doesn't respond, don't use the address. Make sure the appended e-mail addresses aren't dumped in with the rest of your subscriber list until you have received a confirming e-mail.

How to collect the rest of the data you need

So far, you have collected the subscriber's name and e-mail, with permission to send commercial messages. Remember, don't collect anything you don't need. Each additional piece of data gives consumers another reason to abandon the subscription process. To send relevant e-mails in the future, however, you will probably want more than just an e-mail address. Typically you will want the Zip Code, or in most cases, the complete mailing address.

Why the street address? To segment your customers, you need to know something about them, such as age, income, or children—demographic information. You could ask your customers for this, but it may be a nuisance for some of them. As a result, you may lose those who hate providing a lot of personal information.

As pointed out earlier, every company should have a profile and preference page that it links to in every e-mail and on every other site page. This is where you can learn the missing information about the subscriber's address and preferences. Unfortunately, only a percentage of subscribers will fill out these forms. You should have these forms but not make completing them a requirement for receiving newsletters or promotions.

This is where appending demographic data comes in. Services like AmeriLINK and others will append demographic data to any consumer file that has a correct street address for about $0.04 a name (see chapter 2). These data can then be used to segment your customer file.

It isn't illegal or unethical to collect such information or to use it in marketing. You have to use your head, though. Your e-mails should never say, "Since you live in a condo worth more than $400,000" or "Since on October 14 you will turn 46," even if you know both of these things to be true. In your e-mails, use only the information your subscribers have given you themselves. In your segmentation system, however, you can use any information you can collect or append.

Banners, direct mail, TV, print and products

Despite e-mail's success, direct mail is still alive and well. It remains an excellent way to contact people who aren't online. If you do any kind of Internet banners, direct mail, TV, or print advertising, always feature your Web site URL in the message, with an invitation to visit. The URL should also be on every single product you sell and in the instructions that may come with the products. If consumers or businesses are doing business with you, your site URL should be not just easy to find but staring them in the face. Once they come to the site, of course, your "Sign up for e-mails" should be at the top of the page along with an appropriate offer.

A speedy welcome e-mail message

One of the most important parts of the e-mail address acquisition process is the welcome message. This is an e-mail that sets expectations for what subscribers will receive—what kind of content and what kind of frequency. Think of it as your first date with someone special. What do you want to say on that first date that will let this person know what you are really like and what you have to offer? You don't want a one-night stand; you want to build a lasting relationship. That first date is make-or-break time. Go all out. The welcome e-mail should go out within a few *seconds* after the subscriber has successfully clicked on the double-opt-in e-mail message. Some major companies still take two to three weeks to get out their welcome e-mails.

Keep and study your e-mail address sources

One piece of data that must be in every customer database record is the source of the e-mail address. Run periodic reports showing the open, click, and conversion rates of customers by e-mail address source. It may be an eye-opener.

One source may provide unusually good names, while another provides unusually poor ones. Find out how much you spend on each source. Draw some conclusions. Depending on your analysis, you may want to apply a different value to addresses acquired from one source, such as a co-registration agreement, than those acquired from another source, such as your Web site.

If you acquire addresses through paid search, make sure the e-mails acquired are worth what you pay for them.

Dangers of keeping subscribers who don't open e-mail

Permission isn't permanent. After a while, people get tired of receiving your e-mails. They might unsubscribe, or they might click the "report spam" button. This immediately alerts your e-mail provider, which may block future mail addressed to this subscriber and even all of your subscribers with this ISP. So what do you do with inactive e-mail recipients, those who never open your e-mails?

Try something clever, such as "Congratulations! You've been a subscriber to our e-mail newsletter for a year. Happy birthday. Here's a coupon for 25% off." Consumers who open this e-mail are back in the active file and are less likely to report you as a spammer.

If people aren't opening your e-mails, it may be because they switched addresses without telling you. Be careful; some ISPs are sneaky. They use abandoned addresses to catch spammers. For this reason, it's very important to remove abandoned addresses from your e-mail file.

If you have a large group of customers you e-mail who rarely, if ever, open the e-mails, is that a problem? Yes and no. It is very inexpensive to send millions of e-mails, whether the consumers open them or not, so why not send them?

Since they don't open the e-mails, however, they obviously don't consider your messages relevant. They don't want to waste their time reading them. What message does this build in their minds? "Another e-mail from Macy's. What a nuisance." They may be loyal Macy's customers in the stores, but they don't want to read a bunch of promotional e-mails from Macy's. These annoying e-mails damage your brand's image in their minds. While e-mails can build relationships, they can also destroy relationships.

Worse than that, sending e-mails to people who never open them makes you look like a spammer to ISPs and subscribers. To turn your e-mails off, subscribers start clicking the "report spam" button. Gone for good. But not good for you. Better to be proactive: reactivate these subscribers or drop them before your reputation is ruined.

Another concern: your e-mail acquisition staff is acquiring good double-opt-in e-mail addresses, but some other part of your organization is making deals to lend or rent your e-mail list to some other company. The minor revenue from such deals could be nothing compared to legal liability you may be taking on. Unless your privacy policy clearly stipulates this practice and preferably reiterates it in the subscription process, renting or exchanging subscribers' names is totally illegal and carries a huge financial and legal liability. To say nothing of the danger to your reputation with your subscribers and ISPs from the use other companies may make of the names. To avoid this problem, make sure you review in advance all messages that will be sent to your subscribers by any company that uses their names.

Make it easy to unsubscribe

You don't want to trap subscribers into continuing to receive unwanted e-mails by making it difficult to unsubscribe. Every e-mail should have a clearly visible, obvious unsubscribe button somewhere, probably at both the bottom and at the top of the main page. When the subscriber clicks this button, the landing page asks her why she wants to unsubscribe with a simple two- or three-button choice, such as: prices too high, e-mails not relevant, e-mails too frequent.

If she clicks the third button, give her a choice to continue as a subscriber with e-mails less frequently, whether once a week, once every two weeks, or once a month. Better to keep her occasionally than lose her forever. If she tells you e-mails aren't relevant, give her a choice of several types of e-mails, if you have a choice.

By making unsubscribing easy, you keep subscribers from labeling your e-mails as spam. CAN-SPAM clearly stipulates that unsubscribe processes have to be straightforward, without logging in, and be offered through a link in all commercial e-mails. Despite this requirement, there are scores of Web sites and e-mails today that aren't following this simple rule.

The FTC has ruled that you can't require subscribers to go through more than one page during the unsubscribe process. You can't require them to click your unsubscribe survey questions; they must be optional. You can't require subscribers to provide a password to get to the unsubscribe page. You can't ask for their names and addresses in the process. You can, of course, offer them the choice of opting out of just the newsletter they clicked from or out of all your communications.

Gaining e-mail addresses from viral marketing

A successful viral e-mail campaign is a marketer's dream. Your current customers find your products or services so valuable that they electronically recommend them to a friend. In addition to wanting to add names to an e-mail list, marketers want viral campaigns to help with branding, direct sales, and site traffic. We have devoted an entire chapter (18) to this technique. But don't count on viral for more than a percentage of your e-mail list acquisition. Less than 10% of any e-mail file are enthusiasts who will participate in viral marketing, and probably less than 20% of their efforts will result in new subscribers for you. If you do the math, you will see that viral marketing could increase your list by 2%. That is nice but not overwhelming. When acquired, however, these viral names may be more responsive than names acquired any other way.

Partner cross-promotions and co-registration

One third of e-mail marketers have used co-registration at one time or another. When users register for e-mail on a Web site, they see that company's offer as well as yours. By checking an additional box, they register to receive e-mail from both companies. You pay the company doing the registration for the names generated for you. To do it correctly, you should then do a double opt-in to make sure these people really want to hear from you. You may find the money you spent is wasted. Marketing Sherpa reports that the quality of co-registration e-mails is the lowest of any of the many e-mail acquisition techniques.

Making registration fun

Uno's does a great job capitalizing on a new customer to capture more data by using a small carrot—a free pizza. For one promotion, the restaurant created a microsite called the Toppingsfilled Fair, which offered visitors a unique, interactive experience. Through this site, Uno's could interact with customers at home. The customer receives an e-mail that says, "Get Your Free Pizza" and gets her to the site. It doesn't give away pizza; the customer has to earn it by giving more info:

- First name
- Last name
- Postal address
- E-mail address
- Password
- Closest Uno's location
- Frequency of visits

After the customer completes her profile, she's asked to refer her friends. Only then does Uno's send an e-mail with a coupon link. The coupon is custom-published with the customer's name, e-mail address, coupon code, and an expiration date.

In addition to the coupon, the e-mail encourages her to enter a contest to win a prize: "Test Your Skills: Step on up and play the Pizza Puzzler (click here). Click on similar toppings and make them disappear." The interactive game allows you to sign in and check out the top scores and post your own score.

Explain membership benefits

Remember, you must tell potential subscribers what they gain from subscribing to your messages. Nike does a great job of this. In one e-mail in a huge section just below the fold, Nike says:

Join the team. Did you know that as a Nike.com member you get:

- Free shipping on your first order
- Free returns on all orders
- Easy checkout and online order tracking
- Access to exclusive product collections
- A wish list to send to friends & family
- A NIKEID locker to store customized designs
- And much more. Not yet registered? Join Now

Acquire subscribers through customer returns

During the Christmas season, there are two types of consumers: the gift giver and the gift recipient. It is hard to acquire the latter, except when she returns the gift because she didn't want it. Just because the product is returned doesn't mean she doesn't like you; she just doesn't like the product. This is an opportunity to sell her other items during the process. Find a way to turn returns into acquiring a new subscriber and customer.

To make this happen, your marketing and packaging have to tell gift recipients to go online for instructions for returning the merchandise and getting store credit. The recipient goes to your Web site, clicks on the link for returns, and enters the information about her product. The site asks her why she is returning the product.

Suppose the customer clicks "I don't need it." You can show her other products in that category. Show her a list of products with an equal or lesser price, so she knows what she can exchange her gift for without spending more money. Or you can show her more expensive products, with only the upgrade cost. For example, if her gift cost $149, show her something for $199 and display the price as "+$50." This makes up-selling a lot easier, because the price shown is much lower. It shows the consumer's out-of-pocket expense to get the more expensive product. Be sure to provide a button for the customer to sign up to receive information or newsletters about products that are similar to the returned gift.

What if the customer clicks "I want something better or different"? You could show her a product lineup with similar products with different features. Or you could tell her what others who considered this product have bought. Encourage her to sign up for tips and other information about the product line.

And if she chooses "I Already Own This Product," you can show her accessories for the product. You can tell her that "People who bought X also bought Y." And you can get her to sign up for e-mails about the product.

Takeaway thoughts

- You can determine with some accuracy the value of an opt-in e-mail address.
- Capture e-mail addresses in all regular commercial transactions.
- Use the double-opt-in process.
- Your Web site should make registration a big deal at the top, in the middle, and at the bottom of the page.
- Make registration easy and simple.
- You can append extensive demographic data once you have the subscriber's street address.
- Quickly send out welcome messages (not days or weeks later).
- Drop subscribers who don't open your e-mails.
- Make it easy to unsubscribe from your messages.

Notes:

1. "Spam Skyrockets 59% September to November; 91% of All Email is Now Spam," Metrics 2.0, www.metrics2.com/blog/2006/11/28/spam_skyrockets_59_september_to_november_91_of_all.html.
2. Anne Holland, "Stop Bounces with Sales Receipts, Build List 71%" (Warren, RI: Marketing Sherpa, July 2008).

9

Creating Powerful Subject Lines

> Rather than trying to sell people on the value of opening an e-mail, the most effective subject lines simply tell the reader what they have received. Instead of using "Open this now" or "Don't miss out on this opportunity" to get your readers to open the message, simply tell them what your message is about. Some of the most opened permission-based marketing e-mails have subject lines that simply say, "XYZ Widget Co. Newsletter."
>
> Raj Khera, MailerMailer.com.

Subject lines are the single, most-important element in a promotional e-mail. If the subject line isn't relevant, interesting, and stimulating, the e-mail will never be opened, and everything else you have put into the e-mail: interactivity, personalization, and exciting content, will be wasted because no one will ever see it.

You should spend most of your creative energy on the subject line. The copy and offer are important, of course, but the subject line is always more important. Pick the subject first, then write copy that delivers on the subject line's promise. You may even revise the copy you planned to write once you have settled on a winning subject line. Creating a subject line is similar to what editors have to do with a newspaper story. They want to get people to read the article, so they find ways to summarize the story in a few short words.

Today, people open less than half of the e-mails in their inbox. You have to demonstrate that you're providing legitimate, interesting information to the reader. Most recipients look at both the subject and sender lines before they open an e-mail. Their reaction to the subject is influenced by what they know about the e-mail sender, particularly about the sender's trustworthiness. If the reader already knows and trusts the sender, the subject line doesn't have to establish that trust. You can write more freely than if the recipient doesn't know who you are. If messages are going to be opened, more than 80% will be opened

EXHIBIT 09-01 Return Path survey on reasons for opening e-mail

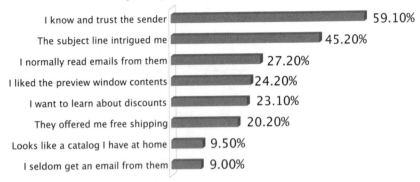

Why I opened the email

I know and trust the sender	59.10%
The subject line intrigued me	45.20%
I normally read emails from them	27.20%
I liked the preview window contents	24.20%
I want to learn about discounts	23.10%
They offered me free shipping	20.20%
Looks like a catalog I have at home	9.50%
I seldom get an email from them	9.00%

within 48 hours after delivery. Fewer than 10% are opened four days after delivery.

Why do subscribers open e-mails?

A Return Path survey[1] on the top reasons consumers open e-mails from retail marketers shows that subject lines are the second reason (respondents could pick more than one answer).

Rules for drafting subject lines

As you draft your subject lines, follow these rules.

Tell rather than sell

The best subject lines tell the subscriber what's inside, while the worst ones try to sell what's inside. Don't make your subject lines read like advertisements. The stronger the commercial pitch in the subject line, the less likely it's going to be opened.

Mike Volpe of HubSpot tested an e-mail promoting a Webinar. He sent three different versions of the e-mail to three randomly allocated list segments, changing only the subject line and first line of the e-mail message. Take a look at the results in Exhibit 09-02 (you can find more information at http://blog.hubspot.com/blog/tabid/6307/bid/2346 /Lessons-from-a-Marketing-Experiment-Email-Marketing-Subject-Lines.aspx).

Why did version two win? Version one's subject line hints of promotion with the dangerous words "free." Version three does the same

EXHIBIT 09-02 HubSpot subject line test results

Subject Line	Headline Within E-mail	% Open Rate	% Click Rate	Grade
V.1 Free Internet Marketing Webinar	Free Internet Marketing Webinar	18.70%	3.10%	C +
V.2 Invitation to Internet Marketing Webinar	Internet Marketing Webinar	21.80%	4.40%	A -
V.3 Special Invitation to Expert Marketing Webinar	Internet Marketing Webinar	21.40%	3.30%	B

thing with "special" and by calling the Webinar "expert." Version two simply says what was inside without selling anything.

Think like a customer, not like a marketer

Your e-mail readers are interested in one thing: what's in it for them? Write with that in mind; write about the benefits that matter to them, not features that matter to you. You want them to spend time reading your e-mail message. Think about why they would want to do that. Then write to them as if you were explaining it to them. Your subject line will be much better.

Don't use first and last names in the subject line

Personalization is very important for e-mail content, but that rule doesn't apply to subject lines. Spammers steal names from the Internet. All they know about the recipient is her name and e-mail address, so they use the names in the subject line: "Arthur Sweetser: an offer just for you." But the recipient is smart enough to know the message is spam.

If you use first and last names in your subject lines you might be considered a spammer. A 2008 MailerMailer study showed that average e-mails with personalized subject lines did worse than those with no personalization at all. The personalized e-mails had a 12.4% open rate and a 1.7% CTR; the nonpersonalized one had a 13.5% open rate and a 2.7% CTR. However, though using a name in the subject line isn't a good idea, localization, such as a city name, does generate higher open rates.

Use your company name in the subject line

Many studies have shown that putting your company name in the sender line and the subject line increases the open rate. JupiterResearch found that including the company name in the subject line increased open rates from 32 percent to 60 percent over a subject line without branding.

Be recognized

An important reason why people open your e-mails is because they recognize you. There are two types of recognition: they recognize the sender, and they've found past messages to be valuable. The opposite may also be true; they have opened your messages in the past and found them to be a waste of time, so they delete them.

Your success in getting any given e-mail opened, therefore, depends on your company's reputation and the quality of your previous e-mails. Your subject line should encapsulate both of these recognition aspects in some way. This recognition is so important that it often produces the same open rates whatever subject lines you use. Recipients' previous experience with your e-mails can be so positive that it overrides anything else in getting your e-mails opened.

Don't forget what you promised at opt-in

We recommend you provide new subscribers with a sample of the e-mails they will get when they subscribe. Over time, though, your e-mails may change; you are always learning what works and what works better. You may gradually get away from what you originally promised. Meanwhile, your standard registration page keeps showing new subscribers stuff you no longer use. Make sure your acquisition link features recent e-mails, so new subscribers will get an accurate picture of what they will receive. Also, as you change e-mail content, put in a short paragraph somewhere that tells readers about the changes you are introducing and how you are always listening to readers and using their ideas.

Test several lines before a rollout

Which subject line will perform best? Your subscribers can tell you—and will tell you by their response. That's why you should have an active testing program. Identifying the best subject line out of a group of them is perhaps the hardest of all calls. In fact, few e-mail experts can consistently guess which subject line will get the best open rate.

If you are a regular e-mail marketer, arrange your schedule so you can plan ahead for the next week's e-mails. Marketing Sherpa reports that 70% of major mailers regularly test subject lines.

Think up two or three good subject lines to introduce your copy. Let's say you will mail to 1 million subscribers next week. Which subject line will work best? If at all possible, send each of your proposed subject lines to a few thousand subscribers who are a cross-section of your intended audience. See which subject line works best. This won't be possible for some subject lines, but do it whenever you can. You may find quite a difference among your subject lines, a difference that could mean tens of thousands of dollars' difference in the response to your mailing. E-mail is so inexpensive and speedy that such tests are possible.

Document and archive both failures and successes. If you don't keep a record, you will make the same mistakes over and over. Plus, you will forget what worked well.

Send the e-mail to yourself

Once you have decided on a subject line, before you roll it out, send it to yourself. Does it grab your attention? Does it stand out from the other messages in your inbox? Does it look interesting and worth opening? Does it look like spam? Many times an e-mail in the inbox looks quite different from an e-mail on the drawing board.

Measure overall results

Don't measure subject lines by opens alone. Sometimes an e-mail with a low open rate has a very high conversion rate. It be that most people weren't interested in your message, but a segment of your audience was really interested. They opened, clicked, and bought. Once you learn this, you might segment your audience and send special messages about products of interest to those who opened the e-mail, while the rest of your audience gets other messages.

Don't use focus groups to test subject lines

Focus groups are expensive and, in our experience, are seldom, if ever, as productive as testing a representative segment of your intended audience. Instead, create a gallery of good and bad subject lines you have used in the past. Record the subject line, open rate, CTR, download rate, and overall conversion rate. Review these data frequently.

Avoid using the same subject repeatedly

Just because a subject line worked well yesterday, doesn't mean it will work well today. Subject line effectiveness changes over time. You can rarely repeat the same subject line with the same audience and get the same good results indefinitely week after week. Since e-mails often stay in subscribers' inboxes for several days, using the same subject line in two different e-mails will get them both deleted faster than if they had had different subject lines.

If you send out a weekly or monthly e-mail and constantly use the same subject line, you may create e-mail fatigue in readers. Worse: if your competitors notice you're using the same subject line repeatedly, they'll conclude it is successful and copy it. At that point, you'll be competing against your own winning technique. For these reasons, you need to keep testing your subject lines and learning.

Avoid certain words

Never put the subject lines in all capital letters, and never use exclamation marks. Free is OK in a subject line, as long as it isn't the first word or capitalized. Most consumers will respond well to free, as long as you are truthful and avoid looking like spam. Spam words like duty free and sex are out, of course. But there are words that aren't on the spam list that may also kill your subject line response, such as *help*, *% Off*, and *reminder*.

Don't use newsletter issue or version numbers

An issue or version number is irrelevant to your readers. It doesn't tell them anything about the great content inside. Use the space instead to tell readers what's inside that is new.

Experiment occasionally with deadlines

You can use urgency and deadlines as part of a planned series of e-mails as well. For example, on a Monday e-mail incorporate "5 Days Left," then on Thursday follow it with "Only 24 Hours Left." There is nothing wrong with these subject lines—if they work and if they are truthful. But don't get in the habit of using deadlines all the time. Subscribers will soon get tired of a sender who is always out of breath.

How long should the subject line be?

Space available for subject lines varies greatly among ISPs and e-mail clients. Exhibit 09-03 lists the space allowed with some of the major ISPs and e-mail clients. If your e-mails are going to subscribers who will read them on handheld devices, you may also want to consider the space that these devices have for subject lines.

Since your e-mails will be sent to your subscribers regardless of the e-mail client, you have two choices: Either you create different e-mails for each e-mail client, or you use the lowest common denominator for the design of your e-mail sender and subject lines.

Besides line length, think about how much subject-line reading your subscribers are willing to do. Just because Yahoo and Excite give you 80 spaces for a subject line doesn't mean you should use all the space available. Here's an 80-space subject line: "Great savings on top

EXHIBIT 09-03 Space available for subject lines by ISP/client

E-mail Client	From Spaces	From Visible	Subject Spaces
Outlook & Outlook Express	User	Name & E-mail	User
AOL 8	16	E-mail	51
AOL Anywhere	16	E-mail	72
Yahoo	30	Name	80+
Hotmail	20	Name	45
MSN	20	Name	45
Eudora	User	Name	User
Excite	20	Name	80
Juno	32	Name	55

User means that the user determines what he will see.

brands in your favorite colors and sizes only until Monday." You can test this, of course, but we don't recommend subject lines this long. Long lines can mean fewer opens.

A MailerMailer study on subject-line length[2] showed the open rates and clicks varied by subject-line length. The study of 300 million e-mails sent in 3,200 permission-based campaigns showed that subject lines of 35 spaces or fewer were opened 20.1% of the time, while those with subjects of more than 35 spaces had open rates of only 15.28%. This means that, if the study is correct, you can increase your open rate by 31.6% by chopping your subject lines to 35 spaces or less.

EXHIBIT 09-04 Opens based on subject line length

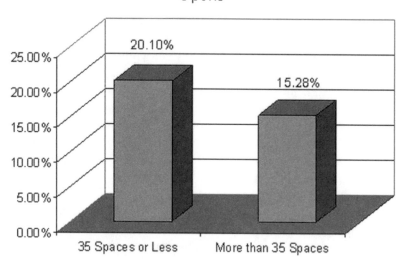

Clicks also varied by subject length. Those with 35 spaces or less had a click rate of 3.28% while e-mails with subject lines greater than 35 spaces had click rates of 2.05%. The difference: you can increase clicks by 60% by shortening your subject lines to 35 spaces or less. This is powerful evidence that shorter subject lines are important to e-mail marketing success.

EXHIBIT 09-05 Clicks based on subject length

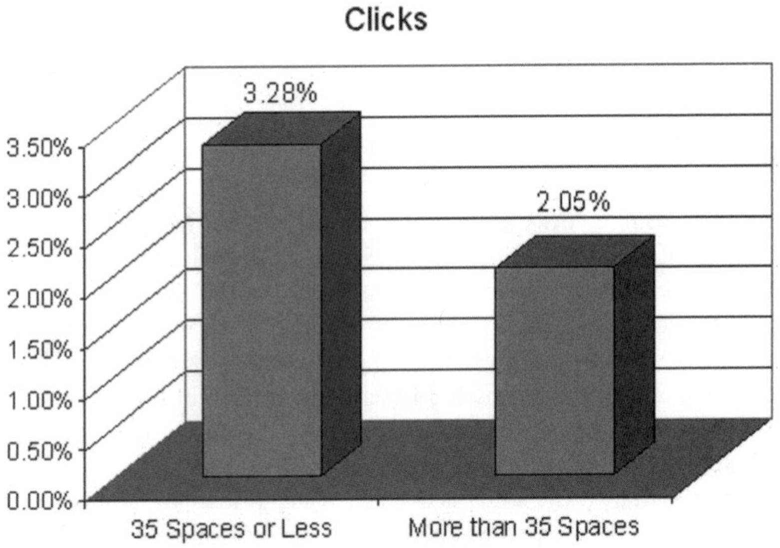

Clicks

Get e-mails opened with authentication
==

We all have too many e-mails in our inboxes every day. One way to weed them out is by considering the sender's trustworthiness. Something from American Airlines, Dell, or OfficeMax is probably worthwhile, as they are trusted sources. How can your company's e-mails get this same kind of immediate acceptance? One way is through authentication. The Authentication and Online Trust Authority (AOTA) has set up a simple system for legitimate e-mail marketers to have their e-mails and brand protected by using its authentication system.

When you authenticate your e-mail messages, you help ISPs identify whether your e-mails are sent by a legitimate company or an imposter, which in turn helps them determine whether to deliver the message to the recipient. Some ISPs use trust icons for authenticated e-mail. Just by virtue of appearing in the inbox, along with the subject line, these icons help assure recipients that they can trust you to be who you claim to be and that they can buy from you with confidence.

A recent AOTA survey showed that AOTA authentication was used on half of the e-mails sent by Fortune 500 consumer brands, half of the Fortune 500 financial-services brands, and half of the 300 top Internet retailer brands. AOTA is used by over 1 million businesses worldwide.[3]

Franklin Electronic Publishers tested the use of McAfee's Hacker Safe logo in its e-mails over seven months. Half of the e-mails contained the logo and half did not. E-mails containing the logo had a 23.8% higher average order size, an 8.1% higher conversion rate, and a 2.15% higher CTR.

Confusing subject lines may not be bad

Pier 1 Imports sent an e-mail with the subject line, "Go Ahead: Party like its 4705!" While this looks like a misprint, the inside copy explained that the coming year on the Chinese calendar, 4706, was the year of the rat, and Pier 1 was offering Chinese furnishings for a Chinese New Year party. This subject line was an interesting beginning for a fun e-mail. E-mails don't need to be serious; they can be lighthearted. There's nothing wrong with a subject line with a sense of humor.

Cyber Monday: a national holiday?

Cyber Monday is the Monday after the Thanksgiving Day weekend—the ceremonial kickoff of the online holiday shopping season in the United States. It was invented by Shop.org for the 2005 holiday season. Comscore research in 2007 showed that 77% of online retailers reported a significant increase in sales that day.[4] Sixty-seven percent of the online retailers tracked by The Retail Email Blog sent at least one promotional e-mail on that day, making it the biggest e-mail marketing day of the year. One quarter of retailers sent at least one promotional e-mail on the Sunday directly preceding Cyber Monday, making it the biggest Sunday for e-mail marketing of 2007. DisneyShopping, Staples, CompUSA, Sears, and TigerDirect used subject lines like: "Click Quick! Cyber Monday Specials End Tonight!"

Watch out for duplicate subject lines

Abercrombie & Fitch and Hollister are owned by the same parent company and use the same creative agency. On the same day, each company sent e-mails to their subscribers with this subject line: "Don't Get Scrooged! Order by Noon Tomorrow." This may have been a good subject line for either company, but sending two different e-mails on the same day with the same subject line may have looked odd to people who subscribed to promotions from both companies. Remember: think like a subscriber instead of like a promoter when planning your e-mails.

Should your subject line feature low prices?

The purpose of e-mails is to generate long-term revenue—in most cases. E-mails should be part of building long-term relationships with customers so they stay loyal and keep buying. Think of how the old corner grocer handled customers walking into his store. Did he always say things like, "We have peaches on sale today," or would he be more likely to say, "I hear the road crews will be working on your street tomorrow."

The second statement provided information that may be useful to the customer and had nothing to do with generating short-term revenue. It built a relationship that produced long-term revenue. It established that the grocer knew who he was talking to, knew where she lived, and thought that the information on the road crews would be of particular interest to *her*. She looks on him as a friend and a trusted source of information, not a vendor always trying to sell her something. Can your e-mails generate that kind of reaction?

Many, perhaps most, e-mail marketers haven't yet woken up to the idea of using e-mails to build long-term relationships with their subscribers, of farming subscribers rather than hunting them. They are like carnival barkers rather than trusted friends. Is that the image you want to create with your e-mails?

Spam checking is essential

More than half the e-mails delivered today are considered spam. This means ISPs will put them directly into a subscriber's spam (or junk) folder rather than into her inbox. Many ISPs have now created a third category: junk suspects. Into this folder may go more than half of what you consider legitimate mail from trusted senders. How do ISPs survey incoming e-mail to determine whether it is spam? Many of them use a program called SpamAssassin or a similar program.

SpamAssassin, free, open-source software, is widely used and is generally regarded as one of the most effective spam filters, especially when used with spam databases. It comes with a large set of rules, and specific fields within the e-mail header and e-mail body are typically searched for particular expressions. If these expressions match, the e-mail is assigned a score based on each test. The total score from all tests can then be used by the end user or the ISP to put the e-mail either in a spam folder or in the customer's inbox. All this is done very rapidly so e-mails can reach their recipients without delay.

Each test has a label and a description, such as "Limited Time Only." If an e-mail contains certain variants of the words *limited, time,* and *only,* it might be assigned a score of 0.3. Any e-mail with a total score from all tests of 5.0 or more is usually considered spam. Other spam tests include invalid message IDs and invalid years and can result in a very high score. Sometimes a single test can classify the message as spam. Depending on the total score, an e-mail can be passed as OK, rejected as spam, or tagged as being suspicious spam. In our daily experience with this program, about half of our legitimate e-mails from business associates and commercial firms are classified by SpamAssassin as junk suspects.

What does this mean for e-mail marketers? First, study SpamAssassin rules and make sure that your subject lines and e-mail copy don't include words that will classify your e-mail as spam. Second, run each proposed e-mail through your copy of SpamAssassin to find out your score *before* you send any promotional or transactional e-mail anywhere.

Takeaway thoughts

- Subject lines are more important than offer, copy, personalization, or interactivity. Without a good subject line, you are dead.
- Subject lines should tell what is in the e-mail rather than sell it.
- In drafting the subject, think like a customer not like a marketer.
- Don't use the subscriber's first and last names. Do use your company name.
- Be sure that readers recognize and remember you.
- Don't forget what you promised to deliver to your subscribers.
- Test several lines before a rollout.
- Send the draft e-mail to yourself first.
- Measure results by conversions and opens.
- Avoid repeating subject lines.
- Keep subject lines to 35 spaces or less.
- Get authenticated.
- Think about long-term, not short-term, revenue.
- Run your e-mail through a spam checker.

Notes:

1. "Email Connections Are Down, But Opportunity to Build Relationships and Increase Sales Is Up" (Return Path Inc., January 2008), http://www.returnpath.net/pdf/holidaySurvey2008.
2. *Email Marketing Metrics Report* (MailerMailer, 2007), http://www.mailermailer.com/metrics/TR-H1-2007.pdf.
3. Kristina Knight, "AOTA: Email authentication has reached tipping point," *Bizreport.com* (February 5, 2008), http://www.bizreport.com/2008/02/aota_email_authentication_has_reached_tipping_point.html.
4. "Cyber Monday Online Retail Spending Hits Record $733 Million, Up 21 Percent Versus Last Year" (comScore, November 27, 2007), http://www.comscore.com/press/release.asp?press=1921.

10

How to Write Compelling E-mails

I always have an image of who I'm writing to in my head. If the e-mail is going to mothers of little girls, I picture a woman I know and her little girl. If it's to a businessperson, I picture someone I know who's in that audience. I think about where they're reading the copy—at their desk, in their home—as well as how they are seeing it—holding a piece of paper in their hand, viewing it on a computer screen, or scanning it on their mobile device. Also important are the distractions they may face while reading it; the copy needs to be interesting enough to gain and hold their attention . . . It's all about putting myself in the shoes of the reader. What's in it for them? Why should they open, read, click, and follow through to meet the objective?

Pat Friesen, direct marketing copywriter

Compelling e-mails require compelling copy. Writing copy for e-mails is an art and a science. Good copywriters like Dave Chaffey, Pat Friesen, and Herschell Gordon Lewis don't come along very often. If you have one on your staff, hang on to her. This chapter won't make you a copywriting genius, but it will fill you in on most of the do's and don'ts that all e-mail copywriters have to know.

Start with a plan

To write compelling e-mails, you must start with a plan for what you are trying to accomplish with the message. What do you want readers to do? Too often e-mails are sent because of the calendar. "We have to get an e-mail out for next week." If that is your reason for writing, readers will notice.

Do you want readers to download something? Buy something? Sign up for something? Whatever it is, it should be *only one thing*. One study showed that e-mails with multiple action items had much lower CTRs than those with single actions.[1] One action item yielded a 56% CTR. Two yielded a 37% CTR, three yielded less than 5%, and four yielded a mere 1.4%. If you have two things you want readers to do, send two different e-mails—and space them a couple of days apart.

The direct mail industry has an adage: choice kills response. If you have several different policies or products recipients could sign up for, in any particular e-mail tell them only about one. As soon as you mention two or more possibilities, recipients will set the e-mail aside and say, "Well, I will have to think about that." They will never get back to it. You will have lost them. That doesn't mean that you can't send them a catalog with many products, for example. But your pitch is for one thing: buy something for this holiday.

Picture your readers in your head

Before you begin, imagine who your readers will be. Picture them reading your e-mail. In writing this book, we have done this as well. We pictured you, our reader, as a person aged 20 to 40 years who has some background in direct marketing. You have been asked by your boss to find out some way to make your company's e-mail program more effective. Maybe you're reading just this book, or maybe you're taking an entire class to learn more. You are reading this book to discover ideas on industry best practices. You want to know what others have done. We pictured you with a yellow marker, highlighting passages in this book that you think would work for your company.

To write e-mails, you need to do just what we have done. Once you can picture your readers in your head, try to imagine what they are thinking when they read your e-mail. What is going on in their minds?

Who are you?

One of the first questions readers ask is, "who is this person writing to me?" Who are you? Are you a company? A mysterious someone hiding behind a bunch of colorful images? The most successful e-mails are written like a conversation between two people, one on one. An excellent way to learn to do this is to read *The Art of Plain Talk* by Rudolph Flesch (out of print, but available through Amazon and Alibris). Here's a quick summary:

- Use short sentences; the shorter the better.

- Use lots of personal references. such as people's names; personal pronouns; and human interest words, such as *man, woman, child, father, mother, son, daughter, brother,* and *sister.*
- Avoid affixes, such as *para-, pseudo-, infra-, meta-, ultra-, hypo-,* and *circum-.* Use root words instead.
- Use a familiar word rather than rare words, concrete terms rather than abstract ones, short words rather than long ones, and single words rather than several ones.
- Use verbs; they give life to a sentence. Use the active voice rather than the passive or subjunctive.
- Be careful with adjectives; adjectives are the enemy of the noun. This is because, very often, if we use the precise noun we don't need an adjective. For example, instead of saying "a large, impressive house" we could simply say "a mansion."

Create the e-mail's author

You can use yourself for the e-mail author or create a persona. The writer should be a person, such as the director of marketing, a product manager, or the CEO. Sign the e-mail and, if possible, add a friendly photo of the sender. When Safeway first started its customer newsletter, it was signed by Bill McDown, a division manager whose picture was featured on the newsletter's first page. When he went to the stores, people often recognized him and came to shake his hand. The first year of the program, he got 3,000 Christmas cards from Safeway customers. If you can equal that, you have a great e-mail.

Also try to give your reader a sense of who you are as a person, what your work involves, and how come you know so much about the products or services featured in the e-mail. Don't talk like a know-it-all; talk like a user or a developer. Tell readers that you have tried the product or service yourself and found that it works for you. Or tell them what you did to develop the product so people would find it useful.

Most e-mails should be conversational. Even for a business audience, don't be too formal. How you speak should reflect your brand personality. For an entertaining consumer product, use a fun tone that's reflected in the vocabulary.

While you are deciding who you are, research the best e-mails. Get your office buddies to forward you the best ones they regularly receive. Make a library of great e-mail ideas. We call these "nuggets." To write this book, we reviewed our library of more than 200 nuggets and have provided the best of them in this book.

Once you have written your copy, read it out loud to yourself. Many times you will find that what seemed good on paper doesn't read well out loud. It should, so change it.

Get the reader involved

The best e-mails are two-way conversations. You can't have a conversation in direct mail. You can have one over the telephone, but phone calls are expensive and too intrusive. Marketing phone calls often make recipients angry. With e-mail, you can have the interaction of a phone call without the annoyance. After all, subscribers don't have to open the e-mails. They can look at the subject line and say, "Let's skip that one." But once they have opened your e-mail, you should somehow make the experience fun and interactive. Look what an enthusiastic subscriber, Dan McCarthy, said:

> I love the daily e-mails from steepandcheap.com. It's a Web site that's focused specifically on outdoor gear. The thing that's great about the e-mails is that they aren't at all focused on the product—they are instead focused on making me laugh or telling me a story, which makes me read the e-mail. As a result, I click on the product link almost every day. There is no other e-mail that gets this much of my attention each day. The bottom line is that they seem to really understand their target audience and know what I'm interested in. The stories are off the wall, and worth reading even if you aren't into outdoor gear!

One way to create interest is to invite the reader to send in articles, questions, or comments to be included in future e-mails. Lots of people like to see their name published, whether online or off-. You can make it possible and generate interest in your e-mails at the same time. To do this, give readers a subject to write about. For instance, if there was recently a conference or industry event, ask readers to write a session summary and send it to you.

Another way to stir up interest is to include a poll or survey in every newsletter, using multiple-choice questions. The topic could be anything of interest to your readers. Give the results in the next e-mail. Subscribers will want to read the next e-mail to see how their responses compared to everyone else's.

Make e-mails interesting

REI's e-mails are filled with outdoor adventures , such as an interview with Peter Potterfield, who shared his experience in hiking New

Zealand, and one with Lauren Reynolds, who shared her advice on running right. Each e-mail features one particular experience plus access to 400 other similar stories. While the reader is scanning one of these adventures, he can check out the deal of the day, the deal of the week, the top sellers, the deals under $20, the Just Added, and a search box that brings up thousands of outdoor gear products. What the reader is getting is adventure. What REI gets in return are opens, clicks, and conversions.

PETCO has another interesting idea: it e-mails letters from a pet to the pet's owner. A typical e-mail might read in the body of the copy, "Jennifer: Louie wrote you a letter. <u>Check it out</u>." Clicking the link leads the subscriber to a page with a cute letter "written" by Jennifer's pet. He tells Jennifer about all the products he would like to have—all sold by PETCO. Jennifer can buy any of them by clicking links in the e-mail.

Create dynamic, personal content

The best e-mails are filled with dynamic, database-driven customer preferences. They have customized subject lines, greetings, offers, or special images inside the e-mail. They strike a responsive chord in readers that helps them realize that you are speaking directly to them as individuals, not to the world in general.

To create dynamic content, you need demographic information about your subscribers, such as zip code, occupation, hobbies, age, household income, or spending habits, and you need to use that information to provide content that speaks to the reader's particular interests. Subscribers like being addressed as individuals.

Dynamic content builds brand loyalty. It can improve a reader's attitudes toward your company. It builds clicks and conversions. To create dynamic content, you need to do most of the things recommended in this book, such as building a marketing database with demographic data about each subscriber. Use that information to create segments with dynamic content related to the interests of subscribers in that segment. Give subscribers choices on the information they receive. This reduces the number of subscribers turned off because they receive nonrelevant e-mails. And include lines like, "Thank you, Arthur, for subscribing on 08/04/2008." Such wording is personal and adds credibility to your e-mails. It helps ISPs identify your message as legitimate, not spam.

Offer wish lists and gift registries

Net-a-porter.com created a series of four e-mails. The first e-mail began, "A Show-Stopping Dress for Every Occasion—Create a wish list and send all your must-have ideas to your loved one." Below this was a "start now" button that took subscribers to a landing page entitled "A Party Dress for Every Occasion." The e-mail concluded with, "This e-mail is part of a series of four daily e-mails. If you would prefer not to receive the rest in the series, please <u>click here</u>."

This series is a version of a "birthday club" series, in which women provide a retailer with their preferences in clothing—sizes, colors, and brands—their birthday, and their husband's or boyfriend's e-mail address. The results are e-mails from the retailer to the men reminding them of their loved one's birthday and suggesting gifts the men could purchase through a link in the e-mail. The brilliance of this technique plays on the fact that most men hate to shop, particularly for women's clothing. Most women love to shop but find it difficult to hint to their significant others what they would really like to receive as a gift.

If you have a series of newsletters that are planned in advance, such as a Christmas schedule, try listing the schedule in each newsletter so subscribers can see what is coming and go back to see what they missed. See Exhibit 10-01 for an example of how Miles Kimball does this. Readers can click on the underlined issues to read something they missed. It helps readers understand how the holiday messages are organized. It is more reader-friendly than just sending e-mails one after the other. Readers may think they are getting too many.

EXHIBIT 10-01 Miles Kimball's Christmas e-mail schedule

Newsletter Schedule

Issue 1: <u>Christmas Gift Ideas</u>	Issue 4: <u>Entertaining</u>
Issue 2: <u>Personalized Gifts</u>	Issue 5: Finishing Touches
Issue 3: <u>Trim the Tree</u>	Issue 6: Last Minute Gifts

Make your e-mail an interactive adventure

SmartBargains.com is one of the most creative, interactive, and successful e-mail marketers on the Internet. Subscribers receive its e-mails every day of the year. Exhibit 10-02 is a sample e-mail that starts off with a treasure hunt. It's hard not to click the X. Price reductions are for today only! Clicking the button takes you to the retailer's home page, shown in Exhibit 10-03.

EXHIBIT 10-02 A SmartBargains.com treasure hunt e-mail

EXHIBIT 10-03 SmartBargains.com home page

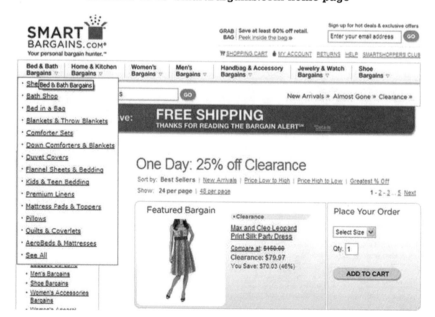

The reader is not aware that in clicking the links in the e-mail, she is actually viewing the home page. It seems to her as if the e-mail she is reading is loaded with links. There are more than 50 links on this page alone. Scroll over one of the tabs in the top navigation bar, and a drop-down list appears with additional links.

In the upper right-hand corner of the home page is an invitation to sign up for "hot deals and exclusive offers." Few Web sites give such a prominent place to the e-mail sign-up box. And the search box is just below the top navigation bar. Search boxes are essential for any Web site. They should be as easy to find as this one is.

Now look at the sorting feature below the "One Day Clearance" headline. Visitors have five options to sort by: best sellers, new arrivals, low to high price, high to low price, and highest percentage off. How handy and interactive!

Each link is an invitation to a new adventure. Just above the "Free Shipping" headline, the visitor has three options. When she clicks on "Clearance," she lands on the Clearance page, as pictured in Exhibit 10-04.

The entire e-mail appears to its readers as a treasure hunt of links. Yet the e-mail itself is small and opens very quickly, since the links are really located elsewhere. This is an extremely sophisticated linkage of an e-mail with a Web site.

EXHIBIT 10-04 SmartBargains.com Clearance

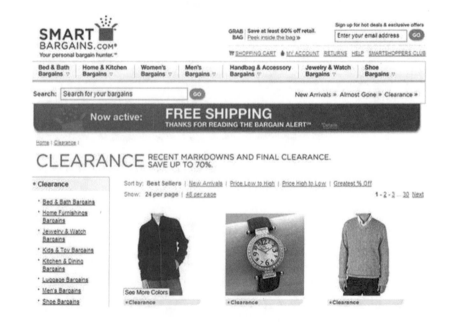

Include an administration center

Every commercial e-mail, whether promotional or transactional, should be a window into your world. From that e-mail, a subscriber should be able to link to anywhere on your site to get information, products, or help. To do this, you must include some administrative items that are easy to find in every e-mail. Don't put them at the bottom in the fine print. Link to them somewhere above the fold, preferably in the same place in every e-mail.

Don't ever tell readers to copy a URL into their browsers. You will lose them. E-mails are supposed to be fun to read, not hard work. Instead, link to the URL you want them to visit.

The administration center should include buttons or links for each of the following:

- Unsubscribe
- Preferences and profile
- E-mails registration
- Forward-to-a-friend functionality
- Phone or e-mail and mail contact to reach the newsletter staff or customer service (CAN-SPAM requires you to put your physical address in all commercial messages)
- Subscriber's account, including status of all previous purchases
- Shopping cart
- Checkout
- Search box for this e-mail and any item of interest from the Web site
- A way for subscribers to comment on a story or product
- Your privacy policy
- Related information
- Shipping and return policies

How to handle images

It is a big mistake to have too many images in your e-mails. Use a combination of images and text, not more than sixty percent of the e-mail should be images. As far as background, no one ever went wrong with white. Colorful backgrounds may be difficult to read and make your e-mail look like spam.

Most subscribers nowadays have broadband can quickly view images included in your e-mails. Some, however, will have trouble. These include:

- People with low bandwidth connections, who may opt not to load graphics
- People using handheld devices
- People with disabilities who use assistive technology, such as refreshable Braille displays or screen readers

To solve this problem, every image in your e-mail should be accompanied by text, which will appear when the image doesn't; this is called an alt attribute.

One important rule for e-mails: *never* send attachments, including PDFs. It creates two problems. First, attachments usually appear suspicious to a spam filter. And second, there is no way to track the action on an attached file. You can't find out if readers opened your attachment or not. The best way to provide information is with a link in your e-mail to the file you want people to see. With a link you won't trigger any filters. And because you'll house the file on your site, you will know how many opened your file and who they were.

Use testimonials

Once you have great testimonials about your company, use them in your e-mails. Don't just collect them and let them sit in a folder.

Some marketers have built entire marketing campaigns around a single testimonial or a group of testimonials. These user stories add credibility, because they come from a customer rather than the marketing department. Use a testimonial as your starting point, then build on its message in the marketing copy. To do this, it's helpful to set up your e-mails as well as your Web site so readers will be encouraged to submit testimonials.

Don't use a testimonial for too long. The writer may change her name or job from that listed in the testimonial. This could become embarrassing for you or the writer.

How the US Postal System uses e-mails

When e-mails first came out, the USPS regarded them as the enemy. After all, many messages sent by e-mail today would once have been sent by direct mail. The USPS, however, has really become expert at e-

EXHIBIT 10-05 USPS address change e-mail

 Address Change Links

- Change your car registration and driver's license address
- Notify the IRS of your move
- Register to vote in your new hometown

 Connect or Reconnect

- Save on Your **Phone** Bill with Vonage
- Order the #1 **satellite TV** service - DIRECTV
- FREE access to 900 games at GameTap
- Cell phones, plans & more: **Wirefly Mobile**

 Save on the Stuff You Need

- Order **labels** online at Current Labels
- Shop for what you want at **Best Buy**
- Shop for **apparel & home** at jcpenney.com

 Get Help with Your Move

- Cards mailed for you at **Movers Postcards**
- Save up to 20% on a Budget **moving truck**
- Choosing a **reputable mover**
- **Homewood Suites**. Make Yourself at Home.

 Get Things Done

- **Poland Spring®** delivery from about $1 a day
- Save on **Boston Globe** home delivery
- Special offer from Brink's **Home Security**
- Check **car insurance** rates at GEICO
- Pay bills with **American Express**
- Wells Fargo **Home Equity** Financing
- Save on **Dry Cleaning** with ZOOTS

New Neighborhood Links

- Look up **Census facts** about your new town
- Continue to receive **Social Security** benefits
- Look up your new **Chamber of Commerce**

mail. Exhibit 10-05 shows a USPS e-mail sent to folks who are moving from one place to another.

Write text specifically for mobile devices

Writing text for a mobile version of your e-mail is very different from writing text for the regular version of your e-mail. A mobile device's screen is tiny—between 2 and 4 inches. When writing the mobile version of your message, visualize your readers. What will they be doing while they read your text? Riding in a cab, waiting for a plane, eating on a train, or being stuck at the wheel of their car in traffic? They are probably operating with one hand, and their attention is somewhere else. They will scan their inbox rapidly and skip most of it.

If you use tracking URLs, you will have to compress them to fit them on the small screen. The messages must be short. Any message over 12 KB may be cut off halfway through. Long sentences force readers to scroll a lot, which can be frustrating. Despite the obstacles, how-

EXHIBIT 10-06 American Airlines cell phone invitation

ever, many subscribers will want to view your important e-mails on their mobile devices.

To get subscribers to sign up for mobile messages, include a mobile option on your Web site and in the admin center in all your e-mails. Before you launch any text e-mail for mobile, send it to yourself to make sure it works on regular cell phones, not just on a smartphone. American Airlines, for example, really plays up, mobile e-mail messages, as can be seen in Exhibit 10-06.

A 10-point e-mail rating system

Now that you have a better idea of how to write compelling e-mail copy, examine your current messages to see how they measure up. Use this 10-point scorecard to rate your e-mails:

- **Personally relevant content.** Use the subscriber's first name in the message body.
- **A clear call to action.** The subscriber should clearly understand what you want her to do after she has read the e-mail.
- **Clear, readable text.** Don't hide your text behind dark colors or confusing images.
- **A meaningful reference to the brand.** An e-mail, after all, is an advertisement. The brand is important for continuity.

- **Obvious and easy navigation and search.** Make search boxes or menus easy to find. The links should be obvious to the readers. They shouldn't be so fancy that the reader is unsure of how to activate what she is looking for.

- **Images that help reader identify with her lifestyle.** Visualize the reader. What images can you show her that will help her identify personally with your e-mail's message?

- **Modular arrangement of the e-mail.** You should be able to easily interchange the e-mail's content based on the reader's or product's dynamics. For example, if you sell bathing suits and you send e-mail to both men and women, the section where the suits are shown should be modular areas so you can switch copy and images based on the reader's gender.

- **Visually appealing overall design.** Look at the e-mail as a whole. Have you created a Michelangelo or thrown together a bunch of unrelated images and fonts?

- **Positive closing call to action.** The closing call to action should make the reader feel good about what she has read. Typically, you should have a well-labeled, obvious button that the reader clicks after she has read the e-mail.

- **Highlighted important offer and call to action.** Most readers won't get below the fold, so important offers and calls to action should be placed above the fold.

Create a company blog

Blogs, short for Web logs, have become ubiquitous, so you absolutely must have one today. A blog is a Web site, usually maintained by an individual or a company, with commentary, descriptions of events, and often graphics and video. Entries, called posts, are commonly displayed in reverse chronological order, and readers are generally able to comment below the post. As of 2008, blog search engine Technorati was tracking more than 112 million blogs.

Your e-mails can't ignore blogs. Before you create your e-mails, consider how blogs can be used to help spread the word about your company and products—and keep from having bad words spread about you on the blogosphere. First, create a company blog. Then, link to the blog on your home page.

What do you put on your blog?

- Articles and guides related to your products

- In-depth product reviews
- New product announcements
- Press releases
- Links to news articles featuring your company or product
- Links to other blogs that mention your company or product
- Video, such as product demos

Once you have a blog, refer to it in your e-mails with a link and text to encourage readers to visit it. Watch your blog and related blogs for news that you can use or react to. Keep up with the bloggers who post comments about your company, brand, products, and so forth.

How to post news with bloggers

If you want to post material on someone else's blog to promote your products, begin by thinking like a blogger. Will the news you want to post inspire readers of a particular blog to comment? Many bloggers will honor time embargoes, so you can send them news in advance of a product release.

Your first step in getting a blogger to post something about you is the same as with an e-mail: the subject line. In your message, tell who you are and mention the blogger's name. Explain why his blog is particularly suited to your situation. Tell him why a post on your topic will interest a typical reader of his particular blog. Facts are more successful than fancy writing here.

After you have sent your pitch to the blogger, give him a chance to think about what you have sent. If you get a response, provide some new and relevant information. You aren't in control; only the blogger can decide what he wants to post. If you have your own company blog, be sure you link to the blog you are talking to. If you have sample products, it might be useful to send some to the blogger along with your pitch.

Don't send the same e-mail to the same person

This is such an obvious rule, you might wonder why we have to mention it. But it happens all the time. Why? Because we are in a rush to get something out to build sales and we grab whatever copy we can find. It is OK on your end, but it looks terrible on the subscriber's end. You will probably lose more subscribers by sending repeat e-mails than you will gain in sales. Here's a real-world example to illustrate what we mean. One subscriber reported this:

> There was no way I was going to be able to forget Valentine's Day this year! Between Jan 22nd and Feb 11th, I received seven e-mails from Proflowers.com reminding me to send my friend Wendy flowers for Valentine's Day again. Each of the e-mails looked almost exactly the same, with only slightly different offers. Here's an example of the subject lines:
>
> - Make Wendy's Valentine's special again! Save 25% on 100 Lily Blooms!
> - Make Wendy's Valentine's special again! Save 25% on tulips.
> - Make Wendy's Valentine's special again! 24 petite roses - only $29.99!
> - Make Wendy's Valentine's special again with 6 Free Roses!
>
> And on it went. The campaigns were nearly exactly the same and by the time I had received the third one, I stopped opening them. I wonder how much thought went into the personalization on this campaign. What if Wendy were an ex whom I just wanted to forget (especially around Valentine's Day) and I kept getting these e-mails with her name in the subject line? It would have helped if they had changed the creative or done something fun or innovative to get my attention. If I wasn't interested in e-mail marketing in general, I would likely have unsubscribed after the second or third one.

Learn from the experts

Before you or anyone in your company begins to write e-mails, be sure you have read what the experts have to say. As a minimum, you should consult these books:

- *On the Art of Writing Copy* by Herschell Gordon Lewis (Amacom, 2007)
- *Total Email Marketing, Second Edition,* by Dave Chaffey (Butterworth-Heinemann, 2006)

Takeaway thoughts

- Successful e-mails come from a person, not a company.
- Base dynamic content on a marketing database.

- The content should be what readers want to hear about, not what you want to tell them about.
- Get readers involved with the subject: use polls, quizzes, and surveys.
- Never send attachments
- Never have more than one call to action in a newsletter.
- Always have an administration center, and at the same spot in the message.
- Have few images on a white background.
- Create a company blog and post new information on relevant blogs.
- Write text specifically for subscribers who want content on their cell phones.

Notes:

1. Joseph Carrabis, *How to Design Your Newsletters* (NextStage Evolution, 2008).

11

Listening to Customers

People don't want to have power only to lose it the instant they exercise it. Yet that's what permission marketing does when permission is asked only at the outset. Unless permission is subject to renewal, then permission is not really empowering. The way to give people control over the marketing to which they are exposed is not to ask for permission, but to ask for provisional permission that periodically must be affirmatively re-extended. Provisional permission is better for marketers, too, because it creates the opportunity for a continuing dialogue between marketers and customers. It also enables a brand to stay fresher in people's minds because it is not something that a person can deal with once, then file away and forget.

Craig Wood, *Coming to Concurrence*

It used to be very difficult and expensive to get information from customers. If you had a survey you wanted them to fill out, you had to get the form to them. Then they had to fill out the form and mail it to a processing center, where clerks keyed the results into a computer, which entered the results into a database. It was very slow, and you were lucky to get as much as 7% of your customers to complete the process. By the time you got the information into your database, the customer may have forgotten all about you.

Today, with e-mail the process is infinitely simpler, cheaper, and more comprehensive. You put a bunch of questions on your Web site or in your e-mails. The subscriber answers the questions and hits "submit." .The data is quality-checked by your software (which will ask the subscriber to fill in any missing data), then put directly into your subscriber database. After the subscriber enters her answers, the data isn't touched by human hands again. You have the data available the same day it is entered, and the cost is almost nothing if you have the supporting software. You can immediately send an e-mail thanking the subscriber for participating and begin what may be a long and profitable relationship.

The trick, however, is to get the subscribers to give you the information you want.

Why would subscribers provide you with information?

We all know people do what is in their own best interest, but do we act as if we know it? For subscribers to spend their time giving you the information you want, they have to receive something. Before you design a survey, therefore, think through the subscriber-motivation process. Create something you can give to subscribers electronically that they consider valuable, such as:

- Downloadable information
- Newsletters
- E-mails about products and sales
- Membership in a club
- Coupons
- A product that they are ordering

Sample subscriber benefits

The Chase Bank paperless statements provide "a convenient and environmentally friendly way to access your credit card statements." Chase will make a $5 donation to the World Wildlife Fund for every card member who goes paperless by April 30, 2009. What's in it for the card member? "Switch to Paperless Statements and you'll also be entered in our sweepstakes for a Natural Habitat Adventures Classic Galapagos Cruise for two—a $12,500 value."

What information do you need?

Before you design a subscriber information form, think through exactly how you can and will use the information you get. Make a list of all the possible information and what you can do with each piece. Then prioritize them, so those at the top of the list will be items you can use every day. A few ways you can use such subscriber information:

- Create subscriber segments based on their needs or interests so your e-mails will be relevant to them
- Send information related to the retail store closest to them

- Send them information they are interested in
- E-mail them as frequently as they want to hear from you

Don't ask for too much at once

Don't ask for too much information at once because subscribers won't give it. They may distrust you and unsubscribe. On the Internet, we are used to asking people for their e-mail address; it is the only way we have communicating with them. On the home page of every Web site—and on any page that links to the home page, marketers must put a box for visitors to enter their e-mail. Of course, if you already have their e-mail address, your site should be smart enough not to ask for it again. Right next to the e-mail request box, tell them they can expect to receive from you. If you will send a newsletter or report, have a link next to the box that says, "Click to see a sample."

When subscribers click the "submit" button, you store the information and immediately send them an e-mail confirming that they really want to receive what they have asked for. How soon should you send this opt-in requesting e-mail? Within a few seconds. Never longer! This is e-mail marketing etiquette.

The confirmation e-mail can ask one or two questions (the top ones on your list) but not too many. It is vital that you get subscribers to confirm the permission to correspond with them.

Many marketers cringe when they hear the phrase *double opt-in.* This confirmation method, however, is very important in preserving an e-mail database's quality. It gives an e-mail marketer the best possible chance to develop profitable subscriber relationships. Exhibit 11-01 is an example of a simple double-opt-in practice that we like from TopButton.com. Right in the e-mail confirmation page, it asks the new subscriber to validate her e-mail address.

Some e-mail marketers ask for much more. Resort vacation exchange company RCI has five pages of preferences with over 100 questions for its members to fill out. Is this too much? RCI has over 3 million subscribing members living in more than 200 countries. It has over 4,000 affiliated resorts located in 100 countries. For members to decide where they want their vacations among these various resorts, perhaps 100 questions aren't too many. RCI has arranged more than 54 million exchange vacations in the last few years.

Now that you have sent and received an e-mail, you can ask more questions. Your subscribers are in a question-answering mood. Strike while the iron is hot. Get the information you need before it is too late.

EXHIBIT 11-01 Topbutton.com welcome e-mail

Registration Notice:

- We're sorry for the inconvenience, but we want to make sure you spelled your email (ahughes@e-dialog.com) correctly. Please double check below.
  If you did spell it correctly, please click on the continue button below.

It's Official - YOU'RE IN!

Congratulations! You've got full-on access to the TOP BUTTON web site and e-mail alerts!

Some of our most exclusive sales are promoted only by mail. So you don't miss a single event or party, fill in the postal information below and you'll also be automatically entered to win an iPod nano.

1. YOUR INFO   2. MEMBER PERKS

E-mail address	ahughes@e-dialog.com	**Zip Code**	33316
First Name	Arthur	**Last Name**	Hughes
Address	2100 South Ocean Drive	**Address2**	
City	Fort Lauderdale	**State**	FL
Mobile Phone	954-767-4558	**Gender**	Male

▶▶ CONTINUE

What to ask for

If you study your business and your customers, you may decide you need only a few, usually not more than 10 or 15 pieces of customer information to enable you to create segments so you can send relevant e-mail messages. The data can be broken down into five categories:

- **Contact information:** name, e-mail, street address, phone number
- **Basic demographics:** gender, age, marital status, income, children, house type
- **Preferences:** product interest, e-mail frequency
- **Attitudes:** viewpoints on pricing, levels of service, and so on

Remember, don't ask for too much information or anything that you don't need in developing relevant e-mails. Some of the necessary information can be gained by appended data (see next section) so you don't need to ask for it. When asking for anything, be sure to let your subscribers know how you will use the data and that their privacy will

EXHIBIT 11-02 Shop It To Me sign-up page

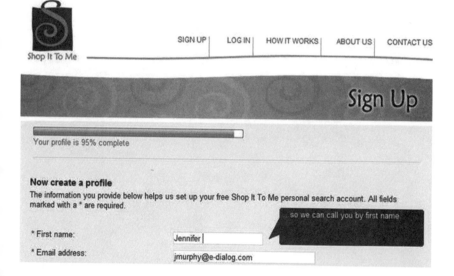

be protected. Let them know how they will benefit from giving you the information.

Shop It To Me does a good job of sharing its intentions in the sign-up process.

Obtaining demographic data

As described in chapter 7, if you have the subscriber's street address, you can get all the demographic data you could want appended to your database file. Since this information is so readily available, you don't need to ask subscribers to provide it.

Is appended data accurate? Not in all cases. Maybe the subscriber just got a promotion last week and his income went up by $15,000. Is that reflected in his personal record in these databases? Of course not. On the whole, these databases' information is probably 80% accurate, good enough for you to create e-mail segments. And it is better in most cases than what you could get from your subscribers. Why? Because much of the information is considered personal and private, so some subscribers will resent or resist providing it. You may lose subscribers by asking for it. They may give you false information. And you may be able to get only a fraction of your subscribers to provide it. By appending data using a compiled database provider, you can get close to a 90% match rate, which is really all you need.

In some cases, however, you may have to ask for demographic data

EXHIBIT 11-03 Parents.com data request

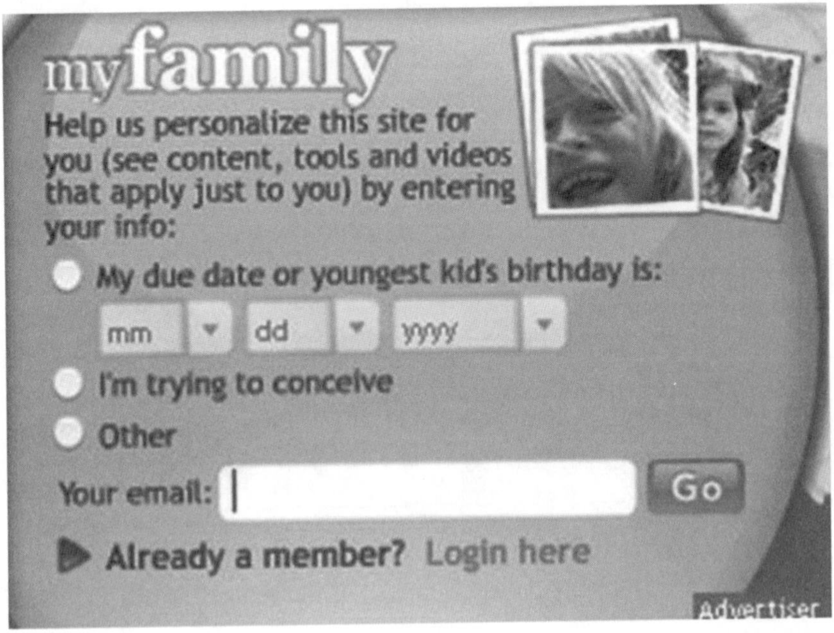

directly: if you're legally obligated to do so or if, in the very first e-mail interaction, you will use this information in a way that will provide immediate value to your subscriber. For example, Jack Daniel's is legally obligated to prohibit access to its online content to anyone under 21, so it has a good reason to ask for date of birth right from the start. Parents.com asks for some very personal information upfront (see Exhibit 11-03) with the purpose of making every site visit personalized to an individual member from the get-go.

Continuing the dialogue

As you begin marketing to your subscribers, you can ask a question or two during the course of transactional and other messages. Before you send an e-mail to any subscriber for any reason, your software should scan the subscriber's database record to see what information is already there. You can compare this information to your list of important pieces of information required for creating marketing segments.

Let's say you sell clothing. The software sees that you are missing the type of clothing this subscriber is most interested in. In your next promotional or transactional e-mail, include a question that will solve this mystery.

Perhaps you are interested in whether this subscriber is keen on see-ing low-cost items, top-of-the-line items, or mainstream items. A ques-tion in the next marketing e-mail will help you to determine what kind of information to feature in the future.

Don't lose the data

Some of your subscribers will become distracted while filling out your forms. When they come back to look at the form, their information will have disappeared and they will have to start over. *Don't ever let that happen.* You will annoy your subscribers and may lose them as a result. Solution: use cookies. Whenever a subscriber begins to fill in a form, save each piece of data and place a cookie on their PC. If they have to log off and come back later, they will be delighted to find the data they entered is still there, waiting for them.

Is this hard to arrange? Sure. So are most of the recommendations in this book. But just because it's hard doesn't mean you shouldn't do it. If your e-mail programmers say what you want is too difficult for them, get some other programmers. Everything we recommend in this book is doable and should be done. Marketing is too important to be made subservient to the abilities of a few programmers. You can quote us on this.

Don't be like IVR

Most subscribers hate interactive voice response (IVR) systems. In most cases, IVR's purpose seems to be to keep the caller from ever talking to a live person. E-mails should be just the opposite of IVR. Whatever the subscriber wants to do should be anticipated with links. In every e-mail, include a search box so the subscriber can search on the site for anything not available in the links, a toll-free number, an e-mail address, and a "live agent" button so the subscriber can have a text chat any time with someone who is knowledgeable and can get things done.

But be warned: don't put advanced features like text chat on your Web site or in your e-mails if you're not prepared to make the experi-ence a pleasure for your customers. You really must have someone sup-porting the customer dialogue around the clock. If you can only cover certain hours, make that clear right next to the input box.

Provide feedback functionality in every e-mail

One of the most frustrating things about a poorly constructed e-mail is the failure to find a way to respond. You read the e-mail (which is supposed to be a one-to-one conversation), and you may really want to get in touch with the person who sent the message. You hunt high and low, but there is no e-mail address or phone number anywhere in the e-mail.

If you really want to listen to your customers, you have to make it possible for them to say something to you—and you have to read what people say. Rule: put feedback functionality, whether an e-mail address or a link to a form on your site, in every single e-mail so you can have a real conversation with your subscribers. Someone in your company should check the feedback daily. It's a courtesy to subscribers who take the time to compliment, complain, ask for information, or point out a problem.

Make the data entry process fun

As you have learned by now, e-mail marketing is a lot of fun. It is highly creative. It calls on you to use your imagination, dreaming up wild ideas that no one has thought of and trying them out. It also calls for keeping up with scores of Web sites, and making use of the thousands of new and great ideas being implemented.

When you design your data-gathering forms, think up interesting or amusing ways to ask for the data and to thank your subscriber after she has entered each piece of information.

Here is where e-mail becomes separated from the corporate Web site. Corporate Web sites are often stodgy and bureaucratic. Committees are formed to review each aspect of the site. Marketers can't introduce new ideas without putting them in front of a sceptical committee. The process takes time, and may be a serious impediment to a creative and exciting Web site.

The same isn't true of marketing e-mails. If you are sending e-mails out every week or every day, no committee has time to oversee what you are doing. So you are free to experiment. You can use your imagination and creativity. Use them. At the same time, be sure to test each new idea. If you try a new approach to data gathering, use an A/B split. Send half of your e-mail recipients the new approach, and the other half the old approach. Keep track of which version each person got. Get a report tomorrow on which got the better response. If the new idea wins, that becomes your control for the future.

Don't ask for information you already have

Many companies ask for the same data repeatedly. Big mistake. Program your software to check every data request in any outgoing e-mail with the data already stored in your database. If the data is already there, don't ask for it again. If, however, the data is quite old, you may ask if their profile or preference has changed. In this case, show them the data you already have and let them decide to change it or leave it. Don't show subscribers a blank form and make them work. Each survey question should be carefully selected for that particular subscriber, not part of a blanket survey. The old corner grocer didn't ask his customers every day what their phone number was or where they lived. Why should you?

Prefill data in any order form

A subscriber has put something in her shopping cart and is ready to check out. She is confronted with a form with about 12 boxes to fill in. If this is an existing customer, make life easy for her: prefill every box you have information for (name, mailing address, shipping address, etc.). Let her know that she can change any box she wants.

The first time your subscriber shops, offer to store her credit card number for her convenience. Ask her to provide a name for her credit card. Tell her why this is safe. When she makes another purchase with you, list her stored credit card numbers by name. She clicks a link beside the name of the card she wants to use and all the credit card information is automatically filled in, except for the three-digit number on the back of her card.

Why should you go to all the trouble to do this? Because you are a professional e-mail marketer! Your goal is to make shopping a pleasure for your customers.

Manage frequency preferences

The Kayak.com travel comparison site does a great job of clearly setting expectations in the first newsletter and throughout its site. Its messages are sent weekly on Wednesdays. The preference center in the e-mail allows subscribers to easily manage what they receive and gives them control:

- Get more!
- Get less . . .
- Make some changes . . .

It also asks for feedback:

- What do you think of Kayak.com?
- Would you recommend Kayak.com to a friend?"

E-mail frequency is such an important subject that we have devoted the next chapter to it. As you know from this chapter, many marketers want to send more e-mails, and most subscribers want to receive fewer.

Organize profiles and preference requests

In setting up the area of your Web site or e-mail that asks for subscriber data, there are several links you should have. Most should be triggered by a button on every page of your e-mail or site, not just the home page.

Make it easy for subscribers to change their e-mail or physical address while they enter the profile information. When they do, tell them the changes have been entered into their database record, and send an immediate e-mail confirming the change.

Make sure subscribers can unsubscribe from all your e-mails at once or each one separately. That way, if they don't want one newsletter, they can still get the others and you won't have lost them entirely. Let your users change the content they receive as their interests change.

The unsubscribe link must be easy and functional, with a simple form asking why they are unsubscribing before they click and leave you forever. Easy means, "click here to unsubscribe," not "send us an e-mail with 'remove' in the subject line." That isn't easy. Don't make them enter an ID and password to unsubscribe. That is an outrage!

Don't wait for more than a few minutes to grant the unsubscribe request, either. Of course, CAN-SPAM allows you 10 business days for to process unsubscribes. *That should not be your guide.* Don't risk annoying your possibly still very valuable offline customers who simply don't want to receive e-mails from you anymore.

As soon as they have unsubscribed, send them a confirmation e-mail or send them to a landing page that says, "You have unsubscribed." Let them know: "You can always come back later—or right now by clicking here."

Be sure there is a viral component in every e-mail. Give all subscribers a chance on every page to forward whatever they are looking at to a friend by entering the friend's e-mail and clicking a button.

If you have a partner who wants to send e-mails to your subscribers, make this clear in the subscription form, giving subscribers a chance to say no. Some subscribers will want the partner information, but many won't and will be annoyed that they are sent more than they wanted. Annoyed with whom? With you!

Provide a link to your privacy policy on the subscription page. They won't bother to read it, but it reassures them that it is there. The DMA has instructions for how to write a privacy policy, which can found at www.the-dma.org/privacy/creating.shtml#form.

Provide a link to customer service and to the "contact us" page. This is just as important as the privacy policy. There is nothing more annoying than wanting to contact the company about some issue and having to search all over the e-mail or the Web site for the proper link. Give subscribers your toll-free number everywhere in your e-mails that they might look for it. Talking to customers on the phone is one of the costs of being in business.

Don't ask for a password unless it is absolutely necessary. Why do subscribers need a password if all you do is send newsletters? It is a nuisance for the user (trying to remember all her passwords) and may lose you subscribers who try to come back later and can't remember the password. If you need a password, make sure your response to a subscriber who has forgotten her password arrives in her inbox within a few seconds of her request, or you may lose her forever. Your goal is to make the process easy for subscribers, not difficult.

Don't ask registrants to invent a nickname for themselves. Always use their e-mail as their ID. People are registered at dozens of sites today. Using their e-mail address makes it much easier than remembering dozens of IDs and passwords.

Provide a list of e-mails *and* a sample of any promotional e-mails or whitepapers that they will receive as a result of registering. Describe the benefits of each item to them with a short paragraph, such as ClickZ does with its subscription page.

EXHIBIT 11-04 ClickZ Experts newsletter subscription form

E-mail: [   ]

ClickZ Newsletters

☐ **ClickZ Experts (HTML)** (preview)
☐ **ClickZ Experts (Text)**

The ClickZ Experts newsletter contains headlines, brief descriptions, and links to that day's columns on the ClickZ site. It's e-mailed every business day. Please note: This is ClickZ's *only* Experts newsletter available in plain-text format. If you are using Lotus Notes, we recommend you subscribe to the text version.

EXHIBIT 11-05 Spiegel Signature Styles

Get customer preferences

To help to segment customers, you may want to find out their preferences regarding your products or services. Spiegel, for example, has a quiz that asks: "What's Your Signature Style? Take our Quiz & Find Out!" On the Spiegel Web site, you answer a dozen or so entertaining questions. Then Spiegel tells you which of six styles fits you best: Modern Romantic, Natural Sophistication, Simple Chic, Relaxed Glamour, Definitely Dramatic, or Understated Elegance. By clicking a link, you see a page for each of those six styles, including fabric and outfit recommendations. Spiegel lets the registrant forward the quiz to friends. Once you know your style, you can get Spiegel e-mails with product recommendations based on that style.

Caution: once you have determined a subscriber's product preferences, put them in her database record and make sure all subsequent e-mails reflect those preferences. Too many marketers come up with a clever idea like this but forget about it in subsequent e-mails, asking subscribers to determine their preferences all over. It destroys the relationship you are trying to create.

The Likert scale for responses

The Likert scales, developed by Rensis Likert in 1932, should be the standard method for survey question responses. It comprises five levels:

- Strongly disagree
- Disagree
- Neither agree nor disagree
- Agree
- Strongly agree

Using the Likert scale, you can compare responses on your surveys with responses to similar questions on other surveys. Likert responses can also be converted into bar charts.

Satisfaction surveys

The best time to conduct an e-mail customer satisfaction survey is when the experience is fresh in subscribers' minds. If you wait to conduct the survey, responses may be less accurate. Your subscriber may have forgotten some of the details or may confuse you with another company.

Using the Likert scale, the basic questions to ask are:

- How satisfied are you with the purchase you made?
- How satisfied are you with the service you received?
- How satisfied are you with our company overall?

You should also ask:

- How likely are you to buy from us again?
- How likely are you to recommend our company to others?
- What did you like about your experience with us?
- What didn't you like about your experience with us?

Don't give up

A consumer reported: "I stayed overnight at the Venetian in Las Vegas recently. Three days after I returned, I received an e-mail asking me to take a survey, an e-mail that I did not notice. Seven days later, they sent a follow-up e-mail. Here was my reaction:

- The survey solicitation was combined with a warm thank-you message, which made me feel exclusive.
- The two-pronged tactic worked! I took the survey after I received the follow-up e-mail.

- The follow-up e-mail made me feel that the Venetian really cared about my opinion. Why else would they bother to send it a second time?

On the other hand:

- The time between the first and second e-mail should perhaps have been shorter.
- The survey did not include an up-sell to book a future stay.

But the fact is that the follow up was a success."

How to use survey answers

The most important part of a satisfaction survey is what you do with the results. There are five basic things you should always do:

- Set up a system to give you the overall results in graphic form. See if your satisfaction ratings are going up or down.
- Find out those things that the customer doesn't like and fix them.
- Respond to all who said anything at all negative. Thank them for their frankness, telling them what you intend to do as a result of their input. You can convert unhappy customers into staunch advocates if you listen to them, correct the problem, and tell them what you did.
- Store the fact of her answering the survey in the subscriber's database record along with the date. *Don't ask her to respond to a similar survey for the next month.*
- Thank all who completed a survey with a short e-mail saying how pleased you are that they took the time to do this and telling them what you have done with the results of past surveys.

Follow-up on survey responses

Netflix customer Shane Sackman contacted Netflix customer service via phone after not receiving a movie he had ordered; he then received a follow-up survey e-mail. "I chose the satisfied option for my answer, which redirected me to a thank-you page with links to customer service in case I had any additional questions," said Sackman. "It was a very simple survey that I appreciated because it showed me as a customer that Netflix cared and that they were constantly looking to improve their service."

The follow-up e-mail:

Dear Shane:

Thanks for recently contacting Netflix Customer Service by phone. In order to serve you better, we would love to hear how we did.

I am **satisfied** with my Netflix Customer Service experience

I am **unsatisfied** with my Netflix Customer Service experience.

Thank you!

The Netflix Team

Customer Jillian Bilodeau experienced amazing customer service from Pottery Barn. She had purchased a few items online from Pottery Barn. When they arrived, she realized the shipment didn't include a hanging rod to hang the products. She called customer service only to find that the rod was actually a separate item and would cost $20.00. "Although the customer service representative was very friendly, she still had to break the news that I would most likely have to pay for the rod along with another $8.00 shipping fee. So, I ordered two rods to hold the three products I originally purchased, now bringing my second order to $40.00 of unexpected fees plus shipping," she said.

"The next day, I received an e-mail asking me to take a survey to evaluate the customer service experience," she continued. "I was honest, explaining how the customer service rep was great, but that I should have been made aware of all items I needed to purchase at once. Two days later, I received a call from customer service explaining how the second shipping fee was waved and that I should expect a $20.00 merchandise credit that I could use online or in stores to make up for the inconvenience. I am very impressed with the customer service I received and now have no negative thoughts towards Pottery Barn . . . any more. The satisfaction survey was no joke and was taken seriously."

Get customer ratings and product reviews

Many Web retailers routinely ask customers to rate and review products they buy. Then they put the customer ratings next to their product offerings on the Web site or in any e-mails describing the product. How important are these ratings? Very important.

Bazaarvoice reported the ability to refine site search results by customer ratings led to 22% more sales per unique visitor on a same-session basis and 41% more sales per visitor on a multisession basis .It also found the return rate of products purchased online with 50 or more customer reviews was half the return rate of products with five or fewer reviews. In a 2007 study, ForeSee Results reported that reviews drove 21% higher purchase satisfaction and 18% higher loyalty than product listings without reviews. EMarketer reported that online UK retailers found their customer retention and loyalty scores rising by 73% once they implemented consumer-generated ratings and reviews. Bath & Body Works found that e-mails with customer reviews had a 10.4% higher average order value, a 7.5% higher CTR, and 11.5% higher sales overall.

In 2007, comScore reported that more than three quarters of review users in nearly every category said the review had a significant influence on their purchase, with hotels ranking the highest (87%).It also reported that 97% of those who made a purchase based on an online review said they found the review to have been accurate. The numerical rating by users is important. comScore also found that consumers were willing to pay from 20% to 99% more for a five-star–rated product than for a four-star–rated product, depending on the product category.

MarketingExperiments tested product conversion with and without customer product ratings. Conversion more than doubled, going from 0.44% to 1.04%, when the five-star rating was displayed with the product.

PETCO found that allowing shoppers to sort products within a category by customer rating led to a sales increase of 41% per unique visitor. It also found that shoppers who browsed the site's "Top Rated Products" page, which features products rated most highly by customers, had a 49% higher conversion rate than the site average and 63% more dollars per order than other site shoppers.

Finally, Forrester Research reported that 71% of online shoppers read reviews, making them the most widely read consumer-generated content.

Word survey questions to educate subscribers

You can teach people with a survey by asking them questions that help them notice things they never noticed before. "Do you prefer option A or option B?" might just be a way of getting people to notice that you even have an option B.

The very act of asking a question may change the experience for the customer. One firm shows subscribers a group of testimonials. The message says, "We hope that when we've completed our job for you, you'll be willing to write one, too." That thought increases the likelihood that people will look for something good to say, which increases the likelihood that they'll enjoy the event.

Be honest in your e-mails

Be honest in your e-mails; subscribers will notice false statements. Lilia Arsenault received an e-mail from Spiegel that began: "Dear Spiegel Customer, as you prepare to celebrate the season, we would like to thank you, our very special customer, for a wonderful year." Spiegel offered 20% off on everything on the site.

Lilia's reaction: "I wish Spiegel was more honest with me. I appreciate being called their 'very special customer,' but I've never shopped with them and probably don't deserve a thank you, so I know that they don't really mean what they said to me. So why not use this opportunity to learn more about me so I do become their 'special customer'?"

Takeaway thoughts

- Before you ask for any information from a customer, figure out how the customer will benefit from giving it to you. Let her know in the e-mail.
- Only ask for information you will need and use.
- Don't ask for too much information at once.
- Consider appended demographic data instead of asking consumers for information.
- Don't lose the data on an uncompleted form.
- Make the data entry process fun.
- Prefill the data on any form.
- Thank customers when they provide you with information.
- The wording of your surveys can educate customers.

12

The Frequency Debate: How Much E-mail Is Enough?

When asked why recipients stopped subscribing to opt-in e-mails, more than one half said the content was no longer relevant, and 40% said they were getting too many offers.

JupiterResearch (2007)[1]

Sixty percent of online retailers conduct between one and three campaigns each month. 32.8% coordinate 4 to 15 campaigns each month; 7.2% conduct more than 15.

Internet Retailer (2007[2])

37.4% of Internet users say they receive more e-mail than they expected when they signed up.

Return Path (2007)[3]

E-mail marketing is so inexpensive that many retailers are seduced into using it too often. Sales figures seem to prove that retailers aren't wrong, either. It seems simple enough: if you send e-mails weekly, then shift to daily, your sales are likely to increase. Doesn't this prove that more is better? Yes and no. Here's why.

Relevance and frequency are related. A relevant e-mail sent too often can lose its relevance effectiveness over time. In a study by Merkle[4], 66% of e-mail users list excessive frequency as a reason to unsubscribe. But the reverse doesn't necessarily hold true. If you send e-mails very infrequently, your customers may forget about you and consider your e-mails as spam when they do arrive.

If you take one thing away from this chapter, it's this: make it easy for subscribers to tell you what they think, and listen to what they say and do. They will usually tell you what frequency is best. Moreover, some of the best communicators of this are your inactive customers.

When your e-mail efforts are perceived as too frequent, you have a problem: your customers, typically the best ones, may unsubscribe or mark your e-mails as spam.

The basic problem relates to the hunting-farming conundrum: should marketers analyze e-mail campaigns or e-mail subscribers? E-mail campaigns themselves are only one side of the equation. The communication's true value is often difficult to measure.

Imagine daily e-mails like a swarm of mosquitoes attacking a group of consumers resting outside a shopping mall. Some of the consumers will get in their cars and go home because of the mosquitoes. Others will go into the mall to shop to escape from the mosquitoes. But instead of studying what the consumers are doing, the e-mail marketers are studying mosquito clouds on the group of consumers. This makes as much sense as an army analyzing the bullets being fired at an enemy rather than what the enemy is planning and doing.

Buyers can be a valuable long-term source of revenue. Your goal should be to woo them, to build long-term relationships with them, to make them happy with your company, your service, and your products. To become successful in the long run, you must analyze and understand all of your subscribers—what their preferences are and how you can create marketing messages that respond to these preferences. If you have a subscriber who might give you $2,000 a year for 10 years and you lose her within a few weeks through excessive e-mails, you have lost a lot of revenue—usually without even realizing it.

How should you determine the proper frequency for marketing e-mails? To answer this question, let's begin with the overall effect on deliverability.

Frequent e-mails can reduce deliverability

Frequent e-mails can generate so many additional unsubscribes and spam complaints that you could end up trading increased short-term gain for a lost long-term revenue, as well as increase list attrition and potentially damage your brand and e-mail reputation. Any additional revenue, leads, downloads, trials, or other desired actions you generate could easily be wasted by the higher costs of replacing lost customers or prospects.

Following is a case study derived from data reported by Kirill Popov and Loren McDonald on The ClickZ Network[5]. Popov and McDonald list the four main reasons for losses due to increased frequency of mailing:

EXHIBIT 12-01 Effect of increasing frequency

Online Retailer Increasing E-mail Frequency	5 Per Month	12 Per Month
Subscribers Start of Year	515,677	515,677
E-mails Delivered	32,161,000	79,890,000
Revenue per Delivered	$0.18	$0.10
Revenue	$5,788,980	$7,989,000
Revenue Per Subscriber	$11.23	$15.49
Unsubscribe Rate	0.740%	1.770%
Monthly Spam Complaints	0.046%	0.646%
Monthly Address Losses	1.53%	3.55%
Annual Loss Rate	18.36%	42.60%
Subscribers Lost in Year	94,678	219,678
Subscribers End of Year	420,999	295,999
Cost of replacing lost subscribers @ $15 each	$1,420,174	$3,295,176
Lost One Year Revenue from lost @ $11.23	$1,062,857	$2,466,105
Cost of e-mails creative & dispatch @ $6/m	$192,966	$479,340
Total present and future costs	$2,675,997	$6,240,622
Net Revenue after present & future costs	$3,112,983	$1,748,378
Lost profits from increasing frequency		$1,364,604

- Additional loss of subscribers
- Cost to reacquire these customers
- Potential lost revenue from lost subscribers
- Higher spam complaint rate that triggers ISP blocks

These were illustrated in their case study, which formed the basis for the numbers shown in Exhibit 12-01[6].

This retailer had annual online revenue of $5.7 million and decided to increase the frequency of his e-mail marketing campaigns from five per month to 12 per month. Revenue increased by 38% to $7.9 million. Popov and McDonald looked more closely at the cost of this $2.2 million increased revenue and found a number of things happened.

The e-mails delivered went from 32 million to almost 80 million. This boost caused the unsubscribe rate to increase, from 0.74% to 1.77%. Reported spam complaints increased from 0.046% to 0.646%. As a result, the retailer lost 219,678 subscribers instead of 94,678 subscribers for the year. This was a serious loss: revenue per e-mail went from $0.18 to $0.10.

These permission-based e-mail addresses cost the retailer an average of $15 each to acquire. To keep his business going, he will have to replace these lost subscribers at $15 each. In addition, each lost subscriber costs the retailer an average annual revenue of $11.23, which he would have received if they hadn't disappeared. This amount was determined by what the company was originally getting per subscriber. Is this $11.23 correct? It could be that the subscribers who unsubscribed were less valuable than the average. On the other hand, sometimes the unsubscribers are more valuable customers than the ones who remain.

At the end of the year, the retailer had less than 300,000 subscribers left with the high-frequency mailing, whereas with the lower-frequency mailing, he had more than 400,000 left.

What this chart doesn't tell is how much the perceived excessive frequency reduces the brand's value in subscribers' minds. When more than 100,000 consumers unsubscribe or otherwise become undeliverable as a result of what they considered to be too many e-mails, what do they think of the retailer who sent these e-mails? Are excessive e-mails not only reducing net revenue but also destroying the brand's image?

Test frequency changes first

Looking at this chart, we can see this retailer lost $1.3 million per year in profits by increasing his mailing frequency. The only way increased frequency will affect your e-mail program is to do the analysis shown here before and after the increased mailing frequency.

Whenever you want to change your e-mail program, begin by making the changes to just a test group. Compare the test group's open rates, CTRs, conversions, deliverability rates, and unsubscribe rates to the control group's. Wait until you convince yourself that your change is a good idea. Then roll it out.

Easier said than done. Increasing frequency from five per month to 12 per month requires an increase in your creative and programming staff. Management won't give you the funds to hire additional staff just for a test. So how can you test additional frequency? If you have your e-mail delivery and part of your creative outsourced to an ESP, you can ask the ESP to help you increase your frequency for the test without you or your ESP hiring additional permanent staff for it.

Of course, increasing frequency isn't always a bad thing. Many companies have the opposite problem: they don't send enough. To determine the right frequency, you need to study your customer situation one segment at a time.

The Email Experience Council's "2006 Retail Email Subscription Benchmark Study" showed that only 7% of retailers gave subscribers any kind of idea how many e-mails to expect. In the study, only one re-tailer, Coldwater Creek, allowed subscribers to choose to receive a monthly e-mail.

Frequency and bounces

Why do e-mails bounce? It may be because subscribers change jobs or e-mail addresses or because they get tired of receiving communications from you. Each of factor is illustrated in MailerMailer data in Exhibit 12.02.[7]

EXHIBIT 12-02 Mail frequency by bounce rate

Mail Frequency	Bounce Percent
Daily or More	2.35%
Few Times a Week	2.02%
Once a Week	2.59%
Few Times a Month	4.91%
Once a Month	5.43%
Less than Once a Month	13.57%

These numbers suggest that if you e-mail people less than once a month, they will forget about you and possibly consider your e-mails to be spam. Regular communications reduce the bounce rate. Using these numbers, you might conclude that daily e-mails are a good thing. But bounce is only one factor to consider.

Two unsubscribe case studies

Take a look at this case study from Dan Wilson on the Email Experience Council's blog:

> A few weeks ago, I enrolled in Saks Fifth Avenue Online Customer Care (I wanted to pay down my Saks Credit Card). At the end of the process, I opted in to receive Saks e-mails. Below is a day-by-day time-line of what ensued from the moment I hit "confirm."
>
> **Day 1:** Opted-in—Redirect to a thank-you page, but no welcome e-mail.
>
> **Day 2:** One day after sign-up, the welcome e-mail arrived. I would've like to have seen it immediately, but a one-day lag time is not the end of the world. I thought the subject line, "Welcome to saks.com. We have a special offer for you" . . . wasn't great, but at least was very

clear and direct. The body of the message contained a call-to-action that included a 10% discount. Pretty good overall.

Day 3: Not 1, but 2 messages from Saks in one day. Oops?

—Message #1: Subject Line—"SAKSFIRST Double Points + From the Heart," received at 10:31AM EST, Valentine's Day call-to-action.

—Message #2: Subject Line—"Get SAKSFIRST Double Points!" received at 3:53PM EST, Double Points call-to-action.

Day 4: Subject Line—"SAKSFIRST Double Points + Have-To-Have Handbags."

Days 5 and 6: Nothing (Super Bowl weekend).

Day 7: Not 1, but 2 messages from Saks. Hard to believe that they would make this same "mistake" only 4 days later.

—Message #1: Subject Line—"Dior . . . Take it Away!" received at 10:08AM EST, Women's Shoes call-to-action

—Message #2: Subject Line—"Video Exclusive! Days 1 to 3 of Fashion Week," received at 4:51PM EST, Fashion Week call-to-action.

Day 8: Subject Line—"Fabulous Valentine's Gifts."

Day 9: Not 1, but 2 messages from Saks. Another "mistake" 2 days after the 2nd one (3rd double e-mail day in past 6 days).

—Message #1: Subject Line—"David Yurman Gifts," received at 9:47AM EST, Women's Shoes call-to-action.

—Message #2: Subject Line—"Day 4 Video of Fashion Week," received at 5:05PM EST, Fashion Week call-to-action.

Day 10: Subject Line—"NEW: Reyes, Wayne . . . + SALE."

Day 11: I clicked on their unsubscribe/change preferences link, fully intending to unsubscribe. But, alas, they did it right! I was able to edit my preferences and elect to receive updates only "Once a Week."

Saved by an unsubscribe option! This is a safety net—a virtual last ditch for you to try to recapture your subscribers' hearts and minds. How many e-mail marketers provide this option? Not enough.

Our second case study compares two companies that did some pretty extensive mailing one year. Exhibit 12-03 outlines the numbers.

Both retail firms had several hundred stores in shopping malls; the numbers here cover only online sales. Both began the year with approximately the same number of registered subscribers in their databases. Company A sent more than 42,000 e-mails, about 72 e-mails per address. Company B sent more than 50,000 more e-mails, about 90 e-mails per address. Company B's higher mailing frequency took a toll on

EXHIBIT 12-03 Two companies with differing e-mail frequencies

	Company A	Company B
Subscribers	586,324	558,128
Delivered	42,407,835	50,173,347
Average E-mails per Year	72.3	89.9
Unsubscribed	43,652	59,031
Percent Unsub	7.45%	10.58%
Online Buyers	58,566	95,036
Percent Buyers	10.0%	17.0%
Total Online Orders	64,910	107,638
Average Order Value	$159.81	$101.77
Total Online Sales	$10,373,267	$10,954,319
Dollar Sales per e-mail	$0.24	$0.22
Sales per Subscriber	$17.69	$19.63
Conversions per e-mail	0.15%	0.21%
Spending per buyer	$177.12	$115.26

its subscription rate: 10.6% of recipients unsubscribed, compared to 7.5% percent of Company A's recipients.

However, 17% of Company B's subscribers became buyers, compared to only 10% of Company A's. The difference in the average order size may have been due to different merchandise rather than a result of less-frequent mailing.

Interestingly, some of the subscribers who unsubscribed had made purchases before they disappeared. The total online purchases of all unsubscribers in each store was close to $1 million (see Exhibit 12-04). The most significant number is the average spend per unsubscriber. Company A's unsubscribers spent an average of $220, whereas all its buyers spent only an average of $177.Company B's lost buyers spent an average of $156, and all its buyers spent an average of $115.

These charts reveal that the lost subscribers were more valuable than the ones who remained. The companies were losing their best customers. Company B was losing 292 customers who bought products four or more times before they disappeared. This kind of analysis shows the hidden costs of increasing mailing frequency.

What can we conclude from these numbers?

• The conversion rate from frequent e-mails was quite low—between 0.15% and 0.21% per e-mail delivered.

• Frequent mailing increased the number of sales.

EXHIBIT 12-04 Two companies' unsubscribes and undeliverables

Company A

Number of Purchases	Unsubs and Undels		
	Buyers	Revenue	$/Buyer
1	3,654	$ 528,140	$ 144.54
2	551	$ 181,528	$ 329.45
3	146	$ 79,704	$ 545.92
4+	156	$ 168,071	$1,077.38
Total	4,351	$ 957,443	$ 220.05
Not Leaving	58,556	$10,373,267	$177.15

Company B

Number of Purchases	Unsubs and Undels		
	Buyers	Revenue	$/Buyer
1	4,054	$ 386,847	$ 95.42
2	753	$ 159,822	$ 212.25
3	262	$ 81,355	$ 310.52
4+	292	$ 207,911	$ 712.02
Total	5,361	$ 835,936	$ 155.93
Not Leaving	95,036	$10,954,319	$115.26

- Frequent mailing probably increased the number of unsubscribes.

Analyze those who leave (through unsubscribing or through becoming undeliverable). If you are losing your best customers, find out why and figure out what you can do about it.

How to keep your best buyers

You know two facts at this point: frequent e-mails increase sales, but they can turn some people off. You can live with losing non-buyers; you can't live as comfortably if you lose frequent buyers, especially if it's because you send them too many e-mails. One way to improve the situation would be to treat your buyers better than your non-buyers.

This obvious solution wasn't easy for either company to adopt. Both were hunters, not farmers. They fell into a trap because all they collected from subscribers in the opt-in process was the subscriber's e-mail and first name. Using that name, they could personalize the greeting in the content, but that was all. Going forward, their buyers got exactly the same e-mails as the non-buyers. The retailers had their buyers' street addresses, of course. They could have appended data and created e-mails with very personal content just for the buyers. Why didn't they take advantage of the situation?

For both companies, the reason is a common one among e-mail hunters: they were so busy creating new e-mails (the traps) that they had little or no staff resources available to create differentiated communications for buyers. Such mass e-mailers typically live hand to mouth. Each e-mail offered deep discounts as inducements for their subscribers. Their management was seeking the least costly way of delivering their e-mails. Any marketer who comes up with the idea of creating different e-mails for buyers will have a tough time convincing management that the extra expense is justified. But numbers don't lie. Amy Black of Constant Contact writes, "According to JupiterResearch, engaging your audiences in more relevant communications could increase net profits by an average of 18 times."[8] (2006). What can you do to get management's attention on this situation?

Frequent e-mails' effect on offline sales

Not shown in these charts are the offline sales attributed to these subscribers. E-mail campaigns sent by companies with several marketing channels, as these two companies have, will impact behaviors in all other channels. Typically, 75% of offline purchases made by customers who are active on the Web(as registered subscribers are) are made after some online research. Unquestionably, subscribers who got these e-mails were prompted (and encouraged) to go to the retail stores to see and try on the clothing before they bought. The offline sales due to these e-mails were significant. No one knows how significant, however. The reason these sales don't show up on these charts is these companies were hunters rather than farmers. They didn't maintain customer marketing databases that showed sales from all channels. Creating such marketing databases would have cost more than $1 million per year. That kind of extra expenditure just doesn't fit into the business model of the heavily discounting mass e-mailer.

How often should you mail?

To answer this question, you have to answer a more fundamental question first: what do you have to say that your subscribers might want to hear? Once you have that clearly in mind, you can explain it to your subscribers during opt-in. However, some subscribers will only be window shoppers at best and will more than likely disappear on you for no matter what you do. You might experiment with the opt-in e-mail to ask them how often they want to hear about your subject, perhaps giving them a choice and letting them dictate the frequency that is right for them.

If you publish news, for example, subscribers might actually want to receive a daily newsletter, plus breaking news occasionally during the day. But most businesses don't publish news, so daily might be an overload. To get the answers you need, set up a preference center that makes clear what your e-mail newsletters or promotions will contain and how often they will appear. Break your content down into several newsletter options: daily, twice a week, weekly, or less often.

Don't bite off more than you can chew. If you advertise daily content, be sure what you send matches the expectations you create in the preference form. To make sure readers actually get what they want, break your subject matter into categories that readers can get their minds around.

For example, you might have four different newsletters and a fifth that is a weekly summary of other four. Some subscribers might opt for the weekly summary. It could have links that take readers back to material in any of the other four e-mails.

Retailers, on the other hand, are providing opportunities to purchase products and services in their messages. The e-mails will contain pictures of the products and links to detailed descriptions. They might have technical information on the products or nostalgia about how they are made. Have a brainstorming session to figure out what you will really give your subscribers so you can make it completely clear in the preference request form. Make sure you explain how often these e-mails will arrive. If you are frank in the opt-in process, there will be fewer disappointments and spam accusations later on. If you send more than your subscribers were expecting based on your preference form, many subscribers will get annoyed, or even angry.

No matter what you promise during the opt-in process, you must honor it throughout the lifecycle of your e-mail relationship with subscribers. Resist the temptation to sneak one or two "can't miss" e-mail messages through. You may get away with it once or twice, but keep it up and you'll pay for your aggression with more spam complaints and less customer engagement.

—Stefan Pollard, ClickZ

Using RFM analysis to measure a mailing calendar's effectiveness

In the absence of other demographic and behavioral data, many mass e-mail marketers use RFM analysis (see chapter 7). RFM can be based on subscriber response (opens and clicks), as well as on actual conversions. In such a situation, many subscribers may be reading the e-mails, then going to a mall to make their purchases.

If you are an e-mail farmer, with a marketing database that includes purchases in all channels, RFM can be a powerful segmentation tool. It can help you decide what the most profitable frequency of mailing for any given group of subscribers is for you. With a marketing database, coding your subscribers by RFM costs you nothing.

RFM tells you who your most responsive customers are. The monetary code tells you who spends the most, and the frequency code points out your most frequent openers and converters. These are people you don't want to lose. If you are worried about losing too many subscribers because of too frequent e-mails, check out your subscribers' RFM cell codes. Check your unsubscribers' and undeliverables' RFM cell codes. Use RFM to make sure you don't lose your best buyers as Company A and Company B did.

Conclusion on mail frequency

Mailing too frequently can be dangerous for your e-mail marketing program. To be sure you are doing things the right way and not losing your most valuable customers, you consider some of the following tests.

In addition to an unsubscribe link, test inserting an "Are we sending you too many messages?" link. When subscribers click this link, tell them how often you have been mailing them. Then offer them the opportunity to reduce or increase mailing frequency or limit mailings to specific topics.

Don't go crazy with this idea. Test it with a few of your subscribers first. Use RFM cell codes to suggest the ones to test this with. You might begin with subscribers with very low RFM codes to see if you could reactivate them.

Another test to try is with unsubscribers; they hold valuable information for you. They have an idea of what is wrong (if anything) with your e-mail program, as far as they are concerned. You have one last shot at these unsubscribers: the "you have unsubscribed" message. Try placing a survey in this e-mail to find out what why they are leaving and what you could do to make your e-mails better. Don't miss this opportunity. Take what you learn very seriously. Think about it, and act on it.

Takeaway thoughts

- About 40% of subscribers think they receive too many e-mails.
- A relevant e-mail, received too often, becomes irrelevant.
- If you increase e-mail frequency, set up control groups to measure the impact on unsubscribes, deliverability, and spam complaints.
- Not mailing enough can sometimes hurt your bounce rate.
- Increasing frequency will probably increase conversions. It may also reduce profits.
- Study the unsubscribers and deliverability of your buyers very closely. Make sure you aren't losing your best customers.
- Treat buyers better than non-buyers. Segment them, send them personalized e-mails, and reward them.
- Study, if you can, the connection between your e-mails and your offline sales. E-mails may have more of an impact on subscriber behavior than your online conversion statistics suggest.
- Code all your subscribers with RFM, and study the results periodically.

Notes

1. "Copy/Content," EmailStatCenter, http://emailstatcenter.com/Copy. html.
2. "Frequency," EmailStatCenter, http://emailstatcenter.com/Frequency. html.
3. Ibid.
4. *A View from the Inbox 2008* (Merkle 2008), http://www.merkleinc. com/user-assets/Documents/WhitePapers/ViewFromTheInbox2008.pdf.
5. Kirill Popov and Loren McDonald, "Calculating the Cost of Increased E-Mail Frequency," The ClickZ Network (June 7, 2006), http:// www.clickz.com/showPage.html?page=3611201.
6. This chart is based on the published case study results but is not the same as the work of Popov and McDonald. We have extrapolated their numbers to illustrate the points in this chapter.
7. *Email Marketing Metrics Report* (MailerMailer, 2007), http://www. mailermailer.com/metrics/TR-H1-2007.pdf.
8. Amy Black, "The Secret to Relevant Email: Segment Your List" (Constant Contact), http://www.constantcontact.com/learning-center/ hints-tips/ht-2008-08a.jsp.

13

The Power of
Transactional E-mails

As a Continental frequent flyer, I've always been impressed with the way it creates messaging that will help make my flight planning and execution easier. Unlike other airlines, Continental makes me feel like a valued customer by sending me e-mail that lets me know about the opportunities to check in online or even check in 24 hours before my flight to ensure I get the best seat. These transactional messages aren't viewed as interruptive at all. They're appreciated . . .

Last week, I was heading to San Francisco and made my reservations as usual. With other airlines I plan on spending 20 minutes digging through e-mail to find my itinerary details and organize everything before I fly. With Continental, I'm lazy. I rely on the e-mail (sent 24 hours ahead of time) with all the nicely packaged details and the opportunity to check in online. When I received the e-mail on my Black-Berry as usual, I saw something new that made me happy. The opening line of the e-mail said, "Wireless customers may check in at http://pda.continental.com/checkin.aspx?PNR=CZFFHD."

Finally! Someone understands the customer is a multichannel creature who doesn't live or function within marketing department silos. This e-mail signified to me that Continental truly understands that its customers leverage different devices to enable a digital lifestyle, and e-mail is much more than copy sent to an inbox. It's an electronic message you receive, regardless of the mode, device, or method you use to read it.

Jeanniey Mullen, ClickZ

Marketers are overlooking the potential revenue contribution that transactional messages can provide. The Direct Marketing Association and Shop.org detail that average order value for retailers is approximately $98. Applying this average order value to an average transactional message volume (e.g., order confirmations), and applying an average three percent revenue contribution from these transactional messages, results conservatively in approximately $2.9 million dollars annually in additional revenue.

David Daniels, JupiterResearch

Transactional e-mails are the most powerful e-mails you will ever send to your customers. They have open rates of 70% to 90%, whereas promotional e-mail's open rates hover around 13%. Transactional e-mails offer you an unparalleled opportunity to communicate and build a lasting relationship with your customers. But you need to concentrate on the contents and method of delivery of these e-mails, as they can really improve your bottom line. In this chapter we will cover the rules that will help you make the most of these e-mails. To be successful, a transactional e-mail should be like a conversation between you and your customer.

There are an unlimited number of types of transactional e-mails. Some include:

- Thank-you messages
- Order shipment
- Satisfaction surveys
- Important purchase information
- Important reminders
- Boarding passes
- Ticket confirmations
- Opt-in e-mail confirmations
- Welcome e-mails
- Service confirmation

Each message gives you a chance to build a strong relationship with your customers and to open the pathway to gaining more information, more loyalty, and further sales. There are some standard links that must be included in all such e-mails. Study this chapter well. It will make you an expert in transaction e-mails—and highly profitable.

How all transactional e-mails should begin

Because this is a transactional e-mail, the message should start with the information about the transaction. There should be no promotional material above the fold or above the transaction text. The subject line should tell subscriber what the message contains (e.g., "Your order has shipped," "Print your boarding pass," etc.). Further down in the message you can include some promotional material. But *never* bury the transactional message beneath a lot of other copy. It *has* to be at the top.

CAN-SPAM is one important reason for beginning your message with the transaction. This law restricts what you can do in transactional e-mails. If you are aware of the restrictions, you can still get a lot of customer-relationship building into your e-mails and stay within the limits of the law. There are really only two basic requirements, which are easy to meet.

First, the subject line should clearly identify the message as transactional. "Your forthcoming trip to San Jose" is clearly about a transaction. "Great deals on sheets and pillows" is clearly not.

Second, the beginning of the text should be about the transaction. No problem. Put the promotional material below the fold, and you are OK.

Include a standard administration section

In Chapter 10, we listed some important links to include in every e-mail's administrative section. These links should be in all transactional e-mails, as well. They provide a window into your world.

If, for instance, your transaction is an introductory welcome, the message should include:

- A personalized greeting
- A warm welcome, explaining some of your products and services
- A link to a sample of the e-mails she will receive
- A link to your privacy policy
- An idea of your mailing frequency
- A link to a page on your site that is relevant to what she signed up for
- An opportunity to buy something else immediately
- A link to a preference page
- A link to a survey

Always use HTML, rather than text

HTML lets you know that readers have opened your message and clicked on links, which a text e-mail can't tell you. By using text, you throw away a golden opportunity to interact with your customers. A

2007 Silverpop study reported that 42% of the transactional e-mails sent by major corporations were sent as text. This is unfortunate for these companies, since HTML transactional messages look better and can be measured.

Text e-mails also can't easily include a logo, which deprives subscribers of the emotional connection to the brand. JupiterResearch estimated that the average online retailer could generate as much as $250,000 annually by improving the delivery and cross-selling functions of its transactional e-mails using HTML[2]:

> Transactional messages, including order confirmations and service related messages, have historically been plain text based messages that are generated from the system that facilitated the transaction. These systems lack the capability to format messages in HTML and include product offers and advertisements, both increasing revenue and brand awareness. However, these legacy transactional systems simply lack the ability to report on critical e-mail measures, such as delivery and response behavior. In fact, deliverability issues with messages such as order confirmations and bank statements will drive customers to contact customer support, consume additional Web site resources, and frustrate the end customer.

Personalize the transaction message

A transaction is always the result of subscriber input: she has asked for something to be sent to her or to be downloaded. Certainly she gave you her name. For this reason, you should use it. The main body of the e-mail should begin with the subscriber's name. Never say "Dear Valued Customer" in a transactional e-mail. In promotional messages you may only know the e-mail, so you can't personalize. But all transactional e-mails can be, and therefore should be, personalized. If you test, you will find that personalized messages produce more clicks and conversions than nonpersonalized ones.

Many retailers haven't learned how to do transactional messages properly. Forty-four percent of the transactional e-mails sent by major corporations weren't personalized in any way, according to Silverpop.

Send them right away

Transaction messages should be sent within 10 seconds of the event that triggered the message. Timing is very important. Your customer has just made a purchase, and she is sitting at her computer waiting for you to send her something. She is in a buying mood *right now*. She may not be in a similar mood tomorrow after she gets her phone bill. In the Silverpop study, only 38% of the transactional e-mails arrived in one minute or less. Twenty-three percent of the e-mails took 10 minutes or more to arrive.

Suggest other products to purchase

This is your best opportunity to communicate with your customers. Transactional e-mails almost always get opened. In planning your transactional e-mail program, estimate what might come from doing transactions properly. E-mail marketers don't do these things out of the goodness of their hearts; they do them to boost sales and customer relationships. Properly designed transactional e-mails can be highly profitable. They arrive at exactly the right time (when the customer is in a buying mood), and they make relevant cross-sale recommendations, which make it easy for the customer to buy then and there.

Despite this situation, 79% of transactional e-mails from major corporations like Nordstrom, Neiman Marcus, Saks, Target, Toys 'R' Us, and Wal-Mart contained *no offer of additional products or services in the e-mail,* according to *Silverpop's How Top Retailers Use Transactional Email* (2007). Even worse, many transactional e-mails from major corporations included a warning not to respond to the e-mail!

How long should it take you to come up with the complementary products to illustrate in the bottom of your transactional e-mails? No time at all, if you have done your homework and have a template ready (see Exhibit 13-01).

When you assemble the creative that illustrates your cross-sell products, use a template like this one. Products can be assembled by intuition (belt, shoes, and coat to go with a dress) or by something more sophisticated based on analysis of similar customers' purchasing experiences, if you are set up for this.

However you do it, you need a lookup table that lists the image location for each item that you sell, along with the image location of its complementary products. The images are automatically inserted into the lower half of any transaction message that mentions its complementary product. The template has space for the other images with suitable wording, such as, "Here's what other customers bought who

EXHIBIT 13-01 Dynamic transaction e-mail template

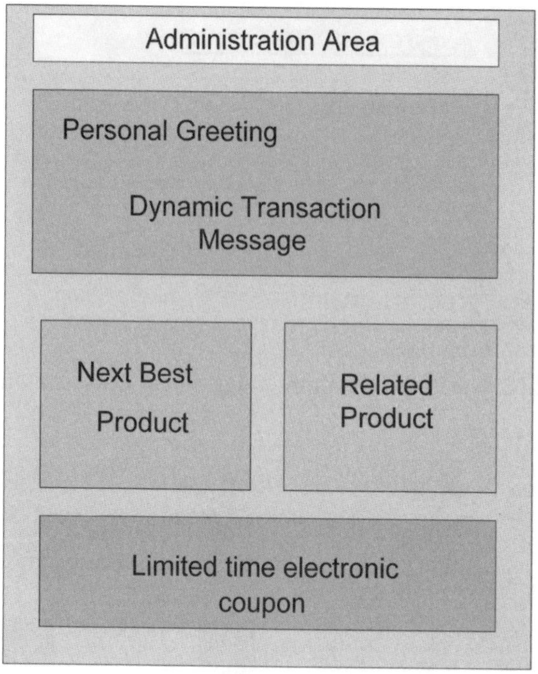

ordered a Yellow Balau Wood Patio Bar Cart. Click on any item to learn more."

Link to relevant Web site pages

How many e-mails have you read that suggest you go to the company's home page or, worse, that you copy the URL into your browser? If you take the first route, you will end up on a page that may have nothing to do with the product you just bought. If you copy the URL into your browser, the company will never know if you visited the page or not.

Everything in e-mail marketing should be measured and tested. Don't ask a subscriber to paste something into her browser or to go to a URL. This is a sure sign that you aren't a very good e-mail marker. Instead, use a link.

In Exhibit 13-02, if the subscribers clicks on either "A Face in the Crowd" or "Recommendations in Classics" (not shown), she is transported to a page where she can learn more from hundreds of additional links. Exhibit 13-03 shows you the "Recommendations in Classics" landing page.

EXHIBIT 13-02 Examples of Links

A Face in the Crowd

Rate this title: ☆☆☆☆☆

Click one of the stars above to rate this movie. Rate movies you've seen to get personalized recommendations based on your ratings.

Recommendations in Classics

EXHIBIT 13-03 Netflix's "Recommendations in Classics" landing page

Include dynamic content

Besides the subscriber's name, the message should use some information from the subscriber's database record to make the content dynamic. For example:

> Thank you, Susan, for your order for a Yellow Balau Wood Patio Bar Cart. We plan to ship your order as soon as possible. We will notify you when it has been shipped.
>
> You may be thinking of other items that might complement your purchase. To help you make up your mind, we have taken the liberty of making some suggestions, based on what other customers who bought this item have also selected. Some of these items are displayed below. You can learn more about and order any one of them by clicking on the images shown below.

This, of course, is what Amazon and Netflix do in their transaction messages. Why should they be the only ones to get the cross sales?

"Dynamic content is the future of acquisition marketing," said Megan Ouellet of Listrak. "Consumers are becoming more savvy and are inundated with too much information to naively respond to generic promotions offering little value. The next generation of e-mail marketing etiquette is sending fewer messages to a larger database, but making every message count with high-impact offers tailored to the needs of the individual. New technologies are being introduced to help marketers easily automate this process."

Let subscribers know what is coming

A good transactional e-mail should be part of a series of messages: a thank-you message, an order shipment information message, a product survey message. Let customers know at the beginning that they will get three messages and what they are. Let them know why you will ask them to rate the product.

Provide a name, an e-mail address, and a phone number

A transactional e-mail can start a dialogue with a customer, leading to a long-term relationship with repeat sales. It is hard to have a dialogue with a company; it is easier to have a dialogue with a person. If possible, then, your transactional e-mail should be from a person and should list an e-mail address and a phone number. The person can be an actual person, or it can be a persona who is supported by your customer service staff. The main goal is for your customer to feel that she is talking to a person and not a computer—someone she can identify with and get in touch with in case something isn't right.

Use transactional e-mails to make your customers' life easier

Before you create a group of transactional e-mails, think about how the messages will affect the customers who receive them. Will they require customers do something difficult? Or will they provide information and reassurance? Consider the transaction e-mail from Microsoft in Exhibit 13-04.

Is this message user-friendly? Take a look at what Microsoft asks this customer to do. If she visits either of the links, she will have to enter the really complex order status ID code. That won't be easy for customers who aren't familiar with the copy and paste functions. Sup-

EXHIBIT 13-04 Microsoft transaction message

Your Order Status ID Code is :

C1F01E5E34C853A7641457EDAD38F20F

You can check the status of your order anytime by doing either of the following:

Visit https://status.microsoft.upgrade.com/orderstatus/microsoft_ics.asp

Visit https://status.microsoft.upgrade.com/orderstatus and enter your Order Status ID Code.

Please do not reply to this e-mail confirmation. It was sent to you through an automated system that is not monitored. If you have additional questions, you can call Microsoft Customer Service Monday through Friday, 8 A.M. to 10 P.M. (Eastern Time), at (888) 218-5617 (toll-free in the United States).

Microsoft

pose the customer thinks something is wrong with the order. The only way she can get ahold of anyone from Microsoft is to read that impossible ID code over the phone to someone. She isn't allowed to reply to the e-mail.

Send transactional e-mails to yourself

Transaction e-mails are typically set up as automatic messages based on orders or transactions received. Sometimes the results are unfortunate, such as "With the 0 **TrueBlue points you've earned as of June 3, 2008,** you're on your way to redeeming your next Award Flight." Sending some e-mails automatically to yourself can help reduce the possibility of embarrassing transaction e-mails.

Why are so many transactional e-mails sent as text?

Talk to any e-mail marketer, and she will agree that HTML messages are more productive than text messages. So why does her company send transactional messages as text? The answer is usually that the text messages come about because of a complex organizational problem typical of many large corporations today.

If you study Exhibit 13-05, you can begin to see the problems. Catalog telesales' software, for example, is connected directly to the shipping department, which ships the orders. The shipping department

EXHIBIT 13-05 Example of a transactional e-mail delivery systems

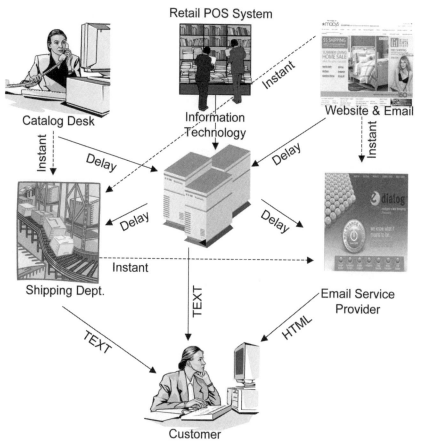

sends a transactional e-mail, which is usually text and normally can't easily include cross-sales.[3] The alternative is for the order to go through IT to the ESP, which can send out an HTML e-mail. But in many cases, IT has database update schedules that result in slow message delivery. IT typically updates the data warehouse on a monthly or weekly basis—very seldom daily or more often.

The same type of problem occurs with online orders placed via e-mail or a Web site. These order channels often have to go through IT to the shipping department. This can result in a text message rather than an HTML message and a warning not to respond, since the shipping department isn't set up to receive and respond to e-mails.

Making the changes necessary to get out instant HTML e-mails that include relevant promotional copy (and that can accept customer responses) usually requires cultural and political shifts within the or-

EXHIBIT 13-06 An ideal transactional e-mail delivery system

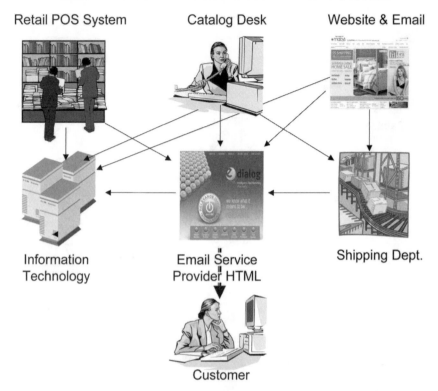

Retail POS System   Catalog Desk   Website & Email

Information Technology   Email Service Provider HTML   Shipping Dept.

Customer

ganization. IT has to accept that messages should go out instantly and that all messages will come from the ESP, not from IT or the shipping departments.

It sounds simple, but in many cases it isn't. To accomplish personalized, dynamic, cross-sale transactional e-mails requires leadership from the marketing department. In many companies, the e-mail function is at such a low level in the organizational structure, that getting the various parties, particularly IT, to listen and accept change is almost impossible. The results outlined in this book that some companies achieve with transactional e-mails can come about only if there is effective leadership in the marketing department.

Fortunately, this situation is changing. Many large corporations have realized the importance of e-mail marketing and have dedicated senior level resources to oversee it. Successful retailers have streamlined this entire process. Shipping departments send electronic messages to the ESPs, which send HTML and can respond to customer inquiries, as depicted in Exhibit 13-06.

To start with, all transactional messages should be sent by the ESP in HTML or multipurpose Internet mail extensions (MIME) format to view on a PC or on a handheld device. To accomplish, this many companies will have to reorganize their e-mail processing procedures similar to this diagram. IT will remain in the loop, of course, but not as a delaying factor. The shipping department won't send e-mails to customers but will send electronic notices to the ESP.

To ensure that all transactional e-mails include a next best product (NBP), a standard administration section, and other features, marketing will need to set up a transactional e-mail template.

E-mails from offline transactions

Now that you know how profitable transactional e-mails can be, you should generate as many as you can. If you have offline sales (retail, wholesale, or catalog), try to capture an e-mail address from each transaction. Your stores' POS system should be set up to accept customer e-mail addresses. Store clerks and call center staff should be offered incentives to ask customers for their e-mail addresses "so we can get in touch with you to let you know if there is any problem with your order" or another valid, helpful reason. If every e-mail address generated from an offline sale is worth $11 to $26 in increased revenue, you can afford to reward any customer contact staff member with at least $5 per e-mail—or give the reward to the customer.

A poorly done transactional e-mail

Now that you know the rules, let's examine a few actual e-mails to find out the right way and the wrong way to do them. Here is a particularly bad e-mail that makes about every mistake in the book. This is an actual e-mail from a large retailer; only the retailer's name was changed. Errors in this message are shown by numbers in brackets, like this: [1].

Dear Valued Customer, [1]

Thank you for placing your order with BillBracket.com. We are currently processing your order 64854019. In-stock item(s) will arrive within 7-10 days [2]. Please add one business day for orders placed after 3:00 p.m. Pacific time [3] and for gift-wrapped [4] or inseamed items [5].

Monogrammed Items: If you ordered an embroidered item, please add one business day to your delivery timeframe [6].

For engraved items, please allow an additional eight to nine days.[7]
For more information, <u>click here</u>.

The status of your items is listed below:

Item name Qty. Size Color Status

Carpenter Jeans, Regular 1 34/30 Med. In Stock OES

Casual Chinos Nano-Tex®—Regular 1 34 Khaki Avail. 12/07/07

If you haven't already, sign up today for a personal Bill Bracket Login Account and you can track this order, plus all future orders![8] (Please note: it may take a day for order status to become available.)

We look forward to your next visit,

Customer Service, [9] Bill Bracket, Inc.BillBracket.com

Check out our new arrivals and find great savings at Bill-Bracket.com. [10] [11]

The errors

[1] This is about an actual order, so Bill Bracket knows the customer's name and should have used it. Also, the e-mail is in text, not HTML.

[2]How does the customer know if the item is in stock or not? Bill Bracket has a computer and a database that is creating this transactional e-mail. The computer has the information about what is in stock at the time the e-mail is sent. If it isn't in stock, the text should say that and tell the customer when it will arrive. If it is in stock, why mention the nonproblem and get the customer worried?

[3] Why should the customer have to know or worry about what the Pacific time was when his order was placed? Bill Bracket's computer knows that and should have added the time to the message automatically.

[4] The item was not ordered gift wrapped, so this sentence should not have appeared.

[5] What is an inseamed item? Why should the customer have to know this and do the arithmetic in his head?

[6] There was no monogramming ordered, so why bring this problem up?

[7] There was no engraving ordered, so why bring this problem up?

[8] The customer has already signed up for a Bill Bracket account. This sentence makes it clear that Bill Bracket doesn't realize this, which isn't good customer relations.

[9] Here was a chance to make the message personal with the name of a customer service rep who was sending the message, someone the customer might identify with and contact if he wanted to.

[10] This was made on the Web site. Why not thank him for using the site, instead of implying he isn't aware of its existence?

[11]Where are the cross-sale suggestions? This was a wasted opportunity. Moreover, the e-mail suggests that the customer go to the site to buy more, but there's no link to the site, not to mention the order was placed on the site.

A good transactional e-mail uses the computer to do the math, to figure everything out, and to present the customer with the complete picture. Customers shouldn't have to do math in their heads or worry about problems that don't exist with their order. Finally, the transactional e-mail should be used for cross sales.

Excellent transactional copy that fails to produce revenue

The following e-mail message has everything, including phone numbers for the insurance company and the service company. It even has a map to show the customer how to get to the service company. However, the message was sent as text, not HTML. There was no reference to what else Liberty Mutual or Safelite has to offer. The cross sales from this e-mail are probably close to zero.

Ms. Williams
LIBERTY MUTUAL INSURANCE
Service Confirmation

Thank you for your recent call to LIBERTY MUTUAL GLASS SERVICE with services provided by Safelite Solutions. This e-mail serves as confirmation that a claim has been reported. You have requested services to be provided by GIANT GLASS.

Your confirmation number is 116653 and your claim number is 0092348300001.

GIANT GLASS will replace your WINDSHIELD for your 2002 HONDA

CIVIC 4 DOOR SEDAN. There is no deductible due at the time of service.

Should you need to change your appointment, please contact our customer service representatives, 24/7, at 800-567-5568. Please have your confirmation number 116653 available when making the call.

Thank you for allowing us to serve you.

LIBERTY MUTUAL INSURANCE and Safelite Solutions

Customer Information—Please correct any information that is in error. If you make any corrections, **click here** to update your record.
Customer Name: Jane Williams
E-mail Address: jane.williams@company.com
Home Phone: 444-444-4444
Work Phone: 555-555-5555
Address: 131 Hartwell Avenue
City/State/Zip: Lexington, MA 02421

Service Information
Shop: GIANT GLASS
Shop Phone: 555-688-8211
Address: 1000 OSGOOD ST (map)
City/State/Zip: NORTH ANDOVER, MA 01845

Vehicle Information
Insurance Claim: Yes
Service Area: 02021
Make/Model: HONDA CIVIC 2002
Service Type: In-Shop
Glass: WINDSHIELD

Danger: IDs and passwords

One of the most annoying aspects of e-mail marketing is the use of customer IDs and passwords. Many subscribers are lost every year because they can't remember their ID on a Web site that they are revisiting. Even more are lost because of the password problem: subscribers click on the link that asks "Forgot your ID or Password" and wait and wait and wait for an e-mail to arrive. They get tired of waiting and you have lost them forever. One problem with this system is that their e-mail client is somewhere else on their PC, so they have to leave your site to view your responding e-mail. How can you deal with this?

One answer is to find a way to send responses to such calls for help instantaneously. But really you should first ask yourself, "Why do we have to have IDs and passwords? What do we gain from this?" Come up with a good answer, or drop the idea. You already know what you lose from having IDs and passwords—many of your subscribers.

If you have to have an ID, the best ID is the subscriber's e-mail. Use that, and that alone, and you can't go wrong. If you have to have a password, make sure you respond to a forgotten password request within a few seconds of receiving the request. If you wait as long as two minutes, you may lose many subscribers forever. Nothing is more annoying than waiting and waiting for a password that never seems to come.

Change of e-mail address

E-mail marketers typically lose 30% to 50% of their subscribers' e-mail addresses every year. Part of this is due to list churn. But a lot of it due to a poor address-change procedure (or no procedure). If you don't make it easy for subscribers to change their addresses, you will lose many of them. You will be throwing away the money you spent to acquire them, plus their future revenue.

Many, if not most, e-mail newsletters today have no obvious way for subscribers to update their e-mail addresses. Some simply say: "If you'd rather not receive this newsletter in the future, click here," without any reference to a possible address change.

Include a link in the admin section in every e-mail that says, "Update your preferences or change your e-mail address.". When subscribers click this link, they see their current e-mail address and their preferences and the ability to change either or both.

After they hit the "submit" button, send them to a landing page that says their changes have been received and they will receive a confirmation by e-mail. Next, send a confirmation e-mail to the new address within a few seconds to make sure it was entered correctly and to confirm any other details the subscriber might have changed. At this time, thank them for making the change and, if possible, reward them with a coupon for a discount or with a download.

Excellent transaction messages

Some marketers are really using transactional messages right. Here is how W Hotels communicated using HTML with a guest.

Two weeks before the stay: it sent an e-mail from the hotel's manager asking if anything could be done during the upcoming stay to make it extra special. The message offered a range of services, including dinner reservations and in-room massages. The tone used was excited.

One week before the stay, the hotel sent an e-mail with a 360° view of the room.

During stay, it sent e-mails sent asking if the customer needed assistance with anything.

Finally, after the stay, W Hotels sent an e-mail from the hotel manager saying thanks and asking for recommendations on improving the overall service. The message contained a survey, asking for overall level of satisfaction.

Delta has an unusually helpful method of contacting passengers about to take a scheduled flight. The e-mail is loaded with helpful links. Here's the copy:

> Want to know what the weather is like in Nashville, Tennessee?
>
> Also, did you know we've added a new flight notification service at delta.com—Delta Messenger—to update you about any flight changes or cancellations. Now you can stay in touch while on the go by:
>
> Choosing the channel: Tell us if you prefer to be contacted via e-mail, phone, mobile device or all three.
>
> Saving your preferences: You only need to enroll in Delta Messenger once. Then, we'll automatically contact you via your preferred method when there is a change to any of your future Delta flights.
>
> Thanks for choosing Delta; we're looking forward to seeing you.
>
> How to—Change your Subscription: click on Profile.
>
> How to—Unsubscribe: click on Unsubscribe.

It's wonderful copy, with useful links. Unfortunately, Delta doesn't get an A+ for this one, because the last line said: "This is a post-only e-mail—please do not respond to this message." What a mistake! Why not a link that permits the traveler to correspond with someone in Delta?

Finally, here is a good example of a transaction message that has everything, including a call to action and a way of ordering again:

Dear Jane Smith:

We wanted to let you know that your size for the following style has arrived in our warehouse:

MBT M Walk Silver Mesh/Synthetic Leather 39 2/3 (US Women's 9) M

Please note that this notification e-mail is simultaneously being sent to other customers as well, so it is possible that your size may sell out again. To purchase this item now, please click here.

P.S. If by the time you receive this e-mail your size has already sold out, simply click here to be notified when your size becomes available again.

How leading e-mail marketers are using transactions

In 2008, JupiterResearch did an important study of 200 leading e-mail marketers[4]. One question asked what features of transactional messaging they were using and what they planned to use. The results are summarized in Exhibit 13-07.

The fact that only 36% are doing A/B split testing should be a cause for alarm. Such testing really costs nothing to do and can yield very useful results. Only 45% are presenting dynamic content—wow!

EXHIBIT 13-07 Transactional tactics used and planned

Tactic	Currently	Plan Soon	No Plans
HTML and images	71%	15%	14%
cross-sell, upsell offers	53%	31%	16%
Dedicated IP Address	50%	28%	22%
Delivery, performance reporting	45%	33%	22%
Dynamic Content	45%	33%	22%
Cart abandon triggers	41%	35%	24%
Report on transactional messages	39%	36%	25%
A/B Split testing	36%	37%	27%
Accreditation	36%	31%	33%
Message authentication	31%	38%	31%
Sponsorship ads	30%	31%	39%

Question: From this list which transactional e-mail tactics do you use currently, and which do you plan to deploy in the next 12 months? N = 200 e-mail marketers 2008 JupiterResearch
StrongMail E-Mail Marketing Executive Survey 9/08

Where have these marketers been? They have been busy shoveling e-mails out the door without having the time or resources to do a good job or measure whether their efforts are working.

Takeaway thoughts

- Transactional e-mails have very high open rates.
- They are an ideal vehicle for promoting cross sales.
- Transactional e-mails should always be in HTML.
- Every transaction e-mail should have personalization, dynamic content, rapid delivery, integrated text, links to the shopping cart, and flexibility and be CAN-SPAM compliant.
- Cross-sale value can be computed.
- Use the subscriber's e-mail address as an ID and respond immediately to lost-password requests.
- Make it easy for the subscriber to change her e-mail or physical address.

Notes

1. *How Top Retailers Use Transactional Email 2007* (Silverpop, January 17, 2007), www.silverpop.com/Printer/silverpop/practices/studies/-transactional_email/index.html.
2. *The Transactional Messaging Imperative* (New York: JupiterResearch, 2008).
3. You may have a sophisticated HTML writing staffer at your ESP or in your marketing department. It is the rare that a company can afford such a luxury in the shipping or IT department.
4. David Daniels, *The Transactional Messaging Imperative: Capitalizing on the Marketing Opportunity of Transactional Email* (JupiterResearch, October 2008).

14

How to Send Triggered E-mails

The amazing thing about triggered e-mail is that it solves a huge execution problem. Setting up and sending several targeted e-mails takes time and effort. If you automate that process, all you have left to focus on is the actual marketing. Imagine that. By "actual marketing," I'm referring to the testing, content tweaking, and creative effort that goes with driving the right responses. The idea of triggered e-mail is not to set up the process, design your e-mails, and then ignore them. Automating these communications takes the pain of execution off your shoulders, so you can focus on the marketing aspects of these communications.

Chris Baggott, *E-mail Marketing by the Numbers*

A triggered e-mail is sent because of something unique that is happening in the receiver's life that he may (his birthday) or may not (his flight is cancelled) know about. For example, in a conversation between a customer and the old corner grocer, the grocer might start out by saying, "How's your boy doing?" knowing the customer's son just started high school. This is different from starting the conversation with, "We're having a sale on smoked ham today." Both are good starts for a dialogue, but the first is triggered by something the grocer knew about his customer. Conversation openers like the first one produced customer loyalty. Today's e-mail marketers tend to fall for openers like the second one. These modern openers may help sell smoked ham, but they don't create loyalty.

"But how," you might ask, "can we learn the kind of personal information about a million subscribers that the corner grocer knew about his 200 customers? We are running a large enterprise here. This is not a corner grocery store!"

It isn't as difficult as it might seem. Using modern e-mail and database marketing techniques, we can develop information to create relevant triggers for e-mails the same way the grocer did: by listening to the customer. Marketers set their systems up to listen for Web visits, registration and preference forms, downloads, and transactions. These events are stored in the subscriber's database record.

Capture a lot of customer events and study them. With experience, you can come up with appropriate conversation openers to match just about any event—just as the grocer used to do with his customers. You then develop business rules configured within the software that takes any event and turns it into a conversation, just as the airlines have done with flight departures.

Trigger types

The transactional trigger

Figure out what the typical transactions are for your business that deserve a message. Certainly asking the customer to rate the product and the purchasing experience should come high on your list.

The Apple stores in the UK offer its customers a choice of a paper or an e-mail receipt for their store purchases. What a wonderful way to capture e-mail addresses and send out a triggered message that is sure to be opened! The clerk asks for your e-mail address so he can send you the receipt. The receipt is, of course, part of the opt-in process.

The pre-event trigger

They bought tickets to a ball game, conference, concert, or Broadway show. The show is three days away. An e-mail reminding them of the event with a map will always be opened. Will the event sponsors be selling T-shirts or CDs at the event? Sell them online in the e-mail to save them time (and ensure they get the one they want!). If you know your customer is going on a trip, a "bon voyage" e-mail will often have an 80% open rate.

In B2B, conference organizers typically provide a preshow attendee list to sponsors. If the list includes e-mails, you have an ideal business audience you know is traveling to the conference. A message asking if the attendee wants to receive e-mails from you—with an idea of what business services you could provide—could be ethical and produce response.

The event trigger

This message reminds attendees of an upcoming flight, a scheduled Webinar, live seminars, or other public events. You can set up a series of messages that are planned in advance.

If you have set up status levels for your customers (e.g., silver, gold, and platinum) with special services and rewards for those who reach each level, you can always get your triggered e-mails opened by mentioning their status. For example, you can announce when the customer has reached a magic threshold. Harrah's, for instance, tells its customers when they are "only one visit away from our Total Diamond reward level." Airlines can do the same thing for people who come close to becoming gold in any given year.

The post-transaction/event survey trigger

After any event or purchase, a satisfaction survey will almost always be opened. Find out how customers liked the product and the purchase process. Get a testimonial if you can, and put it on your Web site and in future e-mails (see chapter 11 for more on customer ratings). While you have their attention, now is the time for some direct listening and selling (more on that later in this chapter). Your first objective should be to get permission for further e-mails, if you don't already have it. The second is to suggest another product that might have a relationship to the one just purchased.

The operational trigger

Operational triggers include double-opt-in notices, password notifications, profile updates, and software updates. Operational triggers can include credit card expiration notices, shipping notices, and customer service responses. Other functions include welcome messages for new customers. Most of these operational triggers will almost always be opened. Make sure you put some personalized promotion *below the fold*.

Exhibit 14-01 is a renewal notice for an old membership. Membership triggers can be tied to other membership statuses as well, such as a monthly statement, loyalty program messages, and length of customer status.

The reminder trigger

These are event triggers based on a key date or the customer's profile. They include birthday reminders, anniversary reminders, wedding reminders, and notices of friends' birthdays.

A birthday is usually an excellent trigger with a very high opening rate. Many companies offer something free on the subscriber's birthday: a dessert, 25% off, or another suitable gift that gets the birthday girl to come in to claim her gift. Baskin Robbins offers ice cream, as

EXHIBIT 14-01 Membership renewal trigger

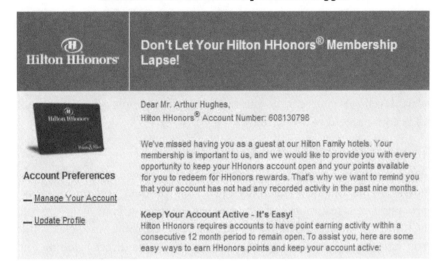

does Safeway. Many restaurants offer a free meal if the birthday boy is accompanied by at least one paying guest.

This should be a standard trigger for any retailer, a trigger sure to be opened. Birthday messages can be personal and provide recognition (see Exhibit 14-04).

EXHIBIT 14-02 Birthday triggered e-mail

Birthday triggers don't have to be confined to the subscriber's birthday, either. Here's one from Woot:

> **Happy Woot Birthday** this month! No, not your regular birthday—the day you signed up for a Woot account. The anniversary is this month. Chances are your so-called friends won't even realize this occasion is happening, much less get you any presents. So here's a gift from your true friends at Wine.Woot to ease the pain.
>
> During this month—and this month only—you may enter the coupon code NEMATIC for $4.98 off shipping on your Woot winery-direct order. It'll only work once, so use it wisely. But don't wait too long. Once we turn the page on our calendar to next month, you won't be able to use it any more.

The sales-cycle trigger

These are event-triggered messages that begin with interest in a product. Triggers can be follow-up messages, product notifications, or information requests. These e-mails get opened because they are related to the rest of the sales process and customers' needs. The customer owns product X 4.0, and release 5.0 just became available. You can send a message letting the customer know 5.0 is available.

The fare-tracking trigger

Many Internet travel sites offer a system that tracks airfares and signals you when a fare matches your ballpark price. Fare Alert allows users to track an unlimited number of trip itineraries and receive e-mail notification when the fare meets or beats a traveler's specified price. Orbitz.com, Expedia, Travelocity, and Kayak offer something similar.

Can these alerts replace spending time on multiple Web sites looking for the right trip price yourself? Carol Sottili tested five sites and found that none "could totally replace a few solid hours of self-directed hunting." But they are a great example of triggered e-mails. Whether it is worth using these sites depends on what you think your personal time spent hunting fares is worth.

The pre-catalog trigger

Catalogers have learned that sending a triggered e-mail announcing the imminent arrival of a paper catalog boosts sales by as much as 18% over just sending the catalog alone. The e-mail can feature the cover of the catalog and have a subject line like, "Look in your mailbox: Exposures catalog." The effectiveness of pre-catalog e-mails has been public knowledge for the past several years, but less than 5% of catalogers use them. Why? We suspect it is because in most companies, catalogs and call centers are in separate departments from Web sites and e-mails. Too bad for them.

The behavioral trigger

Your goal is to match behavior, purchases, actions, and subscriber profiles with a series of customized communications. This is complicated but worth the effort in terms of opens and conversions. If the customer just bought a pair of skis, you might send him an e-mail about ski outfits.

The welcome e-mail

Sending an immediate follow-up to a new subscriber is such an obvious step you might think we are wasting your time telling you do to this. But many well-known and respected companies do a bad job of responding quickly to their new subscribers. According to the EEC's "2006 Retail Email Subscription Benchmark Study," 13% of retailers hadn't sent their first e-mail within three weeks of the subscription date. These delinquent retailers included iTunes, CDW, Sears, 1800flowers, Walgreens, Drs. Foster & Smith, Snap-On, QVC, Sam's Club, Shop.MLB, NFLshop, Niketown, and Reebok.

Welcome e-mails are among the most opened e-mails—second only to purchase-related e-mails. Despite this, many companies fail to use them effectively. A 2008 study by Return Path[1] showed that 60% of companies studied didn't send welcome e-mails at all to new subscribers. Worse, a third of the companies studied failed to send any e-mails of any kind to new subscribers in the 30 days during which the study was conducted. Because of these failures to communicate, many subscribers may forget they subscribed to the e-mail when it does come, making them more likely to hit the "report spam" button. If you wait too long to contact subscribers, you may miss the boat. Subscribers will forget they signed up or will buy from someone else.

In the same study, Return Path found that though 70% of companies asked for more than just an e-mail address at sign-up, three quarters of those who collected the additional information failed to use it to personalize or customize their e-mail messaging.

"It really damages your brand because you're not living up to the expectations you've set," reported Bonnie Malone-Fry, director of strategic services at Return Path. "You've already stated your intentions

EXHIBIT 14-03 Opens and clicks for various types of e-mails

	Opens	Clicks
Welcome E-mails	58%	18.0%
Acquisition E-mails	20%	6.0%
Newsletters	31%	3.5%
Reactivation E-mails	9%	1.8%
Promotional E-mails	9%	0.5%

of making the program more relevant to the subscriber. By not implementing them, there's a huge disappointment factor."

When they get there, however, welcome e-mails are the most opened and the most clicked, as seen in Exhibit 14-03.

Airlines and triggered e-mails

Have you taken a plane lately? If you look around, you will notice that perhaps half of the passengers arrive with boarding passes printed on their home computers. Airlines are sending e-mails to passengers before their flights, encouraging them to do this. Passengers can more quickly check in and frequently pick their seats. They don't have to wait in line for the boarding pass machines. They can directly check their bags or, even better, proceed to security as soon as they get to the airport if they have no bags to check, saving 5 to 15 minutes. It is a great idea that saves passengers and the airline time.

Airlines also save real money, from paper costs to personnel, when their passengers check in online from home. US Airways offered 1,000 bonus miles to anyone who checked in online. The airlines would really like to see everyone start doing this routinely.

Sending travelers e-mails on the day of departure to get them to check in early is an excellent example of a triggered e-mail—a really valuable e-mail service that gets opening rates in the high 90s as opposed to the industry's average of 16% (as discussed in chapter 3). If you can get your subscribers to open your e-mail, that is half the battle.

Boarding passes on cell phones

Continental Airlines passengers in Houston can board flights using just a cell phone or PDA. Instead of a paper pass, Continental and the Transportation Security Administration (TSA) let passengers show a code the airline sends by e-mail to their cell phone or PDA. A TSA screener will confirm the barcode's authenticity with a handheld scanner. The TSA says the electronic pass allows screeners to better detect fraudulent boarding passes.

Air Canada also offers paperless boarding passes on cell phones. The number of fliers using the new procedure doubled each week after Air Canada launched the option. Delta and US Airways soon after developed plans to follow suit.

How airlines use triggered e-mails

A survey of airline triggered e-mails showed how some are using this medium. Delta followed the purchase of a day pass to the Crown Room with a series of e-mails offering trial membership and ability to apply the price of the day pass to the cost of annual membership. US Airways allowed newly reactivated lapsed flyers to recover miles frozen due to inactivity or to trade up to a higher-priority tier in their frequent-flyer program. And American Airlines sends flyers who redeem their miles an offer to purchase additional miles to "reach that next trip."

These triggered e-mails tend to strengthen the personal link between the airline and its members. Each is a message that the traveler recognizes as being uniquely targeted to him

A welcome airline trigger

Dear Lloyd,

Thank you for flying with JetBlue Airways on flight #1218 from Buffalo on May 06, 2008. We apologize that the DIRECTV® was inoperable during your flight.

As a gesture of apology and goodwill, we have issued each customer on your flight a $15 JetBlue electronic Voucher. The Voucher is for you and is nontransferable. JetBlue Vouchers are valid for one year and can be applied towards airfare on JetBlue Airways reservations.

When you are ready to use your Voucher, please visit our Web site at www.jetblue.com. You will have the option to apply your Voucher, using the information below, during the payment portion of your reservation. You may also call 1-800-JETBLUE (538-2583) with your confirmation number D1IJCF for this flight. Please visit our Web site's Help section for more information on how to use your Voucher.

This is an excellent example of e-mail's power to build lasting relationships with customers. It is personal. It recognizes that the service given was not as good as it should have been. It provides a gift that has

EXHIBIT 14-04 Trigger measurements

Triggered E-mails Weight 20%

3	Complex trigger with multiple branching
2	Based on business rules following single path
1	Automated by single business rule
0	Manually executed

real value, as opposed to a simple apology. It encourages the customer to come back.

Triggered e-mails create relevance

Triggered e-mails are important to success with relevance. Triggering amounts to 20% of the total relevance score (see Exhibit 14-04). So figuring out how to trigger e-mails based on a subscriber's lifestyle and events can really pay off in terms of relevance. As a first step, have a brainstorming session to list events that would rate an e-mail in subscribers' minds. Next, figure out how you can easily capture the information needed and store it in your database to support the triggers. Finally, develop business rules to scan the database nightly to yield the occasions for an automatic trigger.

Triggers are so personalized to individuals' lives that we can't possibly have time to create them one by one. We set up the business rules, and they go out automatically, day after day. But be sure you have built in enough daily seeds so you can ensure you aren't sending out ridiculous triggers.

Serious direct listening

Your subscriber is signed up for your e-mails. What's next? It's time for some serious direct listening. You can send an e-mail asking for a few vital pieces of information that will enable you to send triggered e-mails from now on. What kind of questions can you ask? Sears has one of the best sets of questions on the Internet today:

How I feel about brands:
1. I typically buy top-of-the-line brand products.
2. I buy name-brand products at a moderate price.
3. I am always looking for a bargain. I will try any brand if the price is right.

How I feel about technology:
1. I buy products with the latest features and technology.
2. I buy products with mainstream features and technology.
3. I am not interested in technology. Keep it simple for me.

The answers to these questions can dictate your triggered e-mails for months to come. Most e-mail blasts are created by the marketing folks around the idea of pushing some product at a discount. They assume that everyone checks the third boxes in the Sears example. Wrong. Some people do, of course. For those consumers, feature your low price.

But there are many consumers who would check the first box on both questions. They are early adopters. They have the resources, and they want the latest and best. To get these consumers to open your e-mails, your message has to let them know that this e-mail is about a new and interesting name-brand product. Don't even mention the price in your subject line or opening copy to these folks.

And what do you offer to people who check the middle boxes? These people want to go with the herd. What their neighbors will think of the purchase is more important to them than what they paid for it. They want to buy the products everyone else is buying. Here the message is the overwhelming demand for this product. They are in luck that you still have one or two left in stock. That was the philosophy that sold millions of iPods.

Automatic triggering of e-mails

Once a customer has opened an HTML e-mail, you can track what she does while she is reading it. Does she open and click? Which topic does she click on? You can set up a system to automatically send an e-mail based on what she does on your site. For instance, if she puts something in her shopping cart, then abandons the cart, you can send an instant e-mail offering to help her make a decision on the items in her cart. E-loan uses automated e-mails to remind prospects to complete their online mortgage applications or their auto-loan forms. These two types of automated e-mails produced a 300 percent lift in response over a control group. E-loan recaptured a significant number of loans through this process.

Increasingly, marketers are uniting Web analytics with automatic triggered messages to reach potential buyers while they are thinking about a purchase. In this case, e-mail recipients are choosing when the time is right, rather than company marketers. Other examples of such triggered messages include:

- **Incomplete actions:** when the recipient has clicked through but not bought anything; send a campaign offering free delivery for this week only.

- **Reactivations:** when registered consumers haven't opened their e-mails for months; send a "have we upset you?" message with an incentive.

- **Cross-selling:** when people have bought within the last day or two; point them toward complementary products (see chapter 19 for more on next best products).

Triggered e-mail marketing isn't that complicated to set up. The important part is to think through, in advance, what follow-up promotions would be relevant and effective. For example, a gift retailer created a follow-up campaign for everyone who had abandoned her cart over a three-day period with some excellent results. It saw a 50% open rate, of which 50% clicked through to the site and of which 53% converted. This is an overall sales rate of 13.25% for the outgoing e-mails—which is a high level to achieve for any e-mail marketer. The ROI of abandoned shopping cart e-mails makes this marketing method imperative for almost any marketer today.

Advance delivery messaging: the cell phone connection

The Radicati Group expects the mobile e-mail market to grow to $27 billion in 2011[2]. Seventy percent of mobile devices are predicted to be smartphones by 2010. Mobile network carriers are pushing Internet service heavily to improve revenue. Although Internet use is limited to less than 10% of the mobile-device population today, 47% of those who have them use them to access and respond to e-mail.

JupiterResearch estimates that by 2011, 54% of European mobile users will access the Internet on a regular basis. Internet use among US consumers is still very low, but that gap is expected to close rapidly. Why? Consumers have discovered that e-mails on their cell phones can be really useful when they are on the road. Better to get the message while they are traveling rather than miss it and find out about something important after the trip is over.

Because a cell phone is quite different from a PC, marketers should send messages in MIME format to make sure they work well on both

PCs and cell phones. Ask your subscribers if they receive e-mail on their cell phones. Once you know this, you can segment and personalize their messages. Design special messages just for mobile users, such as this one:

> Dear Miss Williams,
>
> When you're juggling a busy life, it's easy to lose track of where you're meant to be, and when. Luckily, our new text message reminder means one thing you don't need to worry about is your Ocado delivery.
>
> A few hours before your groceries are due to arrive, we'll drop you a text message to remind you that we're on our way. We'll also tell you the van registration number and the name of your driver for a little extra peace of mind. And talking of peace, don't worry if you have an early delivery—we'll never send you a text message before 8 am.
>
> So, we might not be able to help you remember your sister's birthday or when to put the bins out, but we can make sure you never forget your shopping again. Well, it beats tying a knot in your hanky, doesn't it?
>
> Tell us what you think by e-mailing demandmore@mailocado.com.

Be sure to give mobile users control of message frequency, however, to avoid angry backlash.

Once you have set up a mobile e-mail program, you can make it a special feature of your brand. If you do this right, you can gain subscribers who are anxious to sign up for triggered messages on their cell phones.

Check trigger accuracy

E-mail campaigns are always checked for accuracy before they are sent out, but triggers are another story. These individual e-mails are sent out every day, automatically, without anyone reviewing them. Over time, however, errors can creep in to your triggered e-mails without anyone realizing it. For example, the e-mail may offer a product or service that is no longer available. A link may have become defunct. The copy may mention an out-of-date event.

How can you make sure that millions of triggered e-mails are correct? Create a seed list for triggered e-mails when they are first set up. Make sure the seed recipients look in their inboxes and check the messages for validity. Since triggered e-mails get opened more often than almost any other e-mail, you *must* make sure they are correct.

Bad trigger e-mails

Adam Tosh got an e-mail alerting him to the upcoming schedule for the University of Portland's men's basketball team. What interested Tosh was the fact that the triggered e-mail was prompting him to buy tickets for a game that had happened the night before the e-mail was sent. Worse, he received this same e-mail at two different addresses.

Tosh also received an e-mail from Ticketmaster telling him that "The ticket(s) you ordered on March 01, 2008 for SEATTLE MARINERS have been printed! They will be shipped to you shortly via US Mail." Tosh noted: "This appears to be a friendly reminder e-mail, with decent personalization, and a reassuring status update that told me 'As of March 24, 2008 this e-mail represents the most current status of your order.'" The problem with the e-mail? He had received the tickets two weeks before the e-mail arrived. "I have to ask," said Tosh, "What exactly was Ticketmaster printing and shipping to me shortly?"

Good trigger e-mails

What follows are three examples of good trigger messages.

Your flight 340 to San Francisco will be delayed by four hours, Mr. Sweetser. We sincerely regret this inconvenience to you. There are several earlier flights with available seating. Click here to get automatically rebooked.

This is a reminder, Mr. Hughes, that you have purchased seats C 13-14 for the performance of Verdi's La Traviata tonight at Lyric Opera of Chicago at 20 North Wacker Drive at 8:00 PM. Click here to print out your tickets, or you can use this e-mail to pick up your tickets at the Reserved Seats window in the lobby

Mr. Sweetser: your prepaid air time on your Boost Mobile phone now stands at 16 minutes. Click here to automatically add 200 minutes to your air time using the credit card you have on file with us.

Why are these good triggers? They are personal. They are timely. They are very worth reading by the subscriber who receives them. They boost customer loyalty and your open rate. If all your e-mails were as good as these, you would have no trouble keeping your subscribers and getting them to read all of your e-mails.

Takeaway thoughts

- Triggered e-mails are sent based on presumed events or subscriber preferences.
- To trigger an e-mail, you need information.
- Direct information comes from the customer in a preference form.
- Indirect information comes from examining the various purchases, Web visits, and transactions that reveal what your customers are thinking about.
- Triggered e-mails get open rates of up to 90%, compared to promotional e-mails, whose open rates hover around 13%.
- A welcome e-mail should be sent to a subscriber within seconds of the subscriber's clicking the "submit" button.
- Other useful triggered e-mails are abandoned carts, store receipts, status-level changes, satisfaction surveys, pre-event reminders, birthdays, catalog arrival, airline check-in, and gift reminders.
- If triggered e-mail aren't watched closely, they can soon get out of date.
- Triggered e-mails are among the most powerful messages you can send. There are small numbers of them, but they off a big ROI.

Notes

1. Bonnie Malone-Fry, "Research Study: Creating Great Subscriber Experiences," *Email Marketing Water Cooler* (Return Path, June 3, 2008), http://www.returnpath.net/blog/2008/06/research-study-creating-great.php.
2. Ken Magill, "Pivotal Veracity Unveils Mobile E-mail Optimization Tool," *Direct* magazine (January 22, 2008), http://directmag.com/email/news/pivotal_veracity_mobile_email_tool_0122/.

15

Interactivity: Make Each E-mail an Adventure

> In face-to-face conversation, you can see if you're holding someone's attention. Is your audience rolling their eyes or glancing at their watches? Or are they smiling and nodding enthusiastically? E-mail interaction gives you the same kind of insight. That sort of trackability is what makes it very different from a postcard or television. Best of all, with e-mail, your constituents can talk back to you. It's as easy as hitting the reply button. When was the last time you were able to talk back to a commercial and have your voice heard? Exactly. You can even take e-mail interaction to the next level by adding forms and surveys.
>
> Chris Baggott, *E-mail Marketing by the Numbers*

Marketing e-mails are both a complement to and a substitute for direct mail. In most ways e-mails are better than direct mail: they cost a fraction of what direct mail costs ($6 per thousand instead of $600[1]) and are delivered four times faster (half a day instead of two days). You can find out what people do with your e-mails (opening, clicking, registering, voting, and buying), which you can't tell with conventional offline direct mail (except for buying, of course). E-mails can be much more interesting through the use of rich media, such as video and audio, and therefore interactive and engaging. From the message, readers should be able to take surveys, research, buy products, ask questions, get answers, and respond to the sender. Done right, marketing e-mails are really wonderful. Few companies are exploiting their full potential. This chapter will tell you how to do this.

What is an interactive e-mail?

Interactivity involves two-way communications. The communication may take the form of data, video, or audio. Instead of remaining passive, the reader becomes an active participant within the experience. Interactive e-mails get the reader doing something. The process helps maintain reader interest and get reader input. Interactivity refers to the degree to which a person can make choices within an e-mail. These choices are based on the rules built into the e-mail. It's also a measure of user influence. The higher the degree of interactivity, the more influence the user has on the form and course of an e-mail.

A good interactive e-mail is very personalized and relevant to the recipient. If the reader is someone already on your customer database, what he sees when he opens an e-mail derives some of its content from his database record or profile. When the marketer uses profile data, the reader is welcomed to the e-mail by the use of his name wherever appropriate—not just in the initial greeting.

What you can do with interactivity

Within an e-mail, you can let the reader:

- Download a report, whitepaper, or manual
- Forward the e-mail to a friend
- Reply to the e-mail
- Find a definition or background information on any subject in the e-mail
- See and complete a form to order a product or to register for e-mails
- See a video, a photo, or an article on the subject
- Go to a Web site
- Take a quiz or a preference survey or vote on an issue

Measuring interactivity

Fifteen percent of the total relevance score is represented by interactivity as explained in chapter 5. The more links you have, the more relevant your e-mails will be to your subscribers.

EXHIBIT 15-01 Measuring criteria for relevance with interactivity

Interactivity	Description	Weight 15%
3	Customer provides preferences, surveys, viral	
2	Limited to purchase or simple question clicks	
1	At least one click	
0	No form of interaction with customer involved	

The importance of linking

Perhaps we should have called this chapter "How to make your e-mails seem short," because that is a distinguishing feature of a really good interactive e-mail. In direct mail copy, nonprofits have found that they got more donations from a 6- or 12-page letter than from a one-page letter. The opposite seems to be true with e-mails, with this exception: to be convincing to a reader, you *do* need a lot of content, but most of it should be on your Web site or a landing page. When a reader first opens the e-mail, she thinks, "Oh, this is a short and easy read. I'll see what it says." While reading the short e-mail, if she has questions or wants to know more, she clicks on a link, which takes her to a Web page with additional content. In a good interactive e-mail, 90% of the total content is accessed by a link rather than actually in the e-mail. Links are the secret to interactivity. They are a wonderful way to get the user actively involved in your e-mail. Instead of just reading it, the reader is now clicking on links.

The other reason for adding links to an e-mail is the direct relationship between clicks and sales. The more recipients click on your e-mails, the more they end up converting and buying. Why is this? Who knows; it is a fact of life. It is like having a conversation with your customers. Why did the old corner grocers chat with their customers? Because they knew that chats build loyalty, which builds sales. This is still true today. So fill your e-mails with interesting links and valuable, relevant content to encourage clicking.

However, there is such a thing as too many links. Moderation is key! Consumers are savvy and understand when they are being pushed into clicking or engaging with something they may not want. Offer links to promote interactivity, but conservatively and within reason. Let readers make the decision to engage. It's as if the grocer chatted with his customers every day, but every time he did he talked about something else he thought they should buy. Ugh! Enough with that.

How do you let readers know there is a valuable link present? Besides the industry practice of underlining them, use wording such as, "Click here to see a client list."

The effect of having lots of links

E-mails with lots of links get more reader interest than e-mails with less links, according to MailerMailer. Analyzing 300 million e-mails sent in 3,200 campaigns in 2007, it found that e-mails with more than 20 links were clicked many more times than e-mails with few links (see Exhibit 15-02).

EXHIBIT 15-02 Clicks as a percentage of e-mails with varying numbers of links.

	Percent Clicks
1-5 Links	1.82%
6-10 Links	1.46%
11-20 Links	2.18%
21+ Links	3.84%

Putting a lot of links in an e-mail takes time and adds complexity to the overall production aspect. But it pays off in terms of reader interest. And that, after all, is what we are trying to accomplish in sending marketing e-mails: stimulating and gaining response.

> The thing about interactive media is that it's just that: interactive. That is, the media is designed and built to allow people to do things and to get results from those actions. I used to work with a phenomenal creative director who, back in 1998, said: "Every click is a wish." What an amazing line. It reminds us that every time someone presses down on that mouse button, she's expecting something great to happen, and the best sites are the ones that deliver on that wish.—Gary Stein, Director of Strategy, Ammo Marketing

Case study: Sears

Sears created a "Sears Football Challenge" in their Columbus Day Sale promotional newsletter. The winners won an expensive Sony Home Theatre System. Registrants each week got an e-mail with a code word needed to enter to add more players to their fantasy team. The more players, the more points you earned. The users with the most points each week earned prizes. They created an entire microsite around the promotion that was actually fun. They did a good job of merchandising on the site that was not intrusive. I had a crappy team, but I kept playing each week (and visiting the Sears site) in hopes that I would do better. What Sears did well with this promotion:

- Fun, interactive microsite
- Lots of user engagement
- Method for getting users to return to the site—to check their standing
- Good product placement—Debra Hultberg

Using cookies to interact with your customers

A cookie is simply a piece of text. It isn't a program. It can't do anything. It is placed on your PC by a Web site and is designed so *only* that Web site can retrieve it. A Web site can't make use of any other Web site's cookies to learn any information about you, because it doesn't have a lookup table that would correspond to any other Web site storage system.

A Web site can use cookies in many different ways. For example, it can greet you by name on its site. It can accurately determine how many people actually visit the site. It can find out how many unique visitors arrived, how many were new rather than repeat visitors, and how often a particular visitor comes to the site.

The first time a visitor goes to a site, the site creates a new ID in its database and puts the ID in a cookie, which it places on the visitor's computer. The next time the user visits the site, the site can update the counter associated with that ID in the database and know how many times the visitor has returned. Sites can store also user preferences in the cookie so it can customize the page appearance for each visitor.

Cookies make it possible to keep track of what you are doing while you add items to your shopping cart. Each item you add to your shopping cart is stored in the site's database along with your ID. When you check out, the site knows what's in your cart by retrieving all of your selections from the database. It would be impossible to set up a convenient shopping system on Web sites without cookies.

When a repeat visitor receives one of your e-mails and clicks through to a preference or order form on your site, he will find much of the form's data, such as name, address, phone number, and e-mail address, are already in the appropriate fields. Why? Because he filled out that data on a previous visit to your site, and you were smart enough to use cookies. Because of cookies, if your reader starts to fill out a form but gets distracted and surfs to another Web site, when he returns to the form he will find his previous entries are still there. How can you do that? By saving all entries in a database record as soon as he enters them and putting a cookie on his PC.

Each time the reader enters something on your form, you store information about that entry in his database record, either his existing record if you have one or a newly created record set up at the moment he opens your e-mail.

Interactive e-mails in action

Amazon and Netflix are perhaps the world's experts at interactive communications. On either site, if you click on a movie or a product, the site immediately suggests other movies or products triggered by what you clicked on. A good interactive e-mail can then remember everything you clicked on, via data feeds collected. When you receive your next e-mail or revisit the corresponding Web site later, the marketer hasn't forgotten your expressed interest. Very few digital marketers, however, have mastered that art.

Recalling recent conversations isn't really so unusual in real life. If you have a conversation with a friend about a movie you saw, you would be shocked if the friend couldn't remember this conversation five minutes later. Yet that is the case with 95% of the Web sites and e-mails today. Their short-term and long-term memories are usually nonexistent. Having a memory or measurement-and-tracking program in place is important to successful interactive e-mail and Web site communication strategies.

Planning an interactive e-mail

When planning an interactive e-mail campaign, ask yourself what you want the reader to do when he looks at your e-mail:

- Buy a product
- See something he will want to forward to a friend, thereby adding to your subscriber base
- Complete a survey
- Register for a newsletter
- Learn more about your products, brand, company, services, and so on
- Download a whitepaper or program
- Do research that leads him in a certain direction
- Share an opinion on the product or service

Once you have a plan for where you are going, the e-mail has to be designed with this plan in mind. When you have completed the e-mail design, read and experience it as you expect your readers will do—to see if the finished product actually produces the results you want. In other words, test, test, and test your campaigns.

Basically, each e-mail should be an adventure, an experience that will make the reader think, "Wow! Am I glad I read that." That is a

EXHIBIT 15-03 Kraft Kitchen's interactive e-mail

 **Quick Cheesy Broccoli**

Prepared entirely in the microwave, this side is both savory and tangy.

▶ add to recipe box   🖶 print recipe

> Goes great with:

Slow Cooker BBQ Short Ribs

hard standard to reach every time, but that should be your goal. If that isn't your goal, you shouldn't be in the e-mail marketing business in the first place.

How the experts do interactivity

One of the experts in interactivity is the Kraft Kitchen e-mail program. It combines mouth-watering photos with plenty of interactive options. Exhibit 15-03 shows one example.

The e-mail arrives with eight pictures of food like the one in Exhibit 15-03. Notice how you can add this recipe to your recipe box, print the recipe, or check out the slow-cooker BBQ short ribs recipe, which leads to further interactivity.

The Book of the Month Club (BOMC) has a Web-based service similar to Netflix's. It always ships for free. All bestsellers are $9.95 when you subscribe, and subscribers create a personalized reading list. As a result, BOMC's e-mails are highly personal and interactive. For example: "Because your reading list is empty, you currently have two credits . . . If any of your reading list titles are out of stock or haven't yet been released, the next available title on your reading list will be shipped. If there are no available titles on your reading list, you will miss your scheduled selection and receive a credit."

Blogs' role in interactive e-mails

Most sophisticated e-mail marketers have blogs for their subscribers. These are Web sites where the companies publish news and information, and readers can publically respond to those posts. Netflix, for example, has created the Netflix Community Blog. On the home page, Netflix welcomes subscribers with: "Hello and welcome to the official Netflix Blog! We the blog authors are various members of the Netflix team. We're also rabid movie fans. We hope this will be a great forum for us to talk about what we are doing, and for you to tell us what you think." On the blog are many posts and literally hundreds of comments from subscribers. (For more on blogs, see chapter 10).

Don't waste a reader's time

If you read letters from the 19th century, you'd be impressed by their length. Not so today. Corporations, of course, send us long official letters. Few consumers, however, send letters through the mail bigger than a few words on a postcard or Christmas card. We communicate by phone or short e-mails. We have so much content coming at us today from TV, radio, newspapers, magazines, banner ads, and e-mails that few of us have a moment's peace in the day. Most people realize that our time is very valuable. We hate to have other people waste it.

Therefore, the rule for consumer e-mails is don't do anything that wastes your e-mail readers' time. If they want content, provide plenty of it, but on your site. Make sure your e-mails can be opened within two or three seconds at the most. To accomplish this, the part that opens should be quite small. The text they see should be able to be scanned in a few seconds.

Contests and sweepstakes

Dell had an interesting interactive e-mail to sell its Inspiron line. It began, "Reveal up to $350 in savings." Readers were given a unique mystery savings coupon code in the message. To use it, they clicked a button, entered the coupon code on a landing page, and found out how much they could save. The majority of the offers were 15% off, but a select few were up to 75% off. The coupon codes were randomly assigned to everyone who opened the Dell e-mail. The e-mail's interactive feature made the response higher than a normal Dell promotion.

American Airlines also came up with an innovative e-mail: a sweepstakes tied to its site feature Price and Schedule. To enter the sweepstakes, readers clicked on an e-mail link to go to a Flash page that demonstrated the feature (and that offered a partner message from Alamo) before they could enter the sweepstakes. The Flash piece was so entertaining that readers didn't mind watching it to get to the entry page. The sweepstakes kept the user engaged through the new feature demo. Result: high reader interest and interactivity.

Interactive reader-review request

REI does a good job of engaging its users and encouraging interactivity online and in its stores. For example, at the bottom of the e-mail it offers a weekly sweepstakes to encourage users to enter product reviews. Product reviews are very effective in selling products. With the short section (see Exhibit 15-04) and small sweepstakes, REI accomplished the following goals:

- Generate click-through to the REI site, which could generate incremental sales
- Encourage product reviews from its e-mail list, increasing the e-mail programs interactivity and overall subscriber engagement
- Increase the number of product reviews on its Web site, a driver for on- and offline sales

Get interactive preferences

What are your readers looking for? The easiest way to find out is by asking them. Don't ask too much. That may turn them off. Ask one or two questions per e-mail. If you want subscribers to answer your questions, make it easy for them. Give them a few bullet choices. Then let them know how many other readers clicked that choice.

EXHIBIT 15-04 REI's call for product reviews

To keep the process interactive, send a personalized e-mail thanking them for answering any question in an e-mail—and tell them what you will do with the information. For instance, if subscribers said they prefer aisle seats, tell them that in the future you will try to assign them an aisle seat as a first option. (Then, of course, you have to have a program to follow through on your promise!) A survey plus a thank-you e-mail can start a great relationship with your customers and make your e-mail really interactive.

One way to increase interactivity is to feature in your e-mails the feedback you received from the questions in your previous survey or poll. This will show that you are listening to readers' comments. Including this feedback and your responses can encourage readers to participate. Acting on feedback from your audience will make you stand out from your competitors.

A Bag A Day Game

Piperlime had the innovative interactive Bag A Day Game in its e-mails. Here is how it worked:

1. The subscriber clicks through from the e-mail to a landing page.
2. She clicks on the calendar link to see which bag is being given away each day until the game ends.
3. She registers or logs in and lands on the game page.
4. She clicks "start," and the bags in the grid will start disappearing (see Exhibit 15-05). If the last bag left matches the one being given away that day, she wins.
5. Next, the subscriber is given the opportunity to check off the bags she likes so she can be sent a reminder to play the game on the day her favorite is being given away.
6. On the same page, she is given the opportunity to forward the e-mail to a friend.

One subscriber said, "I LOVE this idea!! I especially like being able to see the calendar of bag giveaways that lets me decide what days I do or don't care about playing. I also don't have to worry about getting an e-mail about it every day if I don't care every day (or at all)."

Does animation pay off?

Fashion retailer Bluefly Inc. conducted an e-mail marketing test on the effect of animated text within a marketing e-mail on e-mail recipients'

EXHIBIT 15-05 Bag-a-day Contest

behavior. The text in question was "Shhhhh," which scrolled across the message. It was a light-hearted approach to promote a private sale for select Bluefly customers, who made up 35% of the e-retailer's e-mail list.[2]

Using Web analytics from Coremetrics, Bluefly had a 5% increase in CTR for recipients of the animated version (25% of the 35% sample) over recipients of the nonanimated version. But more important, shoppers who received the animated e-mail and clicked through generated a 12% increase in dollars spent per thousand e-mails compared with shoppers who received the nonanimated version and clicked through.

As a result of this success, Joellen Nicholson, director of marketing at Bluefly, decided to use the animation in many more e-mails. Nicholson planned to "change the percentage, giving more people the animation. We will use our analytics to see how the metrics play out to a larger group. We want to see if it still holds true, to see if this animation is a clear and distinct winner . . . We use Web analytics extensively, looking at daily, weekly, monthly and quarterly reports to track e-mail performance."

Hidden interactive pricing

Interactivity preferences vary by regions and products. Luxury goods customers may not care so much about the prices they pay. They want the best. That is part of the idea behind Lancel Paris, whose e-mails don't mention the price of the luxury goods displayed. In a recent e-mail, below the picture of a stain-resistant luxury bag was "Demander le prix de ce produit" ("ask the price of this product"). Clicking the picture pops up a box that asks for the subscriber's name and e-mail address (see Exhibit 15-06):

EXHIBIT 15-06 Ask for the price

Seconds later, you receive another e-mail. The e-mail features an image of the product, the price, and several links to:

- See the product's details page on the Web site
- Find the closest boutique
- Sign up for the newsletter
- Browse the Lancel Web site

This is taking exclusivity to a new level—but it works! Lancel Paris is an e-mail marketing farmer that knows its audience.

Some ideas for interactive e-mails

- Instead of saying "click here," have the button tell what it does: "find out more" or "download now."
- Make links look like a headline. Make them as specific as possible: "Enter here to view the article archives."
- Change the color of links when they are clicked: blue for unclicked and purple for clicked is the industry standard. Links should always be underlined, unless they are part of a graphic.

One-click ordering

One way to make your e-mails interactive is to set up a one-click ordering system on your site. The idea is that you store the customer's name, address, e-mail address, and credit card information from previous orders (with customer permission). When she wants to order something else through your site or e-mail, she can do so with one click—after entering her password. No need for her to reenter information. (Of course, you can't call it "One-Click Ordering," as Amazon.com has the copyright on that term.) For your e-mails, make ordering as simple as possible.

Maintaining linked data

Paper catalogs can lie around a consumer's home for months. It isn't unusual for a consumer to order something from a six-month old catalog. Marketing e-mails, on the other hand, have a shelf life of only a couple of days. Our inboxes fill quickly with old messages. We delete them and get on with life. That is no excuse, however, for an e-mail marketer to delete linked content from his Web site unless it is clearly obsolete (e.g., prices that are no longer valid). E-mail readers are encouraged to send interesting content to their friends and relatives. An interesting video, photo, or whitepaper may crop up in someone's inbox days, weeks, or months after its first use. *Don't delete this content.* What does it cost you to keep old articles, whitepapers, or videos? If you do some research, you will find that you can keep most of your old content on a Web site for years for $1.00 per month or less. Why is this important? Let's take an example.

Suppose you run an annual conference. After the conference, you post 50 whitepapers linked to the conference Web site and send the links to your e-mail list. Scores of attendees and others download these papers. A year later, you are preparing for a new conference. In cleaning up your Web site, you delete all those links to last year's conference whitepapers. What a mistake! Without your lifting a finger, search engines have indexed the materials from last year's conference. A Web visitor a year from now will enter a query in Google and find a reference to one of these whitepapers—except that the paper no longer exists on the Web. Or your e-mail has made the rounds and a recipient clicks on a link to read the whitepaper. Either person might have read the paper, seen that it came from your old conference, and decided to register for the new conference. With conference registrations of $1,500 or more, what is the ROI of keeping old data available? Perhaps $1 to $150.

Interactive speaking avatars

SitePal provides an excellent case study of interactivity. It has developed an avatar, a virtual image of a person that speaks and follows a mouse's movement on a Web site or in interactive e-mail. To increase sign-ups for a small business newsletter, SitePal created an avatar of the newsletter's editor based on her photo and made it move its eyes and mouth so it speaks to site visitors about the newsletter. The avatar was used on 50% of 11,000 site visitors, chosen at random. The visitors who saw the avatar signed up at a rate of 144% more than those who didn't see the avatar.

Video in e-mails

Video in e-mails can increase sales. There is a huge audience for Internet video: 116 million US consumers watched Web videos in the first half of 2008. And video isn't just for a young audience. YouTube attracts all age groups for its video content: 18% are under 18; 20% are 18-34; 19% are 35-44; 21% are 45-54; and 21% are 55 or older.[3]

FirstStreetOnline.com sells gifts, gadgets, and household products aimed at older consumers. The retailer introduced a weekly video called FirstStreetReports in which a mature man provides nontechnical explanations of the products. Sales and conversion rates on those products went up by double-digit percentages, according to InternetRetailer.[4]

HavenHolidays.com conducted a highly successful test of video in its promotional e-mails for its amusement park. After scrubbing the subscriber list to get rid of bounced addresses, online marketing executive Carolyn Jacquest produced a five-minute video showing the park's features. To discover the optimal length, she sent clip sizes to the in-house accounts for its UK-based audience's 10 most-popular Web mail providers or receivers. From the test results, she learned that 20-second clips were optimal for deliverability. The copy at the top of the HTML design was: "Fun Filled Easter at Haven!" A 320×180 pixel video box automatically started rolling when the message was opened. If the subscriber's system didn't let her see the video in the e-mail, she saw a link to a microsite.

Embedding the video e-mails worked. The Easter campaign had a 3.38% conversion rate—50.2% higher than previous non-video campaigns, which were 2% to 2.5%. The 20-second clip had a deliverability rate of 96%, with a CTR of 27%. Including the word "video" in the subject line produced a 14.6% boost for opens.

Unfortunately, a large number of subscribers couldn't view the video because their client (something other than Outlook 2000 or Outlook 2003) didn't show the video in a satisfactory manner. Those subscribers clicked on the Haven microsite to see the video. Despite this failure, the conversion rate improvement is impressive.

Takeaway thoughts

- Successful e-mails should be an adventure for the readers.
- Make e-mails short, but fill them with links to content on your site that each particular reader is interested in.
- Using profile/preference data, e-mails should be personalized and filled with content that, based on past behavior or preselected preferences, readers find interesting.
- When a reader completes a survey, follow it up with an e-mail, thanking him for completing the survey and telling him what you will do with the information.
- When readers enter personal profile data (name, address, e-mail address, credit card, etc.) via a preference center, remember this data (with the reader's permission) and make it available within future communication opportunities, either online or via e-mail, to improve and shorten the overall purchase cycle.
- Interactive means lots of clicks, which equals lots of revenue.

Notes

1. This depends on volume, of course. Once an e-mail has been constructed, you can send it to a million subscribers for about $2 per thousand. With direct mail, you are always paying for printing and postage, so the volume discounts aren't as significant.

2. "Analytics Helps Bluefly With Top Secret Sale" (InternetRetailer, March 13, 2008), http://www.internetretailer.com/dailyNews.asp?id= 25696.

3. Larry Brody, TVWriter.com (November 28, 2006), http://www. screenandtvwriter.com/phpBB/viewtopic.php?=&p=33160.

4. Don Davis, "Raising the Stakes" (InternetRetailer, May 2008) http:// www.internetretailer.com/article.asp?id=26243&ref=ya.

16

Testing to Improve Your Marketing

Almost any question can be answered, cheaply, quickly, and, finally, by a test campaign. And that's the way to answer them—not by arguments around a table. Go to the court of last resort—the buyers of your product.

Claude Hopkins, Scientific Advertising, 1923

Without testing, you will never improve your marketing. You can send out a promotion of 1 million e-mails and get certain open, click, and conversion rates. Was your success good or bad? The only way to know is to compare your results with some previous promotion to the same group to see if you did better this time than last.

But that is a crude way of testing. A better way is to use your best previous promotion as a control. Constantly try to beat your response to that specific best promotion.

Testing's role in relevance

As you recall from chapter 5, the various factors in relevance have different weights (importance) in creating total relevance. Testing is important, but the least (5%) of the total relevance factors. Unfortunately very few e-mail marketers adequately test. They are too busy getting

EXHIBIT 16-01 How to score testing

Testing and Measurement Weight 5%	
3	Attribute ROI to each testing element
2	Multivariant testing resulting in multiple tests
1	Tests one element with single split of audience
0	No testing or measurement of results

out today's e-mails to bother with a test. They may test the subject lines to see how they affect opens. That, of course, is better than nothing. But many are using their intuition rather than a statistically valid test to prove how well they are doing.

If you are going to run a successful e-mail marketing program, you must test. Display a sign prominently in your desk area that says, "Don't send out a single promotion today without building in a valid test *first*."

Here are some rules that you can use to start off right.

Use your best previous promotion as your control

Use your best newsletter as your newsletter control. Select your best welcome e-mail as a second control. Find your winning transaction message as a third control. In other words, for each type of campaign you send out, look for your best and try to beat it.

Define what was best about the control e-mail

Was it opens? Clicks? The lower rate of unsubscribes or the high conversions? Be sure you have a concrete definition of *best*.

Create test groups

This isn't as easy as it sounds. The people in your test groups should be representative of your entire customer base. You will use their responses to your tests as representing how everyone would respond to a similar newsletter or promotion. To define a test group, you need criteria, such as:

- Buyers vs. non-buyers
- Length of time as subscribers
- Source of the subscriber
- Demographics (more about this later)

If you don't have any test groups, you can simply use an A/B split: send version A to half your e-mail file and version B to the other half—and keep track of which group got which version. This is a good way to begin and should give you valid results. It costs nothing to do this, since everyone gets an e-mail.

When you want to get more sophisticated, however, you will need test groups. Why? Suppose version B delivered a 4% conversion rate and version A delivered a 2% conversion rate. Version B is so much better that you will want to use that version from now on. But to test something else, you don't want to risk losing a lot of sales by restricting the number of people who get your best e-mail. You will want to test your new ideas on only a small portion of your database. Hence, a small test group and everyone else is your control.

How many things can you test in one e-mail promotion?

The best test is the single-variable test. Test only one thing with each e-mail promotion. Some people make the mistake of testing many things. Big mistake! In the e-mail marketing business, we are all very busy. We may be sending out e-mails every day. We can build in lots of tests, but when do we have the leisure to study the test results to determine which was the best and what we should do now?

What should you test first?

The first thing to test is always the subject line. This line is all that most people see before they delete your e-mail. If it isn't good, most subscribers won't see anything else. No matter how well your subject line performed in the past, always test another version on a small test group. Your competition is looking at your e-mails, and they may be copying what you are doing. They may have worn out the words that once brought you such success. You want to keep one step ahead of them.

Do a quick subject line test

You have six possible subject lines. Which is the best? Let your readers tell you. Here's how: Create a random 10% of your file, dividing it into six equal segments. Try one subject line on each segment. Mail 'em. Wait six hours. Look at your open rates for each. Then send to the remaining 90% of your file using the winning subject line. This is a very quick way to win the subject line battle early.

What are you trying to prove?

Before any test, write down a statement of what you're trying to prove or disprove by the test. For example: "Our hypothesis is that showing the product price above the fold will produce more conversions than the present system of showing the price only in the checkout process."

Also before the test, determine your decision metrics and the roll-out plans. "If the new e-mail page arrangement increases conversions by at least 10% more than the control, we'll use it in the rollout." After the test, write down your numeric results, your interpretation of their meaning, and your decisions on the next steps.

Keep a test notebook. It becomes your marketing department's shared institutional memory (it is worth maintaining two copies.)

For example, the Motorcycle Superstore found that testing frequency changes allowed it to increase revenues by up to 120%. Next it split its list into groups based on product interests. Each group received customized content in their e-mails. The new segment-based content resulted in doubled open rates and tripled click-through rates.

Separate significant results from the noise

All tests have some element of random statistical noise. To find out what it is, randomly split a mailing list of 10,000 people into two cells of 5,000 people each, and on the same day mail each cell exactly the same e-mail. It is almost certain that one cell by chance alone will have a higher open, click, or conversion rate. Let's say the variation in opens is 15, that is one file gets 15 more opens than the other file. Statistically, this difference amounts to 0.3%. Once you know this, you have established the level of statistical noise. To use this knowledge in future tests, you might use a rough rule of thumb: "a test needs to increase conversion or CTR by more than 1.5 times the level of statistical noise to be considered significant." Any difference, then, less than 4.5% shouldn't be taken as a significant difference (15 times 0.3% is 4.5%).

Assign unique mail codes

To understand your tests, give each e-mail cell a unique mail code. Come up with a system, and record your system in your testing notebook. Write the meaning of each code in a spreadsheet. Your spreadsheet should be available to your marketing team and preserved so you can go back later and check your work.

Don't expect amazing results

If you are doing a lot of tests (and you should), many tests will fail to prove anything significant. That's OK. Be patient and try again. Make sure your management understands that most tests don't produce surprising results. If you have been doing testing for some time, your current e-mail program has been improved by years of step-by-step adjustment, so each additional test may not be earth-shaking. The more successful your testing has been, the harder it becomes to move the needle.

There are still rewarding tests: A hunting-products retailer tested the value of designing the content for images. It tested an all-images design against one that contained images but whose main message was in the text. The retailer found that the second e-mail produced almost four times more revenue. Why? Because it worked well for subscribers who blocked images.

The Quality Paperback Book Club tested two different headlines in its e-mails. One was, "Click here to see . . . " and the other was, "Get . . . " "Get" had a 47% higher conversion rate. How could you possibly know that unless you tested it?

Testing many ideas at once

The rule of testing only one thing at a time doesn't prevent you from trying many different concepts at once. Say your creative staff has developed five different approaches to selling a product using e-mail. Don't have a committee meeting to choose the best one. Divide your subscriber list into five parts and test them all at once. The results may be surprising. One of them may prove to be much better than the other four—a result that your committee members would never have been able to guess and might have rejected because it seemed unusual.

How big should your test group be?

This is a common question, and we have a very good answer. To be sure of statistical accuracy, you should have as a test group, a bunch of subscribers who might generate about 500 responses. What do we mean by responses? You can define it as opens, clicks, or conversions, depending on the situation.

Suppose you have been getting an overall open rate of 12%. You want to try out a new version on a test group. Since you expect 12% opens and you are looking for 500 opens in the test group, your test group should be at least 500 divided by 12% or 4,167.

Set aside time to study every test's results

E-mail marketers' other great sin is the failure to study the results of previous tests. It takes time. It takes imagination. It takes persistence. We worked with the CMO of a large corporation that mailed 25 million e-mails a week. When we began, we asked what the first tests were to be. She answered, "Oh, we don't need to waste our time with tests. We already know what works." Since she was the client, we didn't argue with her. Later, however, we were able to introduce some tests that did about 15% better than the version she was using. She began to see the value of experimentation and testing.

The great thing about e-mail marketing is that test results can often be learned within 24 hours. With direct mail, the results may take weeks. Since good analytic software can give you results so quickly, you have to build in time to study those results and apply them to the next few e-mails. Tomorrow you may be busy getting out the next e-mail. You don't have time to figure out what to do with the results of yesterday's test. That is a shame. You might have learned something valuable.

Testing personalization

Suppose you want to test the effect of personalization by using the subscriber's name in the message's salutation. In one case study, the client had been using a straight message with no salutation or personalization. As a test, it began with "Dear Customer." Just that little change provided a 4.1% lift in the click rate over the previous version. Wow!

Since that little change worked so well, the client decided to dig up the first names of many subscribers and test "Dear [Name]" with a similar offer. However, the entire subscriber list had gotten used to the "Dear Customer" salutation. The offer had to be changed slightly. No matter: with a similar offer, the personalized salutation increased the click rate by 13.0% over the original version. This case study shows the importance of constant testing.

Testing the offer

EVO Gear tested an identical offer of Wake Packages: one version with $50 off and the other with 15% off. Pricewise, the offers were almost identical. However, the $50-off e-mail generated 170% more revenue and a 72% higher conversion rate. Conclusion: many people still don't understand percentages. Everyone understands dollars.

The click-to-open rate

In testing, we have to know what we are using as a measurement. There are three standard measurements: opens, clicks, and conversions. There is a significant additional way of using these numbers that can give you positive results, suggested by e-mail expert Jeanne Jennings of

EXHIBIT 16-02 CTR versus CTO[1]

	Control Group	Test Group
Number Delivered	1,000,000	1,000,000
Unique Opens	300,000	250,000
Unique Clicks	80,000	80,000
CTR %	8%	8%
CTO %	26.70%	32%

JeanneJennings.com: the click-to-open rate (CTO). The CTO can be compiled by dividing the unique number of clicks by the unique number of opens. Exhibit 16-02 offers an example.

In this example the click-through rate (CTR) is identical for the control group and the test group, but the CTO rate of the test group is better because an equal number of clicks was produced from a smaller number of opens. Opens are nice, but clicks are better.

Mistakes you can make in testing

To run a successful test, avoid the following mistakes.

Mistake 1: Making too many changes at once

When you change several items in one version of an e-mail and test it against your control, you won't learn much. Suppose that in the two versions, the layout, promotions, copy, and even products were completely different. Any one change might have helped or hurt response, but putting them all together, you can't tell what was doing what. One change might have helped opens by 10%, but another change in the same e-mail might have reduced clicks by 10%. Rule: test only one element at a time.

Mistake 2: Looking only at conversions

There is a logical sequence for e-mail readers: They are attracted by the subject, so they open the message. They like the way the salutation greets them when they open. The copy is interesting and the offer stimulates them. They click on a couple of links and finally order a product. At any point, your e-mail can fail: bad subject, bad salutation, bad offer, weak link, poor products or pricing, or confusing order form. Which of these things was responsible for the low conversion rate? You will never know if you look at the conversion rate by itself.

Test each part separately. First, select a subject line that works better than others. Then get your best salutation. Now you are ready to try different versions of the copy. You also need to test pricing, then your order form. We never said testing was easy, particularly if you neglect testing elements separately.

Mistake 3: Offering too many choices

There is an old saying in the direct mail business: "Choice kills response." Time after time, direct mail marketers have tested a direct mail piece that offers readers two or more choices against a mail piece that offers only one possible answer: take it or leave it. The one choice always beats more choices. For example, a company selling low-cost tours leading to the sale of a timeshare tried two approaches: "Only $69 for a family vacation weekend in Fort Lauderdale, Florida. Chose any of the following six weekends, and the vacation is yours." and "We have only one available family weekend for $69 left in Fort Lauderdale, Florida: March 12–14. Call right away." The second message always beat the first by a large margin.

Just because you are doing e-mail marketing, don't think you can't learn from the direct mail folks. There are a lot of fundamental truths about marketing that have already been learned. Choice kills response is a fundamental truth. Don't make the mistake of giving readers a choice.

Mistake 4: Not knowing the territory

There is a wonderful song in *The Music Man:* "Whaddaya talk, whaddaya talk? . . . You gotta know the territory." In e-mail marketing, you will get better results if you know who you are sending your e-mails to. Are they affluent seniors or college students? Are they married women or single men? Do they live in big cities or way out in the country? Are they previous buyers or registrants who have never bought anything?

The new elements you test may attract some people but alienate others. If you know nothing about your audience (i.e., you are a hunter who doesn't know the territory), you should stick with big, significant changes in your testing, such as a dramatic ease of navigation or a promotion that is of general interest to all.

If you *do* know the territory (i.e., you are a farmer), then you can show different content to different segments reading your e-mails. Run different tests for each segment. You'll get a cleaner answer on your tests if the population who sees the test is more consistent.

Mistake 5: Testing by committee

The worst group to create an e-mail program is a committee representing different departments in your company. Some people like one idea, and others like something else. You compromise on an e-mail that no one likes very much but has the least negatives. Good ideas are edited out of the process during meetings as being bad ideas before they can be tested. The result is a test that is really an A/A test—there may be a little tweak here or there, but the two versions are really the same.

A better approach is to let your subscribers kill bad ideas and reward good ones. Let your creative people loose to try new ideas. Are you in business to create peace in a committee or to build customer loyalty and sales? After all, it's only an e-mail. Your whole company's reputation doesn't hang on every word. Cut loose. Try something new. Use what you learn.

Mistake 6: Using personalization in the subject line

Since personalization in the body of the e-mail improves clicks and conversions, why not use it in the subject line? At one time that was a good idea, but spammers have ruined it. By now millions of people have received e-mails from unknown people who seem to know the receiver's first and last name. They picked them up from a phishing expedition. If you use the subscriber's name in the subject line, you may be deleted as spam.

Keep a log of your mailing statistics

Tests have to be compared with the results of other tests to know whether you are doing better or worse. Is an open rate of 16% good or bad? It is better than an overall industry average of 13%, but what if your e-mails last year had an opening rate of 28%? You need to know this.

Set up a systematic log of all e-mail statistics that are posted after every e-mail sent out, organized by type of e-mail. It might look something like Exhibit 16-03.

Exhibit 16-03 is the result of a single mailing. It could be created a few days after the actual mailing. Remember, an e-mail's shelf life is usually less than a week. In this example, we compare two different subject lines. Everything else in the two e-mails should be exactly the same if the test is to be valid. Based on this test, you can decide that subject line B is better than subject line A.

Next, we could try two different salutations using subject line B. One might be "Dear Valued Customer" and the other might be "Dear [Name]." We can bet that "Dear]Name]" will win, but we can't predict by how much. If "Dear [Name]" wins, then you can test two dif-

EXHIBIT 16-03 E-mail statistic log

Type of E-mail	Promotion	Promotion	
Name	Cocktail Dress/A	Cocktail Dress/B	
Date	Jun 3 2009	Jun 3 2009	
Mailed	1,172,839	1,172,839	
Delivered	1,129,444	1,138,827	
Del %	96.3%	97.10%	Percent of mailed
Opened	242,830	268,763	
Open %	21.50%	23.60%	Percent of Delivered
Unique Clicks	44,681	54,559	
CTR	18.40%	20.30%	Percent of Opens
COTR	18.4%	20.3%	clicks/opens
Conversions	1,385	1,582	
Conversion Rate	3.1%	2.9%	Percent of Clicks
Total Sales	$169,551	$190,498	
$ Per Delivered	$0.15	$0.17	
Average Order	$122.41	$120.40	
Mailing Cost	$10,555.55	$10,555.55	
Cost per open	$0.043	$0.039	
Cost per click	$0.236	$0.193	
Cost per sale	$7.621	$6.671	
Conv. %	3.30%	4.10%	Conv as % of Delivered
Unsub %	1.20%	1.10%	As % of Mailed
Undel %	2.50%	1.80%	As % of Mailed
New Viral Names	4,877	6,120	
Viral %	0.43%	0.54%	As % of delivered

ferent offers in the body of the e-mail using the winning subject line and salutation.

The examples make the process seem simple, but it isn't that simple. If you have only 2.3 million subscribers, you can't keep sending them the same e-mail advertising the same cocktail dress if you want to remain relevant. Each e-mail will have to be different. The difference will affect your open, click, and conversion rates. That doesn't mean you will never learn anything lasting. You will learn how to create a productive subject line. In time, you will perfect your salutation. Finally you will learn the best way to sell your products.

This chart shows why we say that every single e-mail you send should be a test. Because you can test only one thing with each e-mail, you really need a lot of tests to become an e-mail marketing expert.

Does it seem as if recording each test's results is a lot of work? It is, but not necessarily for you. If you have your e-mail delivery outsourced (and we highly recommend you do this), you can ask your e-mail service provider (ESP) to prepare this chart for you as automatically for every e-mail you send. You can concentrate on the marketing aspect of your e-mail program, leaving the drudgery for your ESP.

Testing by analyzing the audience

The testing we have been discussing has been about the effect of our e-mails on an audience. We haven't defined the audience, other than to say it comprises opt-in registrants. E-mail analysis can be quite sophisticated. It is much more sophisticated than what direct mail marketers can do, because we know so much more. We know that our e-mails have been received, opened, clicked, and purchased from. In direct mail we only know if the recipients bought something.

However, direct mail marketers have become very sophisticated in their audience analysis. E-mailers can do the same thing. In general, though, e-mail marketers haven't done much audience analysis. They are so excited by the instant results they get from the e-mail analysis (from hunting) that they haven't bothered to take the next step (farming). Many of them know nothing all about their audience other than their e-mail address.

However, a rich harvest can come from taking that next step and becoming farmers. We can break our audience down into segments based on a number of factors:

- Type and value of products purchased
- Recency, frequency, and monetary of purchase (RFM)
- Demographics, including:
  —Age, gender, income, wealth, marital status, children
  —Housing type, value, own vs. rent, length of residence
  —Occupation, ethnicity, lifestyle

For e-mail farmers to test, therefore, they must assign segment codes to their subscriber lists, studying the test results by segment. (For more on segmentation, see chapter 7).

If you want to test using demographic data, start with people who have provided you with their home address, either because they have bought something or because you included the address field in your e-mail registration form. Let's say you test 120,000 consumers with appended data, and the data cost you $6,000. You are trying to sell life insurance to a group of existing auto insurance customers. Your goal is to get the e-mail readers to fill out a life insurance application. Exhibit

EXHIBIT 16-04 E-mail results by age range

Age Range	Delivered	Opened	Clicked	Applied	Open %	Click%	Appl %	Success
Under 20	3,305	264	58	5	8%	22%	9%	0.16%
21-40	24,331	4,136	745	171	17%	18%	23%	0.70%
41-55	31,882	11,478	3,214	996	36%	28%	31%	3.12%
56-65	28,774	6,330	2,785	1,114	22%	44%	40%	3.87%
66+	29,773	8,634	3,195	1,757	29%	37%	55%	5.90%
Total	118,065	30,843	9,996	4,044	26%	32%	40%	3.43%

EXHIBIT 16-05 E-mail results by household income

Income Range	Delivered	Opened	Clicked	Applied	Open %	Click%	Appl %	Success
Under $20 K	35,664	9,629	2,359	873	27.0%	25%	37%	2.45%
$21K–$40K	35,663	8,238	2,065	558	23.1%	25%	27%	1.56%
$41K–$75K	20,859	5,006	1,652	661	24.0%	33%	40%	3.17%
$76K–$125K	16,774	6,877	3,439	1,685	41.0%	50%	49%	10.05%
$126K+	9,105	1,093	481	269	12.0%	44%	56%	2.96%
Total	118,065	30,843	9,996	4,044	26.1%	32%	40%	3.43%

16-04 illustrates the type of results you might get from an identical e-mail sent to everyone on your list broken down by age range:

The chart shows us that your message resonated with subscribers ages 66 years or older. You aren't doing well with those under 41. With direct mail, we might conclude that mailing to those under 41 was a waste of money. But with e-mail marketing, we can come to a different conclusion: we keep the message for those 66 and older, but we change our message for the under-41 crowd and perhaps for those 41 to 65. We have a control to beat: get a success rate of 5.9%.

We aren't done yet. Let's look at exactly the same mailing to the same people by income (see Exhibit 16-05). We don't have to mail them again, just compile the statistics in a different way.

From this we can see that the e-mail appealed mainly to people whose income was $76,000 to $125,000. We have a winner here. For other income ranges, perhaps we should change the offer or the e-mail content in some way to improve the success rate. We have an e-mail that appeals to people over 66 whose income is from $76,000 to $125,000.

And we're still not through yet. We could look at the data by gender; women and men have very different reactions to life insurance offers. We could look at people by section of the country or length of residence, and we would get still another picture. People who have lived at a residence for a short time are much more likely to respond to such an offer than people who have lived a long time in their homes. There may be six or more ways to break the audience down based on this one mailing. You will learn something from each chart, but you only had to do one mailing.

Testing by demographics for certain kinds of products and services can be very powerful. Once we know how to write winning subject lines, salutations, and e-mail copy, we can get more deeply into audience analysis testing—that is, farming—a process that can be highly profitable.

Takeaway thoughts

- Every e-mail should be a test. Unfortunately, many e-mail marketers aren't doing enough testing.
- Test only one thing in each test, so you can learn how that one thing affects your results.
- Test the subject line first.
- Study each test's results, and apply what you have learned to future e-mails.
- Test personalization, using the subscriber's name.
- Common mistakes include too many changes at once, too many choices for the reader, and using the subscriber's name in the subject line.
- Have your ESP give you a complete report on each mailing, and save the reports.
- Once you learn to get good subject lines and personalization, test audience segments as a farmer. This can produce very powerful results.

Notes

1. Jeanne Jennings, "Dear John: Tips for Testing Personalized E-Mail Salutations," The ClickZ Network (February 13, 2006), http://www.clickz.com/showPage.html?page=3584001.

17

Customer Retention and Loyalty

Loyalty is the result of our marketing efforts. It's an indicator of how successful we have been with our total marketing effort. We must never forget that loyalty is not the obligation of the customer. Rather, it's the result of us providing such a continuous set of positive shopping experiences for the customer that she chooses to keep returning to do business with us . . .

Brian Woolf, *Loyalty Marketing: The Second Act*

Building Subscriber Loyalty

What is a loyal customer? It is a customer who likes your products and services and who thinks of you first when buying in your category. Loyal customers often have become friends with some of your customer service personnel. Compared to other customers, loyal customers tend to:

- Have higher retention rates
- Have higher spending rates
- Have higher referral rates
- Have a higher lifetime value
- Be less expensive to serve
- Buy higher priced options

Every year, more consumers become experienced Web shoppers. According to Forrester Research, 32% of online shoppers in 2007 had been buying on the Web for seven years or more, up from 18% in 2003. The number of brand-new Web shoppers is decreasing. Forrester Research also reports that only 9% of Web shoppers in 2007 had been shopping online for less than a year, a sharp decline from 16% in 2006. These new shoppers are increasingly female. According to Forrester Research, 55% of the new 2007 shoppers were women.

What do these figures mean to you? They mean that it will become

EXHIBIT 17-01 Retention rate based on years as a customer

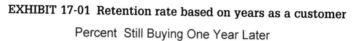

Percent Still Buying One Year Later

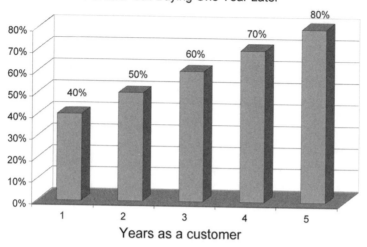

Years as a customer

harder to acquire new subscribers. Your job will be to hold on to the ones you have and to convert more of them to becoming loyal customers.

True customer loyalty is like a successful marriage. It is a relationship in which both parties are satisfied with their relations with each other. They aren't worried that their partner will stop loving them or will run off with somebody else. They will come through misunderstandings and arguments with their relationship intact, even stronger. Developing a bond of loyalty between you and your customers is what e-mail marketing is all about.

Customer loyalty can be measured. The most common measurement is the retention rate: the percentage of people who bought from you last year who are buying from you again this year. Exhibit 17-01 shows customer loyalty with information from a database.

This chart shows that the customers who remain in each subsequent year are more loyal than the total customers in the previous year. Sixty percent of first-time buyers fail to make a purchase in the second year. The 40% who do are the more loyal customers. Half of them will go on to buy in the third year—20% of the original buyers. These 20% are more loyal. By the fourth year, the number of really loyal customers is down to 12% (20% times 60%).

Loyalty can be a function of how subscribers arrive at your Web site. By early 2008, 48% of traffic to online commerce sites and 67% of online sales came from consumers who typed in a retailer's URL or

EXHIBIT 17-02 SmartBargains.com recommendation e-mail

Thank you for your recent order from SmartBargains.com. We hope you are enjoying your latest bargain!

As a followup to your order, we'd like you to answer a few quick questions. They should take you less than one minute to complete, but they are extremely important and allow us to identify ways to continually exceed your expectations.

On a scale of 0 to 10, how likely would you be to recommend SmartBargains.com to a friend or colleague?
(0 = Extremely Unlikely, 10 = Extremely Likely)

☹ 0 = Extremely Unlikely   ☺ 10 = Extremely Likely

○0 ○1 ○2 ○3 ○4 ○5 ○6 ○7 ○8 ○9 ○10

What is the primary reason for the score you gave us?

clicked on a bookmark, according to Coremetrics. These are repeat visitors, the best kind to have.

Would you recommend me?

Frederick Reichheld has one of the best ways to measure customer loyalty. He recommends that companies ask their customers one question: would you recommend me to your friends? The answer is much more indicative of loyalty than satisfaction scores. With automobiles, for example, most satisfaction scores are between 80% and 90%, but the repurchase rate of the same brand is about 35%. Using his basic question, Reichheld developed a Net Promoter Score. To get the score, subtract the number of people who wouldn't recommend you from those who would. The score is often negative. Many companies have used this score to determine how well they are doing and, if negative, to decide what to do about their situation.

The question can easily be asked in an e-mail. SmartBargains.com does a good job of this. It sends out an e-mail to buyers following a purchase as a means of gauging customers' shopping experiences (see Exhibit 17-02).

Increasing the number of loyal customers

There are four basic means of increasing customer loyalty:

- Have high-quality products and services

- Offer excellent customer service and support
- Have a friendly and loyal staff
- Provide excellent, highly personalized, relevant, and rapid communications

If you don't have the first three items, your communications won't save you. But if you do have them, then communications—particularly e-mail communications—become a very high priority for building loyalty and profits.

Loyalty-building communications

Your Web site and your e-mails are the lifeline of your customer loyalty program. To create loyalty-building communications:

- Create personalized, sophisticated HTML transaction messages, and send them out quickly
- Acknowledge all customer input within a few seconds, and fulfill their requests within a few hours
- Ask for customer preferences and modify your communications and services based on these preferences
- Develop trigger messages that treat each customer as an individual rather than as members of a large herd
- Thank customers for their business, personalizing the e-mails with such comments as how long they have been your customers

As you develop your loyalty-building communications, keep in mind how our old corner grocer built customer loyalty. When customers came to his store, he greeted them by name. He started his conversations with topics he believed were of interest to them, based on previous purchases and conversations. The grocer remembered where his customers' lived and how far they had to travel to get to his store. He remembered what they said to him and used it in future conversations. He would point out where the products they wanted could be found in the store, put things aside for them, replace defective products, help them to carry heavy packages, and so on. He congratulated them on birthdays and anniversaries. He remembered how long they had been customers and how much they spent with him. He knew each customer's family members and used that knowledge to suggest products and services.

As you can see from this listing, there are many things that one helpful, intelligent, and caring human being can do for another human

274 • • • Successful E-mail Marketing Strategies

being that result in friendship and—in commercial terms—loyalty. Our database can store a lot of customer data, though not as much as the corner grocer kept in his head, but our goal should be to get as close to what he stored there as possible.

Many of this book's chapters have already explored in depth the types of communications that support customer loyalty, including:

- Communication relevance (chapter 5)
- Listening to customers (chapter 11)
- Communication frequency (chapter 12)
- Transactional e-mails (chapter 13)

Let's see how e-mail messages can be used to build loyalty.

How Nike builds customer loyalty

Here's how Nike built loyalty with one Nike customer:

My fiancé received an interesting e-mail from Nike last week. It was a special invitation to an opening of a NikeID shop in Manhattan. Making an appointment, the customer receives a 45 min. consultation, where he can design as many sneakers as he wants using exclusive and limited color-ways and materials. When Jason called me about his e-mail, I wondered how he was chosen for this exclusive event. Segmentation, of course!

My fiancé is a sneaker fanatic. To pay homage to his fanaticism, we all will be wearing Nike sneakers at our wedding this winter. Due to this we have purchased six pairs of Nike sneakers from NikeID.com in the last two months.

If I had to guess, my fiancé now falls into a "best customer" segment. Nike does not come right out and say, "Hey, thanks for buying all those sneakers last month," but they are letting Jason know they value him as a customer and are showing the perks to being an avid NikeID shopper. This is a win-win; Jason feels special and valued as a customer, while Nike continues to build a relationship with him, strengthening brand loyalty. And not to mention targeting the customer who will most likely purchase at least one pair of sneakers (Jason is already plotting his purchase).

Acting on customer input

If you do your job right, you will have a host of input messages, other than regular orders, from your subscribers every day. They include preferences and profiles, complaints, returns, questions, special requests, and all sorts of other inquiries. How you handle these will determine the level of customer loyalty you can achieve.

The first step is to assign someone to make an exhaustive search of all the types of customer input received in the past three months and categorize them in a number of ways, as shown in Exhibit 17-03.

Come up with your own categories based on actual customer input. It may take some time to fill out this form. It will take even longer to put the business rules in place, both in software and in human actions, to come up with a satisfactory solution to every problem. But this form shows you what you have to do to create customer loyalty. At least twice a year, revisit this form to make sure the solutions you developed are working and that there aren't new categories of problems that need solutions.

Log on as a customer

The next step in achieving customer loyalty is to have a number of staff members log on to your Web site, make purchases, and receive e-mails to be sure you know what your output looks like on the receiving end. Those who log on should be given a list of things to test, starting with the categories listed in Exhibit 17-03, to see just how well you are responding.

Have them search each e-mail received to see if they can get all the information they require. Can they reach customer service through text chat or on the phone? Can they return a product without hassle? Are their e-mails correctly personalized? Are their preferences honored? Is there a feedback e-mail link clearly visible in every e-mail? Does someone check the sending e-mail address daily to read and respond to all feedback received?

Using professional and part-time seeds

Each e-mail should have links to images, input forms, display pages, and so on. The more sophisticated your e-mails, the more intricate your landing pages. A quality-control staffer should routinely test all the links in every outgoing e-mail to make sure they work. But you should

EXHIBIT 17-03 Customer input and disposition

	Frequency Per 100 Customers	Seriousness Scale of 1 to 10	Response Can Be Automated	Response Time Req. Minutes	Solution Method Established	Solution Is Satisfactory?
Preference Survey						
Change of Address						
Change of Name						
Reduce E-mail Frequency						
Product Return						
Missing Delivery						
Billing Error						
Defective Product						
Privacy Problem						
Delay in Response						
Unsubscribe						
Forgot ID or Password						
Not satisfied						
Can't find product on site						
Can't reach cust. service						

also set up an e-mail checking service using both professional and part-time seeds to check e-mails as they are actually received.

Freed Seeds is a professional seeding company that provides comprehensive reports on all your sent e-mails. You can also, at little expense, develop a network of part-time seeds, people who work out of their homes. For a modest fee per delivered e-mail, these people will open each e-mail, click on links, fill out forms, and complete an e-mail effectiveness form that you devise, telling you how everything worked. Ideally, each of your part-time seeds should be a subscriber to a different ISP (AOL, Yahoo, Hotmail, etc.). Some should have broadband, and some dial-up. Some should be set up to receive HTML, and others only text. One of them at least should receive messages on a cell phone.

Why is all this necessary? To assure that your e-mails are doing what you want to build customer loyalty. You may have the best intentions in the world, but if the e-mails don't work properly for recipients, you may be turning many of your subscribers off—and never know about it.

Certified e-mail

An ISP may allow a sender to bypass spam filters when its e-mails are sent to its subscribers for a fee to a certifying service, such as Goodmail Certification. Goodmail is used by AOL, AT&T, Yahoo, Comcast, Cox Communications, Road Runner, and Verizon as part of their filtering services. Goodmail requires six months' of sending history from a dedicated IP for certification, which is one reason using an out sourced ESP is to your advantage. If you are trying to build customer loyalty, having your e-mail certified could be an important step.

Recruiting the right kind of customers

Customer loyalty begins with the subscriber acquisition process. In his book, The Loyalty Effect, Reichheld points out that "some customers are inherently predictable and loyal, no matter what company they're doing business with. They simply prefer stable, long-term relationships."

The book provides dozens of examples of companies who have figured out their loyal customers' characteristics. They have developed simple rules that aid them in attracting the right kind of customer and avoiding the wrong kinds. Some of his examples:

- An insurance company discovered that, for them, married people were more loyal than singles. Midwesterners were more loyal than Easterners. Homeowners were more loyal than renters. Once they found this out, they used the knowledge to guide their acquisition strategy.

- MBNA discovered that people reached through an affinity group, such as doctors, dentists, nurses, teachers, and engineers, were more loyal credit card holders than people reached through general direct mail campaigns.

- Many companies used their databases to learn that customers attracted by low-ball discount offers were more likely to disappear than customers attracted using nondiscounted offers. Low-ball–offer responders tended to leave as soon as the competition made them an even lower offer. Were they different people, or had the offer made them think of the company's products in terms of price rather than value? Who knows. It really doesn't matter. Discounting is not a good way to attract loyal customers.

> For years, retailers have argued that having regularly advertised, deeply discounted prices brings price-oriented customers into their stores but that, over time, these customers convert to regular, profitable customers.
>
> Research done by the Retail Strategy Center Inc., based in Greenville, South Carolina, shows that this widely held belief is a myth. A handful of these customers do convert into "good" regular customers, but the majority actually defects within 12 months of their first shopping visit. I have yet to find a retailer anywhere in the world whose investment in this type of shopper has yielded an attractive return on investment.
>
> —Brian Woolf, *Customer Specific Marketing*

Relationship buyers versus transaction buyers

There are two basic kinds of customers: relationship buyers and transaction buyers. Understanding their differences is important in developing programs designed to build customer retention, sales, and loyalty.

Transaction buyers

Transaction buyers try to engage in comparison-shopping for every transaction. They read the ads, consult the Internet, make phone calls, and constantly shop around. For them, the past has no meaning. They have absolutely no loyalty. Never mind what you did for them before, what is your price today? They will shift suppliers of any product for a few pennies' difference in price.

Transaction buyers usually get little service. Service isn't important to them; price is. There isn't much point in trying to win their loyalty, since they have none to give. E-mail marketing may be ineffective here, only discounting. They are seldom profitable customers, even though they may buy a lot of product and represent an important segment of any market. The best thing that could happen to these transaction buyers would be for them to shift over to buying from your competition. One way to make money with transaction buyers, particularly B2B customers, is to negotiate annual volume purchase agreements. The buyers get a good deal on price, and you get the volume without having to spend valuable marketing and customer service dollars on each transaction.

Relationship buyers

Relationship buyers are the loyal ones. They are looking for a dependable supplier:

- Someone who cares about their needs and who looks out for them
- Someone who remembers what they bought in the past and gives them special services as a reward
- Someone who takes an interest in their purchases and treats them as individuals

Relationship buyers know they could save a few dollars by shopping around. But they also know if they switch suppliers, they would lose something they value highly: the relationship they have built with a dependable supplier that recognizes them and takes good care of them. Many of them also realize there is an emotional and economic cost to shopping around for every purchase. They want to concentrate on being happy and enjoying their purchases, not their haggling ability.

Segmenting buyers

By classifying your customers into these two segments, you can focus your marketing efforts on the one segment that is really profitable: relationship buyers. Your database records the purchases of these buyers and gives them personal recognition and special services. You recognize your gold customers. You communicate with them. You partner with them.

EXHIBIT 17-04 Transaction buyers shifting from supplier to supplier

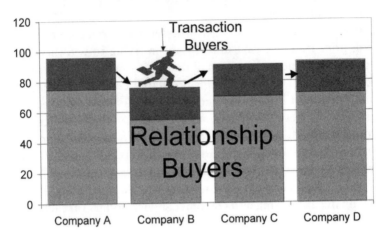

How can you distinguish transaction buyers from relationship buyers? Here's how one retailer does it. New customers are e-mailed a preference survey form. One question asks: "How important are the following in making your decision about where to buy this product? Rank from 1—most important—to 5—least important?" Factors offered are:

- Price
- Service
- Reputation of manufacturer
- Recommendation of a friend
- Company policy
- Previous experience
- Customer service

Those who code price as most important are probably transaction buyers. The others may well be relationship buyers. This can be tested later in other ways.

Your management may insist that most of your customers are transaction buyers. It will point out that when you have a sale, you get more sales. When you don't, the sales decrease. What may be happening, however, is shown on the chart in Exhibit 17-04. Companies, A, B, C, and D have a stable base of relationship buyers who stay with them and a floating group of transaction buyers who jump from company to company, taking advantage of the sales. They never pay full price for anything, and no one makes much money from them. Each company assumes that all of its customers are price sensitive, when in reality, few of their loyal customers are price sensitive at all.

Training your customers

Transaction customers aren't necessarily born that way. They become transaction buyers through environmental exposure and the way they are treated. As suppliers, we may feel we have to take the world as we find it, but that isn't necessarily true. We can ruin a group of customers who are prepared to develop a relationship with us by converting them into transaction buyers. How do we do this? By talking price to them all the time instead of talking services and relationships.

For example, you attract customers by offering discounts. Once you have acquired them, you hold periodic sales and send out e-mails extolling your low prices. What a mistake! You are training your customers to think of your product or service as a commodity whose value can be measured only by price. Once you have implanted this idea in their minds, they will learn to shop around. Soon they will find someone who sells the same product or service for less. In his insightful book, *Customer Loyalty: the Second Act,* Brian Woolf explains:

> Sales always grow when prices are cut. Unfortunately, we now know that new customers attracted by such promotions typically exhibit low loyalty and require constant "price feeding" to keep returning, which means continued lower gross margins. Heavy promotional pricing is not a recommended tactic for building loyalty. Offers to existing customers that reward frequency and spending are far more effective in achieving that goal . . . Several years ago one major US retailer was suffering from the sales doldrums. To address the problem, it reduced prices in its weekly circulars from previous levels. As expected, this triggered higher sales and transactions—but also less customer loyalty. Its best customer numbers, already down 10% from the previous year, continued to fall during the promotional period despite the increased foot traffic. The promotion simply resulted in gaining low margin sales rather than building customer loyalty.

What should you do for relationship buyers?

- Describe what your products do, how various customers use them, how they are made, and new developments in your field.

- Divide your customers into segments and send them different messages.
- Learn their birthdays and send them a card (e-mailed, of course!).
- Periodically write thank-you e-mails for their purchases; don't combine with a pitch for more sales.
- Ask their opinions on your products and services. Put the reviews in your e-mails and on your Web site.
- Create blogs in which your customers can comment. This helps to build a customer community for your company.

Treating buyers better

Many e-mail marketers are so busy getting promotional e-mails out the door that they send the same e-mail to everyone. After all, if you mail daily, with each daily e-mail different from the day before's, you can't do much else.

If you are hunting for sales, as most e-mail marketers are, most of your e-mail subscribers are buying absolutely nothing, a few of your subscribers are buying something, and a fraction of them are buying a lot. This last group represents your loyal customers. These are the ones you want to keep because they provide 80% of your profit. So what should you do?

To maintain their loyalty, you have to treat them better than you do the non-buyers. You can personalize their content. Thank them for their purchases. Offer them something as a reward for being such good customers, like free shipping. You don't want to lose any of them, but you will because that always happens. So divide loyal customers into two groups: a test group and a control group. Do all your experimentation with the test group, sending them all your new ideas. With the control group, do what you have always done: send them the same content that the non-buyers get. Prove to yourself and to your management that treating buyers better—lifecycle management—helps retain your loyal customers.

EXHIBIT 17-05 Lifecycle management contribution to relevance

Lifecycle Management Weight 20%	
3	Part of integration of lifecycle into all e-mails
2	Stand alone e-mail based on one life cycle
1	E-mail used for one occasion: welcome e-mail
0	No recognition of customer lifecycle

As you know, from chapter 5, lifecycle management is a component of relevancy. This chart explains how lifecycle management is scored. Loyalty recognition, basic to lifecycle management, represents 20% of the total score, adding up to relevant e-mails.

Building loyalty in older subscribers

Older Internet users with higher incomes buy more online; 65.6% of consumers over 50 with incomes of $50,000 or more reported they had made at least one Internet purchase in the past year, according to a 2007 survey by Media Audit. This is up from 50.2% in 2004. How do you appeal to these folks?

Recognize their needs. Shop PBS added icons to its site that let visitors increase the font size on product pages. Elderluxe.com moved much of the detail about featured items to the main product page to make it easier to find.

Address their concerns. Data privacy is a greater concern for older shoppers. A Pew Internet & American Life Project survey showed that 82% of those 65 and older say they don't like to give their credit card or personal information to Web sites, compared with 79% of those 50–64, 74% of those 30–49, and 71% of consumers 18–29. The Pew study suggested that finding ways to reduce concern about providing personal or payment information online would increase the percentage of online adults who shop via the Web from 66% to 73%.

FirstStreetOnline puts the HackerSafe and VeriSign security certification symbols on every page and provides easy access to the company's privacy policy, mission statement, and management profiles. Despite these steps, about 25% of customers 65 and older use the phone to place orders, rather than entering credit card information online.

Developing formal loyalty programs

In addition to maintaining customer loyalty through service and communications, you may want to set up a formal loyalty program. By formal, we mean programs where customers fill out an application form and become members. There are basically two types of customer loyalty programs: instant discounts and points accumulation. Both programs are free for registrants.

Instant discount rewards

These programs have been pioneered by supermarkets. They offer members a discount when purchasing certain products, discounts that nonmembers can't get. While they are open to everyone, they particularly appeal to lower-income participants. People join to get the instant rewards these programs offer.

For the retailer, the instant discount programs provide a wealth of information about what each member is spending day by day. Members' purchases can be directed in desired directions. A member who buys a lot but has never bought at the deli, for example, can be offered e-mail coupons good only at the deli, leading her to start buying in a new category.

Some retailers use straddle pricing: cardholders get lower prices on your competitor's advertised specials, while you retain margins on other products. When a regular customer stops shopping, you know instantly because she isn't using her card. You can send e-mails to her to win her back before her alternate retailer becomes a habit. Thus, one by one, you can individually target members to maintain their loyalty.

Points accumulation

These programs have been pioneered by airlines. Instead of discounts, members accumulate points toward future purchases, such as travel, hotel rooms, and automobile rentals. They also offer perks for members who have accumulated lots of points. These members become gold or platinum. These programs are used mainly by participants with higher incomes. People join to get rewards that are more important to them than discounts.

Rewards offered by point accumulation programs include:

- A sense of belonging
- Being treated better, such as service upgrades, club floors, club lounges
- Recognition for their status as members

Marketing e-mails sent to points accumulation program members cover such subjects as:

- How many points the member has accumulated and what she can do with them
- What she has to do to achieve a higher status level (e.g., move from gold to platinum)

- Benefits of encouraging friends and family members to buy from the program sponsor
- Why she should join a related club
- Asking her to provide her profile and preference information so she can receive perks and rewards that appeal to her
- Invitation to post information on a blog
- Invitation to a viral marketing program
- Ability to buy T-shirts, luggage tags, hats, and other brand-identifying products
- Information on company and brand history going back to the founding of the company and including details on how the products are made or developed

How loyalty programs affect attitudes towards financial institutions

Carlson Marketing did a study[1] of more than 2,000 people who statistically represented 2 million financial institution customers. The study showed that:

- Tailored benefits and awards (65%) and communications and offers (59%) that met their personal needs were important factors in choosing a loyalty program.
- Having friendly (73%) and professional (75%) staff was a major factor in determining a customer's primary financial services institution.
- 23% called their primary financial services institution with questions in the last three months, but nearly double that percentage (45%) used the institution's Web site for transactions.
- E-mail and the Internet were preferred over face-to-face interactions when obtaining information (39% vs. 25%) and when accessing customer services (44% vs. 31%).
- 51% would sign up for e-mails from their primary financial services institution if they were offered.

The membership application

All loyalty programs start with a membership application. The customer answers a few questions, such as providing her name, address, and e-mail address. You let her read the fine print about the benefits and regulations of your loyalty program. You send her a welcoming e-mail, in which she confirms her willingness to continue to receive e-mail communications from you.

Companies with both types of loyalty programs have found that starting with the application form, they are able to compile a wealth of data on consumer behavior from the programs, leading to modification in prices, products, and services that improve sales and retention. In addition, using the data, the program managers can create e-mail marketing programs that help build loyalty, increase sales and retention, and reactivate inactive customers.

Loyalty programs, thus, are a win-win situation for consumers and for the companies that offer these programs. Most of today's loyalty programs, like frequent flyer programs, were started before the advent of the Internet and e-mail marketing. Many of the program managers haven't yet caught up with the possibilities that e-mail marketing offers for their loyalty programs.

Social media programs

Faster Internet connections at home and at work have made it easier for millions of people to interact with each other. They are creating their own online content. They are watching online video. In December 2007, a Pew survey found 48% of Internet users watch Web videos, 39% read blogs, 30% post online reviews, and 16% participate in social networking sites like MySpace, Facebook, and Friendster. Social networking and social computing are growing. Consumers today are more connected to other consumers, and they trust other consumers.

In response, some e-mail marketers are adding social elements to their Web sites and e-mails. Social media Web sites like MySpace, Facebook, and LinkedIn have become popular, particularly with younger users, and e-mail plays a large role in them. Social media can represent a great way to capture new subscribers you might not otherwise be able to attract.

If you want to reach young people, go with the flow. Create ways to leverage social networks to promote your e-mail program. For example:

- Create a Facebook page for your company, and capture e-mail addresses on it.
- Use social media sites to communicate news.
- Test messages, calls to action, and creative on social networking sites.

- Use e-mail to drive initial traffic to these sites or your features on them.
- Inform subscribers through e-mail when you launch new social network initiatives.

Before you spend a lot of money on such applications, be wary. Many consumers go to these sites primarily to socialize, not to shop. Ads on social networking sites so far have generated relatively few sales. In 2008. Forrester Research reported that the average cost of an order from an ad on a social network site was $50.11, compared with $19.33 for paid search ads and $6.85 for e-mails to subscribers.

Exhibit 17-06 is an interesting chart. Notice that regular mail always beats e-mail—but not by much—and e-mail beats everything else. The cost of direct mail is about $600 per thousand. The cost of e-mail is less than $10 per thousand. So, for any age group, including seniors, e-mail marketing is more cost-effective than any other direct marketing method.

American Airlines, for example, provides many sources of information for members of its frequent flier program, including:

- E-mails with the flier's AAdvantage account balance showing which miles were posted.
- Personalized e-mails featuring American Airlines product and service news, current promotions, exclusive discount codes, fare sales, travel tips, and special offers—customized for the member.
- Special travel savings bulletins, including discounted weekend fares, special mileage offers, fare sale news, cruises, and vacations.

EXHIBIT 17-06 Messages that lead consumers to buy by age group

Source	15-17	18-24	25-34	35-44	45-54	55-64	65+
Regular Mail	58%	59%	72%	77%	82%	88%	92%
e-mail	42%	56%	65%	66%	69%	79%	73%
Phone	23%	14%	26%	26%	35%	32%	32%
Text Message	13%	9%	10%	4%	2%	3%	0%
Social Networking	12%	10%	11%	5%	3%	1%	1%
Instant Message	11%	5%	7%	2%	4%	1%	0%
RSS	4%	4%	3%	2%	1%	1%	0%

US Internet Users who have purchased due to marketing messages
Feb 2008 n=1,555 who own a mobile phone
Source: ExactTarget 2008 Channel Preference Survey

- AAdvantage partner promotions, partner information, and offers.

Loyalty and affluence

Wealthy consumers are more likely to join points-based loyalty programs. A nationwide survey by Parago showed that high-income households are influenced more by loyalty programs than average income households. More influential than age, gender, or geography, household income proved to be the most indicative of the strength and impact of customer loyalty programs. In total, 94% of high-income households said their membership in a loyalty, rewards, or frequent customer program had a strong to moderate influence on their purchasing decisions, compared to 78% of all consumers.

As income increases, so do the importance and impact of loyalty programs on consumers. Among loyalty program members, 92% of high-income households ($125,000) are actively enrolled in an airline frequent flier program, compared to 51% of all respondents. Hotel program membership showed similar income-dependent results, with 78% of high-income households enrolled in a hotel rewards program, compared to only 35% of the general population.

High-income households differ from other households in the types of rewards they prefer to receive from loyalty programs. Compared to the general population, high-income households are less interested in price discounts and more interested in receiving rewards and recognition for their loyalty. In the Parago study, 39% of high-income households named the special treatment they received from loyalty programs as one of their favorite things. Particularly among male travelers, first-class upgrades, perks, and faster check-in and boarding were more important to them than the free miles.

Loyalty programs affect consumer behavior. According to the survey, 93% of US consumers were willing to depart one hour earlier than needed for a flight if it meant they could fly on their preferred frequent flier airline. Sixty-seven percent of frequent fliers said they would be willing to pay $25 or 5% more for a ticket on their frequent flier airline versus a competitor.

Takeaway thoughts

- Loyal customers buy more, buy higher priced options, and have a higher lifetime value.

- Loyalty is measured by retention rate.
- Loyalty can be increased by good products and services, employees, and communications.
- Loyalty is built by rapid, helpful response to communications. The process should be studied on a regular basis.
- Use professional and part-time seeds for your e-mails.
- Loyalty is helped by attracting the right kind of customers in the first place.
- Transaction buyers have no loyalty; it is hard to make a profit from them.
- Relationship buyers are the loyal customers you want.
- Don't train your customers to think only of price.
- There are two types of formal loyalty programs: discounts and points.
- A key benefit of loyalty programs is the data you can collect on customers, which can be used in communications.
- Points programs attract affluent customers, who want perks rather than discounts.

Notes

1. *Carlson Relationship Builder 2007* (Minneapolis: Carlson Marketing, April 2, 2007) http://www.carlson.com/media/article.cfm?id=427 &group=marketing&subhilite=0&terhilite=0.

18

Viral Marketing

> One of the most powerful, but surprisingly underutilized, tools is the referral program. For generations, companies have witnessed the power of satisfied customers referring products or services to someone they know. However, most companies do not actively pursue referrals, thinking customer advocacy is a phenomenon that occurs naturally, not one that can be encouraged. This hands-off approach to referrals is being pushed aside for something more proactive. In many industries the cost of acquiring customers via traditional marketing efforts is four times what it is to acquire customers through referrals. Renowned business author Frederick Reichheld believes the number of people who are willing to refer your product or service is the single most important customer metric in determining a business's success. He quoted Enterprise Rent-A-Car's CEO Andy Taylor: "The only way to grow a business is to get customers to come back for more and tell their friends."
>
> Chris Moloney, Parago

Word of mouth has always been one of the best forms of advertising. When e-mail marketing came along, word of mouth was given a new name: viral marketing. "Viral" because how it spreads news about products and services is similar to how a virus spreads infections throughout a population.

Everyone is familiar with the chain letter e-mails we receive from friends from time to time. These e-mails are a form of viral marketing. Companies have learned to take advantage of the chain letter concept by encouraging their customers to tell other people about products and clever e-mails they are enthusiastic about. Viral promotions may also take the form of video clips, interactive games, advertisements, images, and text messages.

In the typical situation, an e-mail has something so interesting, amusing, unusual, or valuable, that recipients want to share it with a friend. The marketer makes this easy by featuring an "E-mail this to a friend" button prominently within the e-mail. When this button is clicked, the e-mail client sets up a forward message, just as if the reader had clicked "forward." In some cases. the marketer offers an incentive to forward: "If your friend takes advantage of this offer, your friend will receive X% off on his next purchase."

Should you offer incentives to your advocates?

Mixing love and money is usually a bad idea. Offering customers incentives to spread the work about your stuff is often a mistake, and here's why: you make them feel dirty if they're paid for it. Some things just shouldn't be for sale—friendship, certain kinds of favors, and your recommendation . . . But do you remember the original MCI Friends and Family promotion? It was all about mutual benefit. When you told a friend about the program, each of you got a reduced phone bill. You both benefited, equally and together. It kept the motives pure, it respected altruism, and everyone felt good about it. It was all about sharing the savings, not one person making money off the other. It's still one of the greatest word-of-mouth programs in history.

Andy Sernovitz, *Word of Mouth Marketing*

What is your viral goal?

The most important thing you can ever have, in any strategy, is a clear goal that can actually be achieved and is shared by all stakeholders. With viral campaigns, this is critical. Problem is, some strategists state the method as the goal. Going viral isn't the goal. The goal is to engage the audience in one of two ways: amplification or advocacy.

—Gary Stein, "Go Viral or Bust"[1]

Harvesting e-mail addresses

Once a reader forwards something to a friend, several things can happen. The friend could buy the advertised product. The friend could forward the e-mail to another friend. If you set it up right so that the new folks have a reason to buy from or get in touch with you, you may have harvested the e-mails of some new people: some of your subscribers' friends. But remember: you don't have permission to send e-mails to these friends. You can, however, ethically send one e-mail to each one with a message: "You recently received an e-mail from yourfriend@ISP.com, which featured one of our products. If you would like to periodically receive future e-mails directly from our store, click here."

If you mail to 1 million subscribers and 1% of them forward your e-mail, your mailing will reach 10,000 new potential subscribers or forwarders. That's 10,000 people you probably didn't know about, some of whom will come to your Web site and buy from you. And what did it cost you? Probably nothing. A really good e-mail can thus spread rapidly to reach a large number of new people. Those reached through viral messages are usually *more likely* to buy from you or forward your e-mail than the average original recipient. Why? Because what they received was from a friend, not a firm. They may want to please the forwarder or just trust the fowarder more than a company, so they're more willing to forward it.

Shared benefit

There can be a joint benefit in a forwarded offer. You can offer your subscribers the same deal you offer her friend, such as: "If you both stay at the Hilton in Hawaii, you can each get 10% off the normal daily rate. To be sure you both get this rate, enter this code . . . " In such a situation, there is not only a joint benefit but also a togetherness because each one benefits from the word of mouth. To do this, of course, you must provide a unique code and set up your system to honor those codes. Plus, you will want to measure the number of forwards, opens, clicks, subscribes, and purchases.

For example, "Are you an *in* girl?" was the e-mail query that Sephora used to launch a lead-generating program targeting brand enthusiasts. The point of the interactive campaign was for girls to get their friends to nominate them as "in girls," who would then receive free products to critique. The campaign started with e-mails to Sephora's existing customer base. The recipients then used their social networks to attract new participants.

After forwarding the e-mail to their friends, subscribers received a congratulatory electronic card that invited them to take a trend-spotting quiz. A sample question: "How would you describe your beauty personality? a) I don't touch the stuff; b) You name it, I've tried it; c) Lip balm, mascara and moisturizer only."

Each subscriber was also given a personalized Web page containing Sephora marketing offers and that allowed them to see how many nominations they had received. The girls with the most nominations won. "In girls" received targeted Sephora products in exchange for providing their opinions. By asking customers to reach out to their peers, Sephora had a response rate three times higher than those of its other marketing efforts. The 5% of the girls who asked friends to nominate them managed to recruit 40% of the overall traffic to the program.

Thanking people for their comments

There are hundreds, maybe thousands, of blogs and Web sites where people can comment on products and services. If you deal with the public, chances are there are dozens of comments on your company somewhere. Some are probably good, and some are probably bad. What should you do about it?

Most companies ignore these comments, but intelligent marketers can often make productive use of them. In his book, *Word of Mouth Marketing,* Andy Sernovitz recommends marketers make it a practice of thanking these folks. They will probably be surprised to learn that someone from your company read their comments and took them seriously.

"Why not recruit one of your customer service reps (preferably one who can spell) to be a word-of-mouth service rep?" Sernovitz writes. "Give a low-level frontline staffer the job of proactively searching the Web for any and all word of mouth about your company and your products. When people are praising your company—thank them. When people have a complaint, a rant, a slam—fix it.

"Every problem festering unsolved is another unhappy customer out there spreading negative word of mouth," he continues. "Make it right. Every problem is an opportunity to fix the permanent record, to end your story on a positive note."

Viral Examples

Below are several examples of viral campaigns.

WZ.com's PlayStation sweepstakes

WZ.com created a viral sweepstakes to boost site traffic. The contest gave away four Sony PlayStations. Each entrant received an additional chance to win for every friend he referred. After registering, users were asked to reenter their first and last names and e-mail address. Then they entered a friend's name and e-mail address above an e-mail from them to the friend.

The sweepstakes' viral aspect increased the results by 96 times. People referred their friends who, in turn went to the Web site and referred their friends, so the total number of e-mail addresses collected was 96 times what it had been on previous campaigns, when only existing members were asked to enter the sweepstakes. The program's success led WZ.com to run the contest every month.

Subservient Chicken

Burger King's Subservient Chicken illustrated the fast-food chain's "have it your way" slogan. A man dressed up as a chicken obeys commands you type into a box on the Web site. It was such fun that thousands of people clicked "Tell a Friend" to send e-mails to their friends. It did wonders for Burger King TenderCrisp chicken sandwich sales.

Less than a year after the site's went live, it had 14 million unique visitors. About a month after the TenderCrisp sandwich debuted, Burger King reported that sales increased an average of nine percent a week. Subsequently, the company saw a "double-digit" growth of awareness of the sandwich and significantly increased chicken sandwich sales. The TenderCrisp continues to sell better than the original chicken sandwich.

Successful viral marketing efforts are happy accidents that take on a life of their own. Subservient Chicken had entertainment value, utility, instant gratification, and was unique among its peers.

You've got to be kidding

Quicken offered a "you've got to be kidding" guarantee, whereby customers who weren't satisfied could get their money back without returning the product. Thousands of Quicken users sent e-mails to others about this, and Internet sales of Quicken increased dramatically.

Pepsi extras

PepsiCo rewarded e-mail forwarders through a VIP program within its Pepsi Extras loyalty program. If a subscriber had done enough ad forwards and conversions, the subscriber made it on to the Pepsi VIP list. The VIPs got coupons and other perks via e-mail. Pepsi designated those who forwarded e-mails as influencers. The idea was that forwarding e-mails provided an opportunity to build a deeper connection with people who liked the company, products, and e-mails so much that they are willing to tell their friends and family about it. It worked. An analyst of the Pepsi program had suggestions for those who wanted to copy this approach:

First, choose your subject line wisely. Your e-mail's subject line will determine your open rate and have an impact on your company's brand equity. Next, know where you stand. The devil may be in the details, but your e-mail may be in the spam filter if your domains aren't set up properly or you have a poor reputation. Finally, only send relevant messages. Offers in the e-mail work best when they support the brand or industry you are sending to. You can get more than three times the lift in response if the offer is relevant to the message.

How to create viral marketing e-mails

Viral marketing e-mails are inexpensive and, once programmed, easy to apply. Set up a system and place a "forward to a friend" button prominently in your e-mails. Viral marketing is a good measure of your success as a copywriter. If viral is working, it is because you have something interesting in your e-mails that readers want to pass on. Viral is an easy way to add to your subscriber list, if done correctly. There is always the chance that one of your e-mails will be so creative that it becomes a national sensation. It is like winning the lottery: your chances of winning are low, but since the entry fee is basically nothing, why not enter?

In his book, Sernovitz sums up the essentials for high velocity viral e-mails:

- **Make sure it's forwardable.** Far too many overdesigned e-mails fall apart when forwarded.

- **Write it for the second recipient.** Make sure your e-mail makes sense to pass-along readers who get it from a friend.

- **Capture new talkers.** Every e-mail should have sign-up instructions right in the message.

- **Tell recipients to tell a friend.** Put a big bold call to action right at the top.

- **Be funny.** Put something amusing at the end of every message just to get it forwarded.

- **Tell readers NOT to forward the message.** Works every time. My most-forwarded messages start with the phrase "PRIVATE: DO NOT FORWARD."

Viral jokes

Joke lists provide entertainment and instant gratification. They offer people something they've seen before. Someone reads the joke because it was sent to them; they laughed. Then they sent it on to you. You laughed and sent it on to a friend in the hopes that she will laugh. To use this idea in marketing, put something really funny in your marketing e-mails.

Many of the people on joke lists pass the jokes on to someone else. My value to you increases because I gave you something you could use. I don't ask for anything in return. Keep opening my e-mails because I may do this again.

Chris Bliss became an expert at social networking. By 2008 he had developed over a million hits on his Web site. He did this with no listings, no search engine work, and little effort. He reported recently that he had talked to a friend about floating a clip on the Web, maybe as an e-mail attachment, but he never got around to it. Then it happened on its own. The viral content marketed itself.

Widgets

A widget is a small program usually designed to do one very specific thing. Widgets can exist on a Web site, on a user's desktop, or as a part of an operating system. On Facebook and MySpace, widgets are used by members to personalize their pages. American Airlines launched a marketing widget called Travel Bag that lets Facebook friends share personal tips and travel experiences. AA worked with Microsoft to advertise the widget within Hotmail.com and Window's Messenger, as well as on sites like Digg.com. The idea was to put marketing in the hands of consumers by allowing them to generate lists of best restaurants, gyms, and museums. They could post journals about trips, post photographs, share anecdotes, and keep friends updated.

The widget's viral nature became the marketing tool by which American Airlines hoped to learn more about consumer preferences for travel destinations, restaurants, and leisure activities. If someone shared a list of places to see in Barcelona, Spain, with friends, for example, AA might e-mail both the customer and the friend information on services and flights to the city, along with a 10% discount coupon.

Web 2.0

You can't discuss viral marketing without reference to Web 2.0, a term first used by O'Reilly Media in 2004. Web 2.0 refers to a certain level of interactivity on a site. It includes a social element where users generate and distribute content, with freedom to share and re-use. This sharing produces a rise in the economic value of the Web to businesses, as users can perform more activities online.

How the long tail works

Chris Anderson, editor-in-chief of *Wired* magazine, coined the term *long tail* to explain that through the Internet, products that are in low demand can be listed on Web sites and can collectively have a total sales volume that exceeds the sales volume of the current bestsellers or blockbusters.

EXHIBIT 18-01 The long tail

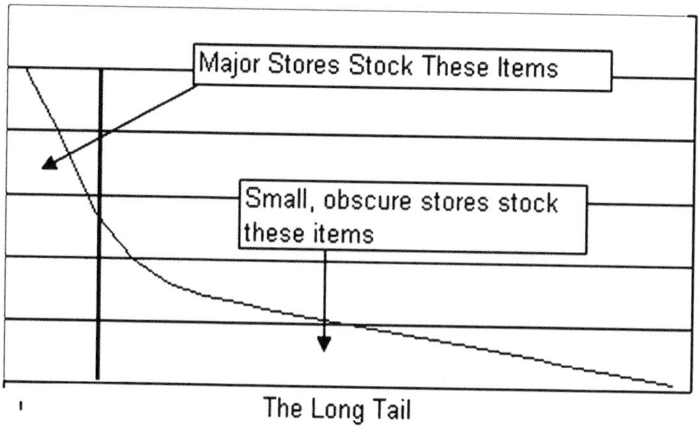

Major Stores Stock These Items

Small, obscure stores stock these items

The Long Tail

There are two reasons why the long tail is so successful: First is that using the Internet, a retailer can have one warehouse for the entire country, instead of the hundreds of warehouses that are required by brick-and-mortar stores. The central warehouse can maintain thousands of less popular items that would be impossible to stock in the traditional retailing system. Second, through links in Web sites and e-mails, it is possible to have access to goods stocked in partner companies, with the partner company fulfilling the orders coming to it from the central Web site.

Examples of Web sites that benefit from the long tail include eBay, Yahoo, Google, Amazon.com, Netflix, and iTunes. According to Anderson, "the future of business is selling less of more." A significant portion of Amazon's sales, for example, come from obscure books that aren't available in brick-and-mortar stores. The total volume of low-popularity items that it sells exceeds the total volume of high popularity items.

The key reason the long tail works is the Internet has dramatically reduced the search costs for products and services. EBay was the first to discover this, followed by Amazon. Google capitalized on it to become the powerhouse it is today. Before the Internet, consumers spent far more time hunting for things than they have to nowadays. So the long tail benefits consumers. But it also benefits business because before the Internet it was very difficult for vendors of obscure items to find customers.

Before Netflix, video rental stores like Blockbuster could only stock a few thousand titles in their stores. Netflix can stock 90,000 titles in a few warehouses. Consumers get a wider choice and less well-known movie producers get a wider audience.

Takeaway thoughts

- Viral marketing involves encouraging customers to send their marketing e-mail content to other people, sometimes providing you with access to the new people.
- You gain wider recognition, more sales, and increase your e-mail mailing list at comparatively little expense.
- Viral marketing is not a sure thing. But sometimes it takes off and results in a major public awareness of your brand or products—without your having to spend any additional resources.
- Viral marketing is basically free. The only requirement is to have a "forward to a friend" button on your Web site and in e-mails and provide an easy routine to forward the content.
- You can send one e-mail to the new addresses gained by viral marketing, asking if they want to receive e-mails from you.

Notes

1. Gary Stein, "Go Viral or Bust," The ClickZ Network (June 3, 2008), http://www.clickz.com/showPage.html?page=3629750.

19

Using Analytics to Boost E-mail Success

In my humble opinion, your customers need to know that Web analytics is hard so they can:

- Plan to spend a reasonable amount of time determining their needs
- Allocate resources appropriately for implementation and deployment projects
- Set expectations with management about when results will begin to appear and what will need to be done with those results
- Make the case to management when they need additional resources, more software, or more time
- Have an appropriate relationship with their vendor, based on clear expectations

Eric T. Peterson

There are two broad methods of using analytics to support e-mail marketing: subscriber analytics (farming) and clickstream analytics (hunting). Both are useful and can be highly profitable.

Subscriber analytics is more than 30 years old and supports most of the marketing methods discussed in this book. They are familiar to anyone who has participated in database or direct mail marketing. Clickstream analysis is very new and only applies to Web sites and e-mails. Because it is so new, many people starting out in e-mail marketing assume that clickstream analysis is all there is. Wrong. If you are going to do subscriber farming, you start with subscriber analysis.

To analyze subscribers, build a database and track what your subscribers are like, what they want, and what they do (see chapter 4). In addition to studying what the subscribers do when they receive your e-mails, study their demographics and offline behavior. Typically, once you have the subscriber's postal address, you can append more than

100 fields of data, such as age, income, presence of children, and time at residence. These data, combined with opens, clicks, and purchase history enables you to create segments, to customize and personalize your e-mails, and to increase profits.

There are several analytical techniques you can use, particularly multiple regressions, chi-squared automatic interaction detector (CHAID) analysis, lifetime value (LTV) analysis, and RFM (LTV is discussed in chapter 6 and RFM is discussed in chapter 7). Here, we'll discuss the basic idea behind regressions and CHAID.

Predictive modeling

Predictive modeling is predicting how a large group of subscribers will react to an offer. With a good predictive model you can determine:

- Which subscribers are likely to buy and which aren't
- Which subscribers are in danger of leaving you and which are more likely to stay
- Which products subscribers are more likely to buy

The ideas behind e-mail marketing predictive models rest on some simple principles. First, segmented subscribers react in predictable ways. This predictability is vital. If everyone had unpredictable reactions to your services and marketing efforts, a model couldn't provide reliable predictions.

Also, clues to expected behavior can sometimes be discerned in subscribers' previous behavior and their demographics. The behavior used in predictions can usually be stored in your database in the form of transactions. The demographics can be appended from an outside source. However, this doesn't always work. It isn't always possible to predict subscriber behavior based on the data you can collect in a database.

Finally, a predictive model is usually developed from the response to previous promotions. It is difficult to run a successful predictive model unless you have already sent a promotion to your subscribers and received a reaction from them. You usually can't just create a model from a file of names and addresses to determine which ones will be more interested in your product. For example, what kinds of customers are more likely to purchase an RV? You can make some assumptions (e.g., over 65, lower middle income), but without the results of an RV promotion to a number of subscribers, you won't be able to build a model that gives you reliable predictions.

Once you have built a model that works, you can improve your open and click rates. The basic use of a predictive model is to concentrate your attention on those subscribers most likely to respond and purchase and avoid promotions to those least likely to respond.

For example, you send a promotion to 100,000 subscribers offering a product and get a 2% conversion rate. Using the promotion's results, you build a statistical model that successfully identifies the characteristics of responders and non-responders. You use that model to score a new batch of 100,000 names. If you mail only to the 50,000 whom the model identifies as the most likely responders, you should get a response rate of more than 2%, perhaps 3% or more. This will be much more profitable for you and will help you avoid sending e-mails to people who aren't interested in this particular product.

Is e-mail subscriber analysis necessary?

Some people maintain that subscriber analytics is useless for e-mail marketing. Their reasoning goes like this: Subscriber analytics was developed for direct mail, where each letter has an in-the-mail cost of $0.50 or more. By sending your promotions to those most likely to buy, you are saving the cost of mailing to those less likely to buy. These savings don't apply to e-mail, where the cost per e-mail is a fraction of a penny. Consider the table in Exhibit 19-01. The table compares direct mail with e-mail marketing. With direct mail, we have a house file of 1 million names. We send a promotion that has an in-the-mail cost of $500 per thousand ($0.50 per piece), including printing and postage. With a 2% response rate and a $30 profit per successful sale, the net profit is $100,000.

We then add in analytics to the mailing program, developing a predictive model that we apply to our file. This model predicts those customers most likely to buy. We drop from the mailing those less likely to buy, half the file, and our sales rate goes up from 2% to 3%. Our net profit has risen by $90,000.

With our e-mail program, we also have 1 million names. Using batch and blast, it costs $10 per thousand ($0.01each) to create and send then e-mails. We get a conversion rate of 0.5%, giving us a net profit of $140,000.

Finally, we look at our e-mail subscriber file using subscriber analytics. We create a model to determine the likelihood of each subscriber to respond to this offer. Using this model, we select the responsive half of the file for e-mailing. *Then* we can take a step we couldn't easily do in direct mail: we segment the responsive subscribers into five groups,

EXHIBIT 19-01 Subscriber analytics results for direct mail and e-mail programs

Comparison of Analytics Results	Universe	Mailed	Cost per Thousand	Promotion Cost	Analytics Cost	Percent Sales	Total Sales	Profit per Sale	Gross Profit	Net Profit
DM Without Analytics	1,000,000	1,000,000	$500.00	$500,000	$0	2.0%	20,000	$30.00	$600,000	$100,000
DM With $10K Analytics	1,000,000	500,000	$500.00	$250,000	$10,000	3.0%	15,000	$30.00	$450,000	$190,000
e-mail without Analytics	1,000,000	1,000,000	$10.00	$10,000	$0	0.5%	5,000	$30.00	$150,000	$140,000
e-mail with $10K Analytics	1,000,000	500,000	$15.00	$7,500	$10,000	1.5%	7,500	$30.00	$225,000	$207,500

each with e-mail copy specifically designed for them. As a result, our conversion rate goes up to 1.5%. Our costs per e-mail has gone up from $10 per thousand to $15 per thousand ($0.015each), but the net profit has gone up by $67,500. (If a service bureau builds your model, you may pay between $5,000 and $50,000 for a model, depending on complexity. An additional expense is the appended data necessary for your model to work.)

There is one other benefit of using subscriber analytics not shown in this table. Because we have eliminated the mailing to 500,000 subscribers whom the model showed were less likely to buy, we have reduced the unsubscribes, undelivers, and spam reports that would have come from those subscribers if we had e-mailed them something they didn't want. These unmailed subscribers are available for a promotion for something that would be more to their liking.

E-mail subscriber analytics, thus, has two benefits: It boosts the conversion rate by letting us send customized e-mails to segmented subscribers. And it helps us avoid sending e-mails to people for whom the promotion isn't relevant, saving them for a promotion they will consider relevant.

Why does direct mail get higher conversion rates?

There are several significant reasons for this. First, a direct mail letter's shelf life is several days. For catalogs, it is several weeks. An e-mail's shelf life is seldom more than one day. The longer the direct mail letter, catalog, or postcard kicks around the house, the greater the chance someone will read it and will buy something from it. It can be carried from room to room. E-mails are almost never printed out. They can't be carried around. They sit with a hundred other e-mails in an inbox where only one or two people in the house ever see them.

Also, everyone in the country gets direct mail. Roughly one-fifth of all US households is disconnected from the Internet and has never used e-mail, according to a 2008 Parks Associates study. Although the number of nonconnected households is slowly going down, age and education remain factors in this divide. One-half of those who have never used e-mail are over 65, and 56 percent have no schooling beyond high school. On the other hand, many Americans over 65 are active responders to direct mail.

Another reason e-mail's conversion rates are low is because of batch-and-blast e-mail hunting campaigns. People are sick of getting too many e-mails. The same isn't true of direct mail. People get only five or six direct mail pieces a day. The average person gets many promotional e-mails a day. Batch and blast reduces the attention span and response rates.

Finally, because of the cost of a direct mail letter, all direct mail today is targeted at people likely to respond. Direct mail is conducted like farming. Because of the low price of marketing e-mails, less than 10% are targeted. Most e-mail marketing is hunting: set a trap out (e-mail blast to everyone) and see what you can catch.

How predictive modeling works

There are some simple steps to predictive modeling. First, do a promotion or use a previous promotion as your base. You will need enough customers in your model to get statistically valid results. A promotion to a few hundred people is seldom adequate as a base. For a typical model, you need about 500 conversions. If, for example, you typically get a 2% conversion rate, you need to send your promotion to 25,000 people (500/0.02).

Next, append demographic and behavioral data to your responders and non-responders. What data should you append to your database? Start with a test file with all possible data appended. Work with it to discover which fields contribute to a successful model, and don't append the rest. You will find that there aren't more than 20 data fields worth appending. Exhibit 19-02 shows the typical data available for appending.

EXHIBIT 19-02 Data available from AmeriLINK for appending

Appended Fields	Millions	Appended Fields	Millions
Age	236	House Value	123
Income	236	Length of Residence	185
Auto Loan	84	Mail Order Buyer	108
Census Data	236	Non Profit Donor	84
Dwelling Type	236	Persons in Household	236
Gender	236	Occupation	90
Glasses Wearers	19	Religion	208
Height	61	Student Loan	22
Weight	55	Wealth	236
Home Ownership	153	Marital Status	236

Now add geographic data. Some of the data in Exhibit 19-02 are demographic (age, income). Some are behavioral (mail order buyer, non profit donor). You can also add geographic data: code people by whether they live in rural areas, suburban areas, or urban areas. You may find differences in people who live in the north, south, east or west. Those who live near the ocean or a lake may differ in their response from those who live inland. Do they have a listed or an unlisted telephone number? For some products, marketers have found that those with unlisted phone numbers respond differently from those with listed numbers.

To this appended data, add previous purchase history with your company.

Next, divide your data into two parts: a test group of 12,250 non-converters and 250 converters and a validation group of 12,250 non-converters and 250 converters (if you're starting with a group of 25,000 subscribers). Both groups should have exactly the same type and variety of people.

Set aside the validation group, and work with the test group to create a model. Discard the outliers. These are customers whose purchases were so unusual that they will distort the outcome. For example, if the average customer bought one or two items for an average sale of $200, an outlier would be a customer who bought 482 items and spent $96,400. You toss out this customer's records in building your model.

Now that you have a file rich with appended data, you are ready to construct a predictive model. As a first step, you will typically use a multiple regression model (we will discuss CHAID later in this chapter). A multiple regression is an equation that describes the relationship between a dependent variable and more than one independent variables. The dependent variable is the purchase that the customer made as a result of your promotion, here 500 bought and 24,500 didn't. The independent variables are the behavior and appended data. Which of the independent variables will be most valuable in predicting who will buy and who won't? That is what the model is designed to find out.

The model is typically run on a PC using analytical software, such as provided by SAS or SPSS. When the model is run, the software applies weights to each independent variable. A weight is a number that indicates how important (weighty) each variable is in predicting the desired result (product purchase). Typically, a weight of 0 means the variable has no discernable influence on the consumer's decision process. A negative weight means the variable influenced the purchase process in a negative way. The higher the negative value, the less likely the person is to buy the product. Higher weights mean the factor is more likely to influence the outcome. A weight of 0.89 for income tells us that this factor is more important than age, which receives a weight of 0.52.

Exhibit 19-03 is a sample table of weights created by a regression model. There were 24 independent variables with weights from –4.88

EXHIBIT 19-03 Weights assigned by a regression model

Variable Description	Effect	Contribution %	Coefficient
Last Product = Other	–	15.87%	–0.8988
Customer E-mail Flag = N	–	14.22%	–0.6856
Sales Item Amount LTD $0–$100	–	12.72%	–0.8494
Last Registration Recency 25–36	+	7.90%	0.5511
Sales Last Order Recency 0–6	+	5.13%	0.5330
Last Registration Recency 7–12	+	5.01%	0.5953
Sales Item Amount LTD $101–$250	–	4.87%	–0.5232
Last Registration Method = Broadband	–	4.06%	–0.4365
Customer Type = Unknown	–	3.66%	–4.8778
Last Registration Method = Dial Up	–	3.57%	–0.4432
Customer Type = Organization	+	3.35%	0.6922
Sales Last Order Recency 7–12	+	2.95%	0.3867
First Registration Method = Paper	+	2.63%	0.2668
Sales Last Order Recency 61+	+	2.35%	0.6308
Sales Last Pay Method = Credit Card	–	2.32%	–0.2889
First Product = Other	–	1.98%	–0.4011
Sales First Order Recency 0–6	+	1.46%	0.6904
Sales Item Amount LTD $251–$500	–	1.22%	–0.2690
Last Registration Recency 0–6	+	1.15%	0.2837
Sales Item Amount LTD $1001+	+	0.96%	0.2885
Sales Last Item Amount $20.00–$39.99	+	0.77%	0.1655
First Registration Recency 25–36	+	0.67%	0.2151
First Registration Use = Business	+	0.61%	0.3022
Sales First Pay Method = Credit Card	–	0.57%	–0.1337
		100.00%	

to 0.69. Some are positive (+), and many are negative (–). If the customer said he didn't want to receive e-mails, he is unlikely to buy the product (–0.6856). Note that almost all the positive variables are related to recency. This table shows us that for this promotion, the e-mail marketer should probably have used RFM and saved the money he spent on modeling.

Using the weights determined by the model, you may want to concentrate on those independent variables that have a high weight in determining the outcome. You can ignore those variables whose weight is very low. So instead of using 30 different variables (age, income, religion, student loan, etc.), you can build your model based on the five or six variables that provide the greatest predictive power. This may save you money later on when you have to append data to a large file.

The final outcome of the model is the algorithm. An algorithm is a

EXHIBIT 19-04 A large test file scored by algorithm into deciles.

Decile #	Mailings #	Responses	Response %	Index
1	15,853	1,085	6.84%	297
2	15,853	640	4.04%	175
3	15,853	564	3.56%	154
4	15,853	390	2.46%	107
5	15,853	286	1.80%	78
6	15,853	279	1.76%	76
7	15,853	193	1.22%	53
8	15,853	142	0.90%	39
9	15,853	69	0.44%	19
10	15,853	9	0.06%	2
Total	158,530	3,657	2.31%	

The index is computed by dividing the average response rate by the actual response rate and multiplying by 100. The index for decile three, then, is 3.56% divided by 2.31% multiplied by 100, or 154.

mathematical routine used to perform computations. In the case of a marketing statistical model, the algorithm usually includes computer code that creates a score for each customer or prospect record. The scores may vary from very likely to purchase to very unlikely to purchase. Exhibit 19-04 shows the ranking of deciles from an actual mailing.

Using the algorithm that emerges from your test group modeling, you can then score the validation group. Remember, the validation group has already been promoted. You know the outcome (see Exhibit 19-05). If the algorithm developed for the test group is going to be use-

EXHIBIT 19-05 A large validation file scored by algorithm into deciles

Decile #	Mailings	Responses	Response %	Index
1	15,984	1,092	6.83%	292
2	16,265	618	3.80%	163
3	15,528	524	3.37%	144
4	15,900	397	2.50%	107
5	16,391	339	2.07%	89
6	15,378	295	1.92%	82
7	15,812	217	1.37%	59
8	15,471	128	0.83%	35
9	18,258	89	0.49%	21
10	13,542	4	0.03%	1
Total	158,529	3,703	2.34%	

ful in predicting, it should correctly identify most of the people in the validation group who actually bought (with a high score) and those who didn't (with a low score). If the algorithm correctly scores the validation group, you have a successful model that can be used to predict customer response in your next promotion.

In example, look how closely the validation group response rates came to the test group. This model was an accurate predictor of response to a large mailing. From charts you can see that the lowest deciles should probably not be mailed to, since the offer wasn't relevant to more than 99% of those mailed.

What if it doesn't work?

If the validation process is unsuccessful, of course, you either have to redo your model or give up the whole process as a bad job. It may be that with the data you have available, a model can't predict the responders. This is very often the case. Modeling doesn't always work.

Often, the answer may not lie in the available data. For example, it could be that purchasers can't be determined by age, income, presence of children, or any standard demographic factor. Suppose you sell cold remedies. It is highly possible that demographic variables won't show a difference between purchasers and non-purchasers. If so, all the modeling in the world won't help.

A general rule: if the solution doesn't seem to make sense to you, it probably doesn't make sense. Modeling isn't magic. It is usually only a quantification of intuitive logic.

A good marketing analyst can sense when something doesn't look right. In my experience, if something looks odd, it probably is odd and isn't real behavior. Sudden changes in trends, steps in the data, spikes, and dips are all potentially symptomatic of artificial impacts on data. If they can't be explained by real-world events, it's worth digging into the data to see if there's anything untoward happening, like changes to the tool's configuration, new site monitoring tools being put in place, changes to the hosting environment, and so on.

Getting good data integrity is not a one-off event. It's an ongoing process. Be wary of the potential impact that changes to your site or tracking environment will have on your data and plan accordingly. Take time to reconcile your data on a regular basis to see if there are any divergent trends. With these basic processes in place, you might avoid that sinking feeling at some point in the future.—Neil Mason, "Analytics Basics: Getting the Right Numbers Right"[1]

What you can do with your model

If you have a model that works, you can use it to segment your subscriber file and generate profits. With predictive models, you can determine who will buy (or not buy) a product or service and which product or service to offer them. You can also determine which customers are most likely to unsubscribe, and when they are most likely to depart.

To start using your model, score the mail file for your next planned promotion of the same product. Then divide the scored file into deciles based on the score. The top decile contains those people most likely to buy, the bottom decile those least likely to buy.

Deciles 6 through 10 are your worst-performing deciles. Avoid sending e-mails to this group. You should, however, mail about 5% of each of these low-performing deciles to prove to yourself and to your management that the model works properly and actually predicts the buyers correctly.

By mailing only the higher deciles, you will get a higher response rate overall and avoid bothering subscribers who aren't interested in the product. By not sending them what they consider to be irrelevant e-mails, your unsubscribe rate should go down.

Modeling using CHAID

CHAID is a classification tree technique that displays the modeling results in an easy-to-interpret tree diagram, going from the top down instead of from the bottom up. CHAID is useful in picking the best prospects for an e-mail marketing effort. But it may be useful to score the remainder of the file using a regression model, if we wish to identify valuable segments.

The segments in the tree diagram can be shown in a gains chart. The gains chart shows how deep into a file you must go to select subscribers who have the results you want in terms of conversion rate. Financial data or assumptions can also be incorporated into CHAID results. When the desired predicted outcome has only two values, such as opener or non-opener, modelers can generate a nominal CHAID model.

Exhibit 19-07 is a small, simplified example of an ordinal CHAID tree diagram. The diagram begins at the top with a box representing

EXHIBIT 19-06 CHAID diagram

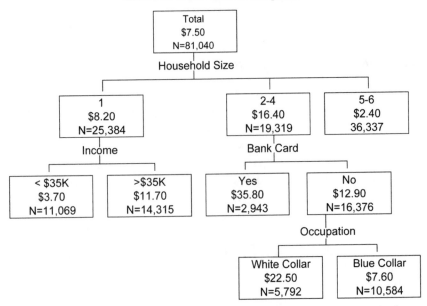

the entire modeling sample of 81,040 households to which a consumer product was marketed via e-mail. Also included in this first box is the average profit per household generated by the initial mailing ($7.50). The CHAID analysis identified household size as the best predictor around which to begin segmenting the prospect market.

We see that a household size of two to four persons returns an average profit of $16.40, which is more than twice the profit generated by a one-person household and nearly seven times the profit generated by a five-to-six–person household.

CHAID then shows us that if a two-to-four-person household has a bank card, the average profit jumps to $35.80. If no one has a bank card, they return an average profit of only $12.90. However, among this non-bank-card group, if the head of household's occupation is a white-collared job, profitability rises to $22.50.

Exhibit 19-07 shows the gains from each segment identified on the CHAID diagram. The fourth column shows the average profit per household for each segment. The fifth column represents this profit number as a relative index, with the average for the entire modeling sample set at 100. The best segment has an index of 476, which means it performs at a profit level of 4.76 times the average for the entire modeling sample and more than 15 times the profitability of the worst segment.

EXHIBIT 19-07 Gains chart from CHAID analysis

1	2	3	4	5	6	7	8	9
Segment ID	Segment Count	Percent of Total	Average $ Value	Segment Index	Cum. Count	Cum. Percent	Cum. $ Value	Cum. Index
3	2,943	3.6	$35.80	476	2,943	3.6	$35.80	476
4	5,792	7.1	$22.50	298	8,735	10.8	$27.00	358
2	14,315	17.7	$11.70	155	23,050	28.4	$17.50	232
5	10,584	13.1	$7.60	101	33,634	41.5	$14.40	191
1	11,069	13.7	$3.70	49	44,703	55.2	$11.70	156
6	36,337	44.8	$2.40	31	81,040	100	$7.50	100

Columns six through nine are cumulative representations of the data from columns two through five: cumulative household count, percentage of modeling sample, average profit per household, and profit index. Among other things, the gains chart shows that the best three segments (segments 3, 4 and 2) represent 28.4% of the total sample, have an average profit of $17.50 per household, and are 2.32 times as profitable as the average sample household.

The gains chart is a handy tool for seeing what levels of expected profitability would result from going increasingly deeper into a subscriber file.

CHAID helps to create market segments. The tree diagram predicts the performance of each segment. This helps e-mail marketers visualize and define market segments. CHAID model algorithms are used to score a master database. As with regressions, new records added to a file can be scored quickly once the basic scoring algorithm is set up.

Descriptive modeling or profiling

Even if predictive modeling doesn't work for you, have a profile done of the actual customers in your subscriber base through descriptive modeling. It is amazing how many companies know very little about their customers. Any modeler can create useful profiles that look like the one in Exhibit 19-08. In this example, we see the household income of the company's customers. It has a much higher percentage of upper-income consumers than the national average.

EXHIBIT 19-08 Household income of customers compared to the national average

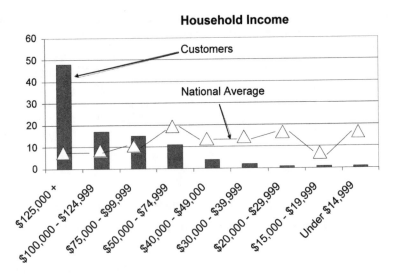

Goals for subscriber analysis

- **Which offers are working and which aren't?** Which products are best to try to cross-sell with others? These insights can help to make sure more visitors convert into customers.
- **Which subscribers are unsubscribing and which aren't?** How much do they spend before they unsubscribe? What have you done that leads people to unsubscribe?
- **Which RFM cell codes produce the most conversions?** Can RFM be correlated with e-mails to make useful predictions?
- **Which source of e-mail addresses produces subscribers who convert, as opposed to subscribers who never buy anything?**
- **Should multibuyers be treated differently from one-time buyers or non-buyers?** What would the difference be?
- **What is the lifetime value of your subscribers?**
- **Are your segments working to help you design better e-mails?** Segments set up at one-time may not be working well today.

Clickstream analytics

Clickstream, or Web, analytics is the science of analyzing what customers do when they read your e-mails or come to your Web site. The goal is to make these e-mails and Web sites more user friendly and encourage more opens, clicks, and conversions. It requires specialized software. It also requires analysts who review the data and come up with methods for using the results to improve the e-mails and Web sites. Web analytics is so specialized that the process should probably be outsourced. It is not simple, easy, or cheap to do. Done right, however, it can have a tremendous return on investment.

How are e-mails tracked?

Little invisible Web beacons are embedded in outgoing HTML e-mails. These beacons are used to track what happens to the e-mail after it arrives. Whenever the user opens the e-mail, the beacon sends a packet back to the server that originally sent the e-mail. This lets the server know that the e-mail has been opened. Similar beacons are embedded in all links within the e-mail. As a result, the organization running the server is informed of all the links the subscriber clicks on.

Using clickstream data

Clickstream data is the history of the links a consumer clicked on when she read your e-mail or looked at your Web site. Storing clickstream data concerns privacy watchdogs, especially since some companies have begun selling users' clickstream data as a way to earn extra revenue. Several companies purchase these data, typically for about $0.40 per month per user. While this practice may not directly identify individual users, it is often possible to indirectly identify them. Most consumers are unaware of this practice and its potential for compromising their privacy. Reputable companies that use major outsourced e-mail agencies highly rated by Forrester or JupiterResearch never sell user clickstream data to others. They advertise that fact on their Web site and in their e-mails. We do not recommend selling clickstream data.

Internal analysis of clickstream data, however, has become essential to profitable e-commerce. It tells you how your e-mails and Web sites are being received by users. It also tells you something about subscriber behavior. You can use clickstream data to create or enhance subscriber profiles. For instance, you could use clickstream analysis to predict whether a particular subscriber is likely to make a purchase from your site. You can also use clickstream analysis to improve subscriber satisfaction with your e-mails and your company.

Using clickstream analysis

Once it is possible to capture what your subscribers are doing when they receive your e-mails, you can use the information to understand

EXHIBIT 19-09 Illustrative clickstream analysis dashboard

Clickstream Analysis of July 13 Campaign									
Delivered	1,874,223 Opens		356,102 Unique Clicks		8,582 Clicks		24,682 Conversions		12,217
Click Category	Subscriber Visits	Avg Pages Visited	Time on Site	% New Visits	Avg Cart Items	Avg Abandon	Items Checkout	Average Item Price	Total Revenue
Childrens	969	1.97	1.48	76.47%	1.2	48.0%	605	$37.44	$22,638
Womens	1,218	2.68	1.52	65.91%	2.2	31.0%	1,849	$108.33	$200,294
Kitchen	787	2.50	2.48	63.63%	2.4	11.0%	1,681	$18.01	$30,275
Stationery	484	2.24	2.22	71.43%	1.3	18.0%	516	$38.33	$19,776
Bargains	1,997	3.11	3.22	44.87%	2.8	12.0%	4,921	$18.32	$90,146
Elsewhere	3,127	1.88	2.01	44.67%	0.9	6.0%	2,645	$4.09	$10,820
Total/Avg	8,582	2.88	2.59	73.40%	2.16	25.2%	12,217	$30.61	$373,949
Annual		1.97	2.01	44.60%	1.77	21.74%		$36.40	
% Change		45.99%	28.66%	64.57%	22.03%	15.92%		-15.91%	

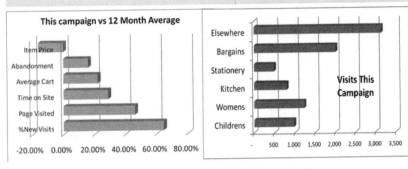

how your e-mails are being received. One of the best ways to under-stand the data is to create dashboards that summarize the subscriber's activity in ways that enable you to make changes to improve your e-mails.

Exhibit 19-09 shows the results of an e-mail campaign that fea-tured five product categories: children's, women's, kitchen, stationery, and bargains. The marketer sent 1.8 million e-mails that produced $373,949 in sales. The chart compares this e-mail to the 12-month av-erage of e-mails sent by the company. The graphs show which site sec-tions were most visited by subscribers, time on site, new visits, abandoned cart percentages, revenue, and average sales.

Your ESP can help you set up your own dashboard ESP. The impor-tant part of the analysis is using the data to improve the e-mails in the future. This is where many e-mail marketers fail today. They are so busy creating and sending new e-mails that they don't take the time to see what was good or bad about the current e-mails, so that they can make their new ones better. In this example, the card abandonment rate in women's clothing is particularly striking. If the abandonment rate could be brought down from 31% to 21%, for example, total sales might go up significantly. Why were so many carts abandoned, and what could the marketer have done about it? Developing and studying such a dashboard is very important to success in e-mail marketing.

Key performance indicators

To create a useful dashboard, begin by identifying the key performance indicators (KPIs) that are important to your business. Then add the reports that contain those KPIs to your dashboard. Which are the most useful e-mail KPIs? Here are several from different industries:

- E-mails sent and delivered
- Percentage of delivered e-mails that are opened
- Clicks compared to other campaigns
- Percentage of opens that are clicked
- Churn rate (percentage of unsubscribes or undeliverables)
- Viral rate (e-mails sent to a friend)
- Opens and clicks by ISP domain name

You may also include:

- Total sales by campaign, month, quarter, or segment
- Profit per delivered e-mail
- Sales per delivered e-mail
- Cost per delivered e-mail
- Average order value (AOV)
- Number of orders
- Conversion rate of opens or click-throughs
- Number of site visits
- Cost per visitor
- Number of leads by entry page
- Average page views
- Length of site visit by source

If you are interested in generating leads for your sales force, you may have these KPIs:

- Number of leads (by product/client type)
- Number of downloads
- Site visits
- Google PageRank

- Cost per lead
- Conversion rate
- Membership, subscriber, or database growth

Using clickstream data to improve e-mail campaigns

Let's use what we have learned in this chapter. Suppose we send a promotional e-mail to 1.5 million customers on Tuesdays and Fridays, which research has shown us to be our best days. Our e-mail program is outsourced to a large agency highly rated by Forrester and JupiterResearch. The e-mail agency has an excellent clickstream analytics staff. For example, they receive reports from the Tuesday mailing on Wednesday. They spend Wednesday afternoon analyzing the results, and their creative team and our creative team spend Thursday redoing the material on the home page based on what the clickstream analysis tells us.

The e-mail, diagrammed in Exhibit 19-10, has eight sections with links. A is a search box. B is a place to change your profile or preferences. C is the main message, a welcome offer. D is a download offer, and E is a discount offer, F is a second main subject area. G is a prod-

EXHIBIT 19-10 Diagrammed e-mail sections

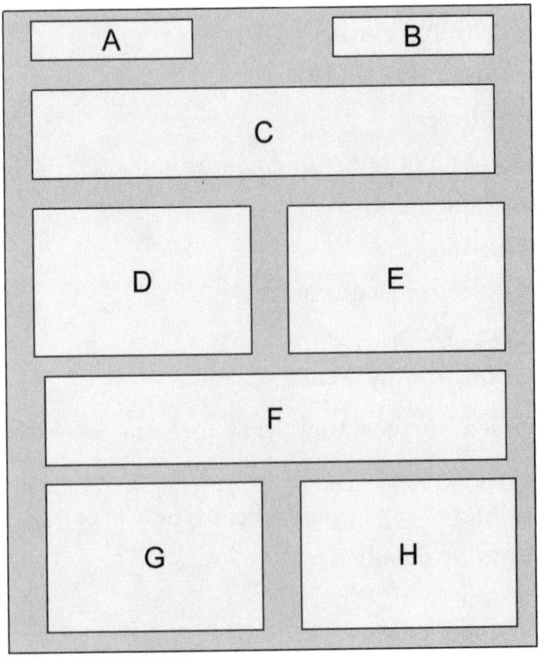

uct directory with links to many other areas, and H is viral information. Clicking on any of these sections leads readers to more information on the site, where there are additional links to click. (A well-crafted e-mail has at least a dozen more links. These complexities are why e-mail tracking is so specialized that it should be outsourced.)

Twenty-four hours after we send those 1.5 million e-mails out, we get a report on the results. We design our dashboard to provide us with information on what the subscribers did with the e-mails we sent. Exhibit 19-11 shows us how we might arrange the statistics.

At first, this chart seems like a bunch of numbers that don't tell us much of a story. Only 3,655 subscribers (0.7% of the openers) clicked as many as eight times on the links. But graphs can help show some productive actions we might take. Exhibit 9-12 shows the first clicks, and Exhibit 9-13 shows the second clicks.

What do we learn from these two graphs? Subscribers go first to the discount offer (section E), which is in the middle of the page on the right. After that, most people appear to go to the search box to find something else, rather than going to the product directory (G) or to another area in the e-mail. We can reasonably conclude they are looking for something that isn't in the e-mail.

What are they are looking for? Our Web analytics can tell us what subscribers put into the search box. If we find that most people are searching for a similar product, that product should be featured in the next e-mail—and we should revise the product directory to include that product, since it clearly isn't there. Besides revising the directory, where in the e-mail should we feature this missing product? What should we displace?

The graphs also tell us that the download offer (D) isn't a winner. It occupies valuable space to the left of the discount offer, our most popular click. We are wasting that space on something of lesser interest to our subscribers. Let's find out what most people are searching for and feature that in space D.

If you can get your e-mail agency to give you dashboard charts like these, you are home free. Get the data, figure out what it tells you, and take the actions suggested. Create profitable e-mail marketing. If you do this correctly, you can correct 90% of what can be fixed using this type of analysis. Don't waste money by trying to fix the remaining 10%.

EXHIBIT 19-11 Clicks on e-mail locations

April 15 Promotion
Sent 1,502,116
Delivered 1,437,223

No Title	Total Clicks	First Clicks (Opens Percent)	Second Click	Third Click (501,223 / 34.9%)	Fourth Click (Unique Clicks Percent)	Fifth Click	Sixth Click (335,819 / 67.0%)	Seventh Click (Unsubs Undels)	Eighth Click	Click (9,823 / 55,070)
A Search Box	291,219	210,004	35,700	27,801	6,300	4,200	3,360	1,680	1,260	420
B Registration	428,662	72,561	12,335	1,887	2,177	1,451	1,161	580	435	145
C Welcome Offer	191,113	310,110	52,719	11,730	9,303	6,202	4,962	2,481	1,861	620
D Download Offer	415,552	85,671	14,564	3,038	2,570	1,713	1,371	685	514	171
E Discount Offer	82,222	419,001	71,230	14,858	12,570	8,380	6,704	3,352	2,514	838
F Second Product	290,884	210,339	35,758	15,414	6,310	4,207	3,365	1,683	1,262	421
G Product Directory	191,337	309,886	52,681	21,977	9,297	6,198	4,958	2,479	1,859	620
H Viral Invitation	291,338	209,885	35,680	12,900	6,297	4,198	3,358	1,679	1,259	420
Total			310,667	109,605	54,824	36,549	29,239	14,620	10,965	3,655

EXHIBIT 19-12 First clicks by priority

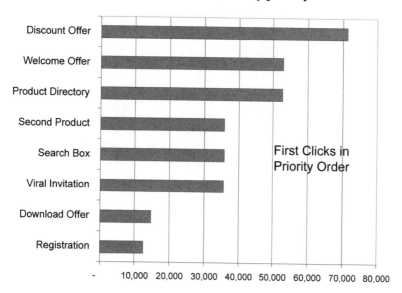

EXHIBIT 19-13 Second clicks by priority order

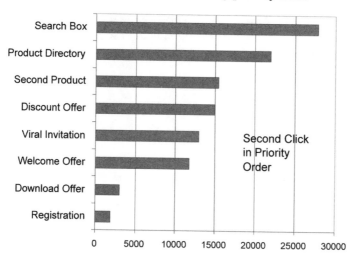

Takeaway thoughts

- There are two broad types of e-mail marketing analytics: sub-scriber analysis and clickstream analysis.
- Subscriber analysis uses multiple regressions and CHAID.

- You can usually accurately predict which subscribers will be interested in your e-mail for a particular product—and which won't.
- Use modeling to ensure your e-mails are relevant to those subscribers you target.
- Clickstream, or Web, analytics tracks user opens and clicks on e-mails by embedding invisible Web beacons in each HTML e-mail.
- Web analytics uses clickstream data to tell you what people are looking at and which people are looking.
- Clickstream analysis involves massive amounts of data, which are usually collected and analyzed by outsourced specialists and put into custom dashboards for e-mail marketers.
- The most important part of analytics is what you do with the results: improving your e-mails and targeting the right subscribers with the right offers.

Notes

1. Neil Mason, "Analytics Basics: Getting the Right Numbers Right, "The ClickZ Network (June 24, 2008), http://www.clickz.com/showPage. html?page=3629993.

20

Business-to-Business
E-mail Marketing

Business-to-business e-mail campaigns . . . show up looking like long-winded, copy heavy, direct mail solicitations. Some have one giant image with marketing-department–focused jargon. Most seem to miss the mark in understanding what may attract the right buyer and how to deliver real value and relevancy to the inbox . . .

Your tone should be much like it would be in a face-to-face meeting with your prospects: direct, professional, and in a manner that makes your audience want to do business with you. Don't waste your time building up to the pitch—state why you are sending this message and what's in it for the recipient.

The message should clearly articulate the purpose and value to the subscribers while making it easy for them to identify and act on any call to action. Don't bog them down with too many cross-promotional messages or secondary marketing messages. Allow them to scan the e-mail and find out what's in it for them.

Your main measurement analysis should not be based on opens and clicks but on how many leads are generated.

Simms Jenkins, Brightwave Marketing

B2B e-mail marketing is completely different from B2C marketing, mainly because of differences in the audience. Businesspeople are intensely interested in their industry—whether the industry is software, hotels, automotive parts, or insurance. They are seldom interested in some other industry. They feel a community spirit within their industry but are also suspicious that others in the industry are trying to learn their secrets and steal their customers. They are usually keenly anxious to know what their competition is doing, planning, and thinking. They are convinced that the competition knows things that they don't.

Depending on their jobs, businesspeople want to know how products are made and how they are marketed. They want to know the details of new products. They gobble up statistics on their industry. And despite a strong desire not to give up any information on their own companies, they are really interested to know details about their competitors—who their clients are and what their prices are. Case studies are of great interest, then, particularly if they explain how they were done and the results are put in terms of numerical improvements: "20% better than the previous method." They will circulate your e-mail with details like this throughout their company.

Your audience consists of two groups of businesspeople: customers (and prospects) and competitors. You can be certain that your competitors will be reading your e-mails, no matter how hard you try to prevent it. Your job is to define your industry for your customers and prospects and be a trusted source of information for them.

Don't make your e-mails vehicles to push your products or your company. Instead, treat your readers as insiders; give them exclusive inside information on trends that you see: new processes, markets, and products (not necessarily yours). And don't assume your audience knows everything you do. You can recycle or reprint valid information from the past or provide extensive links to other sources. When you use industry jargon, always provide a link to the term's definition. Because people change jobs so often today, at least a third of your audience are newcomers who aren't sure what the term means. Make it easy for them to find out. Make them want to open your next e-mail to learn more.

Also, make it easy for your readers to e-mail your content to others in their company. The ideal B2B e-mail will have a huge secondary audience of people within any company. Your readers will often gain internal recognition and status from having found your e-mail and passed it around.

Glossaries of terms and statistics in your industry, sent in your e-mails, will be reprinted and saved. They will be the most widely read and circulated e-mails you can send. They establish you and your company as experts in your field.

Your goal is simply to provide to your readers a source of the most interesting, well-informed information about their industry. As a result, your readers will look forward to receiving your e-mails, will print them out, and will forward them to others. They will see you and your company as experts and leaders in their field. If you can do that, you don't need to sell your products in your e-mails. Your acceptance and reputation will do that. It is then up to your sales force to move in and take the orders.

Administrative requirements

There are a few requirements for every B2B e-mail. You will need:

- A table of contents, so readers can quickly see and skip to whatever interests them.

- A comprehensive search box, so readers can search for any product or piece of news. Constantly improve what this box can do by monitoring what readers put into it.

- A blog for readers to post comments on—comments that will be read by everyone in the industry.

- An "forward to a friend" function that captures the friend's e-mail address.

- An archive box to permit readers to see an index of all previous e-mails.

- Cookies, so you can say greet readers by name in your e-mails.

- A link to the company's history.

- A link to the company's directory, with links to everyone readers may want to get in touch with—including e-mail addresses, phone numbers, and postal addresses.

- A link to product listings, so readers can look up any product.

- A suggestion function, so readers can suggest topics for future e-mails.

- An option for readers to be send shortened text messages to their cell phones.

- A prominent, easy-to-use unsubscribe function.

How you look in a preview pane

B2B marketing subscribers almost all use preview panes when looking at their inboxes. In an EmailLabs survey, 90% of e-mail newsletter subscribers have access to a preview pane, and 69% say they frequently or always use it.

After looking at the sender and the subject line, these readers' eyes peek at what is in your e-mail. This view can make or break your whole e-mail campaign. Design the top left of every e-mail with that pane in mind. If you have a big colorful ad there, the readers will see nothing of interest.

Writing a B2B newsletter

A good B2B e-mail newsletter is like the popcorn, peanuts, and TV that go with the drinks at a bar. While you are in the bar, talking to your friends, you are munching away and keeping your eye on the TV. When you have eaten, watched, and talked for a while, you will order another drink—which is why the bar provides those free things in the first place.

Your newsletter should be filled with articles and information about you or your subscriber's industry, not necessarily about your products. Businesspeople like to keep up on what is going on in their industry. That's why they may want to read your e-mail newsletter. If you can provide interesting content once a month, things that people in their industry want to know about, then your company will always be fresh in their minds. They may also be willing to read something about your products and your company, which could lead to an inquiry and an order.

Your job, therefore, is to come up with the interesting content (the peanuts, popcorn, and TV) so your readers will think first of your company when they need products that your company sells. So what should you write about?

Start by signing up for all your competitor's newsletters. You should know what they are saying so you can say something similar, but better. Be sure to go to all the trade shows and mingle with people there to find out what they are saying and thinking about you and your competitors' products. Use Google and Technorati to read what is being posted on relevant blogs. You will get a lot of material for your newsletter from blogs. Create a blog of your own.

Talk to your sales reps and your customer service. They will give you ideas for content. You can exchange news and articles with other newsletters from companies that don't compete with yours.

But the best source for ideas will be your readers. Give them a space in the sign-up form and in every newsletter for them to suggest topics. One interesting idea: when your subscribers are out of the office, which happens a lot in B2B situations, they usually post an automatic notice saying when they will be back. This notice often includes their current title and other useful information. Read all of these and add the relevant info to your database record.

Mobile versions

The percentage of businesspeople who regularly read business e-mails on their mobile devices is more than 37%. It is essential that any B2B e-mail message have an option for the stripped-down version in every campaign.

Create a mobile version of your newsletter optimized for a phone's screen. Include only a small version of your logo. The rest of the content should be easy-to-read text that can be scanned quickly. In the mobile version, include a link to the full edition of your newsletter so readers can check it out on their desktops.

Many executives today use their smartphones to scan and delete e-mails. If you have a weak message, busy execs will delete your messages while attending a meeting. If, however, you have something interesting to say that shows up in the first three sentences, your e-mail may get saved for the executive to read later.

According to MailerMailer, 74% of all opens occur within the first 24 hours. Since a few recipients will open your e-mail weeks later, however, make sure your images, links, and landing pages remain accessible.

Topics for your B2B newsletters

- Events of interest: trade shows, new product launch, etc.
- Industry calendars
- Interviews with key executives in the industry
- Tips and best practices
- Surveys and reports on the results
- "Ask the expert"
- Regular columns and features
- Top 10 lists
- Six steps to success
- Industry statistics and benchmarks
- Interactive quizzes
- Reader feedback
- Links to resources and Web sites of interest in the industry
- Best-of-class write-ups of the present and past
- Glossary of terms used in the industry
- Case studies
- Opinions on an industry trend
- Common problems in the industry and how some are solving them

Check the clicks on each section of your newsletter to see which are being read and which ones are skipped. Be guided by these clicks.

Creating a business blog

A blog can help humanize your company to customers and the outside world. Blogs are a powerful tool for marketing and promotion. Because they are short, they are easy for your customers to read (and you to write), so customers are more likely to come back daily to see what you might have to say.

With a blog, you can show your customers that your company is made up of ordinary people. If you do it right, you can create a blog without becoming too personal or too formal. Company Web sites are often created by a committee. Blogs are just the opposite.

For that reason, you have to be able to assign one person to write for and manage the blog within written guidelines without formal approval of content every day.

Hewlett-Packard uses blogs to show off its friendly image to the world. The HP Blogging Code of Conduct is an example of how a large corporation handles blogging. It's worth reading, and perhaps emulating. According to the Code:

> HP blogs are written by a variety of employees at different levels and positions in the company, so you can expect many viewpoints. You can also expect the following:
>
> 1. We will strive to have open and honest dialogues with our readers.
> 2. We will correct inaccurate or misleading postings in a timely manner. We will not delete posts unless they violate our policies. Most changes will be made by adding to posts and we will mark any additions clearly.
> 3. We will disclose conflicts of interest.
> 4. Our Standards of Business Conduct will guide what we write about—so there are some topics we won't comment on such as information about financials, HP intellectual property, trade secrets, management changes, lawsuits, shareholder issues, layoffs, and contractual agreements with alliance partners, customers, and suppliers.
> 5. We will provide links to relevant material available on other blogs

and Web sites. We will disclose any sources fully through credits, links and trackbacks unless the source has requested anonymity.

6. We understand that respect goes both ways—we will use good judgment in our posts and respond to you in a respectful manner. In return, we ask the same of you.

7. We trust you will be mindful of the information you share on our blogs—any personally identifiable information you share on a blog can be seen by anyone with access to the blog.

8. We will respect intellectual property rights.

9. We will use good judgment in protecting personal and corporate information and in respecting the privacy of individuals who use our blogs.

Comments:

1. Comments will be reviewed by bloggers before they are posted on our blogs.

2. We will review, post and respond to comments in a timely manner. We welcome constructive criticism. We can't respond to every comment, but will read all of them.

3. defamatory, use profanity, or otherwise violate our policies or Terms of Use.

4. Because our blogs focus on material of general interest to all our readers, we ask that you direct customer support inquiries through our traditional customer service channels or use our IT resource center forums. Using these channels will allow you to get your issues to experienced HP support representatives in a timely manner.

5. Our bloggers will not respond to customer support issues and will not post these comments to their blogs.

Reaching C-level executives

C-level executives are the top executives in any company, including such titles as chief operating officer (COO), chief executive officer (CEO), chief marketing officer (CMO), and chief financial officer (CFO). C-level executives make high-level decisions that can affect millions of dollars. It may be useful to survey these executives so you can present a valuable report to the industry. How can you reach them?

Trying to get these busy executives to take 15 minutes to complete a survey presents two problems: much of the information they have is highly confidential, and they aren't usually in a position to accept anything of monetary value as an incentive for participating in a survey. So what can you do?

One of the best methods was outlined by Claire Tinker at ESL Insights, a marketing intelligence firm. She suggests setting up an executive advisory panel. You can begin with a simple e-mail that says, "You are invited to participate in a business study." The invitation has to spell out what executives will get in return for their investment. You can offer a personal incentive or a donation to a charitable organization, and, more important, an executive summary of the research findings. They will be reading information provided by other C-Level executives who work for their competitors.

To get their participation, the invitation has to come from a C-level executive at your own company. It will seem like two senior executives talking to each other, not a researcher asking questions. When the survey is done, send a summary of the results to the respondents with a thank-you note. The results of this survey could be one of the most valuable e-mails you send all year, besides building a close relationship with the C-level executives who participated.

Takeaway thoughts

- B2B e-mail marketing is completely different from B2C e-mail marketing.
- Since B2B readers are not spending their own money, perks work better than discounts.
- Your goal should not be to sell but to establish your company as a source of industry information.
- It is OK to repeat information from the past.
- Always define your technical terms because your readers will look to you as an authority.
- Study your competitor's newsletters.
- Remember that many of your B2B readers will see your e-mails on their mobile devices.
- Newsletter content should be mostly about industry trends, analyst reports, and whitepapers. There should be very little about your company or products.
- If you're trying to reach an audience of executives, your e-mail should come from someone who is equal to the people you are trying to reach.

21

Building Retail Store Traffic

I can't believe the number of people who are actually walking in our restaurants and redeeming the coupons. Before I tried e-mail, I put a coupon in the local newspaper and had fewer than 10 people redeem it. Then, I put the same coupon in an e-mail and sent it to 400 people and saw 100 of the e-mail coupons redeemed that month! That's an outstanding rate, given that only 400 were sent. I've also tried direct mail and got such a low redemption rate that I won't do it again. The e-mail coupons are being printed and brought in daily and people are fighting to get on my e-mail subscription list.

—Abby Weaver, Marketing Director, Fajita Grill

Most people think of e-mail marketing mainly as supporting online transactions. Actually, e-mails do far more for offline sales than they do for online, as you will learn in this chapter. An Epsilon study reported that 86% of e-mail recipients said that they buy products and services at retail locations as a result of e-mails.[1] Besides online sales, marketing e-mails build the brand and drive catalog sales, phone sales, and brick-and-mortar sales. The percentages will surprise you.

In 2003, cataloger Miles Kimball did a pioneering test of e-mail to stimulate catalog sales. It sent 20,000 catalogs in three waves to previous online shoppers with an accompanying e-mail saying, "Look in your mailbox for . . . " It also sent 20,000 catalogs in three waves without the accompanying e-mail to identical shoppers. Those who received the e-mail spent 18% more per household than those without. Many catalogers now use e-mails to boost catalog sales. By 2007, 82% of 434 catalogers surveyed by the Direct Marketing Association (DMA) were using e-mail promotions. Today, more than 44% of all paper catalog sales are made on the Web, as opposed to phone or mail.[2]

A major video rental chain asked members to provide their e-mail addresses and asked them whether they wanted to receive e-mails about movies. When its list was big enough, it sent e-mail newsletters about movies to 204,000 members every two weeks, holding 16,000 as a control group who didn't receive the e-mails. After six months, the retailer discovered that those who got the e-mails spent 28% more per household than those who didn't. E-mails drive traffic to retail locations.

In 2008, Constant Contact reported that 88% of small-business owners surveyed used e-mails to build sales for Mother's Day. Thirty-seven percent of retailers found flowers to be the most popular gift, and 25% of the gifts were a restaurant meal. Salon/spa appointments, jewelry, and clothing were also popular gifts. Most consumers spent from $25 to $75 on their gifts.

Why e-mails boost offline sales so well

- Direct mail and print are about 100 times more expensive than e-mail ($600 per thousand versus $6 per thousand).
- E-mail can be personalized and customized to individual subscribers.
- E-mails are completely measurable.
- E-mails are useful in building a relationship with individual subscribers.

A Harris Interactive Poll conducted for Yahoo reported that 66% of consumers shopped online before making an on- or offline purchase. Of that group, 75% said that going online to research products and services was their first stop in their holiday shopping experience, and 90% said they had a better overall shopping experience when they researched products online before shopping in-store.

Multichannel customers have high expectations for what they think retailers should do for them. Many of them want to:

- Use loyalty cards, store cards, and gift vouchers through all channels
- Get e-mail updates about special orders when they talk to a call center
- Return products to stores that were bought online
- Find out via the Web whether the item they want is available in any given store

After doing their research on the Web, some shoppers will visit a store to touch and examine the product. They may then return to the Web for further price comparison. Finally, they may order it online or by phone.

Bringing shoppers to store events

Stores have an advantage over an e-mail: in a store, a shopper can use her senses to experience the products firsthand. Store visits also prompt impulse buying. They are ideal for food tastings, cooking demonstrations, instructional workshops, trunk shows, and book signings. For instance, Harry & David held a Gourmet Grilling Sauces Tasting Event and used e-mail to raise awareness. Home Depot promoted a kids' workshop on how to build a birdhouse through e-mail. Toys 'R' Us used an e-mail to promote a 3D Crayola Chalk Art event going on in the store. Saks Fifth Avenue e-mails subscribers a monthly listing of flagship-store events. Macy's sent an e-mail promoting its National Wear Red Day for the American Heart Association; if you wore red to a Macy's store on a given day, you received a 15% off coupon.

E-mails offer unique ways to create in-store traffic. Walgreens announced that it was giving away free 8 x 10 photos for one day only. All you had to do was upload your photo to its system online, then pick up the print at your local store.

Getting subscribers to visit your store

The first step is to capture the subscriber's zip code. You can get this on a Web site, in the opt-in e-mail, or in the welcome e-mail. If you don't have the zip code yet, put a box asking for it in every e-mail you send.

As soon as the subscriber enters her zip code in this box, she should be directed to a landing page showing her the stores nearest to her, complete with name, address, phone, hours, and a map. If there are several stores near her, get her to click the store she normally shops at or wants to shop at. *She should never have to enter her zip code again and should never be asked to.* The only exception is if you find that she actually does her shopping at a retail location other than the one nearest to her home zip code. If that's the case, change her designated store to the one she uses. Most of your subscribers are probably employed. Their preferred store may be closer to their work than their home, so you have to allow for that. Once you do, from then on, their preferred store will be featured in every e-mail you send them.

The e-mail should come from the manager of the subscriber's local store and include his name and photo. The subscriber shouldn't receive e-mails from some big corporation. Each e-mail is a personal message to Susan from Burton Price, Manager of the Macy's store at 2314 E. Sunrise Blvd. Does having a manager's name and photo on a promotional e-mail make a difference in store visits? That is easy to test. The numbers will answer your question.

How to use the store manager's name

If the subscriber's local store is within shopping distance of her home, try a personal greeting to her from the store manager above the fold:

> Susan,
>
> Thanks for subscribing to our e-mails. We'd love to have you shopping in our store.
>
> Next time you are there, look me up and I will show you around. I have a special gift for you. Ask any of the sales assistants in our store. They know where to find me.
>
> Burton Price, Store Manager

Be sure to keep track of the results. It should be well worth the effort.

Of course, sometimes your retail staff turns over so fast that such an e-mail isn't possible or practical. You might make it worse if the customer comes to the store as a result of your e-mail and asks for Burton, only to learn that he no longer works there!

Getting the store location correct

A customer reported: "A major retailer really missed an opportunity to personalize an e-mail. The e-mail offered a class at "my local store," but nowhere in the e-mail did it tell me where my local store was. I went to the bottom of the e-mail and saw an "enter my zip code" field. I entered my zip code, and the link took me to the general store locator page on the retailer's Web site. I had to enter my zip code again. What a waste of time."

The relationship between online and offline sales

In 2008, eMarketer provided a very useful chart showing the relationship between Web-influenced store sales and retail e-commerce sales. The results of the survey were eye-opening, as seen in Exhibit 21-01.

Actual walk-in retail traffic purchases as a result of the Web are about four times the volume of online sales! These Web-induced sales can come about in a variety of ways. Consumers can use search engines or banner ads to find Web sites where they do their research before

EXHIBIT 21-01 Web-influenced retail sales

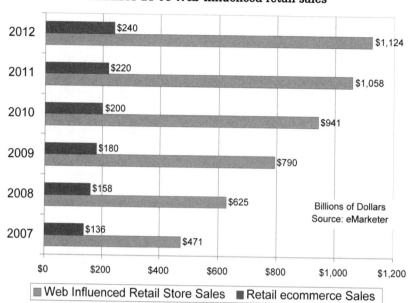

Billions of Dollars
Source: eMarketer

■ Web Influenced Retail Store Sales   ■ Retail ecommerce Sales

going to the retail store. They can also receive e-mails from stores or Web sites where they have shopped or registered and use the information in these e-mails for suggestions that prompt them to visit the local stores to make a purchase. It is really up to the retailer whether he wants to wait patiently until his customers decide to visit his Web site again or to proactively go to his subscribers to tell them what he has to offer that may be of interest to them.

These are powerful numbers. The relationship between e-mails and offline sales shows that for any retailer who wants to send e-mails to potential customers designed to inform them of what is available in his stores, the returns can be phenomenal—even if he does no online business at all.

In 2006, comScore did a study sponsored by Google that found that 25% of Web searchers actually bought an item directly related to their Web search. Among these buyers, 63% completed their buy offline in some manner, either in a retail store or over the phone. The remainder bought the item on the Web.

The study reported that the highest levels of offline buying were video games and consoles (93%), toys and hobbies (88%), consumer electronics (84%), and music/movies/videos (83%). Offline clothing buying reported in the study averaged 65%.

Items in stock in a retail store

How annoying to receive an e-mail promoting an interesting product only to find, when you go to the store, that the item isn't in stock. Some retailers have managed to put links in their e-mails that enable viewers to check if an item is in stock at their nearest store. It saves an hour's fruitless trip—and just might represent the secret to creating more offline sales. If some of your stores have special evening events, your e-mails might let your subscribers know about the events at their local store. Banana Republic does an excellent job of preview shopping events for top customers.

How a retailer becomes Web-savvy

To see just how promotional e-mails can affect overall revenue and lifetime value, let's try what Albert Einstein described as a thought experiment. We will imagine a retailer who started with a profitable business with 350,000 customers who visited his stores twice a year, spending an average of $144 per visit. We will trace this store's possible future based on three scenarios:

- The store has successful retail outlets but no Web site or e-mails.

- The store adds a Web site but doesn't sell on the Web.

- The store adds online sales to his Web site and starts sending e-mails.

Each incremental marketing method has its benefits and costs. Let's first look at the retail-only picture in Exhibit 21-02.

In Exhibit 21-02, the retailer traces the lifetime of 350,000 customers over three years. The 50% retention rate in the acquisition year means that half of those who shopped the first year never come back again. Marketing costs include print ads, promotions, and a loyalty card program, which is used to track visits. The retailer used part of the marketing budget to recognize his gold customers and to try to get the lapsed customers to come back.

The retailer builds a Web site

Spending $1 million, the store built a Web site that features its products, sales, long corporate history, and management team. The chain doesn't sell from the Web site, but visitors can enter their zip code and find the nearest store location. In addition, there is a search box so shoppers can find a product on the site, with pictures and prices. Occa-

EXHIBIT 21-02 Retailer with no Web site

No website Small Retailer		Acquisition Year	Year 2	Year 3
Customers		350,000	175,000	96,250
Retention Rate		50%	55%	60%
Visits Per Year		2	3	4
Total Visits		700,000	525,000	385,000
Spending Per Visit		$144	$150	$155
Total Revenue		$100,800,000	$78,750,000	$59,675,000
Operating Costs	65%	$65,520,000	$51,187,500	$38,788,750
Customer Acquisition Cost	$40	$14,000,000		
Marketing Costs	$4	$1,400,000	$1,400,000	$1,400,000
Total Costs		$80,920,000	$52,587,500	$40,188,750
Gross Profits		$19,880,000	$26,162,500	$19,486,250
Discount Rate		1	1.15	1.36
Net Present Value Profits		$19,880,000	$22,750,000	$14,328,125
Cumulative NPV Profits		$19,880,000	$42,630,000	$56,958,125
Lifetime Value		$56.80	$121.80	$162.74

sionally the store offers coupons on the site, which visitors can print out and bring to the store. The site is listed in the search engines, increasing the possibility of visitors finding the site and searching for products. As a result of all this, the retailer has increased the visits per year (see Exhibit 21-03).

Despite the expensive Web site, the customer lifetime value grew by $24 in the first year, $44 in the second, and almost $60 in the third. First-year revenue grew by more than $27 million.

The retailer sends e-mails and adds online shopping

The Web site has been a success. The retailer now takes the next big step. He collects e-mail subscribers on the Web site and offers incentives to store employees to ask customers for their e-mail addresses. The result, after some effort, is the store has acquired 300,000 e-mail opt-in subscribers plus 200,000 regular shoppers who shopped offline but did not subscribe to e-mails. The retailer begins a weekly series of e-mails to the subscribers, inviting them to come to his store. The e-mails permit shoppers to research, learn of his sales, and print coupons

EXHIBIT 21-03 Retailer with non-e-commerce Web site

Website No Online Sales Small Retailer		Acquisition Year	Year 2	Year 3
Total Customers		350,000	192,500	115,500
Retention Rate		55%	60%	65%
Visits Per Year		2.5	3.5	4.5
Total Visits		875,000	673,750	519,750
Spending Per Visit		$146	$152	$157
Total Revenue		$127,750,000	$102,410,000	$81,600,750
Operating Costs	65%	$83,037,500	$66,566,500	$53,040,488
Customer Acquisition Cost	$40	$14,000,000		
Marketing Costs	$4	$1,400,000	$1,400,000	$1,400,000
Website Costs	$2.50	$875,000	$481,250	$288,750
Total Costs		$99,312,500	$68,447,750	$54,729,238
Gross Profits		$28,437,500	$33,962,250	$26,871,513
Discount Rate		1	1.15	1.36
Net Present Value Profits		$28,437,500	$29,532,391	$19,758,465
Cumulative NPV Profits		$28,437,500	$57,969,891	$77,728,356
Lifetime Value		$81.25	$165.63	$222.08

to use in his stores. The e-mails are a great success and bring in more revenue.

In addition, our retailer begins to sell his products on the Web. Exhibit 21-04 shows how his picture has changed.

His first year revenue is now over $163 million including revenue from online and e-mail-induced sales. We can trace the increase in his sales as he moves up the chain to full online and offline sales with e-mail stimulation in Exhibit 21-05.

The $53 million is pure profit. All the added costs have been included. This example shows how to go about the computation process in moving gradually from offline retailing to full online retailing, supported by e-mail marketing. Use tables like these to begin supporting your e-mail marketing planning. These and all the other charts in this book can be downloaded for free at www.dbmarketing.com.

E-mail coupons vs. FSIs

It is really important to know what your audience is doing. Are they buying? Are sales working? Is relationship marketing working? Are the e-mails important? How much do they drive offline purchases? One

EXHIBIT 21-04 Retailer with on- and offline sales and e-mails

Online & Off Line Sales Small Retailer	52	Registration Year	Year 2	Year 3
Non-E-mail Customers		100,000	55,000	30,250
E-mail Subscribers		250,000	207,500	174,300
Annual Unsubs & Undelivers		17%	16%	15%
End of Year Subscribers		207,500	174,300	148,155
E-mails Delivered		11,895,000	9,926,800	8,383,830
Open Rate		25%	22%	19%
Opens		2,973,750	2,183,896	1,592,928
Conversion Percent of Opens		2.0%	2.3%	2.5%
Online Conversions		59,475	49,793	40,142
Off Line Sales due to				
e-mails	300%	178,425	149,379	120,426
Total Sales		237,900	199,172	160,568
Sales from online and				
E-mail induced retail	$144	$34,257,600	$28,680,768	$23,121,792
Sales from Previous Business		$129,600,000	$112,500,000	$85,250,000
Total Revenue		$163,857,600	$141,180,768	$108,371,792
Operating Costs	65%	$106,507,440	$91,767,499	$70,441,665
Subscriber Acquisition Cost	$40	$10,000,000		
Marketing Costs	$4	$1,000,000	$1,000,000	$1,000,000
Transaction E-mails Per Order	3	713,700	597,516	481,704
Triggered E-mails Per Year	12	3,000,000	2,490,000	2,091,600
Total E-mails Delivered		15,608,700	13,014,316	10,957,134
E-mail Costs				
CPM Incl Creative	$12	$187,304	$156,172	$131,486
Database & Analytics	$4	$1,000,000	$1,000,000	$1,000,000
Website Costs with				
Shopping Cart	$4	$1,000,000	$830,000	$697,200
Total Costs		$119,694,744	$94,753,671	$73,270,350
Gross Profits		$44,162,856	$46,427,097	$35,101,442
Discount Rate		1	1.15	1.36
Net Present Value Profits		$44,162,856	$40,371,389	$25,809,884
Cumulative NPV Profits		$44,162,856	$84,534,244	$110,344,128
Lifetime Value		$126.18	$241.53	$315.27

EXHIBIT 21-05 Improved profits from adding
e-mail and online shopping

Changes from various Efforts Small Retailer	52	Registration Year	Year 2	Year 3
Original lifetime value		$56.80	$121.80	$162.74
Adding a website —				
no online sales		$81.25	$165.63	$222.08
Online, offline and E-mails		$126.18	$241.53	$315.27
Gain from moving to				
advanced marketing		$69.38	$119.73	$152.53
Times 350,000 base customers		$24,282,856	$41,904,244	$53,386,003

way to find these things out is to issue e-mail coupons that can be used online or at any of your retail stores.

By e-mail coupons, we aren't talking about the free-standing inserts (FSIs) found in the Sunday newspaper or that arrive every week in the mail. For the past 50 years, manufacturers and retailers have printed and inserted coupons into newspapers. FSIs account for 84% of all coupons used by consumers in the US, but the average response rate is only about 1.2%. FSIs usually take about three months from the time they are inserted in a newspaper until they arrive back at the manufacturer, who has to redeem them with some sort of payment to the retailer.[3] These coupons are almost never personalized, and it is seldom possible to know who used them—or even where they got them in the first place.

Yet FSIs are big business. In 2007, 257 billion were distributed with an average face value of $1.26.[4] The top categories were consumer packaged goods (e.g., household cleaning products, pet foods, personal products, room deodorizers, snacks, and medicines). The companies involved included Procter & Gamble, General Mills, Johnson & Johnson, Unilever, Nestlé, Kraft Foods, and Kimberley Clark.

Coupons that arrive in e-mails or are downloaded from Web sites are completely different. They can, if used intelligently, permit the advertiser to get instant feedback and to learn a great deal of useful information about the people who use them. Their coupon's average response rate is from 5% to 20%. Subscribers can print them at home and take to a store or they can use them online—with or without printing—with a code entered in the online checkout process.

One advantage of e-mails in driving retail traffic, therefore, is their speed. In its study "Harnessing the Power of E-mail," McKinsey & Company explained why e-mails are so effective at this job. It found that e-mail response rates were 15%, compared to 1% for direct mail. E-mails cost $0.03 to $0.10 per e-mail, compared to $2 for each direct mail piece. And e-mails generate 80% of responses within 48 hours.

The coupon pass-along effect

Once you encourage subscribers to print out coupons at home, they can—and will—pass them along to family members and friends. When someone arrives at your store, ready to buy with a coupon in hand, will your salesclerks turn them down? How you react to this situation depends on how you plan for it. There are two scenarios.

The coupon is meant for only one subscriber

Sally Warren may be a good customer whom you are trying to reward with a special discount or an invitation to *Tuesday Night With the Manager.* You don't want just any subscriber to have this reward. In this case, place Sally Warren's name prominently on the coupon and "This coupon is valid only for Sally Warren." You could ask your sales staff to check IDs.

The coupon is meant for anyone

In other cases, the coupon is a traffic-builder—any traffic. You can design the coupon to be passed around. For these coupons, you might say, "For Sally Warren and her close friends" on the coupon, then accept the coupons from whoever presents them. A big advantage here is if you scan the coupons into your POS system when they are redeemed, you can learn a lot about Sally Warren. She is an advocate who brings traffic into your store. You might send her an e-mail thanking her for doing this. In this situation, when Annette Bricker uses a Sally Warren coupon, you can ask your sales staff to notice this and, while thanking Annette for her purchase, ask her for her e-mail address.

Coach in-store pickup system

Coach sends e-mails to its subscribers inviting them to use the e-mail links to research a handbag, footwear, or accessories and pick up selected items at "your chosen Coach store within 2 hours of purchase (during store hours)." Once the subscriber has located an item, she is invited to click the store-pickup button. She enters her zip code. At this point, the Web site provides her with a list of nearby Coach stores that have her desired item in stock. "Once you have completed the checkout process online, you will receive 2 separate e-mails from us. Your order will be ready when the Pickup E-mail has been sent to you." The two e-mails are the order confirmation e-mail and the pickup e-mail.

This system is very convenient for the shopper. It is a lot easier to research a handbag on a Web site than to drive to a store, park, and wander around looking for something. The shopper gets in her car only when she knows that what she wants is waiting for her. But the system is also very convenient for Coach. It brings shoppers into its stores to pick up their purchases, many of whom will walk out with more purchases than just the one they came for.

Gift cards: a $26 billion business

About 75% of consumers bought a gift card at some time in 2008. More than one-half of consumers wanted to receive a gift card as a present. The average consumer spent about 16% of her holiday budget on gift cards.

Retailers have found ways to turn gift cards to their advantage. Statistics suggest that many gift card recipients don't use all the cash in their cards. Shoppers will use a $50 gift card to make a $36 purchase, leaving $14 on the card. In such cases, the retailer banks the difference. In other cases, according to *JCK Magazine*, the jewelry industry's leading trade publication, many consumers apply their gift cards toward larger purchases and end up spending more than the amount on the card.

In an article in the *New Yorker*, James Surowiecki describes gift cards as a "socially tolerable version" of giving cash. He explained that gift cards are one of the few ways in which the value of the money spent on a gift equals the receiver's perceived value of it. Gift cards can be purchased on the Web but are usually used offline at a store or restaurant.

In addition, gift cards have two extra benefits. First, with permission, the retailer can go back to the gift giver and suggest that she give again at the same time next year. Second, the retailer may send e-mails to the gift recipients who can, with their opt-in permission, be offered a chance to send e-mail gift cards themselves.

Ordering gift cards online

Gifts.com has signed up several hundred companies for which it provides gift cards, including Barnes and Noble, Bloomingdale's, Macy's, Marriott Hotels, Nike, Dick's Sporting Goods, The Gap, Home Goods,

The Sports Authority, Staples, Ticketmaster, and Overstock.com. The system works this way:

1. The gift recipient receives an e-mail with the gift card and a redemption code.
2. The recipient can then browse through the listed merchants to pick one or several retailers to redeem her gift card with. She can redeem her entire gift amount at one store or split it across multiple stores.
3. To redeem her gift, she clicks on the link in the e-mail and enters her claim code on the landing page. She can redeem some of the money now and more later, or spend it all in one shot. (Some merchants send an actual plastic gift card via mail. Others send the card by e-mail.)

The beauty of this system is the gift-giver doesn't have to decide what to give or pick it out and ship it. She doesn't even have to decide what type of gift to give; it is all up to the recipient.

An e-mail to profit from a mistake

An e-mail to subscribers said:

> As a valued Best Buy customer, we want to inform you of an error that will appear in the September 23, 2007, Best Buy ad. On the front cover we mistakenly listed the price of the 50" Panasonic Plasma TV at $1799, before $90 savings. We intended to advertise the 42" Panasonic Plasma TV at $1799, before $90 savings.
>
> Best Buy will not be honoring this price on the aforementioned 50" Panasonic Plasma TV. We apologize for any inconvenience, and we will offer a $100 Instant Rebate on all Plasma Televisions from Sunday, September 23, 2007, through Saturday, September 29, 2007. This Instant Rebate will be deducted from the price you see in the store, including our regular sale prices. Thank you for your understanding. We look forward to seeing you in our store soon.

Here is a wonderful way to take advantage of a mistake to build a relationship with your customers. You aren't the wizard of Oz behind the curtain, but a real person like the Cowardly Lion who makes mistakes and admits it. Look for opportunities like this, and your subscribers will read your e-mails.

Getting subscribers to create shopping lists

Target has developed a unique shopping aid called TargetLists, which is featured at the top of its Web site and in its e-mails. Subscribers browsing their e-mails can click on whatever interests them and have it added to their list. The list can be made available to others—spouse, parents, children, friends. TargetLists can be used at home or in the stores. To browse and select items, customers can scan an item's barcode in the store or click on the item they want to add online.

To make sure gift recipients get what they want, the forms are set up so senders can add specific information about an item in the comments section. They can advise their gift givers about their favorite colors or themes. List makers also can store future gift ideas, track items purchased, find other people's lists, and e-mail their lists to friends and family.

Live chat reached through e-mail

One reason for going to a store, rather than a Web site, is that you can ask a question while there. Sometimes, though, clerks can be hard to find, and when you find them they don't always know the answers.

Toll-free numbers have turned most consumers off because they reach a voice-response system that asks them to "listen carefully." Listening carefully and pushing buttons seldom enables callers to talk to a live person.

The problem can be even worse on the Web when there seems to be no way the customer can reach anyone to talk to. Web customers are very impatient. If they can't find what they want, they simply click their mouse and move on. About three quarters of Web shopping carts are abandoned by customers who never come back. Solution? A live chat button on the site and in e-mails, providing access to a live operator. Live chat software enables operators to interact with customers by talking to them through instant messaging. Chat software lets operators surf online with consumers through technology called co-browsing.[5]

Chat operators can converse with several consumers at once, increasing efficiency, shortening customer wait times, and allowing more customers to receive help.

Many live support software programs provide a customer survey so consumers can rate their chat operator once a chat is over. If the consumer is reading the e-mail with a live chat button after hours, it can be set up to let the consumer leave an e-mail message.

When CompUSA set up a live chat system, it found that 68.5% of viewers who ended up making a purchase chatted while browsing their site. About half of them chatted while they were in the shopping cart stage. Overall, about 10% of the chat sessions converted to a sale, about 10 times its average Web site conversion rate before it installed the system.[6]

Allurent reported that "83% of online shoppers would make purchases if the sites offered increased interactive elements." And Talisma.com reported that esignal.com, which provides real-time online financial market information, found that by using Talisma chat software it reduced inbound phone calls by 50% and enabled agents to handle more than 5,000 chat interactions per month.

User recommendations

After people have bought something, getting them to give you their ratings of the product and the purchase process is highly useful. This should be done in the transaction e-mails after a purchase. Once you have this information, put it on your site and link to it in all e-mails that feature the reviewed product. The link should be labeled "User Reviews."

The results of including user reviews in an e-mail are remarkable. According to a 2007 Marketing Sherpa survey, 86.9% of respondents said they would trust a friend's recommendation over a review by a critic, while 83.8% said they would trust user reviews over a critic's. Nielsen reported that in a survey of 26,486 Internet users, 78% said that "consumer recommendations are the most credible form of advertising." A survey by the JC Williams Group was cited by 91% of respondents as being "the #1 aid to a buying decision." And Prospectiv reported that 70% of online consumers said they use the Internet to research everyday grocery products.

Takeaway thoughts

- Marketing e-mails lead to up to four times as many offline purchases as online purchases.
- To get e-mail subscribers to visit your retail stores, get their zip codes and put the nearest store location in all your e-mails.
- If possible and practical, have e-mails come from a local store manager, with his photo, rather than from some corporate sales staff.

- E-mail coupons, unlike FSIs, can be instantly tracked and traced to the individual e-mail recipient.
- Gift cards, sold through the Web, lead to highly profitable offline traffic and sales.
- Live chat with co-browsing can boost sales both online and off-.
- Buyer reviews help increase conversion and offline sales.

Notes

1. "The Status of US Email Usage In 2007," (Visionarymarketing.com, 2007) http://visionarymarketing.com/articles/emailusage2007.html.
2. Multichannel Marketing in the Catalog Industry (Direct Marketing Association, 2007), http://imis.the-dma.org/Bookstore/ProductSingle.cfm?p=0D440279|DD4D1CDA3951319EF42A00D3DEA36CD0.
3. According to the Texas Grocery & Convenience Association, the retailer has to "count them, sort them, send them to the right place, then wait . . . and wait . . . AND WAIT for the reimbursement check!" (http://www.txgca.org/index.php?p=1_32_Coupon-Program).
4. "FSI Coupons Deliver 257 Billion Offers Worth $320B in Incentives in '07," Marketing Charts(2007), http://www.marketingcharts.com/print/fsi-coupons-deliver-257-billion-offers-worth-320b-in-incentives-in-07-3005/.
5. Co-browsing is a software-enabled technique that allows someone in an enterprise contact center to interact with a customer by using the customer's Web browser to show them something. For example, a B2B customer having difficulty placing an order could call a customer service representative, who could then show the customer how to use the ordering pages as though the customer were using their own mouse and keyboard.
6. Jason Lee Miller, "Study: Live Chat Ups Conversions Tenfold," WebProNews (June 21, 2007), http://www.webpronews.com/topnews/2007/06/21/study-live-chat-ups-conversions-tenfold.

22

Organizing and Managing E-mail Programs

As marketers begin to slowly adopt tactics such as targeting to improve the relevance of their mailings, the use of e-mail throughout the enterprise is also increasing. However, many companies are not yet centralizing their e-mail initiatives, and even fewer maintain rules to control message frequency, analyze subscriber behavior, and coordinate their messaging initiatives across channels and business units. While the market will continue to expand, this lack of sophistication and centralization will amplify the volume of messages that subscribers receive. Without centralization, marketing strategies will be undermined to the detriment of their brand . . . A common strategy cannot be fully realized without enterprise coordination and consensus, and the importance of centralizing e-mail efforts cannot be overemphasized. Executives are clearly beginning to feel challenged in their ability to optimize mailing effectiveness and efficiencies, in part due to the lack of centralization and messaging coordination.

—David Daniels, "Maturation of Email:
Controlling Messaging Chaos Through Centralization"
(JupiterResearch, 2007)

Consumer purchasing channels

Consumers have three basic channels for purchasing products and services:

- Retail stores or outlets
- Paper catalogs or other direct mail packages
- Web sites

EXHIBIT 22-01 Media influence on sales

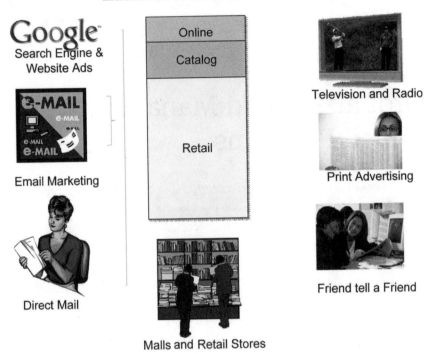

Online sales are growing fast. But they are still a fraction of all retail sales. Catalogs and direct mail produce receive sales by phone, online, and occasionally mail or fax.

Media influence on sales

There are at least seven functions that lead customers to buy, as seen in Exhibit 22-01. E-mail marketing is just one of the many ways suppliers have of getting customers to make a purchase.

Which is the most important? That depends on the product and the situation; it is almost impossible to tell in any situation. Each source of influence plays a part not only in making a sale but also in building the brand, building a relationship with customers leading to retention and loyalty. Exhibit 22-02 shows the various influences on the customer during the sales process. As you can see, search engine marketing is mainly focused on selling a product, whereas e-mail and viral marketing play many different roles. TV is the major brand building engine.

Each medium has different roles in influencing the customer. Television and radio sell the brand and enlightens consumers to the availabil-

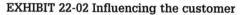

EXHIBIT 22-02 Influencing the customer

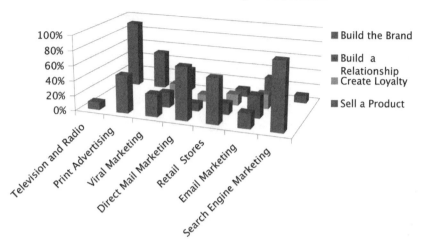

ity of products in retail stores. They get them to the phone, the store, or the Web site. TV and radio's sales impact can't be measured effectively. TV tracking relies on Nielsen annual reports, which are very indirect. Despite the fact that it can't be tracked directly, TV is often very powerful. Good TV ads make many brands household words.

Print advertising sometimes includes coupons, which can be tracked but which are seldom personalized. It can take months before the full effect of print coupons are known. Compare this with e-mail coupons' speed and trackability. E-mail coupon results are known in a few days. Magazine and national newspaper print ads are often used as brand-builders; they are effective in getting consumers to visit retail stores.

Direct mail is more like e-mail than any other medium. It is trackable and effective and often has P&L responsibility. In some organizations, this medium competes with e-mail marketing for budget and influence.

Web sites can be very effective marketing tools—once you can get the customers to visit them. When Web sites first came out, they were thought of as brand builders and were often very stiff and formal. Today, good Web sites are fun to visit and explore.

Search engine marketing has become a major method of advertising and bringing customers to Web sites, where they can learn information and make purchases. With the success of Google, search engine marketing will undoubtedly grow in the future to rival any of the other means of marketing. It is also competing with e-mail marketing for budgeting dollars.

EXHIBIT 22-03 E-mail units in major corporations

Units Responsible for Email

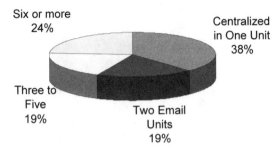

Source: JupiterResearch 2007

E-mails serve a large number of corporate objectives. Besides creating online sales, they drive consumers to visit retail stores—at about four times the rate of sales they produce in online activities. But e-mails do far more than that. E-mails have become key customer relationship management tools. They provide information. They answer questions. They create loyalty. They build the brand. They do everything that TV, radio, print, and direct mail and catalogs can do—and much more. And with through viral marketing, they can boost "tell a friend" to a fine art.

The competing media problem

Many corporate managers are unaware of many of e-mail's functions. As a result, their e-mail programs' effectiveness is less than it could be. Even worse, e-mail marketing is seen as competition by various media silos within a corporation. In many companies, e-mails are sent independently by several different groups. These groups send e-mails to the same subscribers without coordination. It is an internal competitive race. Exhibit 22-03 illustrates the units responsible for e-mail.

In addition to these many units sending promotional and transactional e-mails to the same subscribers, the internal media divisions are often uncoordinated. This situation often leads to overmailing subscribers and to messages that lack a consistent branding and style. In some cases, multiple e-mail units lead to delivery problems, as incorrect mailing practices by one department taints the reputation of the whole company. Decentralization becomes more of a problem as e-mails become central to the company's multichannel strategy.

How e-mail is used within the organization

As you know from chapter 1, a JupiterResearch 2007 survey[1] showed that e-mail marketing is used for:

- Customer service communications (74%)
- Promotional marketing (59%)
- Newsletters (53%)
- Public relations (40%)
- Billing (38%)
- Order confirmation (37%)
- Ad hoc alerts (31%)
- Shipment notices (28%)

These e-mails may emanate from different divisions, and centralizing them may represent a problem. However, the problem must be solved, as subscribers prefer to communicate with an individual within the company who knows them, cares about them, and reads what they say.

The IT problem

The biggest problem for e-mail marketing in most companies, however, doesn't come from competing media. It comes from IT. In many companies, IT stands in the way of effective e-mail marketing. Here is how it works.

When the Web first came along and no one knew what it was going to be used for, the Internet was regarded in many, if not most, companies as technology. This meant the building and maintenance of Web sites was assigned to IT. Of course, as you know by now, Web sites and e-mails are primarily brand-building, marketing, and sales tools. Marketing is dynamic. IT, in contrast, is organized and planned. The IT goal is to write programs that run flawlessly for years. Marketing is lucky to create something that lasts for a few months without change. Eventually, most, but not all, corporate managements have woken up to this situation and moved the Web site and e-mail marketing to the marketing department. In some companies, the battle isn't over yet. The Web site and the e-mail functions are still mixed up in IT.

IT presents another a serious problem for e-mail marketing because of central data warehouses. IT typically maintains the central data warehouse. That has presented a problem for direct mail because database marketing often requires hundreds of data fields (appended demographics, lifetime value, RFM, model scores, etc.), which are essential for segmentation and personalization but aren't related to IT's core functions. Marketing databases need to include prospects and lapsed customers. They need to be updated at least weekly and sometimes daily. All of these functions are constant, unlike regular, periodic functions, like payroll, billing, supply management, order fulfillment, and general ledger. As a result, marketing databases are usually given low priority. For these reasons, the marketing departments have fought to have their marketing databases outsourced to service bureaus, causing IT concern about losing a valuable function.

Even when the marketing database is outsourced to a service bureau, IT usually plays a significant role in central data transfer. Nightly POS data, Web site shopping cart data, and telesales data go through IT before being transmitted to the outsourced marketing database service bureau or anywhere else. This data transfer function doesn't usually represent a problem as long as we are dealing with direct mail to customers. Direct mail typically gets out on a weekly basis. E-mails are another story, however.

To be effective, e-mails have to go out within a matter of seconds after the consumer has made an entry into a Web site or clicked on an e-mail. Daily or weekly updating is just too slow. Consumers want to hear from you while they are still sitting at their PCs or holding their handhelds.

Some IT departments have been reluctant to devote the resources to solving the rapid data transfer problem. In "Maturation of Email," JupiterResearch found that 41% of the companies studied took three days or longer to respond to service-related e-mail inquiries or simply didn't respond at all:

> If organizations centralized their e-mail messaging, rules could easily allow for disgruntled customers trying to remedy a service issue to be pulled out of promotional mailings, at least until the clients' issues are resolved. Centralizing e-mail under one infrastructure would also allow confirmation notices to be leveraged for promotional purposes.

In one company we worked with, when customers signed up for e-mail newsletters, IT needed two weeks to provide the data needed to send them a welcome e-mail. The beginning of regular promotional e-mails may require another week. Outsourced ESPs and outsourced marketing database service bureaus would be waiting to act, but the data wouldn't arrive. Problems like this must be solved if you are to have an effective e-mail marketing program.

How to develop a profitable e-mail marketing program

These problems can be solved, but they take a lot of leadership and work. There are a number of steps that must be taken.

Determine the current e-mail program's net revenue

Many companies haven't yet determined what revenue and profit are coming from their existing e-mail programs. To get the approval and resources for a better program, you first have to build a base of numbers that show what you are currently doing. The steps to be taken have already been outlined in this book:

1. Determine your subscriber lifetime value based on online sales (chapter 6.).
2. Determine what offline sales revenue is produced by e-mails. Try e-mail coupons and querying offline customers on their source of information. A bit of research can yield a picture of the lifetime value of subscribers based on both online and offline sales.
3. Estimate current e-mails' effect in building loyalty, retention, brand, and referrals. Quantify this in terms of lifetime value.

Make a three-year e-mail marketing plan

Armed with information about how your current e-mail program is performing, lay out an aggressive plan for the future. Determine how you can increase on- and offline sales and profits and what resources you will need to achieve those increases. For this plan, assume the current obstacles (silo competition, IT unresponsiveness, slow data, etc.) can be solved. Show what will happen when they are solved. Put the plan together for your executive staff to review. The plan should include:

- The number of opt-in subscribers acquired for each of the next three years, with a plan for reaching these goals
- A viral marketing program, with estimates of success
- The impact of search engine marketing, blogs, social networking, and banner ads
- Customer status levels (e.g., silver, gold, and platinum), with numbers and revenue from each status level
- Increase in the open, click, and conversion rates and average order size from online, offline, and catalog sales as a result of the e-mail marketing program and its features, such as improved cus-

tomer retention, next best product (NBP), viral marketing, test-ing, interactivity, and more relevant communications

- Total profits to be realized by the end of the three years and the ROI on the resources required to achieve the results

List the e-mail program's stakeholders

The units in the company who have an interest in e-mails may include:

- Marketing
- Sales
- Customer service
- Fulfillment, delivery, or installation staff
- Retail store management
- Publicity
- Advertising
- Catalog operations
- Web site designers
- Event planners
- Information technology

Be sure your plan includes satisfying the interests and needs of these units.

List obstacles to achieving plan goals

List your current obstacles to success, such as:

- Slow data delivery, so e-mails are late with time-sensitive infor-mation
- Focus on current sales rather than long-term customer retention
- Opposition to testing
- Low e-mail budget
- E-mail function not being outsourced to an experienced ESP
- E-mail function not centralized
- Lack of a marketing database for personalized e-mails
- Staff and customers not offered incentives to provide e-mail ad-dresses
- Management not realizing what e-mails can do
- Web site and e-mails not coordinated with each other
- Available data subscribers not permitting segmentation, triggers, analytics, or personalization

Come up with a plan for solving each obstacle and an estimate of the costs involved. Your plan will have to include the following types of solutions.

Centralizing the e-mail function. This will be the toughest problem to solve. E-mail is exciting. If your corporation has five or more units independently sending e-mails, without coordinating the subscribers, creating a central e-mail marketing program may be an impossible objective unless senior management believes in centralization and pushes it very hard. You may have to get outside consulting help from a respected authority. According to "Maturation of Email":

> Such a lack of coordination and centralization often leads to over-mailing subscribers and messages that lack a consistent tone in branding and style. Moreover, the prevalence of such a splintered e-mail infrastructure can lead to delivery issues, as incorrect mailing practices by one department could potentially taint the reputation of another. If not coordinated, this decentralization will be further amplified as e-mail messaging becomes more integral to the multichannel strategy.

Rapidly delivering data from consumers to the outsourced ESP. Data from the Web site, the POS system, and the catalog telesales staff must be delivered in seconds after entry so that e-mails can go out immediately.

Solving the IT problem.

Outsourcing the marketing database and e-mail delivery process. The database can be outsourced to a service bureau or to your ESP. According to "Maturation of Email":

> Most companies have yet to deploy a commercially available enterprise-class e-mail system . . . One-third of executives surveyed work with an outsourced provider, and 30 percent use an on-premises packaged application . . . Special attention should also be paid to the recurring costs associated with using an outsourced provider compared with the larger upfront cost of using an on-premises packaged solution.

Devoting sufficient budget to the e-mail program. Again according to "Maturation of Email," "Despite the importance that marketers place on e-mail and the strategic goals they have for it, few companies are appropriately investing in the channel . . . 52 percent stated that e-mail marketing only accounts for 20 percent or less of their budget dollars."

Solving in-house data distribution problems. The Web site should be moved to the marketing staff. The POS system should be upgraded to accept e-mails provided by retail customers, and it should show customer history and NBPs.

Offering incentives to catalog and retail sales personnel. To capture e-mail addresses from customers, offer sales staffs incentives to collect them. You should also offer customers and Web visitors incentives for subscribing to e-mail programs.

Featuring Web site and e-mail subscription benefits. TV and print ads should feature the Web site and e-mail subscription benefits.

Setting up marketing segments and status levels. Segments and status levels should be based on multichannel purchases plus customer preferences and demographics. Gold customers, for example, should be honored by catalog telesales, retail sales, and Web sites based on their multichannel revenue.

Sell your three-year program to management

Getting your program approved may be difficult or easy, depending on your company and your leadership ability. If you have done your homework and built allies within your organization, you can do it. This will be particularly difficult if it involves organizational changes, such as moving the Web site or centralizing the e-mail marketing function.

E-mail marketing program strategy and operations

Armed with approval for your plan, you now have to carry it out. Here are some concepts that successful e-mail marketers have achieved. You will have to do something similar.

Outsource the e-mail delivery function

In its "Maturation of Email," JupiterResearch found that:

> 31 percent of companies surveyed using a homegrown application for their e-mail marketing needs. Homegrown solutions are typically based upon e-mail servers and appliances that are ill-equipped to provide the application functionality, including deliverability and frequency controls, targeting, and measurement insight, that commercial applications provide . . . Given the disparate manner in which e-mail is currently managed as well as the paltry budget dollars that are often assigned to this critical messaging medium, marketers must work to centralize their

efforts as well as align infrastructure and labor resources to align with the importance of the channel

Automate as much as you can

Your ESP should provide you with software that will automate most of your e-mail marketing program, leaving you free to do long-range planning and creative content. All your triggers should be automated. For example, as soon as a person subscribes, a series of e-mails should go out automatically: confirmation e-mail, welcome e-mail, and the start of the promotional e-mails. No one has to do anything. As soon as there is a sale, there are a series of automated transactional messages: thank-you e-mail, product shipment e-mail, purchase process survey, request for product review, thank-you e-mail for the review, and so on. There are automated messages for abandoned shopping carts, subscribers who haven't opened recently, birthday greetings, customers reaching status levels, anniversary of gift purchases, and more.

Test constantly

Every e-mail campaign should have at least one test built into it. To do this, you must develop a testing plan for the next month. You can test subject lines, arrangement of offers above and below the fold, administration section modification, contests, incentives for product reviews, and so on. The most important part of your testing should be a scheduled review every month of test results. The review should answer these questions: What changes in our e-mail program will we make based on what we have learned from tests in the last month? and what new tests will we conduct in each campaign during the next month?

Regularly review e-mail frequency

Are subscribers happy with their current frequency? Tests asking them what they want should be constantly employed and reviewed. Unsubscribing buyers should be queried by e-mail and by telephone to determine what would have induced them to remain as subscribers. Review this monthly.

Review competitive e-mails monthly

Staff members should subscribe to e-mails from all the competition. At the monthly e-mail review session, one staff member should summarize what things the competition is doing that would suggest new ideas for your e-mails. Your goal: be totally informed about what is going on in the e-mail world.

Select the best e-mails as controls

For each type of message (transaction, trigger, promotion, viral, etc.), determine your best previous message, with best defined by such measures as opens, clicks, and conversions. These are your controls. Provide recognition for any staff member who can devise an e-mail that beats the control by a significant percentage.

Set up subscriber controls

Always have a group of subscribers that *doesn't* get your latest new idea, so you can determine whether the new idea really is working and how much better (or worse) it is. Someone needs to be in charge of selecting the controls and making them available on a regular basis.

Run a monthly set of reports

Track lifetime value, NBP, RFM, status level, plus scores of propensity to unsubscribe and propensity to purchase on a monthly basis. You should have each subscriber's current value for these measures and previous values in her database record. Study who is going up and who is going down. See if your e-mail program is making things better or worse. Reach conclusions at the monthly meeting.

Planning for and executing e-mail campaigns

In "Your 10-Point Quality-Control Checklist" for EmailLabs Stefan Pollard wrote, "A successful e-mail launch has a lot of moving parts, and they all need to work together correctly. An effective quality-control checklist will help you spot and correct problems before they can wreak havoc on your list, your deliverability, your reputation and your bottom line."

In both direct mail and e-mail marketing, quality control is crucial. One easily avoided mistake can offend a million subscribers. Whether the job is done in-house or outsourced, check every single promotion before it goes out. There are two parts to the quality control process: the list and the e-mail itself.

Checking the list

For every planned promotion, have a list of selection criteria, such as:

- Choose the audience to be mailed
- Omit those who have unsubscribed
- Be sure buyers are treated differently from non-buyers

- Be sure the frequency agrees with what the subscriber asked for
- Make sure the content is within the subscriber's preferences

As you plan the job, estimate the number of subscribers who meet all these criteria. Let's say that the number is 351,223. When the recipients have been selected, the selection software will give a count of those actually selected. Let's say that count is 397,556. The number is too large by 46,333. Is this something to worry about? Numbers are updated daily so are always changing. The number is 13% larger than it was estimated to be. A difference of 2% might be acceptable, but 13% may not be. The e-mail program manager needs to investigate.

The manager knows five selection criteria were set up, so he has the software quick check of each criterion against the names actually selected. The check reveals that every criterion was met except the fourth. The names need to be selected over again.

Checking e-mail content and setup before delivery

The software should permit an eyeball check of the e-mails as they will look in the subscriber's inbox. A random check should be made of a dozen of these, four taken from the beginning, four from the middle, and four from the end of the list. What should you look for?

When you planned the e-mail, you should have created a list of changes from the standard control. Let's say the list of changes included:

- Under $40 Dress Sale
- Top 10 Summer Must-Haves—Save up to an extra 50%
- Almost Gone Men's Bargains—Priced High to Low

Check each of the e-mails for each change, plus a couple of other standard criteria to be sure that what the subscriber sees is what the subscriber was supposed to see. In particular, check any old links to make sure they still work correctly.

There are two secrets behind quality control: advance planning and systematic checking using a checklist.

The four vital implementation steps

There are four basic steps to setting up an e-mail program with an ESP: discovery, development, testing, and deployment.

**EXHIBIT 22-04 Discovery process in
e-mail marketing program implementation**

Client Implementation	65 days
DISCOVERY	**18 days**
Business and technical requirements	18 days
Document business and technical requirements	15 days
Receive approval on requirements	3 days
Client Configuration Requirements	15 days
Domain Name System set up documents received from client	15 days
Response Management documents received from client	15 days
Outbound Mailing Configuration	15 days
Unsubscribe Template information received from client	15 days
Forward to a Friend Template information received from client	15 days
Proof & Seed Lists Documentation sent to and received from client	15 days
Mailing categories Determined	15 days
Data Intelligence user requirements	15 days
Conversion track requirements	15 days
Conversion Track Business Discovery	15 days
Conversion Track Documentation sent to client	0 days

Discovery

Discovery is the process of finding out what data you have and how that data will be used in to create e-mails for your marketing program. Exhibit 22-04 is a case study that shows how ESPs typically go about this process. Discovery typically takes 18 days.

Development

Development involves creating the programs that will organize the data so that e-mails can be created and sent. The process takes about 33 days and is depicted in Exhibit 22-05:

Testing

Before any e-mails can be set out, there must be a rigorous testing and warming program that assures that all the code developed in the previous step works properly and that the ISPs become used to this new kid on the block. Exhibit 22-06 breaks down the testing phase.

The warming component is needed to assure ISPs that you are a legitimate e-mail marketer, not a spammer. It may seem as if the warming takes a lot of time—and it does, typically 17 days. But without proper

**EXHIBIT 22-05 Development process for
setting up e-mail marketing**

DEVELOPMENT	33 days
Basic Client Configuration	10 days
Domain Name System Records Configured and Tested	4 days
Response Management / ReturnPath set up	7 days
Outbound Mailing Configuration	6 days
Unsubscribe Template setup for each brand	10 days
Forward to a Friend Template setup for each brand	10 days
Proof & Seed Lists set up	5 days
User Defined Functions- Mailing categories set up	5 days
Prepare data specifications	13 days
Data sync specifications (unsubs, campaign, welcome)	5 days
Abandoned cart specifications	5 days
Feedback file specifications	5 days
Welcome trigger specification	5 days
Data model	5 days
Receive sign off on specifications	5 days
Build data schema	3 days
Receive sample data, unsub, welcome, & campaign files	0 days
Write code	20 days
Unsub data sync	10 days
Campaign data sync	10 days
Welcome data sync	10 days
Welcome trigger	10 days
Abandoned cart data sync and trigger	15 days
Feedback file	5 days
Data intelligence dashboard configuration	8 days
Dashboard tools set up	3 days
QA and testing	2 days
Credentials provided to client	1 day
Conversion track configuration	13 days
Conversion Track coding installed by client	10 days
Conversion Track Setup	3 days
Data Management Software Configuration	4 days
Set up basic Data Management profiles	4 days
Creative development	10 days
Receive templates from client	0 days
Set up Welcome creative for each brand	10 days
Set up abandoned cart creative for each brand	10 days

**EXHIBIT 22-06 Testing and warming for
new e-mail marketing program**

TESTING	38 days
Custom testing	31 days
Test welcome trigger	5 days
Test abandoned cart trigger	5 days
Feedback file testing	5 days
Conversion track testing	3 days
Quality Analysis of Data Management Profiles	1 day
Forward to a Friend testing	1 day
Unsub testing	1 day
Response Management testing	1 day
IP Warming / Deliverability Plan	17 days
Week 1 -Two Mailings	3 days
Week 2 - Two Mailings	3 days
Week 3 - Three Mailiings	9 days
Training and Education	1 day
Training on Analytics	1 day
Training on Reporting System	1 day

warming, your e-mail marketing program may get off on the wrong foot, leading to a serious loss of deliverability. Slow and steady is vital for warming.

Deployment

The final phase is deployment, which can be brief since the previous steps have covered all contingencies. The breakout is shown in Exhibit 22-07.

What can go wrong?

Anything and everything. In his "Your 10-Point Quality-Control Checklist" Pollard suggested this sample list:

EXHIBIT 22-07 Deployment of an e-mail program at an ESP

DEPLOYMENT	2 days
Receive and Load master unsub file	1 day
Welcome data sync and trigger	1 day
Abandoned cart trigger live	1 day
Unsub data sync live	1 day

- Blank e-mail
- Misspelled subject lines
- Test messages sent to the whole list
- The wrong image used
- Images missing or broken, even with images enabled
- Coding errors that wipe out all text and images
- E-mail client browser does not render what you sent

Pollard also provided a number of important quality checks, summarized here:

- Check your copy. Paste your copy into a plain-text program and eyeball it. It will look different. This may help to spot errors.
- Check your administration center. CAN-SPAM requires adding an unsubscribe link and your company postal address. Always make sure these elements are included and easy to find. Include telephone numbers, Web site URL, and e-mail address. Make sure subscribers can contact you any way they want.
- Make sure the subject line accurately represents the e-mail message content and that the sender line shows your company or brand name, not an e-mail address.
- Ensure that dates, especially copyrights, reflect the correct year. Having the wrong date makes you look amateurish and sloppy.
- Click every link and link-connected image to make they all work. Make sure each image has an alt tag describing the content.
- Preview the message in a preview pane, with images disabled, in different clients, and on different computer platforms.
- Test-send your message before your roll out, even if you're using a template that has been thoroughly debugged.
- Have one other person who wasn't involved in the launch look it over before you send the e-mail.
- Use a third-party delivery monitoring service, such as EmailAdvisor, to make sure you have the most up-to-date filter quirks checked.

Takeaway thoughts

- Many large companies have several internal units sending e-mails to the same group of subscribers. E-mail marketing should be centralized, if possible.

- Slow data delivery by IT can destroy e-mail program effectiveness. This problem must be corrected.
- To develop an e-mail marketing program, start by determining e-mail's net revenue from all sources—on- and offline.
- Make a three-year e-mail marketing program that includes acquisition, viral, status levels, testing, interactivity, and increased relevance.
- List obstacles to be corrected, including decentralized e-mails, slow data delivery, amateurish in-house production, insufficient budget, and lack of incentives for capturing e-mail addresses.
- Outsource your e-mail to a qualified ESP.
- Automate as much of your e-mail programs as possible.
- Build in a test to every e-mail campaign.
- Subscribe for and study all competing e-mails.
- Create subscriber control groups.
- Do quality control on lists and on e-mail content and setup before delivery.
- Have a monthly review to determine changes needed in your e-mail program as a result of the tests and the success of your previous programs.

Notes

1. David Daniels, *The Maturation of E-Mail* (JupiterResearch, September 17, 2007), 4.

23

The Future of
E-mail Marketing

The supposed convenience of electronic mail, like so many other inno-
vations of technology, has become too much for some people.
Swamped by an unmanageable number of messages—the volume of
e-mail traffic has nearly doubled in the past two years, according to research firm DYS Analytics—and plagued by annoying spam and
viruses, some users are saying "Enough!"

E-mail overload gives many workers the sense that their work is
never done, said senior analyst David Ferris, whose firm, Ferris Research, said there were 6 trillion business e-mails sent in 2006. "A lot
of people like the feeling that they have everything done at the end of
the day," he said. "They can't have it anymore."

Stanford University technology professor Lawrence Lessig publicly
declared e-mail bankruptcy a few years ago after being deluged by
thousands of e-mails. "I eventually got to be so far behind that I was
either going to spend all my time answering e-mails or I was going to
do my job," he said.

He eliminated about 90 percent of his e-mail traffic, but said he
can't quite abandon it entirely. "The easiest strategy is just to ignore e-
mail, but I just can't psychologically do that," Lessig said in an interview.

Mike Musgrove, "E-Mail Reply to All: 'Leave Me Alone,'"
The Washington Post

Wild game hunting and hunting-based e-mail marketing are both in
trouble. The reason for the trouble is there are too many hunters. More
and more companies putting more and more traps (e-mails) in the
woods are reducing the yield (sales) per campaign and are gradually de-
pleting the total universe of profitable game (loyal subscribers), leading

ultimately to the destruction of the entire wild game and hunting-based e-mail marketing industries. What has been happening to hunting-based e-mail marketing?

First, subscriber inboxes are cluttered with too many e-mails—more than most subscribers can possibly read and more than they want. E-mail marketers keep sending more e-mails each year. E-mails that began a couple of times a month became weekly, then semiweekly, then daily. Why? Because of the pressure to increase sales. The more e-mails sent, the more sales. Hence, many marketers' goal is to douse their subscribers with as many e-mails as they possibly can.

Each year, more companies are entering the e-mail marketing business. They see others prospering from e-mails and want to get in on it, too. But open rates are down: year after year average e-mail open rates are less than they were the year before. Average open rates of 40% became 25% and are probably below 13% today.[1]

Users, sick of receiving too many e-mails and not trusting (or being unable easily to find and activate) the "unsubscribe" button, are taking the easy way out. They are reporting that the e-mails they originally signed up for as spam. As a result more and more legitimate marketing e-mails are being designated as spam. According to a study by Merkle[2], 68% of consumers report that the permission e-mails they have signed up to receive have wrongly been identified as spam by filters. The majority of this group (73%) don't care that this is occurring. Spam filters have become an unintentional and often welcome method of reducing the amount of e-mail that makes it to their inboxes. This hurts the whole legitimate e-mail marketing process.

E-mail marketing is suffering from the tragedy of the commons. The tragedy of the commons is an economic trap that involves a conflict over finite resources between individual interests and the common good. It states that free access and unrestricted demand for a finite resource, like public lands or the Internet, ultimately structurally dooms the resource through over-exploitation. Because the Internet is essentially a free resource like unprotected public lands, everyone uses it. No one takes care of it, and gradually it will be destroyed.

The solution: farming

There is only one viable solution to these problems: e-mail marketers who want to survive must shift from being hunters to being farmers. In the 1700s in England, the tragedy of the commons was solved by the enclosure movement: all land was divided up by fences so it could be farmed by individuals who took care of the land and their livestock.

Grazing land was no longer a communal property. We need to do the same today with e-mail marketing.

E-mail marketers must focus their attention on the interests and preferences of identified subscribers, not on creating clever e-mails and campaigns directed at relatively unknown consumers. Marketers must build marketing databases that have a 360-degree picture of each subscriber: her demographics, on- and offline purchase history, preferences, NBP, and segment. Subscribers must be analyzed; sent personal content, greeted by name, and thanked for their business. Customers must be placed in status levels—silver, gold, platinum—and given appropriate appreciation and rewards.

The goal of e-mail farming

The goal is simple: to build our bottom line by learning as much as we can about our subscribers so that we can have regular dialogues with them, just as the old corner grocer had with his customers. Forget about campaigns. Think about building relationships. Farming consists of collecting data and using it to create personal communications: promotions, transactions, triggered messages, loyalty-building messages, thank-yous, viral messages, and membership messages. Every subscriber should be a person we know a lot about, whom we care about, and whom we correspond with. Our e-mails are sent from a real person reachable by e-mail or phone. We put the subscriber in charge of the frequency and the content she wants to receive. We empower her. In return, she loves to hear from us.

How to shift from hunting to farming

Shifting from hunting to farming isn't done overnight. The first step is to decide to become a farmer. Following this must be the creation of a multiyear plan for the transition: who does what, how much it will cost, what to expect in terms of success. There will happen in a series of steps.

Explaining the program to management

Shifting to a farming-based e-mail marketing program is a major change for any company. Initially, it may be expensive. A database has to be built, data acquired, subscribers enrolled and rewarded for providing data. Segments must be created, and segment managers appointed. A budget and a one- or two-year plan must be developed. Finally, this whole process has to be explained to management so they understand it and approve the budget. An outside consultant or ESP strategist can help you develop the plan and educate management. Until you get buy-in, you really can't do any of the subsequent steps.

Building the database

If you lack a marketing database, the existing subscriber database has to be converted into a true marketing database, built on a relational platform with access for both the marketing staff and the ESP using insight-builder software accessed over the Web. Decide what information about each subscriber will be needed for the farming operation. Demographics should be appended to all records that have postal addresses.

Engaging an ESP

If you don't already have an external ESP, now is the time to get one. E-mail marketing is too important to the success of any enterprise to make it an in-house, learn-on-the-job pickup operation. There are a dozen large, experienced ESPs out there reviewed and recommended by JupiterResearch and Forrester Research. Consult these agencies, write a request for proposal (RFP), and started doing e-mail in a professional way. For additional reasons for outsourcing ESP functions, see the discussion following this project list.

Combining on- and offline data

All offline data sources should be investigated, and a means found to combine everything about a particular subscriber in a central database record. This process should probably be outsourced to the ESP or to the external database service provider, since there are usually legacy data ownership issues that will prevent success if the process is tried internally. For example, in many companies, the catalog operation has always maintained its own database and won't give it up. But it doesn't need to. It can just share the data nightly. The same is true of the retail POS system and the Web site maintenance system.

Deciding what data is needed from subscribers

In a series of working sessions, create a list of the inputs desired from each subscriber. The goal is to understand each subscriber and learn what she wants in terms of types of messages, frequency, products of interest, NBP, gifts registries, anniversaries, birthdays, and family obligations. We also want to understand her income, age, wealth, type of housing, ethnicity, lifestyle, and so on. Devise forms for subscribers to enter preference data. For each piece of data, create a business rule to determine how the data will be used to create a dialogue with the customer and to send her e-mails that will delight her.

Give thought to how the data will be made available to sales clerks in retail stores, to call centers, and to catalog sales agents. Many hunting e-mail marketers have no more in their subscriber database than an e-mail address and possibly a first name. To get into farming, you need a lot more from your current subscribers and from all new subscribers. Put campaigns in place to get the subscribers to provide the missing data, particularly their postal addresses, phone numbers, and preferences.

Develop a plan with numerical goals, preferably with rewards for subscribers, segment managers, and other customer contact personnel who can help in the drive. Use the double-opt-in process to be sure all subscribers really want to receive your messages.

Determining segmentation needs

Develop segments based on the data as they come in, rather than on some arbitrary intuitive decision. In the beginning, you can develop a temporary segmentation plan to get started, such as by age, income, click categorization, or type of product purchased. After data have been collected and preference forms filled out, modify segments to be most useful in creating winning e-mails. Appoint segment managers and charge them with thinking up the kinds of communications that will appeal to their groups. Each manager's goals should be developed in terms of percentage increases in opens, clicks, and conversions from her segment, reductions in unsubscribes and undelivers, and overall segment lifetime value and profitability.

Beginning testing at once

Every new idea should be tested using an A/B split or a control group. From now on, no e-mail campaign goes out without at least one test. Each segment manager should give you a list of the tests conducted, the results, and the recommendation for changes and new initiatives resulting from what the tests have established each month. E-mails without tests are a waste of an opportunity to learn something valuable. Tests without analysis and behavior modification are a waste of the information learned.

Collecting case studies

In e-mail marketing, as in real farming, practitioners learn many lessons. Most of these lessons are internalized and not made explicit. If we are to become modern professional farmers, these lessons should be thought about and recorded. After all, agriculture only got to be so efficient because experts wrote down what worked so that other farmers could read about it.

For our e-mail marketing, every account and segment manager should be asked to come up with case studies on a regular basis. Develop a format for the studies: what the situation was before, what was done that was new, how it was tested, the results of the test, the conclusions drawn, and the general applications of what was learned. The results should always include a numerical conclusion, such as "Conversions were 12 per 1,000 e-mails compared to 8 using the previous method."

Collecting examples

Create a library of examples of triggers, transaction messages, content, viral messages, loyalty rewards, and so on. Your library needs to be indexed and accessible to all marketing staff and the ESP so you don't keep reinventing the wheel.

Reviewing the business regularly

Quarterly or semiannually, review your e-mail marketing program. Set up the reviews in a formal way, with adequate preparation of charts, test results, and recommendations for changes. In preparing these reviews, develop the lifetime value of each segment and each segment member, and compare them with similar values from previous reviews. Also study and analyze the results of NBP analysis, viral marketing, reactivation campaigns, status level rewards, contests, games, and interactivity.

Creating a loyalty program

Early on, decide what type of loyalty program would be most profitable for the company and acceptable to the subscribers. Explain it to all current subscribers and all customer contact personnel. Establish enrollment goals.

Using interactivity

Plan and implement interactivity in all messages. The goal is to have every single e-mail become an adventure. Have a live agent available for text chat through every e-mail sent to subscribers. Also include a search box that enables subscribers to look up absolutely everything they might want to know about from any e-mail they receive.

Designing an administrative section

The administrative section should appear in all e-mails similar to the one described in chapter 13.

Designing standard transactional messages

Design standard transactional messages with business rules that put them in place automatically.

Recording data

Make sure your database records the subscriber's NBP, RFM cell code, segment number, and lifetime value. This information should appear whenever the database is accessed by customer service, for e-mail creation, for the Web site, or for reports.

Selecting an ESP

Currently about 56% of commercial e-mails are sent by out-sourced vendors, according to JupiterResearch's *Sending From the Inside*. This is due to the increasing complexity of e-mail deliverability and more services being provided by ESPs. Only 3% of companies that have the functions outsourced are considering moving them in-house. According to JupiterResearch, desiring to gain increased production control by moving to on-premises solutions

> indicates marketers are misguided about on-premises benefits and will likely be disappointed if they rally around this perception . . . production and control issues are typically mired in organizational dysfunction and conflict and cannot be remedied by technology alone.

To that we would add two more reasons. First, complexity and change. The e-mail marketing industry is highly complicated. Not only does involve very specialized software, training, and experience, it is also constantly changing. An in-house staff will find it very difficult to keep up on all the changes in the industry, compared to an ESP with the skills and experience to handle 100 or more different clients.

Second, specialized programs have to be learned. To be competitive in e-mail marketing, a marketing staff has to understand and deploy viral and interactive marketing, segmentation, lifetime value, analytics, triggers, testing, transactional e-mails, and constant experimentation with subject lines. No in-house staff can possibly afford to have experts in even half of those fields, yet without them, they can't produce an e-mail marketing program that will keep up with the top e-mail marketers.

Reducing the cost of e-mail marketing by in-sourcing is really penny-wise and pound-foolish. E-mails are so inexpensive compared to any other form of marketing that the cost is hardly worth calculating. What companies should be thinking about are subscribers' interests and preferences: how you can continue to deliver relevant communications that will build loyalty and sales. Any help you can get in this field from experienced ESPs is usually worth far more than any cost savings you could make by bringing the function inside.

Exhibit 23-01 offers differences between hunting and farming.

EXHIBIT 23-01 Comparing hunting and farming

Functions	Hunter	Farmer
Marketing database	List of subscribers and buyers. Only buyers have postal addresses; no demographics, and no offline history.	Complete marketing database with names; postal addresses; demographics; open, click, and conversion history; includes offline sales from POS and catalog.
Frequency	Daily or twice a week; subscribers offered no choices.	Monthly, semimonthly, weekly, sometimes daily; subscribers given extensive choice.
Segmentation	None; all subscribers get the same message.	Several marketing segments, each with different creative; each has a manager.
Personalization	None or just a personal greeting.	Personal greeting; content based on database record of each individual.
Triggers	None.	Birthday, anniversaries, reminders of previous purchases, suggestions based on purchases, next best products.
Transactions	Thank-you messages, order shipment.	Thank-you messages, order shipment, ordering process survey, product review requests

Functions	Hunter	Farmer
Analytics	Opens, clicks, conversions.	Opens, clicks, conversions, NBP, defection prediction, lifetime value, RFM.
Interactivity	10 links per e-mail.	Extensive links, treasure hunts, games, more than 200 possible links per e-mail, video, text font enlargement, image enlargement.
Cookies	Used for shopping cart.	Used for greeting, shopping cart, form completion, Web site arrangement, personalization automatic store locater.
Relevance	Average about 1.5.	Average about 2.7.
Offline sales	Store locater.	Store locater, letters from store managers, coupons for stores, complete tracking of offline sales by home phone number.
Subject lines	Extensive testing.	Extensive testing.
Subscriber acquisition	From TV, print, search engine, banners, sweepstakes, direct mail.	From TV, print, search engine, banners, sweepstakes, direct mail, viral marketing; double opt-in used; offline sales personnel and catalog sales personnel are offered incentives
Viral marketing	Seldom.	Constant on every e-mail page, with rewards for both subscriber and viral target.
How buyers are treated	Same as non-buyers.	Buyers treated very well by status level, thanked constantly, free shipping for higher levels.
Unsubscribes and undelivers	Loss about 35% per year; no reactivation program.	Loss about 20% per year; follow-up with direct mail to reactivate about 5% of those lost.

Functions	Hunter	Farmer
Creative	In-house.	Promotions in-house, transactions and triggers outsourced to ESPs.
Testing	Subject lines.	Every single promotion and most triggers and transactions; extensive revisions based on test results.
Review of marketing success	Yearly.	Monthly discussions, quarterly formal reviews of every aspect of the programs.
Subscriber input	Preference form; actions and content not based on preference.	Extensive input: preference forms, product reviews, blogs; all outgoing e-mails based on business rules related on subscriber input.
Loyalty programs	None.	Either points- or discount-based.
ROI	$10 per $1 invested.	$80 per $1 invested.

A farewell to the reader

Thanks for coming with us on our journey. We hope that you have learned something useful and that your success with e-mail marketing will improve as a result of some of the lessons in this book. If you want to get in touch with either one of us at any time, e-mail Arthur Sweetser at asweetser@e-dialog.com and Arthur Hughes at ahughes@e-dialog.com. You can also download all the tables and charts in this book at www.dbmarketing.com. We want to help you become an expert in e-mail marketing. It will make us proud to think that we have helped you to do this.

Takeaway thoughts

- Success from e-mails using hunting techniques is getting lower each year.
- Farming, rather than hunting, is the solution.
- Develop a three-year plan to shift to farming subscribers.

- Explain the process to management.
- Build an online and offline database.
- Elicit needed information about and from subscribers.
- Create segments and appoint segment managers.
- Begin to test, collect case studies, and hold quarterly business reviews.
- Set up a loyalty program, plan for interactivity, and create an administrative section.
- Allow live chats and search boxes.
- Calculate NPB, lifetime value, RFM, and segment numbers.

Notes

1. Most industry analysts claim that open rates aren't a valid measurement of e-mail marketing success for a number of reasons, including preview panes, which count e-mails appearing in them as opens, when in fact many subscribers are just skipping through their inboxes, not looking at the preview panes at all.
2. *A View from the Inbox 2008* (Merkle 2008), http://www.merkleinc. com/user-assets/Documents/WhitePapers/ViewFromTheInbox2008.pdf.

Appendix: The Discount Rate

The discount rate is used because revenue, costs, and profits come in over several years. We add them together to get a LTV. Profits to be received in future years aren't worth as much in today's dollars as profits received today, so we have to discount them to determine the net present value of the future profits. To determine the discount rate, we use the market interest rate that marketers' companies are paying. For the charts in this book, we use 8%. You can use another number based on your current business situation.

In reality, however, we double that 8% to include risk. In any long-term business transaction, like lifetime value, there is always a serious risk, such as:

- Interest rates could go up.

- Your product could become obsolete in the next few years and wipe out your expectation of further sales.

- In online commerce, competitors always make marketing a risky business. They could steal your expected customers.

- You could be faced with other business risks, such as a severe economy slump.

For these reasons, we have doubled the interest rate to get the discount rate. The risk factor (rf) is two. You may be able to develop more sophisticated risk factors than (rf = 2), based on your business history. Here is a simple formula to compute the discount rate: $D = (1 + (i \times rf))n$. D = discount rate, i = interest rate , rf = the risk factor, and n = number of years you have to wait. The discount rate in year three, for example (two years from now), is computed like this: $D = (1 + (0.08 \times 2))2$. $D = (1.16)3 = 1.35$.

E-mail Marketing Glossary

The following are the terms you should know to use this book.

A/B split	Dividing a list of subscribers into two parts, with A getting one version of the e-mail and B getting the other.
Acquisition cost	Cost of acquiring an opt-in subscriber's e-mail address.
Administration center	Standard area of e-mail or Web site where users can always find important links, such as unsubscribe functionality, e-mail to a friend, and a search box.
Algorithm	Mathematical formula resulting from predictive modeling. The algorithm is used to score a subscriber database to predict who will open or convert.
Animation	Video, avatars, games, and other interactive links in e-mails.
Appended data	Demographic data, such as age, income, and children, which can be appended to any file that contains a name and postal address.
Authentication	A way of equipping e-mails with verifiable information so recipients know it is from a genuine source.
Avatar	The graphical representation of a user in an e-mail that often moves with the user's mouse.
Bits	Electronic on/off signals. E-mails are broken into bytes, each of which contains eight bits.
Blog	Short for Web log. A blog is maintained by an individual or a company. It combines text, images, links, and other media related to its topic. Readers can leave comments. Most blogs are primarily text but may contain images and video.
Blogger	An individual who maintains a blog.

Bounce	E-mails that aren't delivered for some reason bounce back. The sending server tries several times more before the bounce is considered permanent.
Bytes	Electronic representation of a letter or number. Bytes contain eight bits.
Campaign	Promotional e-mails are usually sent in campaigns. Campaigns are measured by opens, clicks, and conversions.
CAN-SPAM Act of 2003	Establishes the US national standards for commercial e-mail. Requires the Federal Trade Commission (FTC) to enforce its provisions.
CHAID	Chi-squared automatic interaction detector; A decision-tree modeling technique used for predicting subscriber response to e-mails.
Channel	A method of purchasing: online, retail stores, catalogs, phone.
C-level Executives	Top level executives, such as a COO, CMO, or CFO.
Click-through rates	Number of clicks divided by number of opens in an e-mail campaign.
Click	An e-mail reader uses his mouse to click on a link to open it or see a new page.
Clickstream analysis	Series of packets back from e-mail users that indicate opens, downloads, clicks, or conversions.
Client	A computer application, such as a Web browser, that runs on a user's local computer or workstation and connects to the Internet. Microsoft Outlook is an e-mail client.
Collaborative filtering	A method of making automatic predictions (filtering) about the user's interests by collecting taste information from many users (collaborating). The underlying assumption of collaborative filtering is that those who agreed in the past tend to agree in the future.
Control group	A group of subscribers who don't get the test e-mails. Their response, compared with the tested subscribers, determines the success of the test.

Conversion	The desired action the marketer wishes the e-mail subscriber to take, such as to purchase a product or request more information.
Cookie	Text stored by a company on a user's PC that enables a sending server to know that this user has visited the Web site or read an e-mail previously. It enables Web sites to say, "Welcome back, Arthur."
Co-registration	An airline signs up their subscribers as rental car e-mail subscribers.
CTR	Click-through rate.
Cyber Monday	The Monday after Thanksgiving. A great day for e-mail sales.
Dashboard	A custom and useful arrangement of clickstream data from a campaign
Database	The place where data about subscribers is stored. Used to create personalized e-mail content.
Database marketing	The system of storing subscriber data; the central repository for e-mail farming operations.
Deliverability	The percentage of e-mails that reach their destination.
Deliverable	The number of e-mails that are delivered.
Demographics	Data about subscribers, such as age, income, presence of children, and length at residence.
Descriptive modeling	Modeling that describes the demographics and behavior of subscribers. Compare to predictive modeling.
Discount rate	Future revenue is worth less than current revenue. To determine the net present value of future revenue, divide by the discount rate.
Double opt-in	Preferred method of signing up e-mail subscribers. When a person signs up for your e-mails, you send an e-mail to them, asking them to confirm the subscription. The person is not added to your database until she has confirmed she wants your e-mails.
Download	A whitepaper or other document subscribers can get from your site; usually offered in an e-mail.

E-mail farming	E-mail marketing campaigns based on what subscribers want, a result being highly relevant promotion e-mails.
E-mail hunting	E-mail marketing campaigns based on very little knowledge about the recipients.
E-mail marketing	Marketing programs delivered via e-mail.
E-mail service provider	A service that sends and sometimes creates e-mail messages.
ESP	An e-mail service provider:
Focus groups	Groups of consumers asked to discuss their reaction to a proposed product or ad. Not used in e-mail marketing.
Frequency	How often e-mails are sent to subscribers; also how often subscribers open a message, click on a link, or convert.
FSI	Free-standing insert; a coupon that falls out of a newspaper or magazine.
Funnel	The route a prospect takes to reach the marketer's goal, such as buying a product.
Gains chart	A chart showing the advantages of selecting certain subscribers selected by a model.
Gift registry	Preferred gifts listed with a retailer.
Goodmail certification	A system used by some ISPs as part of their e-mail filtering services.
HTML	Hypertext markup language; used to create e-mails and Web sites.
Inactives	Subscribers who have not opened their e-mails in some time.
Interactive e-mails	E-mail filled with links to interesting content.
Internet	A worldwide, publicly accessible network of interconnected computer networks that transmit data using the standard protocols.
ISP	Internet service provider, such as AOL or Yahoo.
JavaScript	A scripting language used for Web development.

KPI	Key performance indicators for marketing campaigns, such as e-mails opened.
Lifecycle	Where the subscriber is in relation to the marketer: opener, buyer, repeat buyer, advocate, lapsed buyer.
Lifestyle	A combination of age, income, housing type, and so on that defines how the subscriber lives.
Lifetime value	The net profit received from a subscriber over a given period of years.
Link	HTML code that, when clicked, leads to a specified URL.
Loyalty program	A program that rewards members for specific actions, such as spending a certain amount of money.
Marketing database	The repository where all the data about subscribers, customers, prospects, and lapsed customers is stored.
Mass marketing	TV, radio, national print ads.
Message transfer agent	A computer program or software agent that transfers e-mail messages from one computer to another.
Microsite	Small Web sites, typically created for a specific campaign.
Modeling	Statistical procedures using multiple regressions or CHAID that are used to predict what subscribers will do based on what similar subscribers did in the past.
Monetary	In RFM analysis, the total amount that the subscriber has spent for products.
MTA	Message transfer agent.
Multibuyer	A subscriber who has bought several times from a company.
Multichannel customer	A subscriber who has bought from more than one channel.
NCOA	National change of address, a service of the USPS that updates the postal addresses of consumers who have moved.

Next best product (NBP)	A statistical technique for determining what product a given subscriber is most likely to purchase next.
One-Click Ordering	A technique used by Amazon.com that permits subscribers to buy any product with one click.
Open rate	The percentage of delivered e-mails that were opened by the recipients.
Operational database	The opposite of a marketing database: the billing database that keeps track of who bought what.
Opt-in e-mail address	An e-mail address of a subscriber who has provided you with permission to send her promotional e-mails.
Outlier	In modeling, those who have bought much more or much less than the average and should not be used in the model.
Packet	Electronic forms that transfer data from one compute to another.
PDF	Portable document format. An Adobe PostScript standard file format that preserves the graphical look of a document.
Permission-based e-mail address	An opt-in e-mail address
Personalized e-mail	E-mail that uses the recipient's name in the text.
Phishing	Illegal attempts to secure information from Internet users through false premises.
POS	Point of sale; a system in store cash registers in stores. POS systems are polled nightly.
Predictive modeling	Statistical systems to predict what subscribers will do based on what others have done.
Preference form	A form that subscribers fill out to tell the company what they would like in terms of products, frequency, and so on.
Preview pane	A function in Outlook that allows users to see a part of the e-mail before they open it.
Prizm cluster	A segment of the US consumers created by Claritas.

Profile form	A form where a subscriber enters her age, income, and so on.
Proof of permission	Proof that you have adhered to the CAN-SPAM Act in acquiring a subscriber's permission to send e-mails.
Random select	Selecting subscribers for an e-mail by an arbitrary method.
Reactivation	Getting lapsed subscribers to become active again.
Recency	In RFM analysis, the most recent date that the subscriber has opened or bought something.
Referral rate	The percentage of subscribers who refer other subscribers. Used in viral marketing.
Relational database	The database system that permits an unlimited amount of data to be acquired about subscribers.
Relationship buyer	A buyer who buys from you because she likes your products, company, staff, and so on, rather than because of the product's the price.
Relevance	The process of creating e-mails that subscribers want to open, read, and take actions that you find profitable. Relevant e-mails make subscribers happy. They open them and read them.
Return on investment	The dollars in profit gained from each dollar invested.
RFM	Recency, frequency, and monetary analysis. An old and highly predictive way of determining who will respond and buy.
ROI	Return on investment.
Router	Computers that send packets to their destinations.
RSS	Really simple syndication; a Web feed used to send subscribers frequently updated content.
Search engine marketing	The process of relying on search engines, such as Google, to bring consumers to your Web site.
Seeds	People (often your employees) to whom you send all e-mails so that you will know how they are received.
Segment	A group of subscribers with similar buying habits.

Sender field	The place in an e-mail where the sender's name and address appear.
Shopping cart	Online purchase system.
Spam	E-mail sent to internet users who didn't ask for or want the e-mails. SPAM is illegal in the US but hard to prosecute.
Status levels	Levels in a loyalty program, such as Gold, Silver.
Subject line	The place in an e-mail where the sender puts the subject of the e-mail.
Suppression file	Database files of unsubscribed e-mail addresses; kept to ensure that they are no longer sent e-mails.
Ten-day rule	If a subscriber makes a purchase within 10 days of receiving a promotional e-mail, you can credit the e-mail with the sale.
Testimonial	Consumers product reviews that can be read by others.
Text chat	A box on an e-mail where viewers can converse with an agent live about the purchase process.
Text e-mail	E-mails that have no HTML coding.
Transaction buyer	A buyer motivated primarily by price.
Transactional e-mail	E-mail related to a purchase, such as thanking the subscriber for a purchase.
Triggered e-mail	An e-mail based on something has happened to the receiver: birthday, anniversary, and the like.
Undeliver	An e-mail that didn't get delivered.
Unsubscribe	A subscriber who has requested to no longer receive your e-mails.
URL	Uniform resource locator.
Validation group	In modeling, a group that validates the model.
Viral marketing	Marketing that encourages subscribers to forward e-mails to their friends.
Web analytics	The study of Web site visitor behavior, including Web traffic, e-mail opens, clicks, and conversions.

Web beacon	An object embedded in an e-mail, invisible to the user, that allows the marketer to see if the recipient has viewed the e-mail.
Weight	The significance of a variable in a model in the outcome. A high weight means that the variable affects the outcome in a strong way.
Welcome e-mail	The e-mail sent to a subscriber after she has signed up to receive your e-mails.
Whitelisting	The process of the subscriber adding your sending address to her address book.
Widget	Small pieces of software that can be embedded in a Web site or placed on a user's computer.

About the Authors

Both of us have had more than 20 years in direct marketing. We love it. You can tell that from this book. E-mail marketing is a wonderful way of making customers happy and bringing new products and concepts to the world.

Before his job as CMO with e-Dialog, Arthur Sweetser spent many years with S&H greenpoints doing in-store, real-time CRM marketing, and online and offline retail promotions and rewards. S&H is the fastest-growing loyalty program in the grocery industry today.

Arthur's prior work includes Gearon Hoffman Advertising in Boston. As partner, he mapped and implemented online strategies for Web businesses in search, education, B2B, and financial services. He repositioned and expanded international market share for the Converse All-Star sneaker by adding color and appealing to the youth market. He spent several years at Ogilvy & Mather, expanding American Express card usage throughout the Midwest, and developed successful marketing strategies for such companies as NYNEX, AMD, Sony Professional Products, and Bank of Boston.

Arthur Hughes is Senior Strategist at e-Dialog. Previously, he was VP/ Solutions Architect at KnowledgeBase Marketing. At CSC Advanced Database Solutions, he worked on the development of the Miles Kimball marketing database. At MSDBM, he developed Gold Digger, a database analytical and campaign builder tool and developed the lifetime value of BMW automobile customers. For MSDBM, he provided strategic advice to RCI, "The Washington Post," Universal Music, Fairfield Communities, and MESH Hotels. Arthur founded the Database Marketing Institute in 1994, giving 28 two-day seminars over six years to over 1,400 database marketing executives. For ACS Inc., he designed and developed marketing databases for Compaq, Nestle, Western Union, Pacific Bell, Air Touch Cellular, CIBA Geigi, Killington Ski Resorts, Land Rover, and many others. Arthur is the author of eight books on database marketing, the most recent being the third edition of Strategic Database Marketing (McGraw-Hill, 2006) and Customer Churn Reduction and Retention for Telecoms (RACOM, 2008). Arthur lives with his wife Helena in Fort Lauderdale, Florida.

Both Arthurs can be reached by readers at: asweetser@e-dialog.com and ahughes@e-dialog.com

INDEX